Mobile Data Visualization

AK Peters Visualization Series

This series aims to capture new developments and summarize what is known over the whole spectrum of visualization by publishing a broad range of textbooks, reference works, and handbooks. It will contain books from all subfields of visualization, including visual analytics, information visualization, and scientific visualization. The scope will largely follow the calls of the major conferences such as VIS: techniques, algorithms, theoretical foundations and models, quantitative and qualitative evaluation, design studies, and applications.

Series Editors:

Tamara Munzner, *University of British Columbia, Vancouver, Canada*

Alberto Cairo, *University of Miami, USA*

Visualization Analysis and Design
Tamara Munzner

Information Theory Tools for Visualization
Min Chen, Miquel Feixas, Ivan Viola, Anton Bardera, Han-Wei Shen, Mateu Sbert

Data-Driven Storytelling
Nathalie Henry Riche, Christophe Hurter, Nicholas Diakopoulos, Sheelagh Carpendale

Interactive Visual Data Analysis
Christian Tominski, Heidrun Schumann

Data Sketches
Nadieh Bremer, Shirley Wu

Visualizing with Text
Richard Brath

Mobile Data Visualization
Bongshin Lee, Raimund Dachselt, Petra Isenberg, Eun Kyoung Choe

For more information about this series please visit:
https://www.routledge.com/AK-Peters-Visualization-Series/book-series/CRCVIS

Mobile Data Visualization

Edited by
Bongshin Lee
Raimund Dachselt
Petra Isenberg
Eun Kyoung Choe

CRC Press
Taylor & Francis Group
Boca Raton London New York

CRC Press is an imprint of the
Taylor & Francis Group, an **informa** business

First edition published 2022
by CRC Press
6000 Broken Sound Parkway NW, Suite 300, Boca Raton, FL 33487-2742

and by CRC Press
2 Park Square, Milton Park, Abingdon, Oxon, OX14 4RN

CRC Press is an imprint of Taylor & Francis Group, LLC

ISBN: 978-0-367-54842-1 (hbk)
ISBN: 978-0-367-53471-4 (pbk)
ISBN: 978-1-003-09082-3 (ebk)

DOI: 10.1201/9781003090823

Typeset in Latin Modern font
by KnowledgeWorks Global Ltd.

Contents

TANJA BLASCHECK, FRANK BENTLEY, EUN KYOUNG CHOE, TOM HORAK, and PETRA ISENBERG

FRANK BENTLEY, EUN KYOUNG CHOE, LENA MAMYKINA, JOHN STASKO, and POURANG IRANI

Preface

WHY MOBILE DATA VISUALIZATION?

Over the last few decades, the field of data visualization has made great strides, devising a slew of visual representations and interactive systems, and amassing a wealth of knowledge in how people perceive different representations and use data visualization systems. Data visualization empowers experts to deal with large amounts of data in their work, playing a critical role not only in data analysis and exploration, through which people find meaningful insights, but also in data-driven storytelling, with which people share and communicate the key insights. However, visualization research has largely focused on the desktop setup even though our computing environments and contexts continually evolve, and hardware and software technologies rapidly advance.

Today, we live in a data-driven world, where big data are generated and captured by computing devices and sensors on and around us. Not only experts but also lay individuals have access to large amounts of data. Affordable wireless data communication services are widely available and new mobile device form factors and hardware capabilities continue to emerge, making the vision of data access for "everyone, anytime, anywhere" reality. Beyond the experts, lay individuals including data enthusiasts can and should benefit from data visualization, accessing and leveraging their data in personal contexts. As such, we witness the growing demand for visual access to data on small portable displays.

A vast number of mobile apps—both commercial apps and research prototypes—already employ data visualization. For example, most commercial wearable devices' companion apps use data visualization to enable people to access their health and activity data collected over time. However, we lack practical guidance for how to design good mobile data visualization, whereas existing guidelines for data visualization and interaction design may not be applicable to mobile devices, especially with novel form factors. This book aims to address this gap by reflecting on what is unique about mobile data visualization in comparison to traditional data visualization, by reviewing what has been investigated, developed, and discovered in mobile data visualization so far, and by envisioning what would be possible in the future.

To that end, the editors of this book organized a Dagstuhl Seminar titled "Mobile Data Visualization" in 2019 and gathered researchers from the visualization, ubiquitous computing, human-computer interaction, and health informatics communities.[1] This book is the main outcome of this five-day seminar: through lightning presentations, interactive tutorials, as well as brainstorming and discussions in break-out sessions, 25

---

[1] https://www.dagstuhl.de/en/program/calendar/semhp/?semnr=19292.

participants exchanged and reflected on experiences around mobile data visualization, and synthesized knowledge on and planned for this important and exciting topic.

In closing, the editors want to emphasize that mobile data visualization is in its nascent stage with great potential and opportunities. We believe that expanding the scope of data visualization to cover mobile environments and contexts will amplify the benefits of data visualization, empowering a broader range of people to make better use of data. We hope this book helps both researchers and practitioners get to know mobile data visualization and inspires them to shape its future.

AUDIENCE OF THIS BOOK

This book introduces key concepts and important aspects on mobile data visualization with an aim to establish the research agenda and discuss the opportunities and challenges for mobile data visualization from both research and practical perspectives.

The primary audience of this book is threefold: (1) students, both at the graduate and advanced undergraduate levels, who desire to gain a better understanding of this emerging topic; (2) visualization designers and practitioners who want to and need to design and develop mobile data visualization for their work; and (3) researchers who aim to expand their research scope to incorporate and leverage this topic while contributing to push the state of the art in mobile data visualization. Additional audiences include educators who want to provide helpful references to their students. This book aims to be accessible to this broad range of audiences although some chapters are written in a more formal academic writing style than others. It does not assume any experience or formal understanding with data visualization, visualization design, mobile computing, and programming. While some chapters refer to others, each chapter stands on its own and one can read the chapters in the order they prefer.

STRUCTURE: WHAT'S IN THIS BOOK

The book consists of nine chapters, which provide interesting perspectives on the various aspects of mobile data visualization. Starting with an introduction to characterize and classify mobile data visualizations (1), a discussion of two central aspects follows: the adaptation to various changes called responsive visualization design (2), and the special repertoire of interacting with mobile visualizations (3). As the computing power and resolution of mobile devices increase, 3D data can play an increasing role in mobile visualization (4). On the other hand, considerably reduced attention spans on mobile devices demand careful design of glanceable visualizations (5). In addition, it is important to know both about the specific methods of evaluating mobile data visualizations (6) and about the logistical, privacy, and ethical challenges involved in their everyday usage (7). Looking into the future, mobile data visualizations can be specifically designed through a human-centered ideation methodology (8) and go beyond mobile devices as we know them, which is envisioned as ubiquitous visualization (9). The following provides a short summary of each chapter.

Chapter 1 An Introduction to Mobile Data Visualization

In this chapter, several characteristics are proposed that help us identify and describe the scope of *mobile data visualization*, which stretches beyond an intuitive understanding of the term. The focus lies on those characteristics that, particularly in their extremes, differentiate mobile data visualization from other forms of data visualization. These characteristics give rise to dimensions of a design space for mobile data visualization, against which instances may be classified and positioned. The chapter discusses a number of examples to illustrate how the design space makes it possible to describe and compare mobile visualizations.

Chapter 2 Responsive Visualization Design for Mobile Devices

The term *responsive* describes aspects of a visualization that automatically adapt to changes in, for example, device characteristics, environment, usage context, or data. The chapter discusses aspects of responsive mobile data visualization, and summarizes the types of change that a visualization must respond to and how they can be sensed on mobile devices. Ten responsive visualization design strategies are reviewed, including adaptations of scale, layout, and visual encoding, as well as attentional cues and specific interactions. The chapter concludes with future research directions pertaining to responsive visualization design for mobile devices and beyond.

Chapter 3 Interacting with Visualization on Mobile Devices

This chapter characterizes how interacting with data visualization using mobile devices, specifically a phone or tablet, differs from analogous experiences using a PC. An overview of the topic is provided, which is organized by interaction modality, beginning with touch interaction and subsequently discussing instances of voice interaction and spatial interaction. As an outlook, the chapter envisions compelling opportunities for future mobile data visualization research, inspired by recent developments in the field of mobile human-computer interaction.

Chapter 4 3D Mobile Data Visualization

This chapter surveys the space of three-dimensional (3D) mobile visualizations, that is, 3D abstract or spatial data on mobile 2D displays or 3D head-mounted displays. As a playful "case study" a scenario from the film *Aliens* is used, where the marines are overrun by aliens in the ceiling, as their mobile visualization device fails to show them the height dimension of the space around them. This example is used to illustrate how different mobile and 3D interaction techniques could have prevented the misunderstanding, using both hypothetical descriptions of the improved movie action and a scientific discussion of these scenarios and their implications.

Chapter 5 Characterizing Glanceable Visualizations: From Perception to Behavior Change

This chapter explores glanceability as an important requirement for several types of mobile visualizations, thereby integrating knowledge from the Vision Sciences, Visualization, Human-Computer Interaction, and Ubiquitous Computing. In mobile contexts, quick information needs are frequently occurring and differ from those in traditional visualizations that are designed for analyzing complex datasets. The chapter therefore discusses specific characteristics of glanceable mobile visualizations, explores different evaluation methodologies, and concludes with open challenges in the design of future glanceable visualizations.

Chapter 6 Evaluating Mobile Visualizations

This chapter discusses the special challenges of evaluating mobile visualizations. Many research goals can be addressed by an evaluation study including validating rapid perception of differences in data or examining the long-term use and impact of visualizations. Different methods, time-scales of research, and participant recruitment strategies are needed depending on the questions that one wants to answer. This chapter explores the literature, discussing a variety of goals and evaluation approaches, highlighting best practices and making recommendations for future approaches to evaluating mobile visualizations.

Chapter 7 Challenges in Everyday Use of Mobile Visualizations

This chapter illustrates challenges resulting from the everyday use of mobile visualizations in three categories: logistical challenges relating to situated use, privacy challenges involved with potential data disclosures, and ethical challenges surrounding increased access and decreased evidence. Despite these challenges, introducing visualizations in everyday life can lead to positive experiences viewing and reflecting on data in their natural contexts. Using scenarios to depict use opportunities, this chapter introduces a set of considerations for designers and researchers looking to develop mobile visualizations for everyday contexts.

Chapter 8 Mobile Visualization Design: An Ideation Method to Try

This chapter discusses and reflects on an ideation methodology that can help imagine future mobile only visualizations through a human-centered design approach. The chapter starts by outlining the general approach of the methodology. Ideation activities of three different design groups are then described to illustrate how one can adapt and adjust the methodology to specific ideation scenarios; and four different ideation activity approaches are presented with example results. The chapter ends with a reflection on the methodology itself and how the flexibility of the methodology can encourage a wide range of ideas to emerge.

Chapter 9 Reflections on Ubiquitous Visualization

This chapter provides an outlook into the future of mobile visualization, where we anticipate to see a growing emphasis on *ubiquitous visualization*. An overview of research in ubiquitous visualization is synthesized from the interviews with four renowned researchers who have explored data visualization in novel settings with new modalities and technologies that go beyond mobile devices. The chapter reports on the discussions and distills important themes and their visions for the future of ubiquitous data visualization. Envisioning scenarios are discussed for this emerging research area, and its specific dimensions are reflected going beyond mobile data visualization.

WHAT'S NOT IN THIS BOOK

Mobile data visualization is a nascent topic. The discussions among the international experts contributing to this book resulted in the nine book chapters briefly summarized above, covering important aspects of mobile data visualization. However, we have not aimed for a complete and holistic overview: other important aspects we did not cover in this book may exist or emerge in the future. In addition, the visualization community is currently short of research and knowledge related to mobile data visualization, and thus we could not provide practical guidelines to mitigate the issues specific to mobile data visualization.

As the the first book on mobile data visualization, this book aims to articulate the different and unique challenges and opportunities that mobility brings to the visualization research and practice. As such, it does not cover the general and broader data visualization. We instead provide a short list of books that can help readers gain better access to the wealth of knowledge and techniques in the field of data visualization that are complementary to this book.

The AK Peters Visualization Series provides several books covering a wide spectrum of visualization, both capturing new developments and summarizing the knowledge gained from all subfields of visualization, including information visualization, visual analytics, and scientific visualization. For example, Munzner's Visualization Analysis and Design [5] is a comprehensive textbook that provides a systematic framework and language to discuss visualization design while providing valuable principles and guidelines. On the other hand, focusing on visual, interactive, and analytical methods, Tominski and Schumann's Interactive Visual Data Analysis [7] discusses criteria and process for designing interactive visual data analysis solutions, while examining the factors that influence the design. Henry Riche et al.'s Data-Driven Storytelling [6] offers an informative and meaningful introduction to data-driven storytelling, storytelling techniques and narrative design patterns along with curated examples, comprehensive discussions on human's perceptual and cognitive foundations, ethics in data-driven storytelling, and workflows to accommodate various organizational structures.

While somewhat outdated now, Readings in Information Visualization [2] provides a useful synthesis of the visualization field along with a collection of seminal papers. Ware's two books Visual Thinking for Design [9] and Information Visualization: Perception for Design [8] collectively offer a comprehensive guidance on how we should display information based on the science of human visual perception.

A few books exist from the mobile computing side. Consolvo et al.'s Mobile User Research: A Practical Guide [3] provides an overview of research methods and approaches to elicit requirements and to understand user behavior for mobile interface design. Bentley and Barrett's Building Mobile Experiences [1] presents an approach to designing mobile apps that leverage mobile devices' capabilities—the Internet-connected, context-aware, and media-sharing. It introduces tools that can be used at each stage of building a mobile application, from concept creation to commercialization, and showcases real-world examples from industry and academia. Khan's Interactive Data Mining Results Visualization on Mobile Devices: Interactive Data Mining Results Visualizations Techniques & Framework for Mobile Devices [4] is based on his PhD thesis that proposes a framework that addresses the issues on how to incorporate data mining on mobile devices, providing ways to visualize a highly specific data (i.e., the data mining results) on mobile devices.

[1] Bentley, F. and Barrett, E. *Building mobile experiences*. MIT Press, 2012 (cited on page xvi).

[2] Card, S. K., Mackinlay, J. D., and Shneiderman, B., eds. *Readings in Information Visualization: Using Vision to Think*. San Francisco, CA, USA: Morgan Kaufmann Publishers Inc., 1999 (cited on page xv).

[3] Consolvo, S., Bentley, F. R., Hekler, E. B., and Phatak, S. S. *Mobile User Research: A Practical Guide*. Morgan & Claypool, 2017. DOI: 10.2200/ S00763ED1V01Y201703MPC012 (cited on page xvi).

[4] Khan, M. *Interactive Data Mining Results Visualization on Mobile Devices: Interactive Data Mining Results Visualizations Techniques & Framework for Mobile Devices*. LAP LAMBERT Academic Publishing, 2013 (cited on page xvi).

[5] Munzner, T. *Visualization Analysis and Design*. A K Peters Visualization Series. A K Peters/CRC Press, 2014. DOI: 10.1201/b17511 (cited on page xv).

[6] Riche, N. H., Hurter, C., Diakopoulos, N., and Carpendale, S. *Data-Driven Storytelling*. A K Peters Visualization Series. A K Peters/CRC Press, 2018. DOI: 10.1201/9781315281575 (cited on page xv).

[7] Tominski, C. and Schumann, H. *Interactive Visual Data Analysis*. A K Peters Visualization Series. A K Peters/CRC Press, 2020. DOI: 10.1201/9781315152707. URL: https://ivda-book.de (cited on page xv).

[8] Ware, C. *Information Visualization: Perception for Design*. English. 3rd. Morgan Kaufmann, 2012 (cited on page xv).

[9] Ware, C. *Visual thinking for design*. Elsevier, 2010 (cited on page xv).

Editors

Bongshin Lee is a Sr. Principal Researcher in the EPIC (Extended Perception Interaction Cognition) research group, part of Human-Computer Interaction Group (HCI@MSR), at Microsoft Research. She received her PhD in Computer Science from the University of Maryland, College Park in 2006. Bongshin conducts research on data visualization, human-computer interaction, and human-data interaction, focusing on the design, development, and evaluation of novel data visualization and interaction techniques. The overarching goal of her research is to empower people to achieve their goals by leveraging data, data visualization, and technological advancements. Bongshin explores innovative ways to help people with different abilities to interact with data, by supporting easy and effective data collection, data exploration and analysis, and data-driven communication. Her most recent research endeavors include personal data visualization, data visualization on mobile devices, inclusive data visualization, and multimodal interaction for data visualization. She is a member of the IEEE Visualization Academy.

Raimund Dachselt is a Full Professor of Computer Science at the Technische Universität Dresden, Germany. Since 2012, he leads the Interactive Media Lab Dresden at the Faculty of Computer Science. He received his PhD in 2004 from TU Dresden and was Professor for User Interface Engineering at the University of Magdeburg from 2007 to 2012. His research interests are at the intersection of natural, multimodal human computer interaction (HCI) and data visualization. He worked extensively in the area of interactive surfaces from smartwatches over tabletops to wall-sized displays and expanded the scope to Mixed Reality interfaces for immersive data analysis. He contributed several novel interface approaches for information visualization. He has co-authored more than 220 peer-reviewed publications and two major German HCI textbooks and received several Best Paper Awards at leading conferences. He has co-organized 17 international workshops at ACM and IEEE conferences, is the head of the ACM ISS steering committee and repeatedly served in numerous chairing and organizational roles as well as a PC member for international conferences.

Petra Isenberg is a research scientist at Inria, Saclay, France in the Aviz team and part of the Computer Science Laboratory of University Paris-Saclay (LISN). Prior to joining Inria, she received her PhD from the University of Calgary in 2010 on collaborative information visualization. Petra also holds a Diplom-engineer degree in Computational Visualistics from the University of Magdeburg. Her main research areas are visualization and visual analytics with a focus on non-desktop devices, interaction, and evaluation. She is particularly interested in exploring how people can most effectively work together when analyzing large and complex data sets on novel display technology such as small touch-screens, mobile devices, and wall displays, or tabletops. Petra is associate editor-in-chief at IEEE CG&A, associate editor of the IEEE Transactions on Visualization and Computer Graphics, has served on many organizing committee roles in various conferences, and has been the co-chair of the biennial Beliv workshop from 2012 to 2018.

Eun Kyoung Choe is an Associate Professor in the College of Information Studies at the University of Maryland, College Park. She received her PhD in Information Science from University of Washington, MS in Information Management and Systems from University of California, Berkeley, and BS in Industrial Design from KAIST. She conducts research on HCI, Ubiquitous Computing, and Personal Informatics. With an overarching goal of empowering individuals, she examines some of the major challenges people face in leveraging personal data, such as data collection, data exploration, and data sharing. Drawing insights from formative studies, she designs novel systems to support personalized data collection and multimodal data exploration for people to interact with data. Her work has been funded by the National Science Foundation, National Institute of Health, and Microsoft Research. She has been serving on the editorial boards of PACM IMWUT and Foundations and Trends in Human-Computer Interaction, and as a Health subcommittee chair for CHI 2021 and 2022.

Contributors

Wolfgang Aigner is scientific director at the Institute of Creative\Media/Technologies at St. Pölten University of Applied Sciences, Austria and adjunct professor at TU Wien, Austria. His research focuses on information visualization and visual analytics, particularly in the context of time-oriented data. He performs research on concepts, methods, and software prototypes that support humans in dealing with large and complex information structures, to make them more comprehensible, facilitate exploration, and enable knowledge discovery.

Frank Bentley is a Distinguished Researcher at Yahoo, with 20+ years of mobile research experience, as well as a Lecturer at Stanford University where he teaches a class called Understanding Users. Frank's research focuses on creating systems for non-technical users to understand and interact with complex datasets from email to news to health information.

Lonni Besançon is a postdoctoral fellow at Linköping University, Sweden. He received the PhD degree in computer science at University Paris Saclay, France. His thesis "An interaction continuum for 3D dataset visualization" received the second prize of the prix de these GDR-IGRV. IIe is particularly interested in interactive visualization techniques for 3D spatial data relying on new input paradigms and his recent work focuses on the visualization and understanding of uncertainty in empirical computer science results.

Tanja Blascheck is a Margarete-von-Wrangell Fellow and works at the Institute for Visualization and Interactive Systems at the University of Stuttgart. Her main research areas are information visualization and visual analytics with a focus on evaluation, eye tracking, and interaction. She is interested in exploring how to effectively analyze eye tracking data with visualizations and the pervasive use of visualization on novel display technologies like smartwatches. She received her PhD in Computer Science from the University of Stuttgart.

Matthew Brehmer is a senior research staff member of Tableau Research in Seattle, where he focuses on information visualization. Prior to joining Tableau, he was a postdoctoral researcher at Microsoft Research, which followed his doctoral research at the University of British Columbia. He is interested in expressive visualization design for communication and presentation, visualization and interaction design for devices large and small, and the visualization of time-oriented data.

Sheelagh Carpendale brings her broad background in fine art, design and computer science to her position as a Full Professor and Canada Research Chair in Information Visualization in Computing Science at Simon Fraser University. By studying how people interact with information in both work and social settings, she works toward designing more inclusive, accessible and understandable interactive visual representations of data. She combines information visualization and human-computer interaction with innovative new interaction techniques to better support the everyday practices of people who are viewing, representing, and interacting with data.

Christopher Collins holds the Canada Research Chair in Linguistic Information Visualization and is an Associate Professor at Ontario Tech University. His research combines information visualization and human-computer interaction, with a recent focus on mixed-initiative and context-aware systems. He is a member of the executive of the IEEE Visualization Conference and has served several roles on the IEEE VIS Conference Organizing Committee.

Tim Dwyer is a Professor in the Department of Human-Centred Computing at Monash University, Australia. He directs the Data Visualisation and Immersive Analytics Lab which explores the role of emerging display and interaction technologies in supporting effective and engaging data analytics to help people understand data and complex systems, and to make better, data-informed decisions. He will co-host the IEEE VIS Conference as General Chair in Melbourne, Australia in 2022.

Daniel Epstein is an Assistant Professor in the Department of Informatics at the University of California, Irvine, where he directs the Personal Informatics Everyday (PIE) Lab. His work examines how personal tracking technology can acknowledge and account for the realities of everyday life, designing new technology and studying people's use of current technology to collect desired data or make sense of it through visualization.

Tom Horak is a PhD candidate at the Technische Universität Dresden and with the Interactive Media Lab Dresden. His work lies in the intersection of HCI and information visualization, with a focus on enabling data analysis on modern devices ranging from smartwatches to large displays. In particular, this includes the combined use of devices to allow for a more natural and flexible way of working with data visualizations.

Pourang P. Irani is a Professor in Computer Science at the University of Manitoba and holds a Canada Research Chair in Ubiquitous Analytics. His research aims at designing, implementing and studying interactive and visualization techniques for in-situ sense-making. His team includes a mix of trainees and students from diverse areas including psychology, physics and maths, computer science, electrical and mechanical engineering to create interactive experiences that foster effective mobile and visual analytics. He is currently leading a network of scientists exploring visual and automated disease analytics.

Tobias Isenberg is a senior research scientist at Inria, France. He received his doctoral degree from the University of Magdeburg, Germany, and held positions at the University of Calgary, Canada, and the University of Groningen, the Netherlands. His research interests comprise topics in scientific visualization, illustrative and non-photorealistic rendering, and interactive visualization techniques. He is particularly interested in interactive visualization environments for 3D spatial data that rely on novel interaction paradigms such as augmented reality, tactile screens, and tangible devices.

Alark Joshi is an Associate Professor & Department Chair of Computer Science at the University of San Francisco. He has published research papers in the field of data visualization with an emphasis on medical imaging and neurosurgical interventions. He has also organized award-winning panels at the IEEE Visualization conference. He was awarded the Distinguished Teaching Award at the University of San Francisco in 2016. He received his PhD in Computer Science from the University of Maryland Baltimore County.

Ricardo Langner is a PhD student at the Interactive Media Lab of Technische Universität Dresden. His research focuses on novel ways of interacting with data visualizations through mobile devices. He is particularly interested in exploring different combinations of devices and types of displays including smartphones, tablets, interactive tabletops, wall-sized displays, and augmented reality headsets.

Lena Mamykina is an Associate Professor of Biomedical Informatics at the Department of Biomedical Informatics at Columbia University. Her primary research interests reside in the areas of Biomedical Informatics, Human-Computer Interaction, Ubiquitous and Pervasive Computing, and Computer-Supported Collaborative Work. Specifically, she is interested in the design of intelligent interactive systems that incorporate computational inferences to aid in individual reasoning and decision making in health.

Charles Perin is an Assistant Professor of Computer Science at the University of Victoria, where he co-leads the VIXI lab. His research interests lie at the intersection of information visualization and HCI, with emphasis on designing and studying new interactions for visualizations and on understanding how people may make use of and interact with visualizations in their everyday lives. He is preparing for his first ultramarathon using visualizations on his smartwatch.

Harald Reiterer is a Full Professor of Human-Computer Interaction at the Department of Computer and Information Science at the University of Konstanz, Germany. The common goal of his research group is to develop new concepts to support the reality-based interaction between humans and computers that accommodate the characteristics of human interaction and cognition as well as the latest technological developments, a blend called Blended Interaction. One essential application domain is Information Visualization, where different blends of 2D and 3D visualizations are proposed using Mixed Reality technologies and Cross-Device Interaction.

John Stasko is a Regents Professor in the School of Interactive Computing at the Georgia Institute of Technology. He is a widely published and internationally recognized researcher in the areas of information visualization and visual analytics, approaching each from a human-computer interaction perspective. His research develops ways to help people and organizations explore, analyze, and make sense of data to solve problems. He has served in multiple organizational roles for the IEEE VIS meeting, and more specifically the InfoVis and VAST Conferences.

Christian Tominski is with the Institute for Visual & Analytic Computing at the University of Rostock, Germany. His research is centered around effective and efficient visualization and interaction techniques for exploring, analyzing, and editing complex data on regular desktops, in multi-display environments, and also on mobile devices. He co-authored three books, including a book on the visualization of time-oriented data in 2011, a book focusing on interaction for visualization in 2015, and a more general book about interactive visual data analysis in 2020.

Jo Vermeulen is a Principal Research Scientist at Autodesk Research in Toronto, Canada. His research interests lie at the intersection of HCI, ubiquitous computing, and information visualization, with a particular interest in novel interfaces that put people in control of their digital environments. In relation to the topic of this book, he has published research on situated visualization, mobile visualization, and on new ways of interacting with data visualizations. At Autodesk Research, he is currently focusing on projects in HCI and Software Learning. He obtained his PhD in Computer Science from Hasselt University (Belgium), for which he received the 2015 IBM Innovation Award.

ADDITIONAL STUDENT CONTRIBUTORS

Magdalena Boucher, St. Pölten University of Applied Sciences, Austria

Peter Buk, Simon Fraser University, Canada

Victor Cheung, Simon Fraser University, Canada

Katherine Currier, University of Calgary, Canada

Foroozan Daneshzand, Simon Fraser University, Canada

Alaul Islam, Université Paris-Saclay, CNRS, Inria, LISN, France

Lien Quach, Simon Fraser University, Canada

Laton Vermette, Simon Fraser University, Canada

Acknowledgments

We, the editors of this book, thank Schloss Dagstuhl - Leibniz Center for Informatics for enabling us to organize the Mobile Data Visualization seminar (19292) in 2019, gathering renowned researchers from the visualization, ubiquitous computing, human-computer interaction, and health informatics communities. We are also grateful for the Schloss Dagstuhl - NSF Support Grant allowing us to sponsor the participation of outstanding junior researchers.

This book was written during the unexpected COVID-19 pandemic. We are immensely grateful to all contributors of this book: they served not only as the authors but also as the reviewers, contributing to the quality of each chapter and making it possible to realize this book while experiencing unprecedented challenges.

We thank Ricardo Langner for designing the beautiful cover with the support of Vincent Thiele.

Last but not least, we are also grateful to Tamara Munzer, the Series Editor for AK Peters Visualization Series, Elliott Morsia, the Editor for Computer Science at CRC Press, as well as Talitha Duncan-Todd, Editorial Assistant at CRC Press, for their guidance and support.

The individual authors of the chapters benefit from various funding sources and would like to thank the following institutions and funding agencies:

- Wolfgang Aigner's work was partly funded by the Austrian Science Fund as part of the VisOnFire project (FWF P27975-NBL), as well as the Federal Government of Lower Austria via the project Dataskop (K3-F-2/015-2019).

- Tanja Blascheck is indebted to the European Social Fund, the Ministry of Science, Research, and Arts Baden-Württemberg, as well as the Deutsche Forschungsgemeinschaft (DFG, German Research Foundation) under grant ER 272/14-1.

- Eun Kyoung Choe's work was in part supported by the National Science Foundation award IIS-1753452.

- Raimund Dachselt was partly funded by the Deutsche Forschungsgemeinschaft (DFG)—project number 389792660—TRR 248 (CPEC, see `https://perspicuous-computing.science`), by the DFG as part of Germany's Excellence Strategy EXC 2050/1—Project ID390696704—Cluster of Excellence "Centre for Tactile Internet with Human-in-the-Loop" (CeTI), as well as EXC-2068—390729961—Cluster of Excellence Physics of Life of Technische Universität Dresden.

- Tom Horak was partly funded by the Deutsche Forschungsgemeinschaft (DFG) under grant 214484876 (GEMS 2.0) and DFG grant 389792660 as part of TRR 248 – CPEC, see `https://perspicuous-computing.science`.

- Daniel Epstein's work was partly funded by the National Science Foundation under award IIS-1850389.

CHAPTER 1

An Introduction to Mobile Data Visualization

Ricardo Langner
Technische Universität Dresden, Germany

Lonni Besançon
Linköping University, Sweden

Christopher Collins
Ontario Tech University, Canada

Tim Dwyer
Monash University, Australia

Petra Isenberg
Université Paris-Saclay, CNRS, Inria, LISN, France

Tobias Isenberg
Université Paris-Saclay, CNRS, Inria, LISN, France

Bongshin Lee
Microsoft Research, USA

Charles Perin
University of Victoria, Canada

Christian Tominski
University of Rostock, Germany

CONTENTS

DOI: 10.1201/9781003090823-1

W E may have an intuitive understanding of what is meant by mobile data visualization. Yet, in the context of data visualization, the term *mobile* can be interpreted in several ways. For example, it may describe visual representations shown on devices that are inherently mobile. It may also describe visualizations meant to react to viewers who are mobile relative to the display. Alternatively, it may describe visualizations that are themselves mobile across devices and screens, or in space.

In this chapter, we propose several characteristics that help us to identify and describe the scope of mobile data visualization. We focus on the characteristics that, particularly in their extremes, differentiate mobile data visualization from other forms of data visualization. These characteristics give rise to dimensions of a design space for mobile data visualization, against which instances may be classified and positioned. We discuss a number of examples to illustrate how the design space makes it possible to describe and compare mobile visualizations.

1.1 INTRODUCTION

Gleaning knowledge from data, so-called data analytics, has become a massive industry. Understanding data is no longer the concern of only government and business, but has become a significant component in the life of most people in the developed world. This rise of data analytics has been driven to a large extent by increased computer automation in every aspect of industry and modern life, as well as by the ease of sharing data over the internet. Given the ubiquitous availability of data, people have turned to, amongst other methods, data visualization as a critical tool to understand, experience, explore, and communicate data.

Data and visualizations can now be accessed from almost anywhere, anytime and a vast array of different devices can allow viewers to see and explore data leveraging visualizations. As such, interacting with data visualization is no longer an activity that can only happen on desktop computers, or even laptops or tablets. Smartphones, fitness trackers, and smartwatches—also, more exotically, e-readers, handheld gaming devices, smart glasses, and even augmented-reality headsets—represent the variety of mobile computing devices available today. It is time, therefore, to reconsider data visualization as it relates to this diversifying ecosystem of possibilities.

Mobile data visualization is a nascent research area that aims to take advantage of the new forms of ubiquitous data analysis and communication offered by technological advancements. Hence, it is perhaps not surprising that a shared understanding of its scope is not yet established among researchers and practitioners. Several well-founded perspectives can be adopted. For example, the term mobile data visualization may refer to *visualizations hosted on devices that are mobile* or *visualizations that react to viewers who are mobile relative to the display.* One might also describe it as *visualizations that are themselves mobile across devices and screens.*

The purpose of this chapter is not to identify a connotative definition but to introduce our interpretation of mobile data visualization and lay a conceptual foundation by discussing its scope. The chapter is motivated by our efforts to build a common understanding, language, and discussion basis. This basis is fundamental to building a community of researchers and practitioners around the topic of mobile data visualization.

We started by collecting several core cases, which intuitively would be considered clear examples of mobile data visualization. The set of core examples was then expanded through in-depth discussions of niche examples for which it is more difficult to agree upon whether they are cases of mobile data visualization. To better articulate **why** we considered certain cases to be *core* archetypal examples of mobile data visualization and others to be *edge* cases that in some way stretch the term, we derived a set of characteristics. With the help of these characteristics, the scope of mobile data visualization can be defined, and existing approaches, methods, and techniques can be discussed and categorized more easily. The dimensions that characterize the scope of mobile data visualization will be described next in Section 1.2. Illustrating the central aspects and also the extremes of mobile data visualization, we will discuss core examples and edge cases in Sections 1.3 and 1.4, respectively.

1.2 CHARACTERIZING DIMENSIONS

As modern computing is both portable and ubiquitous, a data visualization can be *mobile* in many different ways. To facilitate discussions on "mobile-visness," we identify seven descriptive dimensions that are relevant for categorizing existing work:

- Physical data display size

- Data display mobility

- Data source

- Reaction of visualization to display movement

- Intended viewing timespan

- Visualization interaction complexity

- Intended sharing

The dimensions emerged from examining characteristic similarities but also differences of existing mobile data visualization examples. We note that, while we think each dimension has its relevance when discussing mobile data visualization, there are certainly differences in their importance and complexity. In addition, there is some overlap: for example, solutions designed for a rather short *Intended Viewing Timespan* (Section 1.2.5) often also call for a more passive or simple level of *Visualization Interaction Complexity* (Section 1.2.6). Nonetheless, the identified dimensions allow us to reason about existing visualization techniques and devices in terms of mobility. What is more important than thinking about what already exists is to consider the possibility the dimensions' extremes bring, which might give insight into what mobile data visualization might become in the future, with advances in technology and imagination. Let's look at the dimensions in detail.

1.2.1 Physical Data Display Size

Looking at today's mobile devices, it is clear that the *Physical Data Display Size* is an essential aspect. Mobility seems closely related to physical screen size. We distinguish pixel-sized, watch-sized, phone-sized, tablet-sized, monitor-sized, and wall-sized displays as illustrated in Figure 1.1.

(a) pixel-sized (b) watch-sized (c) phone-sized (d) tablet-sized (e) monitor-sized (f) wall-sized

Figure 1.1 *Physical Data Display Size* dimension, ordered from smallest to largest.

Even though we focus on examples of flat digital data displays because they are most common, we acknowledge that non-flat data displays exist, for example, in the context of data physicalization. Another important thing to note is that the size of a data display with respect to a viewer's field of view depends on the viewer's distance to the display. This is particularly evident for augmented reality (AR) and virtual reality (VR) headsets. They are physically in the phone-sized display range but are worn so close to the wearer's eyes that they practically cover all of the wearer's field of view. Here, we care about the physical size of the display representing the data and not the apparent size for the viewer. We also assume that resolution is not a limiting factor as the trend to high pixel density displays continues across form-factors. Moreover, the following categories show that this dimension also has a considerable influence on how users interact with the device and presented information.

Pixel-sized: Very small data displays, in the range of a few to several millimeters fit into this category. Examples include single LEDs that show battery charging levels or error states of a machine as illustrated in Figure 1.1a. There is typically no interaction with these very small displays.

Watch-sized: Smartwatch displays are typically around 3–4 cm wide or high. Some deviate from a standard rectangular form to a circular geometry (Figure 1.1b), which is an interesting design constraint for visualization. Smartwatches are large enough to convey information to someone being relatively close to the display. Interaction is typically direct on the display using touch, through buttons or a digital crown on the device, and sometimes with speech.

Phone-sized: Smartphone screens as shown in Figure 1.1c are now commonly around 15 cm on the diagonal and have a high resolution of more than 150 pixels per cm. Compared to watch-sized displays, phone-sized displays can convey more information but still require a relatively close proximity of the viewer. Interaction is typically direct through the display via touch or through buttons on the device. AR and VR headsets also fit into this category but, by design, cover a large field of view and require dedicated forms of interaction.

Tablet-sized: Tablet-sized data displays (Figure 1.1d) typically have a book-like form factor. These displays can easily show more than one information panel or view, and thus support more complex visualizations. Interaction is typically direct through the display via touch, pen, or through buttons on the device.

Monitor-sized: Monitor-sized displays can cover a fair portion of the viewer's field of view even when the viewer is positioned further away (Figure 1.1e). Visualizations consisting of multiple views become more practical on these displays. While interaction typically is indirect using a mouse and keyboard, modern monitors can also be touch-enabled.

Wall-sized: Large displays commonly used in conference room, control room, or trading floor belong to this category. Wall-sized displays (Figure 1.1f) are large enough for multiple people to comfortably view them from varying viewing distances. If interaction is available (sometimes it is not), it often is direct via either touch or pen input, or indirect through connected devices.

1.2.2 Data Display Mobility

As already noted, a small display size can afford mobility. Another key aspects of mobile data visualization is the *Data Display Mobility*, which captures the movement of the display(s) containing visual representations of data. Fixed, movable, carryable, wearable, and independently moving displays can be differentiated along this dimension. Corresponding examples are given in Figure 1.2.

While the *Data Display Mobility* dimension is generally organized from least mobile to most mobile, the spectrum is not quite linear. For example, the difference between a wearable and a carryable display is fuzzy and fluid. A runner strapping a smartphone showing their running data onto their arm makes the display wearable

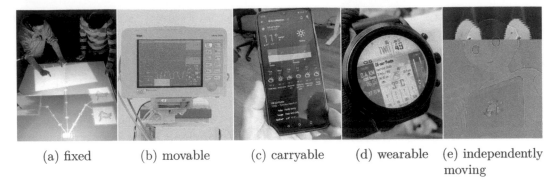

| (a) fixed | (b) movable | (c) carryable | (d) wearable | (e) independently moving |

Figure 1.2 *Data Display Mobility* types ordered roughly from least to most mobile.

while someone else may put their smartwatch showing weather data into their pocket, thereby, carrying it rather than wearing it.

In this dimension we limit our discussion to visualizations that rest on the displays that show them—or that are themselves the data displays (as in physical representations of data, or *data physicalizations*). We do not consider cases in which visualizations move from one to another display. For example, we disregard the scenario of a large display room in which someone analyzes a visualization on a tablet and then pushes the visualization to a shared large display to be worked on with a group.

Fixed displays: A desktop monitor, a tabletop display, a wall-size display, a large data sculpture, a public display—or any other large, typically stationary, data display—all fit in this category. While displays in this category are not inherently mobile, they still may relate different notions of mobility in some way or the other. The digital tabletop display in Figure 1.2a, for example, is set up to accommodate mobile viewers. A fixed display may also react to mobility in the environment, for example, by showing more or less detail depending on a mobile viewer's distance to the display [19].

Movable displays: Displays that cannot be carried for extended periods, but can be moved with the help of some supporting device belong to the category of movable displays. Examples include the display of computers on wheels (COWs) commonly used in hospital settings (see Figure 1.2b), as well as displays and devices, such as the Microsoft Surface Hub 2 that come with a movable stand.

Carryable displays: A data display is considered carryable if it can be moved without supporting devices. Such displays can be easily carried, for example in a bag or a pocket. As everything from a laptop computer to a phone (see Figure 1.2c) belongs to this category, it represents many of today's consumer mobile devices. Consequently, most of the existing mobile visualization research has been conducted in this category.

Wearable displays: Data displays that can be worn on a person and thus do not need to be actively carried belong to this category. Examples include data jewelry, smartwatches (Figure 1.2d), fitness bands, smartglasses, or augmented clothing. Wearable data displays may have a greater degree of responsiveness to user movement or gaze (for example, becoming immediately available when movement is detected) than carryable data displays. This class of devices is becoming increasingly important for visualization research.

Independently moving displays: Data displays that move autonomously or without direct human propulsion belong to this category. Examples include data displays attached to drones or robots as shown in Figure 1.2e. Humans may be controlling the movement remotely, but to the viewers the data displays would seem to be moving independently. See Section 1.4 for existing examples of independently moving data visualizations.

1.2.3 Data Source

In addition to *Physical Data Display Size* and *Data Display Mobility*, it is also possible to distinguish the source of the data being visualized. Some visualizations show pre-loaded data, while others need a connection to fetch data from cloud storage, for example to display weather and stock data. Yet others visualize live data captured from sensors, for example, step counts, GPS, and WiFi signals. It is also possible to combine different data sources, for example, when showing live location data and cloud-based traffic data on a map. Accordingly, we have divided this dimensions into four categories: pre-loaded, connected, captured, and combination (Figure 1.3).

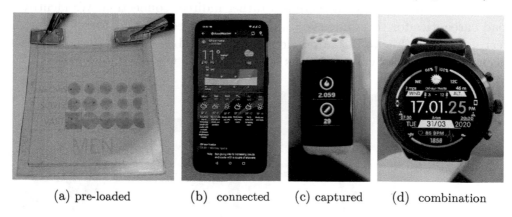

(a) pre-loaded   (b) connected   (c) captured   (d) combination

Figure 1.3 Categories in the *Data Source* dimension.

Pre-loaded data: The data have been previously loaded on the device and thus are static. Pre-loaded data are usually neither time critical nor affected by the environment of the device. The translucent display in Figure 1.3a, for example, can by design only show this and one other dataset depending on the flow of the current through the display.

Connected data: The data arrive dynamically over data connections from online services, such as a WiFi, Bluetooth, or cellular connection. The visualization responds to and may highlight updates to the data. Weather visualizations on smartphones, as in Figure 1.3b, or smartwatches are common examples where data is transmitted from external servers.

Captured data: The data shown in the visualization are generated by the device itself, for example, by capturing them through on-board sensors. Captured data are a form of dynamic data source but without a connection to a server. The mobile device itself needs to mediate the data (i. e., aggregate, filter, or present the data in a consumable form). The fitness band in Figure 1.3c shows captured data as two simple radial progress bars of calories burned and floors climbed.

Combination: It is also common to complement a primary data source with one or more secondary data sources. This is helpful when a mobile device can only partially sense the environment, is not able to process larger amounts of data, or is used in an environment with restricted or limited connectivity. Smartwatches, for example, often show dashboards that combine data captured from the device (battery life) and data from external servers (weather) as shown in Figure 1.3d.

1.2.4   Reaction of Visualization to Display Movement

Another distinctive aspect of mobile data visualization is if and how a visualization changes due to the movement of the display in the environment (not any movement of the viewer). If the visualization changes, the question is if these changes are directly related to the movement or if there is a rather indirect connection. We identify four broad categories for this dimension: no change, indirect change, direct change, and direct + indirect (Figure 1.4). More details on how mobile visualizations may react to movement and other dynamic factors can be found in Chapter 2.

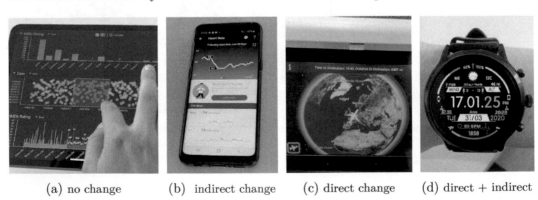

(a) no change   (b) indirect change   (c) direct change   (d) direct + indirect

Figure 1.4 Categories in the *Reaction of Visualization to Display Movement* dimension. *Figure (a) reprinted with permission from Ramik Sadana.*

No change: Visualizations in this category are not linked to and hence do not change on movement of the display. The visualized data typically has nothing to do with potential display movements. An example are movie data as shown in Tangere [34] in Figure 1.4a.

Indirect change: Visualizations in this category change due to movement but they visualize data that is only indirectly related to the movement. In other words, they show and update data that is *affected* by the movement, such as heart rate and EEG signals. Figure 1.4b shows a fitness app's heart rate visualization, in which the heart rate increases when the owner is moving more vigorously.

Direct change: Visualizations that show data being related to the movement directly belong to this category. Movement-related data include step counts, velocity, or position and location as for example in the in-scat display in Figure 1.4c, which shows a plane's location relative to the Earth.

Direct + indirect: Visualizations that show both directly and indirectly movement-related data belong to this category. Smartwatch faces as in Figure 1.4d are a common type of data display dashboard that includes both direct (e.g., step counts) and indirect (e.g., heart rate) visualizations reacting to movement.

1.2.5   Intended Viewing Timespan

Another perspective of mobile data visualization opens up when considering the time available for viewing a visual representation. The *Intended Viewing Timespan* can be decoupled from the screen size and is likely highly related to the context of use. For example, a smartwatch visualization intended for being viewed while running the outdoors will need a different design than a tablet visualization to be viewed while sitting in a comfortable armchair. Similarly, a view on a smartphone has different characteristics when intended for glancing while running compared to focused analysis during a meeting. According to how much time someone spends with a mobile data visualization, we consider the categories: sub-second (glance), seconds, minutes, hours or more (Figure 1.5). More details on glanceable mobile visualizations from the first category will be given in Chapter 5.

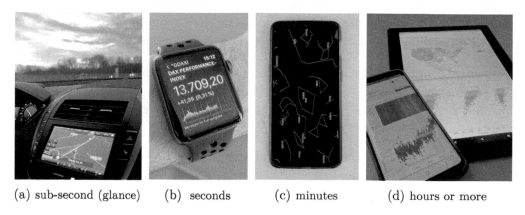

(a) sub-second (glance)   (b) seconds   (c) minutes   (d) hours or more

Figure 1.5 Categories in the *Intended Viewing Timespan* dimension.

Sub-second (glance): An intended viewing timespan of a few hundred milliseconds often arises in situations when people's attention is directed elsewhere and they can only briefly take their eyes away from their primary task. GPS devices in moving vehicles, such as the car GPS in Figure 1.5a, belong to this category.

Seconds: Contexts with relatively simple information needs such as today's or tomorrow's weather, as shown by the app in Figure 1.5b, require visualizations to be read within a few seconds. Visualizations in this category typically support simple comparisons, timelines, and incorporate familiar chart types.

Minutes: Longer analysis times in the range of minutes are expected in visualizations that have more complex information needs. For example, the star map in Figure 1.5c requires viewers to orient the phone at the part of the sky they are interested in and to compare the sky with the representation on their phone. More generally, common tasks required in these contexts are comparing many items, navigating a large dataset, or analyzing multiple attributes.

Hours or more: In-depth analysis of complex data, which require extensive interaction and highly specialized visualization techniques may require viewing timespans of hours or more. For example, dedicated analysis environments such as Tableau Mobile (Figure 1.5d) or tools for situated awareness in law enforcement [30] allow for in-depth data exploration.

1.2.6 Visualization Interaction Complexity

In relation to the impression that mobile data visualization might imply simpler or minimal interaction, this dimension describes the complexity of the main interaction as an interplay between a person and the visualization. Compared to traditional data visualization, mobile data visualization needs to support usage scenarios where people are on-the-go or are engaged in other activities. Analyzing a data visualization may not always be a person's primary task, but rather an auxiliary step to enhance or support other mobile tasks. We categorize four levels of visualization interaction complexity ranging from passive interaction to highly interactive as shown in Figure 1.6. For an in-depth discussion of interaction for mobile data visualization, we refer to Chapter 3.

Passive interaction: The visualizations in this category allow for minimal or no interaction. The focus is on providing pure consumption of information as for the viewer in Figure 1.6a. This category is also related to glanceable visualizations that are characterized in Chapter 5.

Simple view specification: Here, visualizations allow for discrete view switching, which involves changing between the display of different types of data, often also involving a change of representation. The person interacting with a visualization in Figure 1.6b is "swiping" to switch between different representations.

View specification & manipulation: At this stage, visualizations support standard interactions, such as selection, details-on-demand, navigation (for example, with pan and zoom), and so on. The person interacting with a heatmap in Figure 1.6c just selected a single cell to call a tooltip with more information.

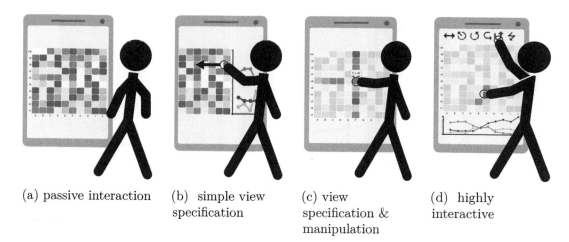

(a) passive interaction   (b) simple view specification   (c) view specification & manipulation   (d) highly interactive

Figure 1.6 Four categories in the *Visualization Interaction Complexity* dimension.

Highly interactive: Visualizations in this category include a broad spectrum of sophisticated interactions. Beyond the types of interactions mentioned above, they may support the full sense-making workflow, including visualization authoring, keeping track of the analysis process, as well as annotation and externalization of insight. For example, the analyst in Figure 1.6d is performing a series of interactions to systematically review information for a group of cells, while bookmarking cells of interest and importance.

1.2.7 Intended Sharing

Mobile data visualizations offer the opportunity for a variety of sharing scenarios, from highly personal use to collaborative use of shared displays. Our focus is on synchronous sharing in which visualizations are viewed at the same time through a shared device or a set of connected devices. Here, we discuss to which extent a visualization is meant to be shared with others: personal use, a few people, larger groups, and the general public (Figure 1.7).

While the intended sharing is affected by the display form-factor (it is more challenging to share a view on a smartwatch than a tablet), these two dimensions are separable. The mobility of the visualization may affect the scenarios in which sharing can take place, for example, from more fixed location-dependent groups at home to dynamically formed opportunistic groupings in a public setting. The sharing might also depend on the personal nature of the data being displayed.

Personal use: The visualization is viewed in a private context, for example, on a small display that cannot be shared with others easily. These visualizations often contain personal data which may have strict privacy considerations or may be of utility only to a single individual. For example, period calendar visualizations or health visualizations such as the migraine visualization in Figure 1.7a are sensitive and meant primarily for a single person.

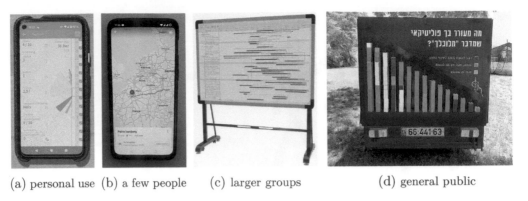

(a) personal use (b) a few people   (c) larger groups   (d) general public

Figure 1.7 Categories in the *Intended Sharing* dimension. *Figure (d) © Ron Levit, reprinted with permission [24].*

A few people: Visualizations can also be for sharing with co-located people in a small group setting, for example, when viewing a map together on a smartphone. In Figure 1.7b, we see a visualization of a visitor's trip progress that can be looked at together with the family.

Larger groups: Visualizations may be shared with larger groups to support teamwork and decision making. For example, the large display in Figure 1.7c can be wheeled into a meeting room to support the coordination of larger group activities by means of a visualization of project plans.

General public: The visualization is displayed in a public setting or can be viewed by many people simultaneously on a personal device. Figure 1.7d shows an example of a public opinion visualization [24]. It can be driven through town and collect data by people passing by.

Overall, we have now presented seven dimensions each with four to six categories according to which mobile data visualizations can be organized. Along the described dimensions, we can mark ranges that are typical for mobile data visualization. We will find small, mobile displays with visualizations that show data that are fetched from the cloud or captured via sensors. Mobile data visualizations will have interactions of moderate complexity and also react to the display movement. A mobile visualization is typically in use only for shorter time spans and also touches upon the aspect of sharing it with others. These seven dimensions also allow us to reason about extremes. For example, a mobile data visualization is not necessary small as can be seen from the truck display in Figure 1.7d. A mobile data visualization might be used only for the fraction of a second on one extreme, for example, when viewers only glance at them as for the navigation display in Figure 1.5a. On the other end of the spectrum, a mobile data visualization might also be used for hours, for example, in the context of supporting law enforcement as in Figure 1.5d.

These few examples already illustrate that mobile data visualization covers a considerable range of designs. We will expand on concrete examples and corresponding categorizations along the characterizing dimensions in the next section.

1.3   TYPICAL EXAMPLES OF MOBILE DATA VISUALIZATION

As mentioned earlier, a crisp definition of mobile data visualization is difficult to articulate, as computing devices converge and propagate to more and more different types of activity. The academic literature and web collections such as MobileVis [32] and Mobile Infovis [35] showcase various mobile data visualizations developed by researchers, practitioners, and technology companies. In this section, we discuss selected examples and relate them to the dimensions presented in the previous section.

We will first look at typical examples of visualizations on smartwatches, phones, and tablets, where most of us would immediately agree they are clearly and intuitively categorized as mobile data visualizations. On the other hand, the dimensions' categories are sometimes blurry and the extremes lead us to examples that point us in Section 1.4 to more creatively think about how mobility affects visualization.

1.3.1   Early Mobile Data Visualizations for PDAs

Research on mobile data visualization began in the nineties [13, 20]. The term mobile computing emerged to describe people's interactions with computing devices that are wirelessly connected, able to exchange information, and portable. With the wide availability of personal digital assistants (PDAs), the topic of mobile data visualization also began to gain momentum [10].

The driving slogan for the works in this early research period was to provide access to information anytime anywhere. The key research challenges were primarily focused on technical issues due to limited computing power and memory. As can be seen in the example on an early PDA in Figure 1.8a, the display capabilities were limited. The display resolution was low (240 × 320 pixels in our example) and early PDAs could display only a few colors—if color was available at all. Therefore, the visualization had to be designed carefully to avoid wasting precious pixels or relying on color-related visual channels. At the same time, the implementation had to be efficient: any overhead by run-time libraries or interpreted languages had to be avoided to keep the visualization reactive and to reduce battery drain.

Another key difference to today's mobile data visualizations is the much lower network bandwidth, causing data to reach the mobile device at a snail's pace. Therefore, the bulk of the information to be visualized had to be stored on the mobile device. Only small pieces of information could be transmitted over the network on demand.

A classic example of a mobile data visualization from this time period is the DateLens [3] (Figure 1.8b). DateLens is a focus+context interface that grants users access to their calendar at any time on carryable handheld PDAs. While PDAs had a form factor that is similar to that of today's smartphones (*Physical Data Display Size*), DateLens had to cope with a screen resolution of only 240 × 320 pixels.

Although some PDAs were equipped with GPS sensors, DateLens did not react to the device owner's mobility (*Data Display Mobility*). The primary input modalities of PDAs were pen-based interaction and dedicated buttons. In terms of *Visualization Interaction Complexity*, DateLens supported a rich set of interactions that allowed users to navigate in time and adjust the focus+context display of the calendar.

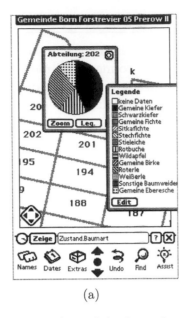

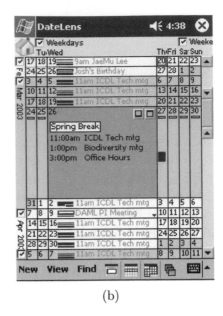

(a)   (b)

Figure 1.8 Early mobile data visualizations on PDAs. (a) Monochrome visualization of forestry-related data on a PDA. Reprinted from Kirste and Rauschenbach [20] with permission from Elsevier. (b) DateLens visualizing a person's calendar [3]. Taken from Windsor Interfaces, Inc. [43] with permission from Ben Bederson.

The schedule visualized in DateLens resided on the PDA, yet, the schedule was not static. It was possible to create new appointments or change or delete existing ones. Naturally, DateLens had an *Intended Viewing Timespan* between seconds (for example, when glancing at the calendar for quick confirmation that there are no upcoming events today) and minutes (for example, when searching the calendar for specific instances of events). Sharing the calendar display with a few colleagues was certainly possible (*Intended Sharing*), but not mentioned in the paper.

DateLens is just one classic example of a mobile data visualization. Visual representations of data can nowadays be found on a wide variety of devices with different form factors. Next, we describe three examples using the most common form factors with high device mobility: smartwatch, smartphone, and tablet.

1.3.2 Mobile Data Visualizations for Smartwatches

When thinking about mobile data visualization, one might picture a small, simple, glanceable visualization on a smartwatch (Figure 1.9). While watch-sized screens are not new, they have gained an increased popularity in recent years with, for example, the Apple watch or Fitbit activity trackers. Recently, we have seen some research efforts in understanding how data and representations are currently displayed on smartwatch faces [18] and how people perceive small-scale visualizations on a smartwatch [7, 15, 27].

Far from the pixelized black and white devices they used to be, smartwatches are becoming powerful computing devices. Despite their small screen size, (high-end)

Figure 1.9 Mobile data visualizations on a Garmin Forerunner 245 watch.

smartwatches can display colorful images at a high resolution (often more than 150 pixels per cm). They are equipped with a state-of-the-art GPS and several on-device sensors, such as accelerometer, gyroscope, and magnetometer. They can be connected to other devices to retrieve and display a wider range of information, including emails, calendar events, and phone call history. This plethora of data being available on smartwatches is a great opportunity for visualization. Smartwatches offer various faces and widgets for people to customize what data to show and how to show them.

Visualizations on GPS watches for runners, as shown in Figure 1.9, are canonical examples of mobile data visualization. The visualizations are on a wearable (*Data Display Mobility*), watch-sized device (*Physical Data Display Size*), and change both directly and indirectly due to movement (*Reaction of Visualization to Display Movement*). The visualized data are typically captured from the device through GPS and sensors, but can be combined with data downloaded from a server (*Data Source*). The visualization design is optimized for on-the-go use while the person wearing the device is running. That said, glancing at the visualization is only a subordinate activity (*Intended Viewing Timespan*). Also the *Visualization Interaction Complexity* is low, mostly involving only passive interaction and simple view specifications. The reason behind this simplicity is obvious: Fiddling with the visualization for too long would increase the risk of tripping or causing other dangerous situations. The visualizations are designed for personal use (*Intended Sharing*). In short, visualizations on GPS watches for runners are a good exemplar of a small, personal visualization, providing glanceable information with limited interaction, for on-the-go use.

1.3.3 Handheld Mobile Data Visualizations

Many existing mobile data visualizations are designed for carryable rather than wearable devices. Examples of existing smartphone visualizations can be reviewed through the web collections, *MobileVis* [32] and *Mobile InfoVis* [35]. Nevertheless, examples of handheld mobile data visualization also include early applications for PDAs (see Section 1.3.1) as well as those for other smartphone-sized tools such as handheld GPS. Just like visualizations for smartwatches, those for handhelds are also designed mostly for personal use.

Smartphones, however, are not as specialized and can be described as a universal personal device with broad functionalities. The successful combination of mobility, portability, and display size as well as the subsequent extended interaction capabilities are reasons why nowadays people are accessing and consuming a majority of digital information with smartphones. The use of smartphones in particular is often linked to actual personal activities and usage scenarios that include a broad range of mobility types: standing at a bus station, sitting on a bench, or lying in bed.

Applications in the context of handheld mobile data visualizations allow people to visually inspect, for example, performance, such as in sports, health measures, such as sleep quality and blood sugar level, product information, such as its components and ingredients, route and navigation information, and departure and transfer times in public transportation. One highly illustrative example for handhelds is Goddemeyer and Baur's Subspotting app [14]. It visualizes the available mobile phone reception along tracks of the New York City Subway. The motivation behind this application is that the expected constant network connectivity of smartphones makes times or places with poor network coverage a challenge for many use cases. The Subspotting app, therefore, shows the previously measured and recorded network coverage for and along a specific route (Figure 1.10), allowing train riders to better understand and decide "where to send the next text or make the next call" [14].

Figure 1.10 The Subspotting app by Goddemeyer and Baur [14] visualizes available mobile phone reception along the lines and stations of the New York City Subway. *Images © 2016 OFFC NY, used with permission from Dominikus Baur.*

With regard to our dimensions of mobile data visualization, this example shows that a visualization on a smartphone (*Physical Data Display Size*) can change due to the movement of the device, both directly and indirectly (*Reaction of Visualization to Display Movement*). The varying strength of a WiFi signal can be displayed during the journey as an indirect indication of position, and the actual physical position on the route can be marked. The *Visualization Interaction Complexity* is at a level of view specification and manipulation: Users can switch between discrete views, and each view also allows for navigation via zooming and panning. The *Data Source* is mainly static and pre-loaded into the application, although dynamic on-board sensor data such as strength of a WiFi signal could be integrated. The visualizations are designed in such a way that the data can be viewed briefly for a few seconds or for several minutes (*Intended Viewing Timespan*). The application and its underlying data are available for the public but the visualizations shown on a device are not designed for sharing (*Intended Sharing*).

1.3.4 Mobile Data Visualizations on Tablet Devices

Tablet devices are like a hybrid of a smartphone and a laptop, with the smartphone's enhanced mobility and touch input and the laptop's larger display. Both companies and developers of data visualization products—for example Tableau, Microsoft Power BI, and Datawrapper—are well aware of the importance of mobile solutions for their customers and, therefore, provide mobile versions of their products as well. Many research examples also are specifically designed for tablet devices, such as Tangere [33, 34] in Figure 1.11a and InChorus [39] in Figure 1.11b, and clearly belong to this core group of mobile data visualizations. At the same time, many of them are expected to be used when the device is in a stationary setting, unlike those designed for smartwatches or smartphones. Visualization research on tablet devices so far has been centered on designing and developing (mostly touch) interactions with existing visualizations rather than developing novel visual representations that might be more appropriate for tablet devices, especially while they are carried around. More details on novel interactions for visualizations on tablet devices can be found in Chapter 3.

(a) Tangere [34]   (b) InChorus [39]

Figure 1.11 Example visualizations specifically designed for tablet devices. *Left image © Ramik Sadana, used with permission.*

Tablet devices and smartphones share a few characteristics (especially from the technical specification point of view): both are carryable (*Data Display Mobility*), can be equipped with a similar set of sensors, can have similar network connectivity (WiFi, Bluetooth, cellular connection), and can have similar pixel resolutions. In addition, in the extreme case, the size of the largest smartphones is close to that of the smallest tablets (*Physical Data Display Size*). However, unlike visualizations for smartphones, those for tablet devices are typically designed for scenarios that require a set of sophisticated interactions (*Visualization Interaction Complexity*) lasting for more than several minutes (*Intended Viewing Timespan*). It is possible to visualize the data captured by a sensor and to react to display movement (*Reaction of Visualization to Display Movement*), for example, a map visualization with the current position overlaid. Visualizations on tablet devices typically allow people to preload (tabular) data to explore from files (*Data Source*). In terms of *Intended Sharing*, they are more for a personal use but since tablet devices are a little bigger than smartphones they can also be shared with a few people, if needed. We note that visualizations—including their visual representation and interaction design—for tablets are not readily transferable to smartphones, which calls for more research on responsive visualization as further discussed in Chapter 2.

Although the first version of the iPad came with a display of 1024×768 pixel resolution in 2010, the resolution has continuously and significantly improved over the last decade: the resolution of the latest iPad devices is as good as (if not better than) laptop displays and desktop monitors. One thing to note is that, as evidenced by the 2-in-1 laptops, the line between tablet devices and laptops has blurred even though tablet devices tend to imply the absence of a mouse and physical keyboard. Somewhat reflecting this hardware trend, earlier visualization research on tablet devices concentrated on showing only one visualization that fit the entire display (for example, TouchWave [2], TouchViz [12], or the initial version of Tangere [33]), while some of the more recent research started to include multiple views (for example, the later version of Tangere [34], SmartCues [40], or InChorus [39]).

1.4 EDGE CASES OF MOBILITY-RELATED VISUALIZATIONS

Apart from the previous examples for smartwatches, phones, and tables, which in a certain way describe the stereotype of mobile data visualization, there are also cases that extend and even stretch the boundaries of what mobile data visualization seems to be in different directions. Likewise, some of these examples also illustrate what mobile data visualization might be in the future.

Sometimes mobility is not in the device itself. For example, an interactive floor [41] is a fixed room-sized device, making it hardly a candidate for mobile data visualization. However, it is linked to the notion of mobility in that it reacts to people's movements. Such an interactive floor can visualize pre-loaded, connected, and captured data, support multiple intended viewing timespans, and allow sharing with a relatively large number of people.

In the following, we will see four more exceptional examples of visualizations in mobile contexts: self-propelled visualizations, visualization in the context of micro-mobility, visualization in hybrid virtual environments, and large movable visualizations.

1.4.1 Self-propelled Visualizations

Devices that can bring themselves to a person to show them a data visualization—rather than the person approaching or simply carrying the device—may seem fanciful, but prototypes of exactly this idea are being tested in research labs. Advances in autonomous robotics are likely to make such devices more and more practical. The appeal of self-propelled billboards to advertisers is likely to create a ready market for such devices, as has arguably been the case for public display walls and projection technologies. Data visualization might be able to take advantage of the same technology.

Yamada et al. [45] developed a self-propelled display device, called iSphere. As shown in Figure 1.12, the iSphere device is a flying drone, surrounded by an array of rotating LED strips to create spherical persistence of a vision display with an effective resolution of 144×136 pixels, at 24 frames per second and with 32 bit color. Despite

Figure 1.12 A more advanced version of the iSphere [45] with an effective display resolution of 760×320 pixels. *Images © 2020 NTT Docomo, used with permission from Wataru Yamada.*

its short battery life (only a few minutes long) and the relatively pixellated image quality, the authors were already able to demonstrate some compelling and potentially important applications—other than advertising. Perhaps the most compelling is the idea of such display drones guiding survivors to safety, or perhaps first responders to survivors, in a disaster situation. The display can show arrows and text, such as "Follow," but it is easy to imagine scenarios involving the display of more complex information to first responders. It is ideal in this scenario, because it does not require the public to have any specifically preconfigured device, it can *actively* get their attention, and its physical presence can be both reassuring and commanding.

The following analysis of the iSphere device according to our seven dimensions of mobile data visualization assumes such a disaster response scenario. The device is independently moving in terms of the *Data Display Mobility* dimension. The *Physical Data Display Size* (88 cm in diameter) is monitor-sized. The *Reaction of Visualization to Display Movement* is direct: for example, displaying information pertinent to the current location, to face the user. *Visualization Interaction Complexity* is passive: while not likely to be interactive (a user should avoid attempting to touch the highspeed spinning LEDs), voice interaction might be a possibility (if a mounted microphone can pickup speech over the motor noise). *Data Source* is a combination of connected and captured, for example, on-board carbon monoxide and thermostat sensor information could be displayed to firefighters. The *Intended Viewing Timespan* is seconds: given the battery life, but also the motor noise, viewing timespan is likely brief. Finally, *Intended Sharing* is general public: this device is intended to be viewed by many people simultaneously in public settings.

1.4.2 Micro-mobility for Visualization

In addition to the dimensions mentioned above, the scope or form of mobility is another relevant and characterizing factor of mobile data visualizations. Most people typically relate mobility of a device to the idea of carrying and using it while they move in the world. However, as with most other physical artifacts around us, we can move mobile devices in a much more local or limited scope. Marquardt et al. [25] write about such micro-mobility, as "the fine-grained orientation and repositioning of objects so that they may be fully viewed, partially viewed, or concealed from other persons." There are several examples, such as Conductor [16], Thaddeus [44], Is Two Enough?! [28], VisTiles [23], or The Role of an Overview Device [9], that all make general use of the mobility of mobile devices but in mostly stationary settings.

VisTiles [23], as an example, is based on the idea of enabling co-located collaborative work with information visualizations by using the combination and spatial arrangement of multiple mobile devices (Figure 1.13). Essentially this allows the use of coordinated and multiple views [31, 42] that are displayed and linked across devices. By repositioning and orientating devices, or by even setting up specific side-by-side device arrangements, users can adapt the interface on the table according to requirements of actual situations.

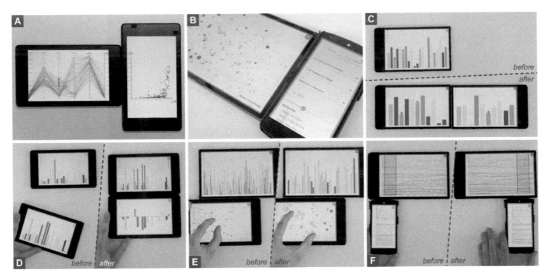

Figure 1.13 VisTiles [23] allows to interact with coordinated and multiple views that are distributed across multiple mobile devices. © *2018 IEEE. Reprinted, with permission, from Langner et al. [23].*

With regard to *Data Display Mobility* and *Physical Data Display Size*, this system works with carryable and phone-sized or tablet-sized devices. *Data Source* is preloaded because devices download and then visualize data. Interestingly, visualization views respond when a side-by-side device arrangement is recognized, which is why the *Reaction of Visualization to Display Movement* is indirect. In contrast to many other core mobile data visualizations, VisTiles's *Visualization Interaction Complexity* is highly interactive and its design considers an *Intended Viewing Timespan* of hours or more. The *Intended Sharing* is personal and—more importantly—for a few people, as colleagues might use such a system collaboratively at a meeting table.

1.4.3 Mobile Data Visualizations in Multi-display Environments

Combining multiple output devices to form enhanced and augmented viewing spaces has long since been an interesting prospect for visualization research. So-called multi-display environments, display ecologies, or hybrid virtual environments offer plenty of display space for visualization and various ways for interactively exploring data [11, 29]. Still more visualization scenarios unfold when considering mobile devices in addition to the mostly stationary devices in such environments.

The appeal of mobile devices in multi-display environments is threefold. First, people nowadays use smartwatches and smartphones regularly, so they are quite proficient in operating these devices [5]. Second, bringing mobile devices to multi-display environments makes it possible to utilize the devices' mobility as well as their output and input capabilities to augment the environment, which in turn can make certain tasks easier to accomplish. Finally, a combination of displays potentially solves problems of sharing information on mobile devices and drastically increases their originally limited display space.

Typically, the devices used in multi-display environment are tablets or smartphones; nevertheless, Horak et al.'s David Meets Goliath [17] show that smartwatches could also be integrated. Mobile devices can be combined with a variety of additional displays and devices. Song et al. [38], Langner and Dachselt [22], Besançon et al. [4, 6], Sollich et al. [37], and Kister et al. [21] envisioned combining spatially-aware tablets or smartphones with large vertical screens (Figure 1.14) for different visualization tasks. Badam et al. developed Munin [1], a framework to seamlessly transition between mobile devices and desktop environments. Instead of large vertical screens, Sereno et al. [36] combined tablets or smartphones with head-mounted displays, while Miguel et al. [26] investigated using such devices in CAVEs.

Figure 1.14 Combining a tablet with a larger vertical screen: *(left)* the GraSp system [21], *image © Konstantin Klamka, used with permission;* (right) Tangible Brush [6], *used with permission.*

In terms of our dimensions of mobile data visualization, the use of mobile devices in multi-display environments spans multiple categories. The *Data Display Mobility* is generally in the range of carryable and wearable, as such devices are flexible and afford direct manipulation for interaction—although other output devices in the environment are usually fixed (table or wall) displays. The *Physical Data Display Size* is, again, likely to be small for mobile devices and large for fixed devices. The combination of different displays often allows users to switch between differently sized visualizations or to augment visualizations with additional contextual information. In terms of *Reaction of Visualization to Display Movement*, the primary purpose is to support direct interaction using spatially-tracked devices. Given the focus of many of these hybrid approaches in supporting highly interactive scenarios, the *Visualization Interaction Complexity* is generally quite high. *Data Source* may be pre-loaded or connected. As many of the examples described above are intended for sophisticated visual analytics, the *Intended Viewing Timespan* is likely in the minutes if not hours—although the weight of handheld mobile devices may be a limiting factor. From the point of view of *Intended Sharing*, there is a span from personal use via the handheld and wearable to shared with colleagues or the public.

1.4.4   Large Movable Displays

Visualizations shown on large movable displays certainly touch upon aspects of mobility, but they are not immediately associated with mobile data visualization. As a thought-provoking exercise, the authors of this chapter sketched the idea of a truck loaded with a large visualization cruising the city to inform the public about certain data. The *visualization truck* is clearly a exceptional case of mobile data visualization. And, it turned out that the idea is not new at all.

In Figure 1.15 on the left one can see visualizations carried by horse-drawn wagons as part of a New York City parade in 1913 [8]. The small print explanation reads: "Many very large charts, curves, and other statistical displays were mounted on wagons in such a manner that interpretation was possible from either side of the street. The Health Department, in particular, made excellent use of graphic methods, showing in most convincing manner how the death rate is being reduced by modern methods of sanitation and nursing."

Fig. 238.   Statistical Exhibits in the Municipal Parade by the Employees of the City of New York, May 17, 1913

Many very large charts, curves and other statistical displays were mounted on wagons in such manner that interpretation was possible from either side of the street. The Health Department, in particular, made excellent use of graphic methods, showing in most convincing manner how the death rate is being reduced by modern methods of sanitation and nursing

Figure 1.15 The left image shows statistical displays on wagons during a 1913 parade in New York [8]. *Image is in the public domain.* The right image shows a truck for collecting participant opinion in the form of a stacked bar chart. © *Ron Levit, used with permission [24].*

A modern example of a visualization truck is shown to the right in Figure 1.15. Ron Levit designed this truck as a 'traveling' data visualization game in which participants could leave their opinion creating a unit-based opinion visualization [24]. While the creation of the visualization would be in-place, the truck could later start moving and show the results of people's opinions.

Large movable displays, here in the form of visualization trucks, are clear borderline cases for mobile data visualization. They are displays that move independently of the viewer (*Data Display Mobility*) and are quite large, even wall-sized (*Physical Data Display Size*). One can envision truck-attached visualizations that are connected to the internet or a GPS device and change due to the truck's movement but in our two examples above, there is no change (*Reaction of Visualization to Display Movement*) and the data is pre-loaded (*Data Source*). The *Intended Viewing Timespan* depends largely on the speed of the truck or wagon but is likely in the minutes and sharing is intended for the general public (*Intended Sharing*). As such, the *visualization truck* is quite different from the core cases we discussed above—but it is in the realm of mobile data visualization.

1.5   SUMMARY AND REFLECTIONS

In this chapter, we addressed the question of what is mobile data visualization. We identified seven dimensions for characterizing mobile data visualization and presented a wide range of mobile data visualizations, ranging from common but typical examples, such as visualizations on smartphones and smartwatches, to more exotic examples, such as drone-mounted visualizations, hinting at a pervasive role for mobile data visualization in a future society. All of our examples have in common that they visualize data in some way, and that they are mobile, but in a variety of senses of mobility. Our set of dimensions is useful as a classification system to describe existing approaches in the context of mobility and visualization. A compact overview of our examples in relation to the characterizing dimensions is provided in Table 1.1.

As computing itself becomes more and more diverse, with devices evolving and shrinking further into clothing and other wearable and flexible forms, and as more and more computing is done in the cloud instead of on local devices, the possibilities for mobile data visualization will continue to grow and diversify. Chapter 9 reflects this with a particular view on ubiquitous visualization.

We struggled with the definition of mobility as it is a moving target. In some sense, everything is mobile depending on your frame of reference. A more serious question that we had to contend with in this chapter was what should be the largest frame of reference that we would still consider mobile? Is a visualization truck as just mentioned mobile? Or, consider the flight path visualization on the seatbacks on an airplane as in Figure 1.16. Is it mobile? The answer in both cases is certainly, yes, they are mobile: the seatback display with respect to the Earth and the truck with respect to the observing bystander. Yet, both examples contradict with our intuition of a mobile data visualization being portable and handheld.

In our considerations of what to cover in this chapter, we have taken a common sense approach: If someone looks at a visualization as intended, would they plausibly

TABLE 1.1 Overview of core examples and edge cases and their relation to the proposed dimensions of mobile data visualizations.

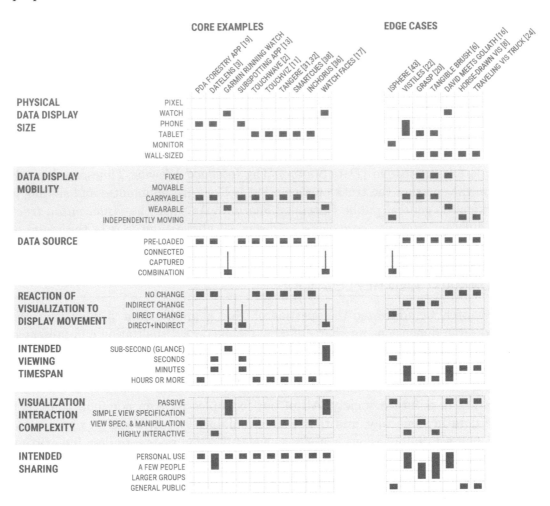

think it is a mobile visualization? If so, we considered it as part of our investigation. We consciously decided to avoid making solid and arbitrary demarcations of what is and is not mobile data visualization by defining our seven dimensions. The degree of inclusion in the class of mobile data visualizations is then a spectrum with fuzzy borders across these dimensions. It is not about whether something is strictly in or out, but certainly some examples are more clearly mobile data visualizations than others. Our intention is not to find a narrow definition which limits what is considered mobile data visualization, but to present our interpretation and to help suggest in what ways mobile data visualization might grow in the future.

There is still a reductive decision implicit in the choice of only seven dimensions. Other dimensions of description are certainly possible; another dimension we might consider is *utility*. For example, at some point wearable visualizations become more decorative jewelry than useful data displays. An edge case even more exotic than those

Figure 1.16 The flight path visualization in the entertainment system on a passenger airplane. They are mobile with the plane with respect to the planet, but the observer is usually (approximately) static with respect to the visualization.

considered in Section 1.4 is the DNA ring.[1] This ring is a wearable physicalization of one's DNA, but it is likely more a conversation starter than something that really informs about the structure of the underlying data. However, it is still mobile (it moves around) and it is still a representation of the data.

Despite many possibilities associated with mobile data visualization, there are also many challenges, which are reflected in the chapters of this book. For example, as we have seen, display characteristics may vary considerably, and thus data visualization researchers can no longer limit their research to the assumption of a relatively large and flat screen. Chapters 2 and 4 will pick up this aspect by discussing responsive visualization design and 3D mobile data visualization, respectively. Similarly, mobile data visualization calls for new ways of interacting with visual representations of data. As will be explained in Chapter 3, interaction for mobile data visualization can be based on a variety of input modalities available on mobile devices, which is an opportunity and a challenge at the same time. Chapter 8 presents an ideation method that might help in creating new mobile data visualization experiences. So, for those interested in the field of mobile data visualization, the possibilities are wide open and exciting.

ACKNOWLEDGMENTS

We thank Harald Reiterer, who was part of our discussion group on "What is mobile data visualization?" and contributed to the preparation of this chapter. We are also very grateful for the helpful comments and constructive critiques given by Tanja Blascheck, Matthew Brehmer, Sheelagh Carpendale, Eun Kyoung Choe, Raimund Dachselt, Alark Joshi, and John Stasko during the writing of this book chapter.

REFERENCES

[1] Badam, S. K., Fisher, E., and Elmqvist, N. "Munin: A Peer-To-Peer Middleware for Ubiquitous Analytics and Visualization Spaces". In: *Transactions on*

---

[1]http://dataphys.org/list/jewellery-shaped-by-dna-profile/

Visualization and Computer Graphics (TVCG) 21.2 (Feb. 2015). **Open Access version:** `https://www.researchgate.net/publication/273161089`, pp. 215–228. DOI: `10.1109/TVCG.2014.2337337` (cited on page 21).

[2] Baur, D., Lee, B., and Carpendale, S. "TouchWave: Kinetic Multi-Touch Manipulation for Hierarchical Stacked Graphs". In: *Proceedings of the Conference on Interactive Tabletops and Surfaces (ITS)*. **Open Access version:** `https://innovis.cpsc.ucalgary.ca/innovis/uploads/Publications/Publications/Baur2012ITS.pdf`. New York, NY, USA: ACM, 2012, pp. 255–264. DOI: `10.1145/2396636.2396675` (cited on page 18).

[3] Bederson, B. B., Clamage, A., Czerwinski, M., and Robertson, G. G. "DateLens: A Fisheye Calendar Interface for PDAs". In: *Transactions on Computer-Human Interaction (TOCHI)* 11.1 (Mar. 2004). **Open Access version:** `https://www.microsoft.com/en-us/research/wp-content/uploads/2004/03/tochidatelens.pdf`, pp. 90–119. DOI: `10.1145/972648.972652` (cited on pages 13, 14).

[4] Besançon, L., Issartel, P., Ammi, M., and Isenberg, T. "Hybrid Tactile/Tangible Interaction for 3D Data Exploration". In: *Transactions on Visualization and Computer Graphics (TVCG)* 23.1 (Jan. 2017). **Open Access version:** `https://hal.inria.fr/hal-01372922`, pp. 881–890. DOI: `10.1109/TVCG.2016.2599217` (cited on page 21).

[5] Besançon, L., Issartel, P., Ammi, M., and Isenberg, T. "Mouse, Tactile, and Tangible Input for 3D Manipulation". In: *Proceedings of the Conference on Human Factors in Computing Systems (CHI)*. **Open Access version:** `https://hal.inria.fr/hal-01436206`. New York: ACM, May 2017, pp. 4727–4740. DOI: `10.1145/3025453.3025863` (cited on page 21).

[6] Besançon, L., Sereno, M., Yu, L., Ammi, M., and Isenberg, T. "Hybrid Touch/Tangible Spatial 3D Data Selection". In: *Computer Graphics Forum* 38.3 (June 2019). **Open Access version:** `https://hal.inria.fr/hal-02079308`, pp. 553–567. DOI: `10.1111/cgf.13710` (cited on page 21).

[7] Blascheck, T., Besançon, L., Bezerianos, A., Lee, B., and Isenberg, P. "Glanceable Visualization: Studies of Data Comparison Performance on Smartwatches". In: *Transactions on Visualization and Computer Graphics (TVCG)* 25.1 (Jan. 2018). **Open Access version:** `https://hal.inria.fr/hal-01851306`, pp. 630–640. DOI: `10.1109/TVCG.2018.2865142` (cited on page 14).

[8] Brinton, W. C. *Graphic Methods for Presenting Facts*. **Open Access version:** `https://archive.org/details/graphicmethodsfo00brinrich`. The Engineering Magazine Company, 1914 (cited on page 22).

[9] Brudy, F., Budiman, J. K., Houben, S., and Marquardt, N. "Investigating the Role of an Overview Device in Multi-Device Collaboration". In: *Proceedings of the Conference on Human Factors in Computing Systems (CHI)*. CHI '18. **Open Access version:** `https://eprints.lancs.ac.uk/id/eprint/89679`. Montreal QC, Canada: ACM, 2018, 300:1–300:13. DOI: `10.1145/3173574.`

3173874. URL: http://doi.acm.org/10.1145/3173574.3173874 (cited on page 20).

[10] Chittaro, L. "Visualizing Information on Mobile Devices". In: *Computer* 39.3 (Mar. 2006). **Open Access version:** http://hcilab.uniud.it/images/ stories / publications / 2006 - 03 / VisualizingInformationMobile _ IEEECOMPUTER.pdf, pp. 40–45. DOI: 10.1109/MC.2006.109 (cited on page 13).

[11] Chung, H., North, C., Self, J. Z., Chu, S. L., and Quek, F. K. H. "VisPorter: Facilitating Information Sharing for Collaborative Sensemaking on Multiple Displays". In: *Personal and Ubiquitous Computing* 18.5 (2014). **Open Access version:** http://infovis.cs.vt.edu/sites/default/files/visporter_ puc.pdf, pp. 1169–1186. DOI: 10.1007/s00779-013-0727-2 (cited on page 21).

[12] Drucker, S. M., Fisher, D., Sadana, R., Herron, J., and schraefel m. c. "TouchViz: A Case Study Comparing Two Interfaces for Data Analytics on Tablets". In: *Proceedings of the Conference on Human Factors in Computing Systems (CHI)*. **Open Access version:** http://citeseerx.ist.psu.edu/viewdoc/ summary?doi=10.1.1.362.7241. New York: ACM, 2013, pp. 2301–2310. DOI: 10.1145/2470654.2481318 (cited on page 18).

[13] Encarnação, J. L., Frühauf, M., and Kirste, T. "Mobile Visualization: Challenges and Solution Concepts". In: *Proceedings of the Conference on Computer Applications in Production and Engineering (CAPE)*. **Open Access version:** https://www.researchgate.net/publication/2785242. Boston: Springer, 1995, pp. 725–737. DOI: 10.1007/978-0-387-34879-7_75 (cited on page 13).

[14] Goddemeyer, D. and Baur, D. *Subspotting*. Web site. 2016. URL: http:// subspotting.nyc/ (cited on page 16).

[15] Goodman, S., Kirchner, S., Guttman, R., Jain, D., Froehlich, J., and Findlater, L. "Evaluating Smartwatch-Based Sound Feedback for Deaf and Hard-Of-Hearing Users Across Contexts". In: *Proceedings of the Conference on Human Factors in Computing Systems (CHI)*. **Open Access version:** https://par. nsf.gov/biblio/10172669. Honolulu, HI, USA: ACM, 2020, 279:1–279:13. DOI: 10.1145/3313831.3376406 (cited on page 14).

[16] Hamilton, P. and Wigdor, D. J. "Conductor: Enabling and Understanding Cross-Device Interaction". In: *Proceedings of the Conference on Human Factors in Computing Systems (CHI)*. **Open Access version:** http://www.dgp.toronto. edu/~dwigdor/?acm=http://dl.acm.org/authorize?N96405. Toronto, Ontario, Canada: ACM, 2014, pp. 2773–2782. DOI: 10.1145/2556288.2557170 (cited on page 20).

[17] Horak, T., Badam, S. K., Elmqvist, N., and Dachselt, R. "When David Meets Goliath: Combining Smartwatches With a Large Vertical Display for Visual Data Exploration". In: *Proceedings of the Conference on Human Factors in Computing Systems (CHI)*. **Open Access version:** http://users.umiacs. umd.edu/~elm/projects/david-goliath/david-goliath.pdf. Montreal

QC, Canada: ACM, 2018, 19:1–19:13. DOI: 10.1145/3173574.3173593. URL: http://doi.acm.org/10.1145/3173574.3173593 (cited on page 21).

[18] Islam, A., Bezerianos, A., Lee, B., Blascheck, T., and Isenberg, P. "Visualizing Information on Watch Faces: A Survey With Smartwatch Users". In: *Short Paper Proceedings of the Conference on Visualization (VIS)*. **Open Access version:** https://hal.inria.fr/hal-03005319. Los Alamitos: IEEE, Oct. 2020. DOI: 10.1109/VIS47514.2020.00038 (cited on page 14).

[19] Jakobsen, M. R., Haile, Y. S., Knudsen, S., and Hornbæk, K. "Information Visualization and Proxemics: Design Opportunities and Empirical Findings". In: *Transactions on Visualization and Computer Graphics (TVCG)* 19.12 (Dec. 2013). **Open Access version:** http://www.kasperhornbaek.dk/papers/InfoViz2013_ProxemicVisualization.pdf, pp. 2386–2395. DOI: 10.1109/TVCG.2013.166 (cited on page 6).

[20] Kirste, T. and Rauschenbach, U. "A Presentation Model for Mobile Information Visualization". In: *Computers & Graphics* 20.5 (Sept. 1996). **Open Access version:** http://www.rauschenbach.net/Publications/docs/cag96.pdf, pp. 669–681. DOI: 10.1016/S0097-8493(96)00041-6 (cited on pages 13, 14).

[21] Kister, U., Klamka, K., Tominski, C., and Dachselt, R. "GRASP: Combining Spatially-Aware Mobile Devices and a Display Wall for Graph Visualization and Interaction". In: *Computer Graphics Forum* 36.3 (June 2017). **Open Access version:** https://mt.inf.tu-dresden.de/cnt/uploads/Kister_GraSp_EuroVis17.pdf, pp. 503–514. DOI: 10.1111/cgf.13206 (cited on page 21).

[22] Langner, R. and Dachselt, R. "Towards Visual Data Exploration at Wall-Sized Displays by Combining Physical Navigation With Spatially-Aware Devices". In: *Poster Proceedings of the Conference on Visualization (VIS)*. **Open Access version:** https://imld.de/cnt/uploads/Langner-2018_PhysNav-SpatialMobiles_InfoVis2018-Poster.pdf. 2018 (cited on page 21).

[23] Langner, R., Horak, T., and Dachselt, R. "VisTiles: Coordinating and Combining Co-Located Mobile Devices for Visual Data Exploration". In: *Transactions on Visualization and Computer Graphics (TVCG)* 24.1 (Jan. 2018). **Open Access version:** https://imld.de/cnt/uploads/Langner_VisTiles_InfoVis17.pdf, pp. 626–636. DOI: 10.1109/TVCG.2017.2744019 (cited on page 20).

[24] Levit, R. *Traveling Datavis Game*. Web site: https://www.ronilevit.com/traveling-dataviz-game. 2018 (cited on pages 12, 22, 23).

[25] Marquardt, N., Hinckley, K., and Greenberg, S. "Cross-Device Interaction via Micro-Mobility and F-Formations". In: *Proceedings of the Conference on User Interface, Software, and Technology (UIST)*. UIST '12. **Open Access version:** http://debaleena.com/courses/cs522/GroupTogether-UIST-2012.pdf. Cambridge, Massachusetts, USA: ACM, 2012, pp. 13–22. DOI: 10.1145/2380116.2380121 (cited on page 20).

[26] Miguel, M. M., Ogawa, T., Kiyokawa, K., and Takemura, H. "A PDA-based See-Through Interface Within an Immersive Environment". In: *Proceedings of the Conference on Artificial Reality and Telexistence (ICAT)*. **Open Access version:** `https://www.researchgate.net/publication/4304401`. Los Alamitos: IEEE, 2007, pp. 113–118. DOI: `10.1109/ICAT.2007.41` (cited on page 21).

[27] Neshati, A., Sakamoto, Y., Leboe-McGowan, L. C., Leboe-McGowan, J., Serrano, M., and Irani, P. "G-Sparks: Glanceable Sparklines on Smartwatches". In: *Proceedings of the Graphics Interface Conference (GI)*. **Open Access version:** `https://doi.org/10.20380/GI2019.23`. Kingston, Canada: Canadian Human-Computer Communications Society, 2019. DOI: `10.20380/GI2019.23` (cited on page 14).

[28] Plank, T., Jetter, H.-C., Rädle, R., Klokmose, C. N., Luger, T., and Reiterer, H. "Is Two Enough?! Studying Benefits, Barriers, and Biases of Multi-Tablet Use for Collaborative Visualization". In: *Proceedings of the Conference on Human Factors in Computing Systems (CHI)*. **Open Access version:** `https://kops.uni-konstanz.de/handle/123456789/42030`. Denver, Colorado, USA: ACM, 2017, pp. 4548–4560. DOI: `10.1145/3025453.3025537` (cited on page 20).

[29] Radloff, A., Tominski, C., Nocke, T., and Schumann, H. "Supporting Presentation and Discussion of Visualization Results in Smart Meeting Rooms". In: *The Visual Computer* 31.9 (2015). **Open Access version:** `https://www.researchgate.net/publication/264868629`, pp. 1271–1286. DOI: `10.1007/s00371-014-1010-x` (cited on page 21).

[30] Razip, A. M. M., Malik, A., Potrawski, M., Maciejewski, R., Jang, Y., Elmqvist, N., and Ebert, D. S. "A Mobile Visual Analytics Approach for Law Enforcement Situation Awareness". In: *Proceedings of the Pacific Visualization Symposium (PacificVis)*. **Open Access version:** `https://engineering.purdue.edu/~elm/projects/ivalet/ivalet.pdf`. Los Alamitos: IEEE, 2014, pp. 169–176. DOI: `10.1109/PacificVis.2014.54` (cited on page 10).

[31] Roberts, J. C. "State of the Art: Coordinated & Multiple Views in Exploratory Visualization". In: *Proceedings of the Conference on Coordinated and Multiple Views in Exploratory Visualization (CMV)*. **Open Access version:** `https://kar.kent.ac.uk/14569/`. Los Alamitos, CA, USA: IEEE, 2007, pp. 61–71. DOI: `10.1109/CMV.2007.20` (cited on page 20).

[32] Ros, I. *MobileVis: Examples of Data Visualization Usage on Mobile Devices*. Website. Accessed December 2019. 2014. URL: `http://mobilev.is/` (cited on pages 13, 15).

[33] Sadana, R. and Stasko, J. "Designing and Implementing an Interactive Scatterplot Visualization for a Tablet Computer". In: *Proceedings of the Conference on Advanced Visual Interfaces (AVI)*. **Open Access version:** `http://citeseerx.ist.psu.edu/viewdoc/summary?doi=10.1.1.473.6882`. New

York, NY, USA: ACM, 2014, pp. 265–272. DOI: 10.1145/2598153.2598163 (cited on pages 17, 18).

[34]   Sadana, R. and Stasko, J. "Designing Multiple Coordinated Visualizations for Tablets". In: *Computer Graphics Forum* 35.3 (June 2016). **Open Access version:** https://www.cc.gatech.edu/~stasko/papers/eurovis16-mcv.pdf, pp. 261–270. DOI: 10.1111/cgf.12902 (cited on pages 8, 17, 18).

[35]   Sadowski, S. *Mobile Infovis and Dataviz Pattern: Best of Data and Information Visualisations for Mobile Devices.* Web site: https://mobileinfovis.com/. 2018. URL: https://mobileinfovis.com/ (cited on pages 13, 15).

[36]   Sereno, M., Besançon, L., and Isenberg, T. "Supporting Volumetric Data Visualization and Analysis by Combining Augmented Reality Visuals With Multi-Touch Input". In: *Poster Proceedings of the European Conference on Visualization (EuroVis).* **Open Access version:** https://hal.inria.fr/hal-02123904. Eurographics, 2019, pp. 21–23 (cited on page 21).

[37]   Sollich, H., von Zadow, U., Pietzsch, T., Tomancak, P., and Dachselt, R. "Exploring Time-Dependent Scientific Data Using Spatially Aware Mobiles and Large Displays". In: *Proceedings of the Conference on Interactive Surfaces and Spaces (ISS).* **Open Access version:** https://imld.de/cnt/uploads/biovis.pdf. Niagara Falls, Ontario, Canada: ACM, 2016, pp. 349–354. DOI: 10.1145/2992154.2996779 (cited on page 21).

[38]   Song, P., Goh, W. B., Fu, C.-W., Meng, Q., and Heng, P.-A. "WYSIWYF: Exploring and Annotating Volume Data With a Tangible Handheld Device". In: *Proceedings of the Conference on Human Factors in Computing Systems (CHI).* **Open Access version:** https://www.researchgate.net/publication/221518364. New York: ACM, 2011, pp. 1333–1342. DOI: 10.1145/1978942.1979140 (cited on page 21).

[39]   Srinivasan, A., Lee, B., Riche, N. H., Drucker, S. M., and Hinckley, K. "InChorus: Designing Consistent Multimodal Interactions for Data Visualization on Tablet Devices". In: *Proceedings of the Conference on Human Factors in Computing Systems (CHI).* **Open Access version:** https://arxiv.org/abs/2001.06423. New York: ACM, 2020, 653:1–653:13. DOI: 10.1145/3313831.3376782 (cited on pages 17, 18).

[40]   Subramonyam, H. and Adar, E. "SmartCues: A Multitouch Query Approach for Details-On-Demand Through Dynamically Computed Overlays". In: *Transactions on Visualization and Computer Graphics (TVCG)* 25.1 (Jan. 2018). **Open Access version:** http://haridecoded.com/images/papers/smartcues.pdf, pp. 597–607. DOI: 10.1109/TVCG.2018.2865231 (cited on page 18).

[41]   Vermeulen, J., Luyten, K., Coninx, K., Marquardt, N., and Bird, J. "Proxemic Flow: Dynamic Peripheral Floor Visualizations for Revealing and Mediating Large Surface Interactions". In: *Proceedings of the Conference on Human-Computer Interaction (INTERACT).* **Open Access version:** https://hal.archives-ouvertes.fr/hal-01610802/. Cham, Switzerland: Springer, 2015, pp. 264–281. DOI: 10.1007/978-3-319-22723-8_22 (cited on page 18).

[42] Wang Baldonado, M. Q., Woodruff, A., and Kuchinsky, A. "Guidelines for Using Multiple Views in Information Visualization". In: *Proceedings of the Conference on Advanced Visual Interfaces (AVI)*. **Open Access version:** http://citeseerx.ist.psu.edu/viewdoc/summary?doi=10.1.1.34.7883. Palermo, Italy: ACM, 2000, pp. 110–119. DOI: 10.1145/345513.345271. URL: http://doi.acm.org/10.1145/345513.345271 (cited on page 20).

[43] Windsor Interfaces, Inc. *DateLens Calendar*. Online. 2004. URL: www.windsorinterfaces.com/datelens.shtml (cited on page 14).

[44] Woźniak, P., Lischke, L., Schmidt, B., Zhao, S., and Fjeld, M. "Thaddeus: A Dual Device Interaction Space for Exploring Information Visualisation". In: *Proceedings of the Nordic Conference on Human-Computer Interaction (NordiCHI)*. Helsinki, Finland: ACM, 2014, pp. 41–50. DOI: 10.1145/2639189.2639237. URL: http://doi.acm.org/10.1145/2639189.2639237 (cited on page 20).

[45] Yamada, W., Yamada, K., Manabe, H., and Ikeda, D. "ISphere: Self-Luminous Spherical Drone Display". In: *Proceedings of the Conference on User Interface, Software, and Technology (UIST)*. UIST '17. Québec City, QC, Canada: ACM, 2017, pp. 635–643. DOI: 10.1145/3126594.3126631. URL: https://doi.org/10.1145/3126594.3126631 (cited on pages 18, 19).

CHAPTER 2

Responsive Visualization Design for Mobile Devices

Tom Horak

Technische Universität Dresden, Germany

Wolfgang Aigner

St. Pölten University of Applied Sciences, Austria

Matthew Brehmer

Tableau Research, USA

Alark Joshi

University of San Francisco, USA

Christian Tominski

University of Rostock, Germany

CONTENTS

DOI: 10.1201/9781003090823-2

W ITH the proliferation of mobile devices, people can now interact with data visualization on smartphones, tablets, and smartwatches. Although these new devices offer the opportunity to visualize data in mobile contexts, most visualization techniques used in practice were originally designed with desktop displays in mind. These desktop-oriented techniques are often ill-suited for mobile devices due to differences and restrictions in display size, aspect ratio, and interaction capabilities. Furthermore, mobile usage is contingent upon many contextual aspects, such as one-handed interaction, unstable movement, or noisy surroundings. The combination of these factors require that data visualization design must be *responsive* to device constraints and dynamic usage contexts.

This chapter is about *responsive data visualization design* for *mobile devices.* We use the term *responsive* to describe aspects of visualization that adapt automatically to various factors, such as changed device characteristics, environment, usage context, data, or user requirements. Given the theme of this book, we focus on mobile devices, although it should be noted that responsive visualization design is also applicable to non-mobile devices, such as PC displays of varying size, tabletop displays, and large wall- or projector-based displays. We discuss aspects of responsive mobile data visualization as well as its relation to existing visualization concepts in Section 2.1, before contrasting it to responsive *web* design in Section 2.2. Section 2.3 summarizes the types of change that visualization must respond to and how they can be sensed on mobile devices. We then review ten responsive visualization design strategies in Section 2.4, including adaptations of scale, layout, and visual encoding as well as attentional cues and specific interactions. Finally, Section 2.5 describes possible future research directions pertaining to responsive visualization design for mobile devices and beyond.

2.1 CONTEXT

Over the course of the last decade, a new class of mobile devices has become ubiquitous in our daily lives. A key characteristic of these devices is their mobility, allowing people to access visualized information anywhere and anytime. However, visualizing the information appropriately remains a challenge, due in part to how mobile devices vary considerably in their display and interaction capabilities, even within the same device class. For example, display sizes of tablets can range from 4.8 to 13 inches. Smartphones typically have an aspect ratio of 16:9, but there are also phones with aspect ratios of 3:2 or 21:9. Even the familiar form factor of rectangular displays can no longer be taken for granted with the advent of circular smartwatches. The heterogeneity of mobile devices makes it virtually impossible to design one-size-fits-all visualization solutions. Embracing a responsive design mindset is a way to keep development cost down while catering to the needs of different devices and usage contexts. We will come back to this idea of "Develop Once, Deploy to Many" in Section 2.5 of our chapter.

Moreover, an increase in mobility and connectivity means that it is possible to use a mobile device across many diverse contexts that are quite unlike those envisioned or typically considered in visualization design. Interactive visualization designed for mobile usage might be used on a bumpy bus ride, in a relaxed position on the couch, on the go while leaving the office, under bright sunlight, or in the dim light of a crowded elevator. In all of these situations, the visualization must allow people to satisfy their information needs and fulfill their interaction intent. Unfortunately, contemporary visualization design is usually optimized for only a small number of contexts. For example, news graphics teams typically produce variants of a visualization for desktops, tablets, and phones instead of creating a single responsive design [47, 79]. This is in contrast to the develop-once idea mentioned before.

To account for the different device properties and usage scenarios, we must design visualizations that adapt automatically. This realization has been apparent for several years in discussions pertaining to *scalability* and particularly those about display scalability [89]. This realization gained momentum with the rise of *responsive web design*, where web pages adapt their layout automatically to the browser viewport. However, while it is now common for web pages to follow a responsive philosophy, for visualization design often no adaptations are applied at all. Recently, Wu et al. [100] studied various visualizations and found that over 73% of them faced at least one issue when being displayed on mobile devices. As a solution, Wu et al. proposed a framework that automatically fixes the detected issues. An alternative to fixing broken visualizations at run time is to implement responsive behavior already at design time, which will allow for incorporating more suitable strategies.

To recap, *responsiveness* denotes the ability of a visualization design to adapt to changing contexts. Responsive behavior can be triggered both by explicit changes invoked by a user or by implicit changes sensed in the environment. For example, a stock ticker mobile application might provide a more detailed chart when the user rotates the device from portrait into landscape mode. Or consider how a personal fitness application might automatically activate a special mode with increased button and font sizes when it detects usage while in motion, for example, when riding a bus.

This chapter discusses responsiveness for mobile data visualization in greater depth. The visualization research and practitioner communities provide a few starting points for this topic, but there remains a clear need for a structured investigation of *what* might trigger automatic visualization adaptation, as well as *how* the adaptation can manifest.

2.2 RESPONSIVE DESIGN VS. RESPONSIVE VISUALIZATION DESIGN

Despite the web design community's recent embrace of responsive and mobile-first design approaches, the visualization community has yet to establish responsive design principles to a similar extent. This is not to say that the visualization community has ignored mobile usage scenarios, as many visualization techniques have been developed for smartphone, tablet, and watch interfaces (quite a few of these are profiled throughout this book). However, these existing techniques tend to focus on single contexts rather than on varied and dynamic usage contexts. Existing literature on responsive visualization design [51, 46, 57] is primarily concerned with implementation aspects and how responsiveness can be achieved using web technologies in particular. However, systematic examinations from a conceptual perspective are rare [21, 36] or predate the smartphone era [34, 22, 71].

Over the past two decades, the fields of mobile user interface design and web design have faced an increasing heterogeneity of devices and capabilities. The sheer number of possibilities quickly made it impossible to create designs tailored for each platform and thus a more adaptive approach was deemed necessary. To realize this, designers had to relinquish some control over specificity of their applications.

In 2010, three years after the release of the first iPhone, Ethan Marcotte attracted much discussion with his *"Responsive Web Design"* blog post [63], in which he introduced three pillars of responsiveness:

- **Fluid grids**: relative grid specifications based on percentages rather than pixels and changing of grid layouts based on interface constraints (such as converting a three-column layout to a single-column layout).

- **Flexible images**: the percentage-based sizing and automatic creation, caching, and delivery of device-appropriate images.

- **Media queries**: a part of the CSS specification that allows web apps to inspect the physical characteristics of the device.

While one might argue that data visualized on a mobile display should be considered as an image with respect to responsive web design [64], this argument falls short. A visualization is more than just an image: it is a complex and structured object in itself. It differs from an image in terms of composition, data-dependency, interactivity, and scalability.

Consider for example the inner composition of a chart. Simply scaling down or changing the aspect ratio of a chart is not merely a technical question of size and resolution, but rather that the content and representation need to be carefully adapted. Let's take a simple bar chart as an example; while the bars themselves might be easily scaled down, the same strategy cannot be applied for data or axes labels to the same extent. For these elements, adjustments such as repositioning, abbreviation, or partial omission might be more suitable.

Also unlike images, interactivity often plays a vital role in visualization [90]. The visualization community has developed countless techniques for selecting, annotating, aggregating, filtering, and partitioning data points, as well as techniques for navigating along data dimensions and modifying visual encoding channels [68]. To achieve responsive visualization design, these interaction techniques must also be adapted in addition to the visual representation.

Visualization is unlike image content also in that the visual representation is explicitly determined by the underlying data. Particular combinations of visual representation and dataset may not be amenable for displays of varying size.

This brings to mind the topic of *scalability*, which is one of the key challenges of visual analytics research [89]. This aspect not only concerns questions of visual representation that depends on the available screen real estate or the number of visual elements to display. It is also very much related to other device constraints such as the often limited processing power or lower network bandwidth of mobile devices. These can make it hard, for example, to store large datasets or run complex data analytics pipelines on the device itself.

We reiterate that *responsive visualization design* cannot be thought of in the same way as images are treated in responsive web design. Responsive visualization must respond to various changes and it must adapt in one or more of the various ways described below. While many of the approaches from responsive web design are applicable in responsive visualization design, we acknowledge the roles of data and the separable components of visualization content.

Responsive mobile visualization is the synthesis of *responsive design* and *visualization design for mobile devices*. Körner's [57] definition of the former implies an adaptation of appearance and behavior, including interaction, to a user's device. As discussed in Chapter 1, *mobile visualization design* encompasses several criteria, including the size and the mobility of the data display and reaction to movement.

In bringing responsive design and mobile visualization together, we address interactive visual data representations that adapt their appearance and behavior to changing factors. This means that responsive mobile visualization must account for changes in data (e.g., small vs. large data sets), the user with their visualization and interaction literacy, the device type and its capabilities, its usage (e.g., whether it is held in portrait or landscape mode), and the environment (e.g., comfortable home use vs. use on a shaky bus).

Although we consider responsive mobile visualization broadly, we focus on devices ranging from smartwatches to smartphones and tablets. We do not address augmented or virtual reality devices such as stereoscopic and head-mounted devices, which are discussed in Chapter 4. Nor do we discuss responsive visualization design for tabletop- and wall-based displays due to their limited mobility aspects. Lastly, collaborative usage scenarios are out of scope as well.

2.3 FACTORS IMPACTING VISUALIZATION DESIGN ON MOBILE DEVICES

As stated before, responsive mobile visualization must be able to adapt to a variety of factors, such as device properties, usage context, or data characteristics. Accordingly, we categorize them into five types of factors: device factors, usage factors, environmental factors, data factors, and human factors. All these factors can significantly impact how well a person can perceive and interactively analyze the visualization content and thus the data. Therefore, it is necessary to examine in detail what these various factors are and how they can be sensed or inferred in the context of responsive visualization design.

2.3.1 Device Factors

 Although our focus is on smartwatches, smartphones, and tablets, this is nonetheless a broad spectrum of devices. The most visually prominent difference across these devices is **display size**. Display sizes can range from only dozens of pixels up to resolutions similar to desktop devices. Notably, "size" can be considered in two ways: as a virtual unit expressed in pixels and as a physical unit in centimeters. In responsive web design, often only the virtual size is considered. However, in visualization design, we argue that the physical size and the pixel density is highly relevant. Similarly, the **aspect ratio** of a display can differ significantly, even within a usage session, such as by rotating a device from landscape to portrait mode. Moreover, many smartwatch displays now incorporate non-rectangular shapes. As many visualizations are sensitive with respect to size and aspect ratio, the device characteristics can prove to be challenging when bringing visualizations to them.

The current approach to handle different display sizes is using breakpoints: hard-coded width values at which content is adapted in some way; between these breakpoints, the content is simply scaled to fit the width [64]. For visualization design, this strategy might not be sufficient to avoid negative effects with respect to readability and graphical perception [16, 97]. To optimize for graphical perception, designers must consider other device factors such as color support, contrast, or refresh rate. Such factors are particularly important when considering devices with alternative display technologies such as e-ink [48, 56].

 The **interaction modalities** supported by mobile devices are also relevant to responsive visualization design: a different modality might require a different interaction mechanism to be implemented. As the default, current smartphones support touchscreen input. While being a very direct form of interaction, touch is prone to the so-called *fat-finger problem* [85] and can hinder the interaction with small elements. Similarly, the lack of mouse buttons (e.g., for right click) makes it necessary to think about alternatives, with touch gestures or pressure-sensitive touch being common ones. Pen- and stylus-based interaction has also become more prominent in recent years with devices such as the Samsung Galaxy Note or the Apple iPad Pro. Pens can offer higher precision allowing for interaction even with fine details in a visualization. In addition to on-screen interactions, mobile devices offer further input modalities such as hardware buttons (a camera button, a back button, or rotatable controls for watches), spatial interaction (such as tilting recognized through built-in sensors), or speech input. A more complete overview of the interaction with mobile devices is given in Chapter 3. For the purposes of our discussion, it suffices to say that when a device's most prominent input modality is atypical (particular when not an on-surface input), adaptations to the visualization design will likely be required.

Finally, the devices' specific **hardware and software** can add limitations to a visualization interface as well. Supported software features defined by the mobile operating system and, particularly for web visualizations, the mobile web browser can notably differ between devices. Similarly, connectivity and performance-related hardware components (such as the CPU, GPU, RAM, storage) can influence the speed of interaction as well as how much content can be loaded and rendered. These factors may also impact battery life differently across devices, where high power consumption will drain the battery until a point at which the operating system will limit the performance to extend battery life.

2.3.2 Usage Factors

When using a mobile device, interaction is no longer only shaped by device factors but also by how and in which **posture** a person is using the device. With desktop computers, the usage is consistent: one is facing the monitor and typically using mouse and keyboard. In contrast, mobile devices can be used in a variety of ways: either hand held, placed on a table, or even body-worn as with smartwatches; while sitting, standing, or lying down; and with one or two hands [8, 30, 31]. In consequence, the viewing angle, orientation, and distance to the display can differ, which likely affects readability of the visualized content.

Further, whether the device is lying flat on a surface, wrist mounted, or hand held will affect the **interaction style** and potentially the precision of a person. On a steady device, small marks can be selected more precisely than on a handheld device, which can slightly move when interacting. The way in which we hold a device also determines which parts of the interface or visualization are easy to reach. For example, when holding and using the device with just one hand, content in the opposite display corner of the hand is typically harder to access [31]. In general, the usage type is closely coupled to device factors such as size, weight, and interaction modalities [32, 102]. Switching from a one-handed usage to a two-handed usage often comes with rotating the device from landscape to portrait orientation, affecting the aspect ratio available for the visualization content.

2.3.3 Environmental Factors

Beyond the control of a person using a mobile device are changes in their surrounding environment. These changes can also impact interaction with visualization content directly as well as indirectly via changes in usage as responses to changes in the environment. For instance, consider that one's environment can be in motion when **on-the-go**, such as when traveling inside a bus, train, or car. Jostling around within a busy train can reduce one's ability to read or interact with the visualization. Further, one might be transitioning to one-handed usage if the other hand is holding on to a safety bar during the ride. In addition to movement, crowdedness can also impose limitations. For example, voice-based input and auditory output are hardly feasible in crowded spaces.

For direct impacts of the surrounding on the visualization content, consider the differences between **indoor and outdoor environments**. In outdoor environments, the lighting situation is dynamic and often problematic for visual perception, such as direct sunlight or dark surroundings in the early morning; both situations may require the display brightness to be adjusted. Variable and insufficient lighting affects the readability of visualizations, especially concerning hue and contrast perception [95]. Other encoding channels might be used to compensate for these deficiencies, or an information display could be simplified for mobile and outdoor environments.

2.3.4 Data Factors

 As for visualization design in general, the **structure and size** of a dataset determines which visualization techniques are appropriate [91]. In particular, when displaying large amounts of data, one must consider the viewer's ability to read, understand, and interact with the visualization. These challenges are further amplified with mobile devices and their often small screen sizes. For instance, visualization of many data points as individual marks can lead to rendering performance issues and a lagging interface on a mobile device. At the same time, selecting such marks can also become challenging due to the reduced precision with touch input [94] or when marks are overlapping.

Similarly, transferring large amounts of data via mobile data connections has also an impact on performance. As loading the whole dataset may require too much time, it is possible to subsequently load chunks or only aggregated data with detailed information only being loaded on demand as in *progressive* visual data analysis approaches [6, 35]. However, as the quality of mobile data connections may degrade during a session, loading additional information might not be possible later on.

2.3.5 Human Factors

 Finally, the person using the mobile device can also contribute constraints to the visualization design. Levels of visualization literacy, subject matter knowledge, attention span, and motivation vary tremendously between people; individuals also learn and change over time. For instance, one may be more motivated to interact with own personal health or finance data via a mobile device than with court case data from a remote county. It can therefore be helpful to think in terms of a person's goals or tasks. For example, one might want to casually browse through a dataset, look up a specific aspect or value, or compare multiple entities. According to Brehmer and Munzner [17], such characterizations of tasks can explain *why* a person requires visualization, and the visualization design must answer *how* a person can complete the tasks using the offered visual encodings and interactions.

An elaborate visualization design may be impractical for some combinations of user and content, though the same design may be appropriate for other combinations or after an initial learning period has elapsed. While a deeper discussion of individual differences in visualization literacy, attention span, motivation, and expertise are beyond the scope of this chapter, it is nevertheless helpful to consider these factors during the process of responsive visualization design.

2.3.6 Sensing and Inferring Multiple Factors

Responsive visualization design for mobile devices requires a way to infer the factors described thus far. Contemporary mobile devices can detect a surprising amount of information relating to these factors. Many device properties, such as the display size, pixel density, and available interaction modalities can be accessed via calls to the operating system or mobile web browser. These can also include WiFi, Bluetooth, and cellular network signal indicators that report the type and strength of network connections available to the device.

In addition, there are a variety of sensors available that can detect changes in the device's usage or environment [45]. Motion and position sensors (e.g., accelerometer, gyroscope, gravity sensor, geomagnetic field sensor) can detect the change of velocity and the relative orientation of the device. Thus, these can indicate if a device is placed on a surface or is handheld, as well as in which posture and orientation it is used. Some devices also offer pressure sensors indicating the amount of pressure one is applying to the touchscreen or on the sides of the device. Both can also be used to detect certain usage styles such as one-handed or two-handed usage.

Today's devices can also sense environmental factors. Ambient light sensors detect the intensity of the light falling into the screen, thus, indicating how well content can still be read and if adjustments of color themes or screen brightness could be beneficial. Additionally, the clock of the device can also be used to adapt visualization content for different times of the day, such as night modes in wayfinding apps. Location sensors such as GPS can calculate the location of the device, which can then be used to load further information on the individuals' surroundings (e.g., on-campus, suburban area, crowded space). In combination with WiFi signals, the location can be inferred more precisely, particularly when indoors. Besides image and video capture, the cameras of devices allow for object, bar/QR code, and face detection or—with depth cameras—for capturing the room properties as well. These can further characterize the surroundings and, for example, indicate if other persons are glancing at the content.

Finally, mobile devices can provide indicators of human factors. Besides user profiles capturing the literacy and expertise of a person, biometric sensors of smartwatches and fitness bands can be used to infer the physical state of the user by sensing, for example, heart rate or oxygen saturation. In stressful situations, visualization content could then be simplified in response. From a security perspective, fingerprint or facial detection can be required for unlocking the device, and thus, guarantee secure access to sensitive data.

Although the quality of these sensors will vary in fidelity and can sometimes only provide a rough indication, modern mobile devices can likely infer many of the dynamic factors discussed in this section, which leads us to a discussion of how to respond to them.

2.4   RESPONSIVE VISUALIZATION DESIGN STRATEGIES

Visualization designers have many strategies at their disposal with respect to responsiveness, and they often apply more than one strategy in combination in any given instance. In providing an overview of these strategies, due to the vast combinatorial space of specific applications, data types, and visual representation techniques, we cannot guarantee a completely exhaustive list of strategies. Furthermore, new mobile devices and sensing technologies may bring about new strategies in the years to come. As for now, our overview also relies heavily upon the work of visualization practitioners who have spoken or written about responsive design, as there is little research literature devoted to this subject, despite an interest in workshops [23, 60] and tutorials [12, 96] targeted at visualization researchers. Work by Hoffswell et al. [47] is a recent and notable exception, which described a system for responsive visualization design based on the documented practices of news graphics designers.

Our discussion largely remains agnostic to implementation, as language- or platform-specific guidance with regard to responsive visualization design is unlikely to remain current, whereas we can expect the strategies themselves to hold for a longer time. Nevertheless, we direct readers interested in web-centric implementation details to Hinderman [46] and Baur [12], who introduce techniques for CSS, HTML, and SVG, Möller [66], Bremer [18], and Körner [57] for D3.js, as well as O'Donovan [70] for React. Similarly, we do not offer substantial commentary on interactive environments and tools for responsive visualization design. For a perspective on responsive visualization design tooling in newsrooms, we refer to an example from Bloomberg News [79]. Existing visualization tools support responsive design to varying degrees, such as Tableau's configurable layout designer [24] or Datawrapper's options for responsive embedding [29]. From the research literature, Hoffswell et al.'s interactive responsive visualization design tool [47] provides a suite of features that could be incorporated into other visualization design environments, such as multiple concurrent previews of different device profiles, or the ability to customize the visualization design for a specific device without affecting the design choices for other devices.

The classes of strategies considered in this section (see Figure 2.1) include changes to the following: scale, aspect ratio, layout, level of detail, amount of data, annotation, attentional cues, animation, visual encoding, and interaction. Our discussion of these strategies complement and expand upon those that Hoffswell et al. [47] used to label a corpus of responsive news graphics, which included resizing, re-positioning, adding, modifying, and removing visualization elements such as axes, legends, marks, and labels. Many of the examples that correspond with these strategies are instances in which a desktop experience is converted to a mobile one, but we must stress that these strategies can also be applicable in the opposite direction, between different mobile devices, or between different states involving the same device, such as by changing contexts or by changing the orientation in which the device is held. Similarly, the motivation for applying adaptations within the examples is most commonly facing a reduced display space. However, all strategies could also be provoked by a changed information need of the user, for example, when selected aspects have to be communicated easily and quickly.

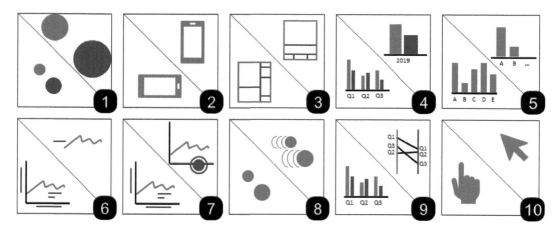

Figure 2.1 Responsive visualization design strategies considered in this chapter. Changes to: 1. scale; 2. aspect ratio; 3. layout; 4. level of detail; 5. amount of data; 6. annotation and guides; 7. attentional cues and dynamic guides; 8. animation and streaming data; 9. visual encoding; and 10. interaction.

Of course, there is also a strategy of doing nothing: taking no responsive design action whatsoever or preventing viewing experiences from certain device profiles. Both approaches are bound to frustrate viewers [100], though the latter approach may be practical in the context of online research experiments, such as in Brehmer et al.'s mobile-only comparisons of time-oriented visualization techniques [16, 15], or Schwab et al.'s comparisons of panning and zooming techniques [81], where control over participants' viewing experience was essential to the experimental design. Finally, we preface our overview with a caveat that not all strategies may be available to the designer, as some will require specific types of devices [61] and/or specific forms of sensing, as summarized in the previous section.

2.4.1 Scale

 The first strategy we consider is that of scaling content to fit within a physically smaller display. Despite their smaller size, contemporary mobile phones are equipped with high-resolution displays; consider the iPhone 12 Pro Max (released in Fall 2020) has a resolution of 2,778 by 1,284 pixels, resulting in more pixels per inch than the display of the latest 16-inch MacBook Pro released in 2019 (3,072 by 1,920 pixels). Given this high resolution, it is possible to scale visualization content initially intended for larger displays. However, this strategy breaks down if the visualization involves text, which will become illegible when scaled down [96], and thus one strategy is to apply different scaling functions to non-text content and text content [18], while another might involve abbreviating text labels in a systematic and consistent manner [83]. It is also ineffective to apply scaling if the visualization is to be interactive, particularly if interaction targets are individual marks or axes. Consider that as much as 92% of mobile phone usage is carried out while holding the device in portrait mode [74], so even a static visualization containing no text elements might be successfully scaled down for viewing in landscape mode. However, further scaling for portrait mode viewing may reduce its interpretability and it will make poor use of the full display height. As a consequence, scaling is a better strategy for visualization content that already has a tall aspect ratio [18].

Finally, we must consider that pure geometric scaling has been shown to incur a perceptual bias [97], and that leveraging an adaptive perception-based approach for resizing visualization might be warranted, as proposed by Wu et al. and realized in their ViSizer system [101] (see Figure 2.2). Other approaches exist that selectively scale text and image content from documents based on salience and uniqueness, which are also known as one instance of semantic zooming (see Woodruff et al. [99], Lam and Baudisch [58], or Teevan et al. [88]). However, these may not be appropriate for visualization content as they can fundamentally distort size and position encodings, except for visualizations that do not employ these encoding channels. Due to these drawbacks, scaling content is often combined with one or more of the other strategies described below, such as changing the layout or aspect ratio of content. If other strategies are unavailable, designers should at least allow viewers to zoom and pan the content, though they should realize that if sustained or repeated viewing is expected, this panning and zooming will quickly become tedious [96].

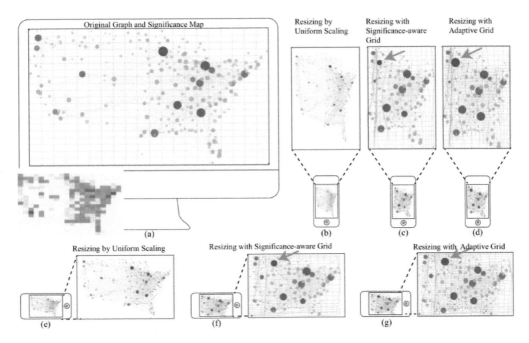

Figure 2.2 Wu et al.'s ViSizer system [101] scales visualization content according to either a significance-aware grid or an adaptive grid. The green arrows indicate where the two approaches produce different results. *Image © 2013 IEEE, reprinted, with permission from [101].*

2.4.2 Aspect Ratio

Since most mobile phone usage is carried out while holding the device in portrait mode [74], it is prudent to make good use of this taller aspect ratio. As a result, one approach is to simply rotate content that was otherwise designed for viewing from a landscape PC monitor. However, text should remain unrotated to ensure its legibility [12]. A simple example of this strategy is converting a vertical bar chart into a horizontal one [20]. Some designs are agnostic to changes in aspect ratio, as the absolute spatial position of marks is not meaningful, such as in circle-packing diagrams or force-directed node-link diagrams [18], where only the relative positions of marks to one another is meaningful. Some chart types are not amenable to mere rotation; for example, rotating a map reduces viewers' ability to recognize familiar geographic features, while rotating a scatterplot would violate conventions of reading direction, with higher values typically proceeding from left to right and from bottom to top. Line charts also resist rotation, due to the convention that the horizontal axis represents time proceeding from left to right.

As an alternative to rotating content, it might therefore be tempting to fill the entire display height. This approach may be appropriate for some chart types but not others. For example, a map can simply show additional territory above and below the focal area, though as Hoffswell et al. [47] report from their interviews with news graphics designers, geographies such as the continental USA are more amenable to a landscape presentation. For line charts and chart types with continuous axes, such a change in aspect ratio can negatively affect perception [43, 87]. Of course, visualization designers need not to use the full display height; in many cases, a square aspect ratio is sufficient, and it is indeed the norm in mobile social media applications such as Instagram [7]. Finally, it should be noted that while the orientation of a device may impact the aspect ratio of a chart, this may not always be the case; consider that a change in orientation can alternatively result in an updated layout of content within a display without affecting the aspect ratio of individual content elements.

2.4.3 Layout

Until this point, our discussion has largely assumed a single piece of visualization content. This content seldom appears in isolation in practice; visualization may be accompanied by text, control panels, images, or additional visualization elements. We must therefore consider composite layouts consisting of multiple charts, documents consisting of interleaved and/or side-by-side text and visualization, and small multiple designs. Hoffswell et al. [47] refer to this as as re-positioning views, though we consider the broader scope of re-positioning visualization in relation to other content, such as text blocks that reference visualization. In the simplest case, a single row of content arranged horizontally for viewing from a desktop can be stacked vertically [12, 18]. However, consider the more typical case in which content can be seen as occupying a two-dimensional grid, such as in a small multiples design. It is the designer's responsibility to establish adaptive grid layout rules that anticipate different screen sizes and aspect ratios [12, 46]; perhaps a grid of six columns is ideal for a desktop display while a grid of two columns is ideal for a mobile display. As a consequence, content that is displayed simultaneously on a desktop display will cascade off-screen when viewing from a mobile display. Unfortunately, information can no longer be compared at a glance, and viewers' comparisons must rely upon memory. Furthermore, interactive brushing and linking across views is not as useful when the linked views are off-screen, unless there is some visual prompt that directs viewers to that off-screen content [10, 39]. Despite this drawback, vertical scrolling is commonplace, fluid, and fast [26], and dashboard creation tools such as Tableau now provide layout guidance for mobile devices [24], in which the default mobile layout involves stacking content vertically. Scrolling a stacked series of charts interleaved with other content (such as text or images) is often preferable to alternative off-screen layouts, such as swiping or tapping page advance through a series of charts, as these interactions are less common than scrolling and may not be discoverable by viewers [41].

2.4.4 Level of Detail

 Another strategy is to simplify and reduce the amount of detail in the visualization. This can be useful when the data are large or the screen space is limited as well as in response to human factors, such as different tasks or literacy being relevant in the current context. While Munzner [68] distinguishes several ways to manipulate the level of detail, we focus on a subset of approaches that we see as being particularly relevant to the topic of responsive visualization design. First, a designer could convert one chart into several charts by **faceting** on a dimension of the data, such as faceting a grouped bar chart into a series of bar charts, each displaying one of the group categories. This approach's disadvantage is that marks that were previously sharing axes can no longer be compared directly, and the newly introduced faceted views may not be simultaneously visible, necessitating scrolling or paging. If faceting is undesirable or unavailable, it may be possible to change the level of detail of a visualization via **aggregation**. This strategy is particularly evident in mobile maps, where aggregation is employed as a form of cartographic generalization [62, 96], such as aggregating counties into states and states into countries. **Reclassification** is a related concept, in which the number of categories or quantitative bins is reduced and consolidated, such as the reclassification of elevation levels in maps. Both aggregation and reclassification can be employed for other forms of visualization beyond maps. Examples of aggregation include a bar chart showing values per week which are then aggregated into bars per quarter, or clusters of adjacent points in a scatterplot that are aggregated and replaced with cluster points, or re-scaling quantitative attributes as ordinal ones. As for reclassification, examples include reducing the number of bins in a histogram, or consolidating categories in a color legend.

2.4.5 Amount of Data

To simplify visualizations incorporating many marks for a smaller display, designers can also remove marks in a systematic way via filtering and sampling. Hoffswell et al. [47] document more than two dozen examples of news graphics where marks are removed when converting a desktop graphic to a mobile one. The example they cite is one by which marks are removed from a symbol map about oil spills based upon a filter that sets a minimum threshold value on the size of the oil spill, and this threshold may vary depending on the size of the display. Another approach to reducing the amount of data is sampling based upon a statistical process. Whenever filtering or statistical sampling is employed, it is critical to inform the viewer that this has taken place as a responsive design measure, with some indication or ability to see what has been elided from view.

Yet another form of sampling is curatorial in nature and is appropriate only for communication-oriented visualization scenarios where there is a series of insights to be communicated to the viewer. In such cases, it could be that the entire visualization is visible from a desktop while a sampling of cropped areas of interest are visible from a mobile display. An example of this is a radial arc visualization by Sadowski [78], in which the entire interactive visualization is the desktop experience while a series of static zoomed-in regions of the arc diagram presented alongside descriptive text is the mobile experience.

2.4.6 Annotation and Guides

Charts, graphs, maps, and other forms of visualization present several types of visual elements to a viewer [54, 47], including at a minimum some data-bound marks and usually also some visual guides manifesting in the form of legends, axes, and grids. In communicative visualization scenarios such as in news graphics, there are also often several forms of annotation [75], such as additional text labels and attention-directing graphical cues such as arrows, color highlights, and shapes. Adjacent to a chart we might also find peripheral annotation such as titles, captions, source accreditation, and other footnotes. In their survey of responsive visualization design in news graphics, Hoffswell et al. [47] show that annotation and guides are often re-positioned, simplified, or removed altogether. Similarly, in a survey of visualization thumbnail links used in online news landing pages and in social media posts, Kim et al. [54] examined the differences between these thumbnails and visualizations appearing within the bodies of articles that they link to, finding that annotations and guides are removed and sometimes replaced with images.

These surveys are helpful in that they illustrate that there is no single order of precedence for re-positioning, simplifying, or removing annotation and guide elements; in some cases, a critical annotation for a single data mark may be more important to retain and emphasize than an axis, and thus the strategy of manipulating annotation and guides will vary greatly across instances. We also acknowledge that these existing surveys are biased toward communicative news graphics. In exploratory data analysis contexts, a systematic or rule-based approach to manipulating annotation and guides across devices may be warranted, such as in Andrews' demonstrations of responsive scatterplots, bar charts, and line charts [4, 5]. In an example of a responsive line chart (see Figure 2.3), Andrews and Smrdel [3, 5] show that as the display size decreases, axis labels first rotate and then are progressively removed at equal intervals, until they are removed altogether. Finally, axes and titles are removed altogether, leaving only a sparkline [93] with annotated endpoint values. Such bare representations are then also known as micro visualizations, word-scale visualizations, or glyphs, but have been shown to still be effective in communicating relevant data aspects [13, 38, 40].

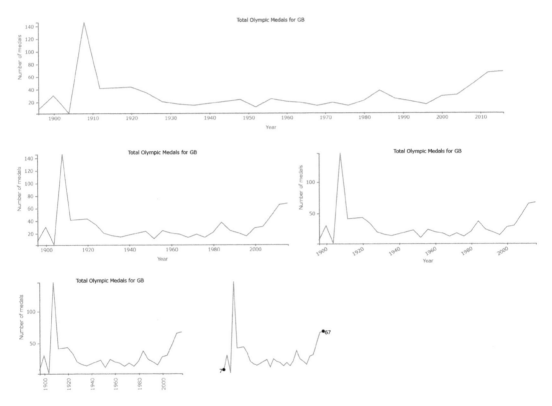

Figure 2.3 Screenshots of Andrews's responsive line chart example at five sizes [3]. With decreasing screen width, axis ticks and labels are gradually reduced, rotated, or removed completely. *Screenshots used with permission.*

2.4.7 Attentional Cues and Dynamic Guides

In contrast to the approach of modifying or removing annotation and guides, there is also a strategy of adding annotation, guides, and other cues to a visualization to support viewing from a small-screen device. For instance, while it may be feasible in desktop viewing experiences to display a large and detailed chart in its entirety, a mobile experience might augment a cropped, zoomed-in version of the chart with a minimap view of the entire chart [22]: a form of focus + context

or overview + detail. An alternative to the minimap approach is to add graphical annotations that indicate the distance to and relative orientation of areas of interest that are currently off-screen [10, 39]. Moreover, labels can play an important role for understanding the visualized information. Fuchs et al. [37] present dedicated algorithms for labeling technical drawings on mobile devices. Similar approaches could also be applied to label for example node-link diagrams in mobile viewing contexts.

2.4.8 Animation and Streaming Data

As with the removal vs. the addition of annotation and guides, we are similarly aware of cases where an animated design for desktop viewing becomes static when viewed from a mobile device, as well as cases in which the opposite occurs. An animated visualization of continuously streaming data may require more processing power than what a mobile device could provide, or a full set of animation controls may take up too much space in a mobile display, and thus a series of static snapshots or a looped animated "Data GIF" [42, 86, 84] may be a suitable compromise in a mobile viewing context. There are also cases in which a static small multiple design intended for desktop viewing becomes a looped Data GIF for mobile viewing. This is advocated by the NPR news graphics team [14], for example, in their article about the growth of Wal-Mart stores in suburban areas [69]. Despite the apparent appeal of Data GIFs in such instances, there is evidence to suggest that static small multiples in mobile visualization design can elicit comparably accurate perceptual judgments [15]. Ultimately, animation can be engaging and memorable, particularly in a communicative news graphics context; however, it can also be distracting and disorienting, so designers should exercise caution. It is entirely possible to craft effective combinations of visualization and animation in both desktop and mobile viewing contexts, as evidenced by the apparent popularity of content incorporating responsive "scrollytelling" [41].

2.4.9 Visual Encoding

Until this point, each of the strategies we have mentioned assumes little, if any, change to the visual encoding. However, this potentially drastic strategy of changing the fundamental design is sometimes warranted, though as Hoffswell et al. [47] show, it is not a popular approach, at least in news graphics design.

Still, an early approach to adapting the visual encoding to display properties has been proposed by Radloff et al. [73]. They use a primary mapping that is consistent across devices and a redundant secondary mapping that varies depending on the device. They successfully tested their approach with a scatter plot being used on a large, regular, and small display.

Bremer [18] cites an example from her own project portfolio, in which a radial paired dot plot is converted into a slope chart. Camoes [20] gives us several additional examples of how a bar chart might be better presented as a strip plot, how a paired bar chart could be transformed into a slope chart, or how a population pyramid could be transformed into a set of overlaid population curves. In each case, the latter is optimized for mobile displays without resorting to sampling or filtering the data. These examples should prompt designers to pause and consider whether a particular encoding design choice for mobile viewing is a better one to use across all viewing platforms, and that a mobile-first design approach may lead designers to more responsive designs relative to a desktop-first approach.

In addition to the mentioned approaches that select and replace a visualization technique as responsiveness measure, dynamic and smooth adaptation methods like *semantic zooming* can be used. Another form of semantic zooming (selective scaling) was already mentioned as a possible tactic in the section on *Scale* earlier. In the context of *Visual Encoding*, a different flavor might be applied: Depending on the available display space or zoom level, the visual encoding can be changed smoothly. For a time series representation, the visualization could smoothly morph [77] from a line plot to a horizon chart [44] when the height of the graph falls below a certain threshold. Such mechanisms can also be used within local zoom areas in focus+context techniques. For example, cells in a matrix visualization can be scaled up to embed charts revealing details about the underlying data [49]. Interestingly, the embedded charts themselves can behave responsively by adapting to the available display space.

Finally, let us revisit the easy choice to disallow mobile viewing, which we know to be frustrating for viewers. An alternative would be to replace a visual encoding with a simple table of the data, or at least a tabular summary [96]. For example, while a node-link representation of a network may be appropriate for larger displays, a sorted tabular representation of nodes may be more appropriate for mobile displays [33].

2.4.10 Interaction

Last but not least, we address the topic of responsive interaction design for visualization. As interaction with visualization on mobile devices is the subject of the next chapter, a thorough discussion of techniques will not be examined here, nor will we attempt a mapping of desktop to mobile interaction techniques. Instead, we offer some high-level comments with respect to responsive interaction design for visualization.

First, there is the question of whether interaction is necessary. This question is perhaps more relevant in the context of communicative news graphics, as newsrooms such as *The New York Times* have reported how rare it is for viewers to interact with these graphics [1], leading their deputy graphics director Archie Tse to declare that the often best visual storytelling is static [92]. While interaction remains to be a topic of debate within the visualization practitioner community [2, 11], entirely scroll-based interaction remains to be a popular design choice across devices [41]. For another example, tooltips that reveal themselves upon hover interaction will be inaccessible to mobile viewers, so fixed tooltips or tap-to-reveal tooltips may be preferable for those viewing from a mobile device [12]. Similarly, a slider below a chart provides another way of revealing additional guides, annotations, or details-on-demand [27].

In non-communicative or exploratory visualization contexts, interaction is often essential to the analytical process [91], and thus it is necessary to rely upon discoverable interactions that allow for similar levels of exploratory behavior across platforms. Scrolling, panning, and zooming work well across platforms, data types, and visual encodings, and initial zoom and pan positions can provide cues that such interaction is possible [18]. The selection of individual marks (e.g., dots in a scatter plot) can prove difficult though due to the smaller screen and depending on the input modality. One approach to tackle this problem is increasing the interactive area of a mark by a few pixels beyond its graphical representation [82, 25, 98]. Yet, for dense visualizations this approach might not be sufficient. In such cases, an invisible Voronoi tessellation can be used to define the interactive areas [19].

This concludes our discussion of possible strategies for responsive mobile visualization. Next, we shed some light on open challenges and research opportunities.

2.5 CHALLENGES AND OPPORTUNITIES

Responsive design is crucial to the success of visualization on mobile devices. While we have pointed to strategies and examples of responsive design applied to visualization that may benefit practitioners and researchers alike, it is also our intent to inspire future research. In this section, we revisit the major challenges and opportunities pertaining to responsive visualization design that should be tackled in future research.

2.5.1 Develop Once, Deploy to Many

Many projects incorporating visualization are tailored to a particular class of device. Developing multiple versions of a visualization project for different devices is expensive [79], particularly if it involves interactivity [92]. In practice, this repeated effort and cost either limits the deployment across devices or results in a drastic simplification of the visualization design, such as by removing interactivity altogether. A responsive design mindset from the outset of a project can facilitate a *develop-once, deploy-to-many* process, which can keep development costs down. However, such a mindset is seldom part of a visualization designer's training. Existing visualization design models such as the nested model [67], the visualization design triangle [65], or the five design sheets method [76] do not explicitly consider the aspect of responsiveness. Responsiveness must become an integral part of visualization design pedagogy so that novice visualization designers learn to approach responsiveness in a systematic way. This requires a rethinking of not only basic charts in isolation, but also the combination of multiple representations in more complex visualization applications. Being responsive is more than fixing visualizations for mobile use [100]. It involves thinking about adaptations at all stages of the visualization design, from requirement elicitation to summative evaluation.

2.5.2 Guidelines for Responsive Visualization

While a responsive mobile visualization mindset can reduce the need for redundant parallel development effort across devices, we acknowledge that the design space for responsive visualization is substantial. We further contend that a foundation of responsive web design is helpful but not sufficient for responsive visualization design. As we showed in the previous section, a visual representation can be adapted in various ways to account for different aspect ratios or display sizes, not to mention different usage scenarios. In responsive web design, grids are often used as a guiding principle. However, for visual representations of data, grids alone might not be sufficient. Unfortunately, the visualization research literature thus far does not provide any substantial guidance beyond responsive web design. While Wu et al. [100] provide a good overview of the most common issues when displaying visualizations on mobiles, we still lack support for avoiding these issues when designing a responsive visualization in the first place. Future research should investigate and expand upon the strategies and practices described in the literature and propose a set of evidence-based guidelines.

2.5.3 Evaluating Responsiveness

The process of evaluating visualization is challenging and can assume many forms [59]. While evaluating visualization on mobile devices is discussed at length in Chapter 6, we take this opportunity to comment briefly on the evaluation of responsiveness in particular. Evaluation of responsive visualization design does not necessarily require large human factors studies. Instead, it seems to be viable to evaluate responsiveness using a set of evidence-based heuristics and guidelines. It may also be possible to quantify differences in the amount of information conveyed in different manifestations of visualization design across devices. Given a possible quantification, automated tests for detecting information loss from larger to smaller devices may be feasible. Finally, one could imagine an evaluation protocol that draws from Kindlmann and Scheidegger's algebraic process for visualization design [55], in which given a set of competing responsive visualization design strategies, the effects of small variations in a dataset could be quantified across different devices profiles for each strategy. This process would culminate in an identification of a strategy that results in a balance between legibility and discrepancy across devices.

2.5.4 Authoring Support

Embodying responsive visualization design guidelines or heuristics in authoring tools is another possible direction for researchers and tool builders. Many web design tools assist developers with templates and device emulators, allowing them to quickly generate prototypes and refine them interactively. While some visualization design environments and languages offer prescriptive guidance (such as the Vega Lite editor [80]), many existing visualization tools do not provide dedicated support for responsiveness. Tableau provides a mobile layout designer and automatic layout for dashboards [52], though other strategies beyond layout manipulation are not offered within this environment. Going forward, researchers and tool builders should identify ways of surfacing other strategies and aspects of responsiveness and into visualization languages and interactive authoring tools. Hoffswell et al.'s recent prototype tool [47] for responsive visualization design is a promising step in this direction (see Figure 2.4), incorporating several of the strategies that we summarized above.

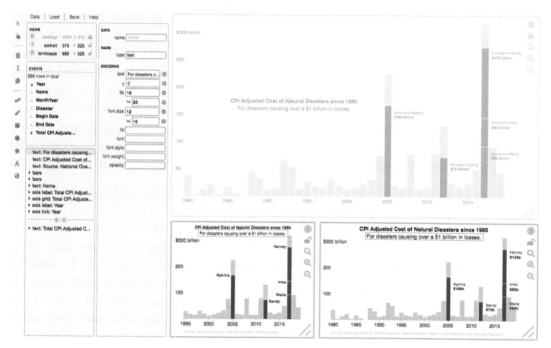

Figure 2.4 Hoffswell et al.'s recent prototype tool [47] for responsive visualization design allows one to preview multiple chart sizes simultaneously. *Image © 2021 Jane Hoffswell, used with permission.*

2.5.5 Responsiveness for New Devices

Achieving responsive visualization design on tablets, phones, and watches is already feasible, though often laborious, and it has become a core concern of visualization design. Yet, emerging and future display technologies will challenge existing approaches to responsiveness. New devices will have properties and characteristics that enable new types of changes that responsive visualization design must take into account. For example, we do not yet have a good understanding of how responsive visualization design could manifest with flexible bendable displays (such as the Samsung Galaxy Fold), not to mention shape-changing displays, which can transform in ways not yet examined in the research literature. Furthermore, upcoming mixed reality technologies might require a special kind of responsiveness, as display constraints no longer exist in the same sense, while the interplay with the real world will put up new ones. The prospect of such devices will be discussed in greater detail later in Chapter 9 of this book. For now we can conclude that identifying responsive visualization strategies for new devices is an exciting direction for future research.

2.5.6 Cross-device Responsiveness

Promoting responsiveness as an integral part of the design process will not only enhance mobile visualization; it will also facilitate multi-device visualization, where multiple heterogeneous displays (large and small, stationary and mobile) are operated in concert to see and interact with representations of data. In multi-device settings, visual representations (or parts of them) can be moved seamlessly from one device to another [72]. For example, if a smartphone is too small to make details sufficiently visible, a throw gesture could transfer the visualization onto a larger device [28]. Responsive visualization design is integral to the impression of seamless continuous interaction across devices. While we have recently seen research dedicated to ensuring responsive visualization design in multi-device environments [9, 50], more research could build upon this work and examine how multi-device responsive visualization design might generalize across contexts and data types.

2.5.7 From Technical to Contextual Responsiveness

Responsiveness as discussed thus far is contingent upon device capabilities and states, such as the size and aspect ratio of the display or the device orientation. In addition to these technical aspects, there are contextual aspects as well, though these are seldom considered in responsive visualization design. Visualization designers and researchers should continue to investigate how mobile visualizations could respond to changing human factors and changing environments. For instance, some wayfinding, music, and podcasting apps infer that the device is in a moving vehicle and offer a simplified driving mode interface not to distract the driver. However, more can be done to infer these changes of state. For instance, wearable devices such as watches could infer a person's mental and physical state. While current technology enables us to determine whether a person is stressed, determining whether they are in flow or immersed in an application remains challenging. Gaze detection via front-facing phone cameras might be useful in this regard [53]. For any given application, designers should determine the possible states that people could be in and what the typical state transitions might be, and design suitable responsive transitions for these state changes.

2.5.8 Make Responses Understandable

Finally, visualization designers should strive to make responsiveness transparent and understandable to the user. Because responsiveness is a form of automatism, the rationale and effect should be predictable and reproducible. For instance, one should be able to determine why a visualization responded to a change in the way it did, as well as be able to understand how a new visual representation is related to a previous representation. The latter aspect could be addressed by smoothly animating visual representations that changed due to responsiveness. The former aspect, that of making the rationale behind responsiveness transparent, requires additional effort. In current manifestations of responsive visualization design, responsiveness is hard-wired into the system. Making it explicit would allow designers to explain the inner workings to the user on demand. Finally, allowing for the responsiveness to be configurable would allow users to tune it to their preferences.

2.6 SUMMARY

While responsive web design is an established practice, responsive mobile visualization design has received comparatively little attention to date. With this chapter, we shed some light on this topic by looking at factors that impact visualization usage as well as possible design strategies. In conclusion, we reemphasize that responsive visualization design involves challenges beyond those encountered in web design: First, visualization content is more sensitive to changes in size, aspect ratio, and interaction modalities, so this content cannot be simply scaled down to fit the screen width. Second, this sensitivity also means that it is not enough to consider the display-related factors in isolation (as is typical in responsive web design), but also the usage context and the environment where the viewer is located. As a consequence, designers require additional context-aware strategies to provide effective visualization. While practitioners have provided an initial set of strategies with respect to how to design responsive visualization, the visualization research community should continue to investigate novel ways to address the challenges of responsiveness on mobile devices and beyond.

ACKNOWLEDGMENTS

We thank Harald Reiterer and Dominikus Baur for their valuable input during the initial discussions at Schloss Dagstuhl.

REFERENCES

[1] Aisch, G. *Data Visualization and the News*. Information+ Conference presentation. https://vimeo.com/182590214. 2016. URL: https://vimeo.com/182590214 (cited on page 50).

[2] Aisch, G. *In Defense of Interactive Graphics*. Blog post. https://aka.ms/aisch-blog. 2017. URL: https://aka.ms/aisch-blog (cited on page 50).

[3] Andrews, K. *Responsive Data Visualisation*. Online examples of responsive visualizations: https://projects.isds.tugraz.at/respvis/. 2018. URL: https://projects.isds.tugraz.at/respvis/ (visited on 11/27/2020) (cited on page 48).

[4] Andrews, K. "Responsive Visualization". In: *Proceedings of the CHI Workshop on Data Visualization on Mobile Devices*. **Open Access version:** https://mobilevis.github.io/assets/mobilevis2018_paper_4.pdf. 2018 (cited on page 48).

[5] Andrews, K. and Smrdel, A. "Responsive Data Visualisation". In: *Poster Proceedings of the European Conference on Visualization (EuroVis)*. **Open Access version:** `http://ftp.isds.tugraz.at/pub/papers/andrews-eurovis2017-rdv.pdf`. 2017. DOI: `10.2312/eurp.20171182` (cited on page 48).

[6] Angelini, M., Santucci, G., Schumann, H., and Schulz, H.-J. "A Review and Characterization of Progressive Visual Analytics". In: *Informatics* 5.3 (2018). **Open Access version:** `https://www.mdpi.com/2227-9709/5/3/31/pdf`, 31:1–31:27. DOI: `10.3390/informatics5030031` (cited on page 40).

[7] Atkinson, H. *Charting New Territory: How The Economist Designs Charts for Instagram*. Medium article, online. 2020. URL: `https://tinyurl.com/economist-instagram-charts` (cited on page 45).

[8] Bachynskyi, M., Palmas, G., Oulasvirta, A., Steimle, J., and Weinkauf, T. "Performance and Ergonomics of Touch Surfaces: A Comparative Study Using Biomechanical Simulation". In: *Proceedings of the Conference on Human Factors in Computing Systems (CHI)*. **Open Access version:** `http://resources.mpi-inf.mpg.de/touchbiomechanics/CHI15Surfaces.pdf`. ACM, 2015, pp. 1817–1826. DOI: `10.1145/2702123.2702607` (cited on page 39).

[9] Badam, S. K. and Elmqvist, N. "Visfer: Camera-Based Visual Data Transfer for Cross-Device Visualization". In: *Information Visualization* 18.1 (2019). **Open Access version:** `https://karthikbadam.github.io/assets/data/visfer.pdf`. DOI: `10.1177/1473871617725907` (cited on page 54).

[10] Baudisch, P. and Rosenholtz, R. "Halo: A Technique for Visualizing Off-Screen Objects". In: *Proceedings of the Conference on Human Factors in Computing Systems (CHI)*. **Open Access version:** `https://www.researchgate.net/publication/2557993_Halo_a_Technique_for_Visualizing_Off-Screen_Locations`. ACM, 2003, pp. 481–488. DOI: `10.1145/642611.642695` (cited on pages 46, 49).

[11] Baur, D. *The Death of Interactive Infographics? Medium*: `https://aka.ms/baur-medium`. 2017. URL: `https://aka.ms/baur-medium` (cited on page 50).

[12] Baur, D. and Stefaner, M. *Everything Except the Chart: Responsiveness + Mobile Support*. IEEE Visualization Tutorial; slides: `http://webvis-do.minik.us/#/responsiveness`. 2018. URL: `http://webvis-do.minik.us/%5C#/responsiveness` (cited on pages 42, 45, 46, 50).

[13] Beck, F. and Weiskopf, D. "Word-Sized Graphics for Scientific Texts". In: *Transactions on Visualization and Computer Graphics (TVCG)* 23.6 (2017), pp. 1576–1587. DOI: `10.1109/tvcg.2017.2674958` (cited on page 48).

[14] Boyer, B. *Data Viz Solutions: Small Multiples on Desktop, GIFs on Yer Phone!* Tweet. 2015. URL: `https://twitter.com/brianboyer/status/583311823245561856` (cited on page 49).

[15] Brehmer, M., Lee, B., Isenberg, P., and Choe, E. "A Comparative Evaluation of Animation and Small Multiples for Trend Visualization on Mobile Phones". In: *Transactions on Visualization and Computer Graphics (TVCG)* 26.1 (2020). **Open Access version:** `https://hal.inria.fr/hal-02317687`, pp. 364–374. DOI: `10.1109/TVCG.2019.2934397` (cited on pages 43, 49).

[16] Brehmer, M., Lee, B., Isenberg, P., and Choe, E. "Visualizing Ranges Over Time on Mobile Phones: A Task-Based Crowdsourced Evaluation". In: *Transactions on Visualization and Computer Graphics (TVCG)* 25.1 (Jan. 2019). **Open Access version:** `https://hal.inria.fr/hal-01857469`, pp. 619–629. DOI: `10.1109/TVCG.2018.2865234` (cited on pages 38, 43).

[17] Brehmer, M. and Munzner, T. "A Multi-Level Typology of Abstract Visualization Tasks". In: *Transactions on Visualization and Computer Graphics (TVCG)* 19.12 (Dec. 2013). **Open Access version:** `http://www.cs.ubc.ca/labs/imager/tr/2013/MultiLevelTaskTypology/`, pp. 2376–2385. DOI: `10.1109/TVCG.2013.124` (cited on page 40).

[18] Bremer, N. *Techniques for Data Visualization on Both Mobile & Desktop.* Blog post. 2019. URL: `https://tinyurl.com/bremer-responsive` (cited on pages 42–45, 49, 51).

[19] Bremer, N. *Using a D3 Voronoi Grid to Improve a Chart's Interactive Experience.* Blog post. 2015. URL: `https://www.visualcinnamon.com/2015/07/voronoi.html` (visited on 11/19/2020) (cited on page 51).

[20] Camões, J. *Efficient Screen Real Estate Management: Improving Data Visualization for Small Screens.* Presentation at the European Commission Conference on New Techniques & Technologies for Statistics (NTTS). Video: `https://tinyurl.com/camoes-ntts`; slides: `https://tinyurl.com/camoes-ntts-slides`. 2019 (cited on pages 45, 49).

[21] Chittaro, L. "Designing Visual User Interfaces for Mobile Applications". In: *Proceedings of the Symposium on Engineering Interactive Systems (EICS).* ACM, 2011, pp. 331–332. DOI: `10.1145/1996461.1996550` (cited on page 36).

[22] Chittaro, L. "Visualizing Information on Mobile Devices". In: *Computer* 39.3 (Mar. 2006). **Open Access version:** `http://hcilab.uniud.it/images/stories/publications/2006-03/VisualizingInformationMobile_IEEECOMPUTER.pdf`, pp. 40–45. DOI: `10.1109/MC.2006.109` (cited on pages 36, 48).

[23] Choe, E. K., Dachselt, R., Isenberg, P., and Lee, B. "Mobile Data Visualization (Dagstuhl Seminar 19292)". In: *Dagstuhl Reports* 9.7 (2019), pp. 78–93. DOI: `10.4230/DagRep.9.7.78`. URL: `https://drops.dagstuhl.de/opus/volltexte/2019/11636` (cited on page 42).

[24] Cogley, B. W. *Tips for Creating Mobile Dashboards With New Automatic Layouts for Tableau.* Blog post. 2019. URL: `https://tinyurl.com/cogley-tableau` (cited on pages 42, 46).

[25] Conversy, S. "Improving Usability of Interactive Graphics Specification and Implementation With Picking Views and Inverse Transformation". In: *Proceedings of the Symposium on Visual Languages and Human-Centric Computing (VL/HCC)*. IEEE, 2011, pp. 153–160. DOI: 10.1109/VLHCC.2011.6070392 (cited on page 51).

[26] Cotgreave, A. *5 Questions to Ask When Designing a Mobile Dashboard*. Blog post. 2019. URL: https://tinyurl.com/cotgreave-tableau (cited on page 46).

[27] D'Souza, T., Nistala, P. V., Bijayinee, S., Joshi, S., Sakhardande, P., and Nori, K. V. "Patterns for Interactive Line Charts on Mobile Devices". In: *Proceedings of the European Conference on Pattern Languages of Programs (EuroPlop)*. ACM, 2017, 1:1–1:13. DOI: 10.1145/3147704.3147727 (cited on page 50).

[28] Dachselt, R. and Buchholz, R. "Natural Throw and Tilt Interaction Between Mobile Phones and Distant Displays". In: *Extended Abstracts of the Conference on Human Factors in Computing System (CHI)*. **Open Access version:** https://imld.de/cnt/uploads/2009-CHI_Throw-Tilt.pdf. ACM, 2009, pp. 3253–3258. DOI: 10.1145/1520340.1520467 (cited on page 54).

[29] Datawrapper. *How to Embed Charts*. 2020. URL: https://tinyurl.com/datawrapper-embed (cited on page 42).

[30] Eardley, R., Roudaut, A., Gill, S., and Thompson, S. J. "Designing for Multiple Hand Grips and Body Postures Within the UX of a Moving Smartphone". In: *Proceedings of the Conference on Designing Interactive Systems (DIS)*. ACM, 2018, pp. 611–621. DOI: 10.1145/3196709.3196711 (cited on page 39).

[31] Eardley, R., Roudaut, A., Gill, S., and Thompson, S. J. "Investigating How Smartphone Movement Is Affected by Body Posture". In: *Proceedings of the Conference on Human Factors in Computing Systems (CHI)*. ACM, 2018, 202:1–202:8. DOI: 10.1145/3173574.3173776 (cited on page 39).

[32] Eardley, R., Roudaut, A., Gill, S., and Thompson, S. J. "Understanding Grip Shifts: How Form Factors Impact Hand Movements on Mobile Phones". In: *Proceedings of the Conference on Human Factors in Computing Systems (CHI)*. ACM, 2017, pp. 4680–4691. DOI: 10.1145/3025453.3025835 (cited on page 39).

[33] Eichmann, P., Edge, D., Evans, N., Lee, B., Brehmer, M., and White, C. "Orchard: Exploring Multivariate Heterogeneous Networks on Mobile Phones". In: *Computer Graphics Forum* 39.3 (2020), pp. 115–126. DOI: 10.1111/cgf.13967 (cited on page 50).

[34] Encarnação, J. L., Frühauf, M., and Kirste, T. "Mobile Visualization: Challenges and Solution Concepts". In: *Proceedings of the Conference on Computer Applications in Production and Engineering (CAPE)*. **Open Access version:** https://www.researchgate.net/publication/2785242. Boston: Springer, 1995, pp. 725–737. DOI: 10.1007/978-0-387-34879-7_75 (cited on page 36).

[35] Fekete, J.-D., Fisher, D., Nandi, A., and Sedlmair, M. "Progressive Data Analysis and Visualization (Dagstuhl Seminar 18411)". In: *Dagstuhl Reports* 8.10 (2019), pp. 1–40. DOI: 10.4230/DAGREP.8.10.1 (cited on page 40).

[36] Fuchs, G. "Task-Based Adaptation of Graphical Content in Smart Visual Interfaces". PhD thesis. University of Rostock, 2011. DOI: 10.18453/rosdok_id00000937 (cited on page 36).

[37] Fuchs, G., Luboschik, M., Hartmann, K., Ali, K., Strothotte, T., and Schumann, H. "Adaptive Labeling for Interactive Mobile Information Systems". In: *Proceedings of the Conference on Information Visualisation (IV)*. IEEE, 2006, pp. 453–459. DOI: 10.1109/IV.2006.17 (cited on page 49).

[38] Fuchs, J., Isenberg, P., Bezerianos, A., and Keim, D. "A Systematic Review of Experimental Studies on Data Glyphs". In: *Transactions on Visualization and Computer Graphics (TVCG)* 23.7 (2017). **Open Access version: https://hal.inria.fr/hal-01378429**, pp. 1863–1879. DOI: 10.1109/tvcg.2016.2549018 (cited on page 48).

[39] Games, P. S. and Joshi, A. "Visualization of Off-Screen Data on Tablets Using Context-Providing Bar Graphs and Scatter Plots". In: *Visualization and Data Analysis*. Vol. 9017. **Open Access version: https://www.cs.usfca.edu/~apjoshi/papers/Games_Joshi_VDA2014.pdf**. International Society for Optics and Photonics. 2014, pp. D01–D15. DOI: 10.1117/12.2038456 (cited on pages 46, 49).

[40] Goffin, P., Boy, J., Willett, W., and Isenberg, P. "An Exploratory Study of Word-Scale Graphics in Data-Rich Text Documents". In: *Transactions on Visualization and Computer Graphics (TVCG)* 23.10 (2017). **Open Access version: https://hal.inria.fr/hal-01389998**, pp. 2275–2287. DOI: 10.1109/tvcg.2016.2618797 (cited on page 48).

[41] Goldberg, R. *Responsive Scrollytelling*. The Pudding. 2017. URL: https://tinyurl.com/pudding-responsive (cited on pages 46, 49, 50).

[42] Groeger, L. *Data GIFs*. NICAR Tutorial; slides. 2017. URL: http://lenagroeger.com/datagifs/%5C#/ (cited on page 49).

[43] Heer, J. and Agrawala, M. "Multi-Scale Banking to 45 Degrees". In: *Transactions on Visualization and Computer Graphics (TVCG)* 12.5 (Sept. 2006), pp. 701–708. DOI: 10.1109/TVCG.2006.163. URL: http://dx.doi.org/10.1109/TVCG.2006.163 (cited on page 45).

[44] Heer, J., Kong, N., and Agrawala, M. "Sizing the Horizon: The Effects of Chart Size and Layering on the Graphical Perception of Time Series Visualizations". In: *Proceedings of the Conference on Human Factors in Computing Systems (CHI)*. ACM, 2009, pp. 1303–1312. DOI: 10.1145/1518701.1518897 (cited on page 50).

[45] Hinckley, K., Pierce, J., Sinclair, M., and Horvitz, E. "Sensing Techniques for Mobile Interaction". In: *Proceedings of the Conference on User Interface, Software, and Technology (UIST)*. ACM, 2000, pp. 91–100. DOI: 10.1145/354401.354417 (cited on page 41).

[46] Hinderman, B. *Building Responsive Data Visualization for the Web*. Wiley, 2016. URL: http://responsivedatavisualization.com (cited on pages 36, 42, 46).

[47] Hoffswell, J., Li, W., and Liu, Z. "Techniques for Flexible Responsive Visualization Design". In: *Proceedings of the Conference on Human Factors in Computing Systems (CHI)*. ACM, 2020, pp. 1–13. DOI: 10.1145/3313831.3376777 (cited on pages 35, 42, 45, 47, 49, 53).

[48] Holman, D., Burstyn, J., Brotman, R., Younkin, A., and Vertegaal, R. "Flexkit: A Rapid Prototyping Platform for Flexible Displays". In: *Adjust Proceedings of the Symposium on User Interface Software and Technology (UIST)*. ACM, 2013, pp. 17–18. DOI: 10.1145/2508468.2514934 (cited on page 38).

[49] Horak, T., Berger, P., Schumann, H., Dachselt, R., and Tominski, C. "Responsive Matrix Cells: A Focus+Context Approach for Exploring and Editing Multivariate Graphs". In: *Transactions on Visualization and Computer Graphics (TVCG)* 27.2 (2021). **Open Access version:** https://ieeexplore.ieee.org/document/9226461, pp. 1644–1654. DOI: 10.1109/TVCG.2020.3030371 (cited on page 50).

[50] Horak, T., Mathisen, A., Klokmose, C. N., Dachselt, R., and Elmqvist, N. "Vistribute: Distributing Interactive Visualizations in Dynamic Multi-Device Setups". In: *Proceedings of the Conference on Human Factors in Computing Systems (CHI)*. **Open Access version:** https://imld.de/cnt/uploads/Horak-Vistribute-CHI2019.pdf. ACM, 2019, 616:1–616:13. DOI: 10.1145/3290605.3300846 (cited on page 54).

[51] Jehl, S. *Responsible Responsive Design*. A Book Apart, 2014. URL: https://abookapart.com/products/responsible-responsive-design (cited on page 36).

[52] Jindal, S. *Take Your Mobile Dashboards to the Next Level With These New Features*. Blog post. 2019. URL: https://tinyurl.com/jindal-tableau (cited on page 52).

[53] Khamis, M., Alt, F., and Bulling, A. "The Past, Present, and Future of Gaze-Enabled Handheld Mobile Devices: Survey and Lessons Learned". In: *Proceedings of the Conference on Human Computer Interaction with Mobile Devices and Services (MobileHCI)*. ACM, 2018, 38:1–38:17. DOI: 10.1145/3229434.3229452 (cited on page 54).

[54] Kim, H., Oh, J., Han, Y., Ko, S., Brehmer, M., and Kwon, B. C. "Thumbnails for Data Stories: A Survey of Current Practices". In: *Short Paper Proceedings of the Conference on Visualization (VIS)*. **Open Access version:** https:

//arxiv.org/abs/1908.06922. IEEE, 2019, pp. 116–120. DOI: 10.1109/VISUAL.2019.8933773 (cited on page 47).

[55] Kindlmann, G. and Scheidegger, C. "An Algebraic Process for Visualization Design". In: *Transactions on Visualization and Computer Graphics (TVCG)* 20.12 (2014), pp. 2181–2190. DOI: 10.1109/TVCG.2014.2346325 (cited on page 52).

[56] Klamka, K., Horak, T., and Dachselt, R. "Watch+Strap: Extending Smartwatches With Interactive StrapDisplays". In: *Proceedings of the Conference on Human Factors in Computing Systems (CHI)*. CHI '20. **Open Access version:** https://dl.acm.org/doi/10.1145/3313831.3376199. New York, NY, USA: ACM, 2020, pp. 1–15. DOI: 10.1145/3313831.3376199 (cited on page 38).

[57] Körner, C. *Learning Responsive Data Visualization.* Packt Publishing, 2016 (cited on pages 36, 37, 42).

[58] Lam, H. and Baudisch, P. "Summary Thumbnails: Readable Overviews for Small Screen Web Browsers". In: *Proceedings of the Conference on Human Factors in Computing Systems (CHI)*. ACM, 2005, pp. 681–690. DOI: 10.1145/1054972.1055066 (cited on page 44).

[59] Lam, H., Bertini, E., Isenberg, P., Plaisant, C., and Carpendale, S. "Empirical Studies in Information Visualization: Seven Scenarios". In: *Transactions on Visualization and Computer Graphics (TVCG)* 18.9 (Sept. 2012). **Open Access version:** https://hal.inria.fr/hal-00932606, pp. 1520–1536. DOI: 10.1109/TVCG.2011.279 (cited on page 52).

[60] Lee, B., Brehmer, M., Isenberg, P., Choe, E. K., Langer, R., and Dachselt, R. "Data Visualization on Mobile Devices". In: *Extended Abstracts of the Conference on Human Factors in Computing System (CHI)*. ACM, 2018, W07:1–W07:8. DOI: 10.1145/3170427.3170631. URL: https://mobilevis.github.io (cited on page 42).

[61] Lee, B., Dwyer, T., Baur, D., and Veira, X. G. "Watches to Augmented Reality Devices and Gadgets for Data-Driven Storytelling". In: *Data-Driven Storytelling*. Edited by Riche, N. H., Hurter, C., Diakopoulos, N., and Carpendale, S. A K Peters Visualization Series. A K Peters/CRC Press, 2018. URL: https://aka.ms/dds_book (cited on page 43).

[62] MacEachren, A. M. *How Maps Work: Representation, Visualization, and Design.* The Guilford Press, 2004 (cited on page 46).

[63] Marcotte, E. "Responsive Web Design". In: *REMOVE* (2010). Issue No 306. URL: https://alistapart.com/article/responsive-web-design/ (cited on page 36).

[64] Marcotte, E. *Responsive Web Design.* A Book Apart, 2011. URL: https://abookapart.com/products/responsive-web-design (cited on pages 36, 38).

[65]   Miksch, S. and Aigner, W. "A Matter of Time: Applying a Data–Users–Tasks Design Triangle to Visual Analytics of Time-Oriented Data". In: *Computers & Graphics* 38 (2014). **Open Access version:** http://www.ifs.tuwien.ac.at/~silvia/pub/publications/miksch_cag_design-triangle-2014.pdf, pp. 286–290. DOI: 10.1016/j.cag.2013.11.002 (cited on page 51).

[66]   Möller, R. *Some Simple Tricks for Creating Responsive Charts With D3*. Blog post. 2015. URL: https://tinyurl.com/moller-responsive (cited on page 42).

[67]   Munzner, T. "A Nested Model for Visualization Design and Validation". In: *Transactions on Visualization and Computer Graphics (TVCG)* 15.6 (2009), pp. 921–928. DOI: 10.1109/TVCG.2009.111 (cited on page 51).

[68]   Munzner, T. *Visualization Analysis and Design*. A K Peters Visualization Series. A K Peters/CRC Press, 2014. DOI: 10.1201/b17511 (cited on pages 37, 46).

[69]   NPR Staff. *The Urban Neighborhood Wal-Mart: A Blessing or a Curse?* NPR News. 2015. URL: https://aka.ms/npr-walmart (cited on page 49).

[70]   O'Donovan, D. *D3 and React — A Design Pattern for Fully Responsive Charts*. Nightingale. 2019. URL: https://tinyurl.com/odonovan-nightingale (cited on page 42).

[71]   Qiao, L., Feng, L., and Zhou, L. "Information Presentation on Mobile Devices: Techniques and Practices". In: *Progress in WWW Research and Development*. Edited by Zhang, Y., Yu, G., Bertino, E., and Xu, G. Vol. 4976. Lecture Notes in Computer Science. Springer, 2008, pp. 395–406. DOI: 10.1007/978-3-540-78849-2_40 (cited on page 36).

[72]   Radloff, A., Lehmann, A., Staadt, O. G., and Schumann, H. "Smart Interaction Management: An Interaction Approach for Smart Meeting Rooms". In: *Proceedings of the Conference on Intelligent Environments (IE)*. IEEE, 2012, pp. 228–235. DOI: 10.1109/IE.2012.34 (cited on page 54).

[73]   Radloff, A., Luboschik, M., Sips, M., and Schumann, H. "Supporting Display Scalability by Redundant Mapping". In: *Proceedings of the Symposium on Visual Computing (ISVC)*. Springer. Springer, 2011, pp. 472–483. DOI: 10.1007/978-3-642-24028-7_44 (cited on page 49).

[74]   Reddy, R. *Smartphone vs Tablet Orientation: Who's Using What?* Blog post. 2017. URL: https://tinyurl.com/reddy-mobile (cited on pages 44, 45).

[75]   Ren, D., Brehmer, M., Lee, B., Höllerer, T., and Choe, E. K. "ChartAccent: Annotation for Data-Driven Storytelling". In: *Proceedings of the Pacific Visualization Symposium (PacificVis)*. IEEE, 2017, pp. 230–239. DOI: 10.1109/PACIFICVIS.2017.8031599 (cited on page 47).

[76]   Roberts, J. C., Headleand, C., and Ritsos, P. D. "Sketching Designs Using the Five Design-Sheet Methodology". In: *Transactions on Visualization and Computer Graphics (TVCG)* 22.1 (Jan. 2016), pp. 419–428. DOI: 10.1109/TVCG.2015.2467271 (cited on page 51).

[77] Ruchikachorn, P. and Mueller, K. "Learning Visualizations by Analogy: Promoting Visual Literacy Through Visualization Morphing". In: *Transactions on Visualization and Computer Graphics (TVCG)* 21.9 (2015), pp. 1028–1044. DOI: 10.1109/TVCG.2015.2413786 (cited on page 50).

[78] Sadowski, S. *Crafting a Custom, Mobile-Friendly Data Visualization. The Design Process, From Science Paper to Responsive Interactive. Medium.* 2015. URL: https://tinyurl.com/sadowski-responsive (cited on page 47).

[79] Sam, C. "Ai2html and Its Impact on the News Graphics Industry". In: *Proceedings of the CHI Workshop on Data Visualization on Mobile Devices.* 2018. URL: https://tinyurl.com/mobilevis-sam (cited on pages 35, 42, 51).

[80] Satyanarayan, A., Moritz, D., Wongsuphasawat, K., and Heer, J. "Vega-Lite: A Grammar of Interactive Graphics". In: *Transactions on Visualization and Computer Graphics (TVCG)* 23.1 (2017), pp. 341–350. DOI: 10.1109/TVCG.2016.2599030 (cited on page 52).

[81] Schwab, M., Hao, S., Vitek, O., Tompkin, J., Huang, J., and Borkin, M. A. "Evaluating Pan and Zoom Timelines and Sliders". In: *Proceedings of the Conference on Human Factors in Computing Systems (CHI).* ACM, 2019, 556:1–556:12. DOI: 10.1145/3290605.3300786 (cited on page 43).

[82] Sears, A. and Shneiderman, B. "High Precision Touchscreens: Design Strategies and Comparisons With a Mouse". In: *International Journal of Man-Machine Studies* 34.4 (1991), pp. 593–613. DOI: 10.1016/0020-7373(91)90037-8 (cited on page 51).

[83] Shimabukuro, M. and Collins, C. "Abbreviating Text Labels on Demand". In: *Poster Proceedings of the IEEE Conference on Information Visualization (InfoVis).* **Open Access version:** http://hdl.handle.net/10155/1228. 2017 (cited on page 43).

[84] Shu, X., Wu, A., Tang, J., Bach, B., Wu, Y., and Qu, H. "What Makes a Data-Gif Understandable?" In: *Transactions on Visualization and Computer Graphics (TVCG)* (2020), pp. 1492–1502. DOI: 10.1109/tvcg.2020.3030396 (cited on page 49).

[85] Siek, K. A., Rogers, Y., and Connelly, K. H. "Fat Finger Worries: How Older and Younger Users Physically Interact With PDAs". In: *Proceedings of the Conference on Human-Computer Interaction (INTERACT).* Vol. 5. Springer, 2005, pp. 267–280 (cited on page 38).

[86] Singer-Vine, J. *DataGIFs.* Pinterest board. 2017. URL: https://pinterest.com/jsvine/datagifs/ (cited on page 49).

[87] Talbot, J., Gerth, J., and Hanrahan, P. "An Empirical Model of Slope Ratio Comparisons". In: *Transactions on Visualization and Computer Graphics (TVCG)* 18.12 (2012), pp. 2613–2620. DOI: 10.1109/tvcg.2012.196 (cited on page 45).

[88] Teevan, J., Cutrell, E., Fisher, D., Drucker, S. M., Ramos, G., André, P., and Hu, C. "Visual Snippets: Summarizing Web Pages for Search and Revisitation". In: *Proceedings of the Conference on Human Factors in Computing Systems (CHI)*. ACM, 2009, pp. 2023–2032. DOI: 10.1145/1518701.1519008 (cited on page 44).

[89] Thomas, J. J. and Cook, K. A. *Illuminating the Path: The Research and Development Agenda for Visual Analytics*. IEEE, 2005 (cited on pages 35, 37).

[90] Tominski, C. *Interaction for Visualization*. Synthesis Lectures on Visualization 3. Morgan & Claypool, 2015. DOI: 10.2200/S00651ED1V01Y201506VIS003 (cited on page 36).

[91] Tominski, C. and Schumann, H. *Interactive Visual Data Analysis*. A K Peters Visualization Series. A K Peters/CRC Press, 2020. DOI: 10.1201/9781315152707. URL: https://ivda-book.de (cited on pages 40, 51).

[92] Tse, A. *Why We Are Doing Fewer Interactives*. Malofiej conference presentation; slides. 2016. URL: https://tinyurl.com/tse-malofiej (cited on pages 50, 51).

[93] Tufte, E. R. *Beautiful Evidence*. Graphics Press, 2006 (cited on page 48).

[94] Wang, F. and Ren, X. "Empirical Evaluation for Finger Input Properties in Multi-Touch Interaction". In: *Proceedings of the Conference on Human Factors in Computing Systems (CHI)*. ACM, 2009, pp. 1063–1072. DOI: 10.1145/1518701.1518864 (cited on page 40).

[95] Ware, C. *Information Visualization: Perception for Design*. San Francisco, CA, USA: Morgan Kaufmann, 2004 (cited on page 40).

[96] Watson, B. and Setlur, V. "Emerging Research in Mobile Visualization". In: *Tutorial Proceedings of the ACM Conference on Human-Computer Interaction with Mobile Devices and Services (MobileHCI)*. slides: https://goo.gl/hBH9sT. ACM, 2015, pp. 883–887. DOI: 10.1145/2786567.2786571 (cited on pages 42–44, 46, 50).

[97] Wei, Y., Mei, H., Zhao, Y., Zhou, S., Lin, B., Jiang, H., and Chen, W. "Evaluating Perceptual Bias During Geometric Scaling of Scatterplots". In: *Transactions on Visualization and Computer Graphics (TVCG)* 26.1 (2020), pp. 321–331. DOI: 10.1109/tvcg.2019.2934208 (cited on pages 38, 44).

[98] Wigdor, D. and Wixon, D. *Brave NUI World: Designing Natural User Interfaces for Touch and Gesture*. 1st. San Francisco, CA, USA: Morgan Kaufmann, 2011 (cited on page 51).

[99] Woodruff, A., Rosenholtz, R., Morrison, J. B., Faulring, A., and Pirolli, P. "A Comparison of the Use of Text Summaries, Plain Thumbnails, and Enhanced Thumbnails for Web Search Tasks". In: *Journal of the American Society for Information Science and Technology (JASIST)* 53.2 (2002), pp. 172–185. DOI: 10.1002/asi.10029 (cited on page 44).

[100] Wu, A., Tong, W., Dwyer, T., Lee, B., Isenberg, P., and Qu, H. "MobileVisFixer: Tailoring Web Visualizations for Mobile Phones Leveraging an Explainable Reinforcement Learning Framework". In: *Transactions on Visualization and Computer Graphics (TVCG)* 27.2 (2021). **Open Access version:** https : //arxiv.org/abs/2008.06678, pp. 464–474. DOI: 10.1109/tvcg.2020. 3030423 (cited on pages 35, 43, 51, 52).

[101] Wu, Y., Liu, X., Liu, S., and Ma, K.-L. "ViSizer: A Visualization Resizing Framework". In: *Transactions on Visualization and Computer Graphics (TVCG)* 19.2 (2012), pp. 278–290. DOI: 10.1109/TVCG.2012.114 (cited on page 44).

[102] Zhang, Y., Buxton, W., Hinckley, K., Pahud, M., Holz, C., Xia, H., Laput, G., McGuffin, M., Tu, X., Mittereder, A., and Su, F. "Sensing Posture-Aware Pen+Touch Interaction on Tablets". In: *Proceedings of the Conference on Human Factors in Computing Systems (CHI)*. ACM, 2019, 55:1–55:14. DOI: 10.1145/3290605.3300285 (cited on page 39).

CHAPTER 3

Interacting with Visualization on Mobile Devices

Matthew Brehmer

Tableau Research, USA

Bongshin Lee

Microsoft Research, USA

John Stasko

Georgia Institute of Technology, USA

Christian Tominski

University of Rostock, Germany

CONTENTS

W E are now capable of interacting in various ways with data visualization on mobile devices. In this chapter, we characterize how interacting with visualization using a mobile phone or tablet differs from analogous experiences using a PC. We provide an overview of the topic organized by interaction modality, beginning with touch interaction and subsequently discussing instances of spatial interaction and voice interaction. As an outlook, we envision compelling opportunities for future

DOI: 10.1201/9781003090823-3

mobile data visualization research inspired by recent developments in the field of mobile human-computer interaction.

3.1 FOUNDATIONS

The high resolution displays of current mobile devices allow you to see minute levels of detail in visualization content. Many devices are also built with powerful processors, capable of not only representing thousands of data points simultaneously, but also of responding to changing data, a changing surrounding environment, and a changing stream of interactions with the device, as described in Chapter 2.

Mobile phones and tablets have screens of varying size and aspect ratio, as well as different sets of sensors, and these differences affect how you interact with these devices. Despite these differences, the current ecosystem of two mobile operating systems (iOS and Android) incorporate a consistent set of interactions across devices. On the one hand, the consistency can make interactions easier to discover, on the other hand, it may limit innovation in mobile interaction design.

In this chapter, we do not constrain ourselves to existing conventions, but turn to research activities that envision possible futures in which you might interact with visual representations of data in unprecedented ways. An overarching assumption of this chapter is that you want and often need to interact with data visualization via a mobile device: that there exist circumstances in which you are unsatisfied with static visual representations of data, and that you become frustrated when you cannot interact easily or at all, such as when a website tells you to revisit the page from a PC [14]. The data that you interact with on your mobile device may be highly personal and immediately relevant to your surrounding environment. Your location, your health and activity data, your personal finances, and the local weather forecast are all examples of personal data that you might already regularly interact with via your mobile device. We assume that there are various occasions in which you are genuinely curious about these data, for example, to make comparisons that inform your decision-making, or to examine anomalous values and possible trends.

The intent to engage further and interact stands in contrast to cases in which all that is required is a succinct representation of data designed for quick monitoring tasks and glanceability, cases that are discussed at greater length in Chapter 5. Mobile interaction also stands in contrast to cases of passive consumption in communicative visualization scenarios, such as when viewing news graphics. There was ample experimentation with interactive news graphics during the first half of the 2010s, however this enthusiasm tapered in the second half of the decade following reports of how little people interact with news graphics beyond scrolling [2, 118].

One response to this realization has been to expand the capabilities of scrolling to trigger various events in a visual representation of data, often referred to as scrollytelling [119]. Another response has been to incorporate viewers' personal information as a form of interaction, such as detecting their location or soliciting personal details from viewers, such as their education, income, or occupation; both approaches can be used to generate custom views of a dataset that people might be more inclined to engage with.

Another interesting invitation to interact has appeared in data journalism focusing on trends or correlations, where the viewers are prompted to first guess the trend by drawing it [3]. According to Nguyen et al. [82], this format allows the viewers to externalize and test their own beliefs. Graphic elicitation of viewers' beliefs via drawing is particularly well-suited for mobile touchscreen devices. Similar approaches to engage a large mobile audience with news stories that incorporate visualization will continue to evolve in the coming years as media agencies strive to seek a balance between development cost and value for the viewers.

This chapter presents an overview of recent advances in interacting with visualization via mobile devices. We focus on mobile phone and tablet devices; we do not consider watches or other wearable devices such as bands, rings, or head-mounted augmented reality displays, though we do comment on their potential in our discussion of future opportunities later in Section 3.3. We do, however, mention a few compelling examples of handheld mobile augmented reality, as well as one example when a mobile device is used in conjunction with head-mounted augmented reality system called FieldView [124].

We organize our overview according to interaction modalities: touch interaction, spatial interaction, and voice interaction. We anticipate that people will continue to interact via these modalities in future devices, and accordingly we hope that this chapter be read as an overview of multimodal interaction possibilities for mobile data visualization. Due to the rapidly evolving and ephemeral nature of mobile software, of which there tends to be no archival description, we concentrate on mobile interaction with visualization as described in peer-reviewed archival research literature. Yet, where relevant we also refer to commercial mobile applications and compelling instances of mobile interaction with visualization designed by practitioners.

Before we proceed with our overview, it is necessary to establish context about interactive visualization and interacting with mobile devices. We also realize that the scope of this overview has foundations in several areas of research, each with an associated body of literature and a research community, and we refer interested readers to these communities where relevant.

3.1.1 Interacting with Visualization

The history of creating visual representations based on data and using them to perform analyses and communicate insights to others is a rich tapestry spanning millennia and cultures. Until a few decades ago, the act of interacting with visualization entailed drawing, engraving, or sculpting representations of data, and then examining and manipulating static physical media. With the advent of computers, interacting with visualization meant interacting with dynamic media. But what makes interactive visualization different from other interactive media, such as video games, illustration tools, or word processors? The answer is simultaneously a difference in one's intents and a different set of interactions needed to satisfy these intents.

Looking back on the past three decades of visualization systems and research papers, many researchers have proposed typologies [21, 44, 102, 128] of intent and interaction that offer some consensus, at least at an abstract level, of what makes interacting with visualization distinct from interacting with other media forms. At the level of intent, people want to analyze, monitor, and communicate aspects of data, and to ask questions or anticipate questions that their audience might ask. In many circumstances, the specific referents of these questions cannot be specified a priori. Similarly, the data may also have a dynamic nature, where new data may provoke new questions. As a result, a single static representation of data often does not suffice.

Therefore, many interactive visualization tools allow people to navigate across their data, to filter them and select subsets of interest, to sort them, to change the way they are represented, to adjust how these representations are arranged, and to augment these representations with their insights [117]. How these interactions manifest vary from one visualization tool or environment to another [116], and as Dimara & Perin [32] note, multiple interactions might redundantly support the same intent. As observed by Lee et al. [71], Jansen and Dragicevic [54], and Roberts et al. [93], computer-mediated interactions with visualization, until relatively recently, involved interacting with only a mouse and keyboard.

3.1.2   Interacting with Mobile Devices

You might recall a time where mobile devices came with a hardware keyboard and a trackball for interaction. Nowadays, mobile devices are typically equipped with a multi-touch display, perhaps one that can even detect the amount of force with which you press on the screen, and with a small number of hardware buttons around its periphery. In addition, there are various other ways by which you interact with your mobile device in contrast to how you might interact with your PC, and it can be helpful to discuss the gamut of possible interactions for what follows below.

First, many mobile devices are equipped with accelerometers, light sensors, pressure sensors, and multiple cameras. These sensors make it possible to detect events such as changes of position and orientation in space, your grip and hand posture, touch events with varying levels of pressure, or the appearance of a face. Second, microphones allow you to speak, record, and sample audio. Third, some mobile devices are compatible with a pen or stylus, allowing you to write, sketch, and make fine selections. Fourth, many mobile devices provide haptic or vibrotactile feedback, either as a means to provide notifications or as a means of indicating that an interaction was recognized by the device. Finally, many mobile devices have various levels of geolocation tracking via GPS, WiFi, and Bluetooth. While it is true that many laptop PCs ship with geolocation awareness, a camera, and a microphone, they tend to be stationary when in use; it is the mobility of phones and tablets that expands the interactive potential of these sensors.

After the introduction of the iPhone in 2007, several touchscreen interactions have become familiar to us, and their effects can often be predictable when using a new mobile application. Consider the many contexts in which you tap, pinch, swipe, and tap & hold. However, beyond common touch actions, there are fewer conventions among the other modalities of interaction that we have listed. As a consequence, designers must consider creative strategies for ensuring the discoverability and learnability of these interactions.

In differentiating the ways in which people interact with mobile devices relative to how they interact with PCs, we must also consider the potentially different contexts of interaction. When you interact with a PC, you are often sitting or standing still. You may be in a professional setting, in your home office, or in a classroom, and you typically commit to longer sustained periods of interaction. In contrast, the contexts in which one interacts with mobile devices are more heterogeneous in terms of their surrounding physical environments, the relationships between other people and devices, and the cadence of interaction. Consider, for instance, that work contexts are becoming increasingly situated and collaborative, where mobile phones and tablets are often sufficient to perform tasks. Regardless of whether one finds themselves in a professional or casual setting, interaction with a mobile device may be more intermittent and fleeting than with a PC.

Despite the different usage contexts for mobile devices and PCs, we note that the distinction between laptop PCs and tablets is beginning to blur. For instance, some Microsoft's Surface devices [77] and others like it are equipped with touchscreens and can be converted between laptop and tablet modes. Meanwhile, tablets such as Apple's iPad Pro [5] boast screens as large as laptops, powerful hardware capabilities as good as many PCs, and peripheral keyboard attachments. These hybrid devices provide affordances to combine bimanual touch- and gesture-based direct manipulation with conventional keyboard, mouse, and trackpad interaction in the context of both WIMP- (Windows, Icons, Menus, Pointer) and post-WIMP interfaces.

We also note that the distinction between larger smartphones and tablets is also blurring, as evident by the use of the *phablet* moniker for the former. The overview we present in this chapter is a retrospective on the past decade of research, where most of the examples that we consider are associated with a specific device type. As a collection, however, the examples we cite along with our commentary may inform interaction design for and future research involving these emerging classes of devices that blur the boundaries between laptop and tablet or tablet and phone.

With this brief initial description of interaction on mobile devices, let us next look at interaction for mobile data visualization in detail.

3.2 OVERVIEW

On the one hand, we have a foundational understanding of how people interact with visualization. On the other hand, we have a foundational understanding of how people interact with mobile devices. This overview examines the intersection of these interactions; and while the research pertaining to interacting with visualization on mobile devices predates multitouch-enabled phones and tablets (e. g., [57, 22, 43, 51, 30]), our overview focuses on research published since 2010. Table 3.1 summarizes our overview.

It is also worth considering what remains outside of this intersection. Are some interactions with visualization incompatible with mobile devices? In Chapter 2, we encountered several strategies and related challenges for responsive visualization design, which include modifying the interaction design for different device profiles. However, given the breadth of interactions in the research literature, there may be

TABLE 3.1 A chronologically-ordered summary of the specific projects that we reference in our overview and the main device form factors associated with these instances: ▢ = phone; ▢ = tablet; 🖥 = large display; 👁 = head-mounted display. We also denote the modalities of interaction that each project incorporates: 👆 = touch (+✎ = pen); 🎤 = voice; ✛ = spatial (📹 = using cameras, 📍 = using (geo)location).

Project (Year)	Reference	Device(s)	Modalities
Tangible views (2010)	Spindler et al. [107]	▢ 🖥	✛
TouchWave (2012)	Baur et al. [13]	▢	👆
TouchViz (2013)	Drucker et al. [34]	▢	👆
Kinetica (2014)	Rzeszotarski & Kittur [95]	▢	👆
Tangere (2014-16)	Sadana et al. [96, 97, 98]	▢	👆
GraphTiles (2015)	Bae et al. [8]	▢	👆
Subspotting (2016)	Baur & Goddemayer [12]	▢	👆 ✛(📍)
TouchPivot (2017)	Jo et al. [56]	▢	👆(+✎)
GraSp (2017)	Kister et al. [61]	▢ 🖥	✛
VisTiles (2017)	Langner et al. [67]	▢ ▢	👆 ✛
Ranges over time (2018)	Brehmer et al. [20]	▢	👆
SmartCues (2018)	Subramonyam & Adar [111]	▢	👆
Visfer (2019)	Badam & Elmqvist [7]	▢ ▢ 🖥	✛(📹 📍)
AffinityLens (2019)	Subramonyam et al. [112]	▢	👆 ✛(📹)
Pan + zoom eval. (2019)	Schwab et al. [101]	▢ 🖥	👆
FieldView (2019)	Whitlock et al. [124]	▢ 👁	👆 ✛(📍)
Pressure sensing (2019)	Wang et al. [123]	▢	👆
MARVisT (2019)	Chen et al. [27]	▢	👆 ✛(📹)
InChorus (2020)	Srinivasan et al. [108]	▢	👆(+✎) 🎤
Orchard (2020)	Eichmann et al. [36]	▢	👆

some that are unlikely to apply in mobile contexts, and others may be difficult or tedious to perform, or they may be difficult to discover, having no precedent in other application contexts. For instance, visualization authoring often requires a series of interactions to select data, apply transformations to the data, and specify a visual representation; would people be willing to perform this series of authoring interactions via a mobile device? Another activity that often entails a series of interactions, photo editing, has until recently been reserved for PCs. However, mobile photo editing with apps like Instagram is now commonplace. Could visualization authoring similarly become an activity that people carry out using a mobile device?

There are also some interactions with mobile devices that are incompatible with visualization. For instance, there are interactions that do not involve looking at the display, such as silencing notifications, adjusting volume controls, or interacting via auditory or haptic channels (we do not discuss data sonification and its haptic analog in this chapter). Finally, we must acknowledge that the limitations of contemporary devices may impose constraints on what interactions people can perform involving visualization, and we return to this topic at the end of this chapter.

As mentioned above, the overview skews heavily toward instances of interacting with visualization via mobile devices as described in archival research literature. We acknowledge that the marketplace of mobile applications incorporating interactive visualization features is growing and evolving. Major business intelligence software vendors such as Microsoft [76], Tableau [114], Qlik [91], MicroStrategy [79], and Thoughtspot [115] all have mobile versions of their visualization solutions as of the time of writing, and these take various approaches to interacting with visualization. There are also many mobile-first or responsive news graphics that feature interactivity to some extent; Ros [94] catalogued several throughout the mid-2010s. However, the ecosystem of applications and responsive interactive news graphics is highly ephemeral, and written accounts of their interaction design choices are uncommon.

We organize our overview according to *interaction modality*. At the same time, we acknowledge the additive nature of interaction modalities; spatial or voice interaction usually accompanies, rather than replaces, touch interaction. As suggested by Table 3.1, nearly all of the projects that we surveyed incorporate touch interaction. Spatial interaction receives the next most coverage, while voice is discussed to a lesser extent, this being a reflection of its prevalence in the research literature on visualization and mobile devices.

3.2.1 Touch Interaction 👆

Research examining the potential of multi-finger touch interaction for visualization started to accumulate around the beginning of the 2010s, following the commercialization of new touchscreen technology and touchscreen tabletop displays in particular and early research by Isenberg et al. [52], Frisch et al. [38], and North et al. [84]. With the introduction of the iPhone in 2007 and the iPad in 2010 as well as the popularization of multi-touch mobile devices, visualization researchers and designers turned their attention to smaller devices.

There are several challenges associated with touch interaction for visualization via mobile devices. First, there is the fat finger problem, the mismatch between the size of graphical marks and human finger tips. This problem is particularly acute with small visual elements that are to be selectable on a mobile phone or tablet, as for example when picking individual points from a scatterplot or narrow segments from a stacked bar chart. Interaction designers therefore face a trade-off between the minimum visibility of marks and their selectability: if all marks are to be easily and directly selected via touch, they must be suitably large, akin to a button. Yet, using larger marks is infeasible in many situations, and thus designers must consider alternative approaches, such as a multi-step or hierarchical selection upon touching a region with the visualization, which may involve selection from a modal menu panel or a modal zoom lens of the touch area, such as in Kinetica [95] or Tangere [96]. Adding larger invisible touch targets or an invisible Voronoi tessellation around small marks is another approach to support interactive selection [14]. Zooming in as a prerequisite to individual mark selection is also possible as a last resort.

A related challenge is the simultaneous visibility and selectability of targets due to occlusion from the finger or hand. If selection has no visible consequences within the remaining unoccluded area of the display, such as via a lens widget, the result of the selection can only be known once the finger or hand is moved away.

Unintended touch is another challenge, particularly for touch surfaces whereupon people may rest their hands or at least the base of their palms, for example, when laying a mobile device flat on a table. Accidental touch may also occur when a mobile device is held in one's hand or positioned at an inclination. The reduction of screen bezel widths across devices in recent years may exacerbate this problem. Also problematic is misinterpreted touch, in which one touch gesture is confused for another, such as confusing a two-finger pinch with a two-finger rotation. Both forms of touch recognition error continue to be problematic for touchscreen interfaces.

Given the limited vocabulary of touch and the restrictions on touch target size, interacting with visualization via mobile devices is often reliant upon menus and explicit modes of interaction, such as alternating between navigation and selection. However, sufficiently large menu interfaces often occlude content on small screens, and different interaction modes are difficult to discover. As a consequence, the number and variety of unique touch interactions tends to be small in most instances, which often forego the ability to select individual marks.

One of the major challenges presented to visualization designers with respect to touch-based interfaces is the relative lack of unique, differentiable gestures for initiating different operations. While it is possible to use more complex multi-finger or bimanual gestures, these are correspondingly more difficult to discover and remember, and are likely more difficult to perform, especially on handheld devices. For example, consider a simple swipe gesture. A designer may associate swiping along an axis to select visual marks in a view or swiping could pan the view to show other data ranges. Both of these mappings are possible, but the gesture must be uniquely assigned to one operation. Mapping tasks to interactions is a non-trivial problem in general; a deeper discussion is provided by Gladisch et al. [41]. While some gestures have become familiar over time, Isenberg & Hancock [53] caution that new gestures are difficult to perform, memorize, and discover. Instead, they advocate for postures that re-use and combine simpler interactions for direct parameter control, and that such postures are easier to remember and discover than a set of gestures.

This section on touch interaction is structured according to device class: tablet or mobile phone. For each class, we profile several notable projects with touch interaction of different complexity. At one end of the spectrum, we have tapping, holding, or double tapping, which do not involve any motion. As we increase the complexity, we encounter actions such as pulling to refresh or swiping, both of which involving motion along a single direction. Gestures such as pinching to zoom, lassoing to enclose, and dragging to reposition often involve motion along two dimensions. Finally, the projects in our list include single-handed as well as bimanual interaction, wherein the dominant hand may be holding a pen or stylus to either draw, write, point, or select.

Touch Interaction on Tablets

Since the release of the iPad in 2010, a number of visualization research projects have examined the potential of this form factor and the touch interaction it affords.

With **TouchWave**, Baur et al. [13] introduced a set of multi-touch interactions specifically tailored for directly manipulating stacked area charts on tablets without relying on widgets and mode switches. To keep the touch interactions simple, they started with established touch interactions (e.g., tap, tap & hold, pinch, swipe) as much as possible, and then expanded the set by incorporating multi-finger gestures, some involving motion and others not (see Figure 3.1). TouchWave also leverages contextual information where the interaction occurs to provide more appropriate response and feedback, such as a single tap on the background canvas to invoke a vertical ruler perpendicular to the horizontal time axis, superimposed with text annotations revealing the value corresponding to each band at the selected time point. The system reacts differently for vertical and horizontal scaling that uses the same pinch gesture: the context is compressed while the focus region is expanded in horizontal scaling, while vertical scaling magnifies the vertical axis uniformly to keep the relative sizes of the layers intact.

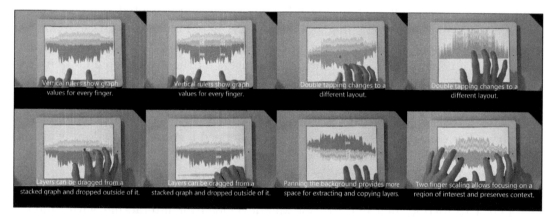

Figure 3.1 With **TouchWave**, Baur et al. [13] introduced a set of touch gestures for manipulating stacked area charts on tablets. *Video stills courtesy of Dominikus Baur, used with permission; watch the full video at* `https://youtu.be/tZ1EJoY8HCk`.

In the **TouchViz** project, Drucker et al. [34] designed and compared two interfaces for working with bar charts on tablet devices. This comparison is notable given the recent blurring between WIMP and post-WIMP interfaces for devices that straddle the boundary between laptop and tablet, as described above. To develop a set of post-WIMP gestures for their *FLUID* interface, Drucker et al. conducted a structured brainstorming session, where they chose to focus on the gestures that involved manipulation mapped directly onto objects on screen. Similar to TouchWave before, the post-WIMP *FLUID* interface strove to minimize the use of buttons and controls, ensuring that all gestures occur on the chart itself. In contrast, the alternative WIMP interface featured the same interactions accessed via buttons and menu commands (see Figure 3.2). Unsurprisingly, the *FLUID* approach was predominantly favored by study participants.

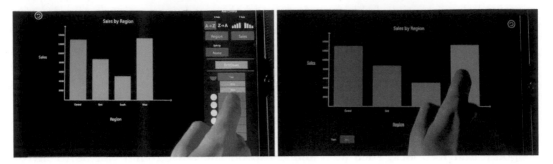

Figure 3.2 In the **TouchViz** project, Drucker et al. [34] compared a WIMP interface using menus of buttons (left) with a *FLUID* direct manipulation touch interface (right). *Video stills courtesy of Ramik Sadana, used with permission; watch the full video at https://vimeo.com/57416758.*

Kinetica [95] is a touch interface for unit charts, in which each data point is represented by a small circular mark.[1] The system implemented a physics-based interface in which a person's fingers and gestures acted on those marks, giving the impression that one can directly push or sweep marks around the display as if they were a set of colliding particles. Placing two fingers on the display could specify two control points for a histogram or a bounding box for a scatterplot. Overall, the system employed a number of custom gestures which applied to the unique physics-based view it provided. Not all of Kinetica's gestures involved direct and continuous manipulation of marks. For example, a spiral-shaped swipe defined a spiral curve along which to position marks, though the marks would only move to fit the spiral curve after the gesture was completed. Moreover, common task such as changing the color, size, and position of marks still required a traditional control menu.

The **Tangere** system [96, 97, 98] was developed for interacting with different types of charts, including line charts, bar charts, parallel coordinates, and scatterplots (see Figure 3.3). The two primary goals were: (1) making touch gestures to invoke operations as simple as possible and (2) keeping them consistent across the different types of charts, the latter goal distinguishing it from the systems reviewed above.

In Tangere, a lasso around a set of marks selects them and swiping on an axis selects items in the spanned region, while tapping & holding, and dragging on an axis initiates a sort. Unlike PCs, modifier keys (e. g., shift, control) are not readily available on tablets to expand the set of operations. To expand the types of selection that could be performed, Tangere used bimanual interaction instead. A person typically holds a tablet with their non-dominant hand and performs touch gestures with the other dominant hand. In Tangere, the thumb of the non-dominant hand can touch the edge of the display while holding it (see Figure 3.3 right). This touch, called a "clutch," acts as a type of modifier to change the functionality of the touch gesture being performed with the other hand. For example, normally a touch gesture on a

---

[1]A video of Kinetica (© 2014 ACM) is available at https://youtu.be/70YcGiKrmEg.

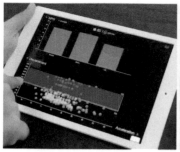

Figure 3.3 **Tangere** [96, 97, 98] featured actions compatible with multiple chart types, including linked highlighting or brushing across multiple views. In a later version of the system, one could "clutch" with the non-dominant hand to modulate the action performed by the dominant hand, akin to holding down a shift or control key with a physical keyboard (right). *Video stills courtesy of Ramik Sadana, used with permission; watch the full videos at* https: //vimeo. com/195348951 *and* https: //vimeo. com/195349037.

data item replaces the prior selection by this new item. With the clutch engaged, the new item can instead be added to the selection. Tangere employs the clutch operation with touch, drag, and pinch gestures to provide a broad set of different operations.

With the emergence of pen-enabled devices, researchers have started investigating the use of pen and touch in the context of data visualization. Although some smartphones (e. g., the Samsung Galaxy Note series) are equipped with a digital pen, existing research has thus far been conducted with tablets. We note that Frisch et al. [38] examined pen and touch interaction on stationary tabletop devices; while some tabletop interactions may be applicable to tablets and smaller devices, the focus of this overview remains on mobile devices. We refer to the union of both pen and touch interactions and not necessarily simultaneous pen and touch interaction.

In their **TouchPivot** system, Jo et al. [56] designed pen and touch interactions to support data exploration on tablet devices for novices (see Figure 3.4). Unlike other systems, TouchPivot deliberately incorporates WIMP interface components to leverage their familiarity and accessibility to novices. In addition, to facilitate understanding of data transformations such as pivoting and filtering, TouchPivot displays a data table and a chart together, keeping them in sync. To devise a gesture set that novices may easily understand and use, Jo et al. started from a survey of pen and touch gestures used in 13 previous studies to support data exploration. To keep their gesture set as small and simple as possible, they decided to use three touch gestures (tap, tap & hold, and drag) and four pen gestures (tap, simple stroke, lasso, and write).

Extending the concept of clutching, TouchPivot employs a fan menu to enable rapid exploration; dragging along the arc of the fan at the bottom left corner provides access to data columns, enabling people to pivot the data by the focused column and preview the distribution of values in the preview area in the bottom right part. Lifting

Figure 3.4 **TouchPivot** [56] featured a fan menu for the thumb of the non-dominant hand, and pen gestures for both tables and charts. *Video stills courtesy of Jinwook Seo, used with permission; watch the full video at* $https://youtu.be/Q6quofDiO7I$.

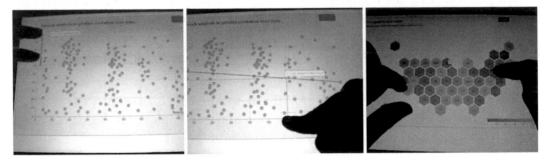

Figure 3.5 In **SmartCues** [111], touch gestures annotate charts with text labels, color highlights, reference lines, and shaded reference bands. *Video stills courtesy of Hariharan Subramonyam, used with permission; watch the full video at* $https://youtu.be/xeQPOmFfn5Q$.

a thumb from the fan menu confirms the pivot operation, updating the data table and moving the chart to the main chart view in the top right part.

Touch interaction with the table on the left side mimics the mouse interaction currently used on a PC. For example, a drag gesture pans the table view. In addition to writing with the pen, TouchPivot also employs a few pen interactions for manipulating the table. For example, drawing a vertical line stroke on the table sorts the data table and the chart based on the corresponding data column, while drawing a lasso on the table highlights the corresponding records in the scatterplot.

Subramonyam & Adar's **SmartCues** [111] tablet application featured a touch interaction vocabulary for selecting and annotating charts with text labels, color highlights, reference lines, and shaded reference bands (see Figure 3.5). This vocabulary involves one- and two-finger gestures on axes, marks, and legends in bar charts, line charts, scatterplots, and tilemaps. Earlier in this section we encountered reference lines and text labels in response to a touch gesture in TouchWave; SmartCues takes this further, toward a more complete chart annotation system akin to desktop-based tools like Click2Annotate [26] or ChartAccent [92].

To summarize, we began this section with TouchWave and TouchViz, which considered touch interactions for a single type of chart. Kinetica introduced us to physics-based interactions with particle-like marks that could be reconfigured into a wide variety of layouts. With Tangere and TouchPivot, we saw both an evolution of how to use the non-dominant hand via clutch interactions and fan menus, as well how to interact consistently across multiple chart types and tables. TouchPivot added pen gestures to our growing tablet interaction vocabulary. Finally, SmartCues focused our attention on annotation and the ability to easily identify and compare values via a small set of gestures. However, all of these projects considered a tablet form factor, leading to the question of whether the interactions that we have discussed will be compatible when we reduce the display dimensions to that of mobile phones.

Touch Interaction on Phones

Though much of the recent research pertaining to touch interaction with visualization on mobile devices has been carried out using tablets, we now review some of the research incorporating visualization and touch interaction on mobile phones.

Beyond considering a mobile phone form factor, **GraphTiles** [8] also stands out in that it considers graph data, whereas our previous examples visualized tabular data in bar charts, line charts, and scatterplots. With GraphTiles, one could swipe to navigate a tile-based node representation featuring superimposed link lines, and tapping & holding would select a node, thereby permitting a faceted search based on the selected node's attributes (see Figure 3.6a). More recently, Eichmann et al. [36]

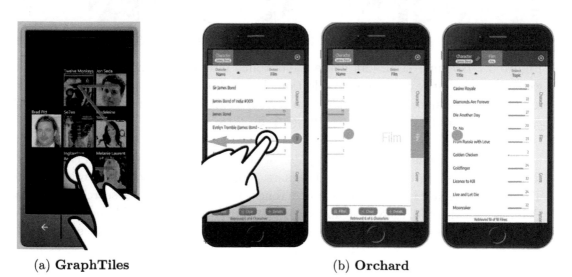

(a) **GraphTiles**   (b) **Orchard**

Figure 3.6 (a) **GraphTiles** [8] and (b) **Orchard** [36] are mobile applications for navigating and exploring network data, such as the relationships between films, actors, and directors. *GraphTiles image courtesy of Ben Watson, used with permission from [9]. Orchard video stills courtesy of Bongshin Lee, used with permission; watch the full video at $https://youtu.be/moCXZuoFYYw$. Hand gesture icons by GestureWorks ® [40]* (ⓒⓕⓞ *2018*).

envisioned another touch-based interface for navigating multivariate networks. With their **Orchard** application, one can scroll vertical lists of nodes and horizontally swipe to pivot a graph by link category, thereby building up a graph query trail (see Figure 3.6b). Both applications avoid a conventional node-link representation in favor of designs that more easily support touch interaction on a small display.

Many of the projects discussed above involve interactions for selecting one or more individual marks. An alternative to selecting marks is selecting regions wherein marks appear. In Brehmer et al.'s visualization [20] of ranges over time on mobile devices, some configurations of the application involved the simultaneous display of dozens or hundreds of individual marks, and a single tap interaction would trigger a rectangle, wedge, or concentric band selection spanning or intersecting multiple marks, which could be repositioned via dragging (see Figure 3.7). The three geometric manifestations of the selection region remained a fixed size irrespective of the granularity of the data and the number of visible marks, and the size of this region was adequately large enough for single-digit touch selection.

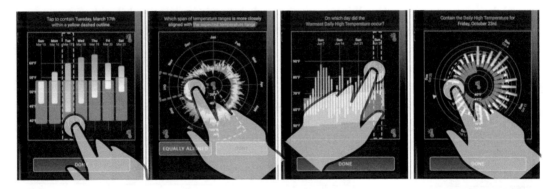

Figure 3.7 Brehmer et al. [20] made use of touch interactions that trigger rectangle, wedge, or concentric band-shaped selection. *Video stills courtesy of Matthew Brehmer, used with permission; watch the full video at* https://vimeo.com/354107502. *Hand gesture icons by GestureWorks® [40] (cc⊕⊚ 2018).*

Recent mobile devices are now capable of detecting touch pressure and can expose degrees of pressure to interaction designers. Apple refers to such interaction as 3D Touch, while Huawei refers to it as Force-Touch. Interaction design researchers such as Pelurson & Nigay [87] have begun exploring the potential of variable-pressure touch on mobile displays, leading to new interactions for navigation [29] and text selection [4, 25, 42]. The implications for interacting with visualization via mobile devices have not been fully examined, and we are unaware of visualization research or existing applications that incorporate tapping and pressing to varying degrees of pressure as an isolated gesture. Notably, Wang et al. [123] explored the use of pressure-based touch interaction for 3D visualization on mobile phones (see Figure 3.8), however the tap and press interaction preceded a drag gesture, which was mapped to continuous 3D navigation, where a light press/drag corresponded with X-Y rotation and a hard press/drag corresponded with X-Y translation. We revisit the topic of pressure sensing and opportunities with novel device capabilities in Section 3.3.5.

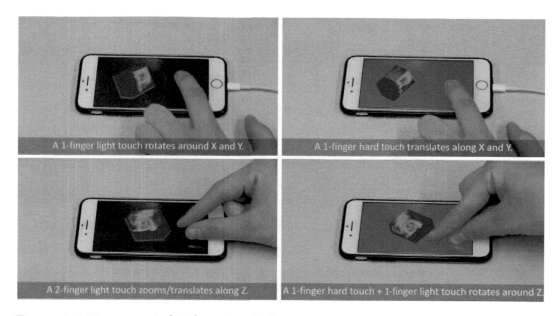

Figure 3.8 Wang et al. [123] explored the use of pressure-based touch interaction for manipulating 3D visualization content. *Video stills courtesy of Lonni Besançon* *(☺①); watch the full video at* `https://youtu.be/nSRhj2ulCNU`.

Panning and zooming are fundamental operations when exploring time-oriented data [1]. This led Schwab et al. [101] to comparatively evaluate alternative gestures for panning and zooming under varying degrees of navigation difficulty (see Figure 3.9). Consider, for example, how tapping twice in short succession has various repercussions across applications. In some cases, a double tap is unintended and is treated like a single tap. In others, it is ignored altogether. Interestingly, Schwab et al. found that while a continuous pinch to zoom is best in most cases, brushing along an axis and dragging orthogonally to an axes are effective in some circumstances, particularly when the difficulty of the navigation is high, where the index of difficulty of a navigation event can be computed according to the distance between the origin position and the target position and the specificity of the target.

Despite the many pan and zoom alternatives examined by Schwab et al. [101], the vocabulary of touch actions used by researchers for interacting with visualization on mobile phones is smaller than that of tablets. With mobile phones, we have yet to encounter instances of two-handed gestures for interacting with visualization such as Sadana & Stasko's clutch action [98]; nor have we seen pen-based input akin to that of TouchPivot [56]. In our discussion of opportunities below in Section 3.3, we revisit the topic of enlarging an interaction vocabulary and we consider new possibilities for mobile phone interaction based on recent mobile HCI research, as well as possible interactions afforded by new and forthcoming mobile phones.

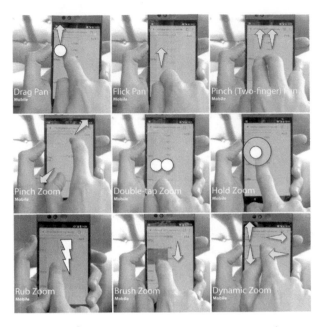

Figure 3.9 Schwab et al. [101] compared alternative gestures for panning and zooming representations of time-oriented data on mobile phones. *Video stills courtesy of Micha Schwab, used with permission (we added the icon annotations); watch the full video at* https://multiscale-timelines.ccs.neu.edu.

3.2.2 Spatial Interaction ✛

In contrast to touch interaction, which involves interacting *on the device*, spatial interaction is about performing the interaction *with the device* by manipulating its position and orientation via movement. Spatial interaction with mobile devices also evokes the related concept of *tangible interaction*, which can be broadly interpreted to involve physicality and embodiment, according to Boy [19] and Maher & Lee [73]. The scope of tangible interaction encompasses far more than we are prepared to discuss here. For example, it even includes interacting with instrumented objects and environments, such as how Chan et al. [24] and Ebert et al. [35] detected the stacking, sliding, and dialing of acrylic discs and cubes across the surface of capacitive touchscreen tabletop displays. In both cases, the discs and cubes are directly linked to digital artifacts displayed on the table, and their movements map to functions in the tabletop application. In the context of visualization, discussion of tangible interaction brings *data physicalization* [55] to mind, however many physical renderings of data are not instrumented with sensors and thus are not capable of responding to changes in position or orientation.

As it relates to our current discussion of visualization on mobile devices, Spindler et al. [106] note that unlike the discs and cubes used by Chan et al. [24] and Ebert et al. [35], a mobile device is simultaneously a display for visual representations of data and the tangible object of interaction. This section will outline the interactions that are possible when mobile devices are used in this way, detecting changes in position and orientation via motion sensors, cameras, and (geo)location tracking.

Spatial Interaction using Motion Sensors

A basic requirement for spatial interaction is the ability to track a device's position and orientation in space relative to its environment. This can be accomplished using sensors within the device itself or via external sensors, such as infrared trackers installed in a room. In theory, 6 degrees of freedom (6-DOF) are used, where three spatial coordinates define the device location and three angles define its orientation. However, the practical use of these degrees of freedom is limited. On the one hand, the available sensor technology might limit the precision with which spatial position and orientation are measured. On the other hand, the human motor system naturally limits possible movements and the precision with which they are performed. In the following, we assume that tracking delivers reasonably good results and that spatial interaction design takes human factors into account.

Given the aforementioned assumptions, Spindler et al. [107] showed that mobile devices can be used for spatial interaction in various ways. Figure 3.10 shows three examples, where so-called **Tangible Views** are used to explore parallel coordinates, node-link diagrams, and space-time cubes. The two basic operations are movement and rotation of the device, which can in turn be combined to form gestures.

 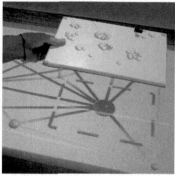 

(a) Parallel coordinates.   (b) Node-link diagram.   (c) Space-time cube.

Figure 3.10 Spindler et al.'s [107] **Tangible Views** applied to different visualizations. *Images from [117] licensed under* ⓒ①.

Basic movement and rotation. Before using device movement for interaction, it is necessary to define a reference space for movement. This involves determining whether movements are measured relative to the current device position or relative to absolute coordinates in a fixed reference space. Relative measurements are typically applied when a mobile device is used in large open environments, while absolute measurements are feasible in smaller spaces, such as in the **GraSp** project [61], where one moves a mobile device in front of a larger display (see Figure 3.11).

In principle, moving a device changes its position in 3D space, which would enable users to control three visualization parameters. However, adjusting a 3D position precisely is difficult given the properties of the human motor system. Therefore, it makes sense to constrain movement interactions, and the resolution with which positions are tracked can be reduced. Spindler et al. [105] observed that people can

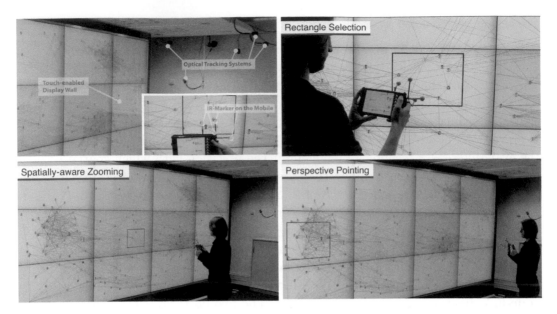

Figure 3.11 In the **GraSp** project [61], spatial movements with the tablet modulate what is visualized both on the tablet and on the larger display. *Video stills courtesy of the Interactive Media Lab Dresden; watch the full video at* `https://youtu.be/ 1LeBSZBL0Qk` .

reach up to 44 different vertical positions reasonably well. Moreover, they can consider movements with respect to 2D reference planes, usually the horizontal and vertical planes in front of them. An example is the **VisTiles** project [67] (see Figure 3.12), in which several mobile devices placed on a table form an ensemble of visualization views that are dependent upon their distance and orientation relative to one another.

In general, the rotation of a mobile device is considered to take place around the device's center of gravity. Again, while three independent dimensions are theoretically possible to control the visualization, it is common to apply constraints to make rotations practically feasible. For example, the rotation could be constrained to one or two dimensions. Moreover, the angle of rotation might be limited based on the situation; for example, rotating a handheld device around the axis of the forearm is limited to less than 180 degrees. 90 degree device rotation often toggles between portrait and landscape viewing modes in mobile applications. One example appeared in a previous version of the Apple's iOS Stocks app; though this feature no longer exists in the current version of the app (at the time of writing), rotating from portrait to landscape increased the size of the line chart for the currently selected stock and hid the list of other stocks.

Spatial gestures. A new perspective on spatial interaction opens up when considering device movements and rotations as paths through space and time: they can be used within the limits of the tracking system and the human motor system to define gestures that correspond with adjustments to visual representations shown on a mobile device. That is, interaction is not based on a single vector with up to six dimensions (3D

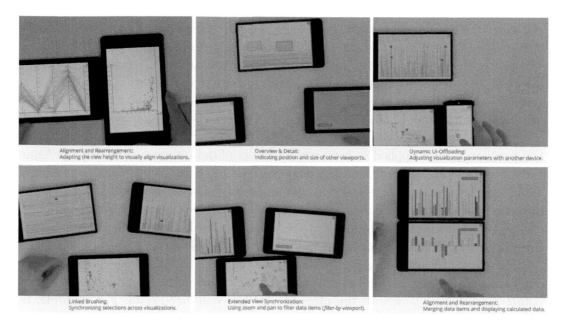

Figure 3.12 **VisTiles** [67] are an ensemble of connected mobile devices that maintain a shared awareness of their relative positions and orientations, as changes to either modulate both what is shown as well as the interaction affordances on each device. *Video stills courtesy Interactive Media Lab Dresden, used with permission; watch the full video at https://youtu.be/8MxPAMKmkSM.*

position and 3D rotation), but on a timed sequence of vectors, where the sequence contains the current position and rotation plus previous positions and rotations and their corresponding timestamps. While it is the users who perform the movements and rotations, it is the task of the visualization designer to define a set of reference paths, so-called gestures, to be matched with the user input.

The space of possible gestures is immense, as any of the six degrees of freedom can be performed and combined with any timing. This has implications for the practical use of gestures, especially, on the discoverability of gesture-based interaction in visualization interfaces. While there are techniques for assisting users in drawing stroke gestures with touch or pen [11], no such techniques exist for spatial gestures. Ideally, spatial gestures are simple to perform, easy to remember, and do not induce any substantial fatigue. Detecting gestures is a non-trivial problem, which reaffirms the need to keep gestures simple. As Spindler et al. [107] indicate, there are two relatively simple spatial gestures for handheld mobile devices for interacting with visualization, namely tilting and shaking.

The tilt gesture corresponds to a brief rotation of the device around the forearm axis and a subsequent return to the default device orientation, as demonstrated by Dachselt & Buchholz [31]. It can have a positive or negative sign, depending on the direction of the rotation. Tilting can be used to navigate a visualization in a step-wise manner, where each tilt corresponds to a single step. This can be useful, for example, for switching between different pages of a visual representation. Additionally, the step size can bear meaning, whereby tilting with a larger angle could be mapped to bigger steps in the interaction. The shake gesture literally requires the device to be shaken. This corresponds to a change in the device position at high frequency, where the direction of change switches frequently from a positive to a negative sign. The shake gesture is applicable for interactions that convey a *"No, I don't want this"* intent. For example, a shake could be used to dismiss the current visualization layout and request that the system generate a new one. Another example could be to reset a filter that has previously been applied to reduce the number of data items on the display. Again, the duration and energy of the shake could be used as an additional channel of control. The shake and tilt gestures are only two examples of what is possible with spatial interaction with the device displaying visualization. Depending on the type of device and data being visualized, different gestures can be used; Chapter 4 will touch upon aspects of spatial interaction in the context of 3D mobile data visualization.

The advantage of interacting spatially with the same device on which visualization content is displayed is a high degree of directness. However, device movements and rotations influence how well the user can see the visualized data. For example, by tilting the device, we lose the ideal perpendicular view on the device. When shaking a device, it is naturally hard to see any details in the visualization. This can be critical in cases where the interaction results in only subtle changes of the display, which might go unnoticed. It is therefore important to ensure that any feedback to spatial interaction addresses these issues.

Spatial Interaction using Cameras ◼◀

Many contemporary phones and tablets feature high-resolution front-facing and rear-facing cameras; both can be used as additional inputs for spatial interaction.

One use of a mobile camera is position-based transfer of visualization content across devices. The **Visfer** project [7] envisions a set of networked displays, which might include mobile phones, tablets, PCs, and large wall-sized displays (see Figure 3.13). The large displays could be divided into multiple views, and each view is augmented with an animated QR code. Using a mobile phone or tablet, one can move the device to point the camera at a QR code and to transfer content from the large display to the smaller one. Several types of content transfer are possible, including a responsive adaptation of the large display view to the aspect ratio of the smaller device, a transfer of the view specification, or a transfer of summary-level data, thereby allowing the smaller device to display a different yet related view to what is shown on the large display.

Camera-based spatial interaction can also be used to navigate and manipulate virtual objects in mobile augmented reality. One example is **AffinityLens** [112], which is an application for affinity diagramming with physical sticky notes augmented with QR-like codes (see Figure 3.14). Detecting these tags and their related note content via the camera, the application can highlight note categories and text search results. It can also generate chart overlays that summarize note content, including word clouds, line charts, and bar charts. Another example is **MARVisT** (or Mobile Augmented Reality Visualization Tool) [27], which allows people to create and view unit charts

Figure 3.13 With **Visfer** [7], one can transfer visualization content from a large display to a tablet or phone via the use of QR codes. *Video stills courtesy of Karthik Badam, used with permission; watch the full video at* https://youtu.be/KG1YqwlePGA.

Figure 3.14 Affinity diagramming is augmented with **AffinityLens** [112], in which alternative visual summaries of sticky note content is shown on the tablet or phone via the use of QR-like codes detected by the device's camera. *Video stills courtesy of Hariharan Subramonyam, used with permission; watch the full video at* https://youtu.be/p9WNlBOrQEo.

of 3D glyphs distributed within a volume (see Figure 3.15). We return to the chart authoring aspect of MARVisT below in our discussion of future opportunities.

Finally, mobile cameras can be used to detect hand gestures, which could in turn modify the visualization, such as by triggering navigation or selection. In our discussion of future opportunities in Section 3.3.5, we refer to two projects (ARPen [122] and Portal-ble [90]) that involve the capture of gestures performed with the hand that is not holding the device. Alternatively, these gestures could be performed by some other person who is visible to the camera.

Spatial Interaction using (Geo)location ♀

Spatial interaction may also involve changing the position of a mobile device at a much larger scale, thereby necessitating the use of a geolocation sensing. Mapping applications such as Google Maps are canonical examples in which visual representations of alternative trajectories, arrival estimates, accidents, and traffic congestion are updated in response to your change in location. Similarly, fitness applications such as Runkeeper [6], Fitbit [37], or Strava [110] encode trajectory paths over the course of a run or cycle, overlaying these on a map. Another notable instance of location-based

Figure 3.15 **MARVisT** [27] is a mobile augmented reality visualization authoring tool, in which it is possible to encode the size of virtual marks based on real objects detected in the scene and subsequently place marks via spatial gestures. *Video stills courtesy of Zhutian Chen, used with permission; watch the full video at* `https://youtu.be/cbtbJXwpwdk`.

Figure 3.16 In **Subspotting** [12], one's change in location along New York City's subway lines updates an egocentric visual representation of cellular connectivity. *Video stills © 2016 OFFC NY, used with permission from Dominikus Baur; watch the full video at* `https://vimeo.com/153013236`.

interaction with visualization on a mobile device is **Subspotting** [12], in which a representation of cellular connectivity along the New York City subway system is updated in response to one's location along a subway line (see Figure 3.16).

Online news articles, mobile versions of websites, and mobile apps can also request geolocation information about the viewer as a means to provide personalized content (for example, consider the OECD Better Living Index [85]). Geolocation sensing could also be used to support *context-dependent interaction* or responsive interaction design for visualization on a mobile device, such as by disabling or simplifying interaction while the location of the device is changing rapidly, which is typically indicative of moving in a vehicle, as described earlier in Chapter 2.

Our final example of spatial interaction is **FieldView** [124], a research project that involves visualizing location-specific data on mobile device displays as well as in head-mounted augmented reality; currently, our focus is on the former, as we return to the latter in our discussion of future opportunities below. In the mobile instantiation of FieldView (see Figure 3.17), multiple visual representations of data aggregated over a spatial grid allow forest ecologists, wildfire fighters, search and rescue teams, and others working in similar roles to ensure coverage of a territory and to add or

Figure 3.17 FieldView [124] combines data entry and mapping using a mobile phone with head-mounted augmented reality visualization. *Video stills courtesy of the CU VisuaLab, used with permission; watch the full video at* `https://youtu.be/pHfdbId4Gis`.

edit location-specific data, thereby updating any corresponding visualization. In a sense, this form of interaction is reminiscent of strategy video games whereby the "fog of war" is lifted via change in location, whereupon more of the territory and its attributes become visible.

3.2.3 Voice Interaction 🎤

Voice interaction has intrigued designers for decades, such as Bolt's *"Put-that-there"* interface (1980) [18] or Bartlett et al.'s Itsy pocket computer (2000) [10]. It has the potential to address challenges in interaction design for mobile visualization use cases, where access to mouse and keyboard is missing and the display size is small [70]. Researchers have recently envisioned compelling scenarios that facilitate and augment data exploration on mobile devices by leveraging speech input. Srinivasan et al. [109] describe a novel tabular data manipulation scenario on tablet devices, discussing ways to complement direct manipulation via touch or pen with minimalistic speech input. Choe et al. [28] envisioned a novel way to help people explore their personal data on smartphones by incorporating speech interaction and Kim et al. recently realized this approach with their Data@Hand [60] application. Exploring self-tracking data often involves specifying date and time, or their ranges. While this is tedious to do on mobile devices with existing widgets, such as calendar and clock controls, people are already comfortable and familiar with specifying dates and times with speech.

Recently, Srinivasan et al. [108] developed **InChorus**, a multimodal interface that incorporates pen, touch, and speech to facilitate data exploration on tablet devices (see Figure 3.18). InChorus was designed to address two fundamental issues. First, most of the prior research of data visualization on tablet devices have been optimized for a specific visualization type, such as stacked graph, bar chart, and scatterplot. This could cause conflicts and inconsistencies when we need to design a system that supports multiple types of charts. Second, when constrained by only pen and or touch, systems face increased reliance either on menus and widgets or on complex gestures as the number and complexity of operations grow.

Figure 3.18 **InChorus** [108] is a multimodal tablet-based visualization tool that incorporates pen, touch, and speech interaction. *Video stills courtesy of Bongshin Lee, used with permission; watch the full video at* $https://youtu.be/cyOVSmUP\_98$.

To design multimodal interactions that function consistently across multiple visualizations, InChorus brings speech interaction into pen and touch interaction: the directness and precision of pen and touch is complemented by the freedom of expression afforded by speech. Each of the three input modalities can work individually for the operations that fit their inherent characteristics. However, what makes InChorus unique is that the three modalities can work together to provide a novel and more fluid interaction experience. For example, combining speech with touch in a meaningful way can help people perform a more powerful action with a simpler interaction because touch can provide a deictic reference to a speech command. Finally, for many operations, InChorus provides multiple ways to complete the operation using different input modalities. This flexibility helps to accommodate individuals' personal preference. We revisit the topic of multimodal interaction in our discussion of future opportunities in the next section.

At this point, we end our overview of interaction for mobile data visualization. We have seen numerous examples of touch-based interaction on tablets and mobile phones, approaches to spatial interaction at local and global scale, and initial results of voice interaction. While the reviewed solutions already illustrate a wide range of possibilities, there is still more to investigate in the future.

3.3 FUTURE OPPORTUNITIES

We see several promising directions for future research and design with respect to interacting with visualization using mobile devices. We now reflect on the interaction vocabulary for mobile visualization and speculate on the future of multimodal interaction, multi-display interaction, mobile visualization authoring, and visualizing data in mobile augmented reality. While the latter two categories of opportunities are relatively nascent topics of discussion within the visualization community, we are not the first to discuss the former categories of opportunities; see Langner et al. (2015) [66]. Beyond visualization, we also look outward toward the broader human-computer interaction research community: to recently proposed mobile interactions and mobile technologies appearing at venues such as the CHI, UIST, and MobileHCI conferences.

For each new development with respect to interacting with visualization on mobile devices, one challenge will be evaluation, and as both Games & Joshi [39] and Blumenstein et al. [17] have observed, evaluation methodologies may need to be adapted to consider mobile devices and contexts. The crowdsourced evaluations of zooming and panning on mobile devices by Schwab et al. [101] and of mobile-specific visual encodings for range data by Brehmer et al. [20] may serve as useful precedents in this regard, however some forms of interaction may require more controlled experimental environments and direct researcher supervision. The topic of evaluating visualization on mobile devices is addressed in greater detail in Chapter 6.

3.3.1 Consistency and Expressivity

Given the diversity of our overview, it appears as though we are in the early days with respect to interaction design for visualization via mobile devices, in that various interactions map to different intents and have different effects across applications. In other words, there is no standard set of consistent interactions with visualization on tablets and mobile phones. Part of this heterogeneity can be attributed to the variety of data types and visual encodings in use, which have their own set of affordances independent of display device. Further complicating matters is the ongoing technological evolution of the devices themselves. Our overview focused heavily on touchscreen devices introduced since the advent of the iPhone in 2007, and since that time, various multi-touch, pressure-based touch, and spatial interaction techniques have appeared. Some touch interactions have attained a more consistent meaning than others in this time, such as pinching or spreading two fingers to zoom content or pulling down to refresh content. However, as Schwab et al. [101] show in their comparison of zooming gestures, there are several other gestures associated with zooming. Likewise, one application's panning gesture could be another application's selection or brush highlighting. In applications with multiple possible interactions, designers may opt for multiple interaction modes, such as a selection mode and a navigation mode, or they might resort to a combination of gestures and a conventional interface of menus and buttons, akin to the TouchViz WIMP interface [34]. In these cases, the discoverability of individual interactions or interaction modes is an important concern for designers.

While acknowledging the challenges associated with the discoverability and consistency of interactions, it is also exciting to expand the vocabulary for interacting with visualization via mobile devices. We can look to the mobile human-computer interaction literature and to particular application domains for inspiration. For instance, consider a dialing touch gesture, one that evokes rotary phones or the classic iPod's scroll wheel; Moscovich & Hughes [80] and Smith & schraefel [104] showed that this gesture can be used to navigate text documents, and thus could be applied to navigating any continuous data dimension. Similarly, drawing a convex hull via multiple touch points could be useful to select content in scatterplots or node-link diagrams, particularly on larger tablet devices. Finally, mobile map and wayfinding applications have provided a rich set of interactions that could be applied to other forms of data, such as two-finger scrolling to tilt the viewing plane or two-finger rotation to toggle egocentric perspectives on content.

3.3.2 Multimodal Interaction

Many of the examples cited in our overview above feature multiple simultaneous modalities of interaction, though by examining each modality individually, this might not have been apparent. As Table 3.1 shows, instances of spatial interaction and voice interaction also tend to involve touch interaction. For instance, the InChorus system [108] incorporates touch input, pen input, and voice input. The additive nature of these modalities leads to the question of how designers should assign interactions to modalities, and whether interactions should be exclusive to one modality or should they be redundantly accessible via multiple modalities [41]. Once again, as this aspect of mobile visualization design matures, we may see more variety in the allocation of interactions across modalities and in turn a need for consistency, particularly as applications incorporating multimodal interaction move from the domain of research to commercial or publicly-available applications.

3.3.3 Multi-device Interaction

Designing for multi-device, multi-person environments leads to questions of how an interaction might differ across several heterogeneous devices, or how the repercussions of one person's interaction with one device might manifest on other devices in the environment. If multiple views of a single dataset are distributed across displays, we arrive at the possibility of collaborative brushing and linking and other interactions that support mutual awareness and signalling. Linked navigation and selection across displays is another promising aspect of multi-device interaction with visualization. For instance, Voida et al. [120] envisioned a multi-device system involving an iPod touch and a tabletop display, in which the former is used both to view focused content in greater detail and to interact with the content using higher-fidelity multi-touch gestures afforded by the iPod touch. More recently, Berge et al. [15] demonstrated how a large wall-mounted screen could display an overview while a coordinated mobile phone could display a detail view of a subset of the overview, while Kister et al. [61] and Langner & Dachselt [65] showed how a detail view could be determined based upon the distance and relative orientation of a phone or tablet to the display. Langner et al. [68] would go on to demonstrate a multi-device system that supports both direct touch manipulation as well as remote interaction via a mobile phone for triggering details on demand views as well as highlight lenses and rulers for a wall-based visualization dashboard. Besançon et al. [16] demonstrated the use of spatial and touch interaction with a mobile phone to act as a remote for a paired large display, involving the visualization of 3D volume data, which called for 6-DOF navigation and the orientation of a 2D cutting plane across the volume. This intersection of 3D data visualization and mobile devices is discussed in greater detail in Chapter 4. Finally, Vistribute [49] takes us beyond tablets and mobile phones, being a framework for allocating interactive visualization elements across various types of displays, from mobile phones and tablets to PCs and wall displays.

Multi-person, multi-device environments are still an emerging area of visualization and human-computer interaction research. A study by Plank et al. [89] revealed that people are not accustomed to collaborating with visualization content distributed over a set of coordinated tablet devices. To overcome a legacy bias of working with single devices in isolation, visualization researchers and designers should identify a set of discoverable interactions for coordinating displays with corresponding attentional cues for promoting collaboration. Frameworks such as VisTiles [67] and Vistribute [49] are promising in that they may provide infrastructure for this research, which may in turn reveal new compelling use cases for multi-device interaction.

3.3.4   Visualization Authoring

Mobile devices are capable of sensing and storing various types of data, including motion, usage, location, sound, and images. Automatically-recorded data can also be augmented or complemented with manually-recorded data. In addition to many commercial self-tracking applications, some amateur "quantified-self" enthusiasts develop mobile data collection processes and applications. Mobile applications such as OmniTrack [59] allow people to track the data of their choosing, with options for specifying the type and granularity of the data. However, while OmniTrack and other self-tracking mobile applications allow people to record various forms of data, there are few options with respect to configuring or authoring visualizations of the data; if provided at all, visualization in these applications allow for little customization or control over visual encoding design choices. While there may be some convenience in being able to make visualization design decisions from the device that captured the data, self-tracking enthusiasts seeking to perform in-depth data analysis are likely to export their data from the device and visualize it using a PC.

There is evidently an opportunity to design effective mobile visualization authoring interactions. Tableau's Vizable iPad app [113] took an initial step toward mobile visualization authoring, though it required connections to external data sources rather than to data captured by the device itself. Mendez et al. [74] suggested a scenario for mobile visualization authoring in which people would take photographs of charts encountered in the physical world using a phone or tablet app. The app would infer its data relations and allow for the manipulation of these relations as new or augmented visual encodings.

Another opportunity is to bootstrap mobile visualization authoring via the capture of autographic visualization [86], or visible material traces of real-world phenomena such as air pollution or sea level change. One could imagine an interface wherein it would be possible to define position, size, or color scales and encode image or video content relative to these scales.

Lastly, we arrive at the intersection of mobile visualization authoring and mobile augmented reality, instantiated in the MARVisT system [27] described above. MARVisT allows people to specify visual encodings of unit charts via a mobile touch interface, while individual units can be placed within a 3D volume via touch or spatial interaction; the resulting unit charts can be navigated via spatial interaction.

3.3.5   Inspiration from Mobile HCI

By focusing primarily on visualization-related research projects in our overview, we have only scratched the surface of mobile interaction design research and the work of mobile interaction design practitioners. While our focus has until this point been on the intersection of mobile interaction design and data visualization, we now point to several recent developments in mobile HCI that can potentially be applied to future visualization research and design.

Interaction with visualization on smartwatches. Although we excluded smartwatch and other wearable devices from our overview, there are nevertheless opportunities here worth noting. Building off of earlier work by von Zadow et al. [121] that envisioned a wearable sleeve interface for interacting with a large wall display, Horak et al. [48] designed a system incorporating multiple smartwatches and a large wall display, wherein watches could store and display a subset of data based on touch and proxemic interaction, or they could act as a filter and remote control for the large display. To accomplish this, the system required a vocabulary of touch gestures for both display types, which are modulated by proximity to the display.

Smartwatch spatial gestures are steadily becoming more familiar, such as moving one's wrist to face upward, which reveals the watch's home screen. Seyed et al. [103] have also considered new gestures for smartwatches, such as flip, slide, or detach. We also see opportunities to apply voice interaction to smartwatch visualization, as well as opportunities for pen or stylus interaction with smaller watch displays, perhaps via a finger-mounted stylus, such as the one demonstrated in the NanoStylus project [127]. Finally, there may be new interaction modalities to consider with smartwatches. For example, the MyoTilt project [64] uses electromyography allowing a smartwatch wearer to manipulate display content via a combination of arm tilt and forearm muscle engagement.

While smartwatch visualization interaction is still relatively uncommon, a review of this research area along the lines of our present overview may be worth undertaking in the near future.

Gaze interaction. Researchers have been examining the potential of eye gaze interaction on mobile devices for over a decade [33]. Initially, such interaction required specialized eye-tracking equipment, while contemporary front-facing cameras on mobile phones and tablets are now capable of eye-gaze tracking without any hardware modification, as demonstrated by Khamis et al. [58]. To our knowledge, there has yet to be a demonstration of eye gaze interaction with visualization for mobile devices.

Pose and grip interaction. Pfeuffer et al. [88] explored thumb + pen interaction on tablet devices: similar to the clutch and fan menu described above, the dominant hand's pen actions are supported and augmented by thumb interaction with the non-dominant, device-holding hand. For example, to enable quick access to available options such as menu items, they employ thumb marking menus that can be operated by the thumb even while holding a device. To alleviate the issue caused by the thumb's limited reach, they integrate indirect touch input with virtual handles, which were introduced in earlier work by Wolf & Henze [126]. Pfeuffer et al. demonstrated that thumb + pen techniques can be applied to manipulate and analyze data in spreadsheets on tablet devices: they focus on the common actions people perform with cells in spreadsheets, such as copy-paste, formatting, or data editing. In this project, the pen always writes (or draws), while touch always manipulates content, following a design mantra advocated for by Hinckley et al. [46]. To our knowledge, we have yet to encounter a mobile application incorporating both visualization and bimanual pen+touch interaction.

Also promising are prototype devices that can detect changes in the positioning of one's hands relative to the device, whether or not they are touching the device. Zhang et al. [129] demonstrated how to improve pose and grip sensing by augmenting devices with sensors placed along the bezel of the screen. Similarly, Hinckley et al. [45] demonstrated the ability to detect a finger hovering over the screen. It would be fascinating to experiment with how such techniques could be applied to visualization tools, such as Tangere [98], which remains to be a rare example of bimanual touch interaction with visualization on a tablet. For instance, grip and hover detection could be a way of eliciting tooltips for marks on a mobile display.

Mobile augmented reality. Recent developments in mobile augmented reality (AR) interaction also offer exciting prospects for visualization with mobile devices. ARPen [122] and Portal-ble [90] are instances in which the non-dominant hand is holding the mobile device as an AR lens, while the dominant hand interacts with virtual objects using a pen in the case of ARPen and using freehand gestures in the case of Portal-ble. Both cases require specialized hardware (a custom pen in the former case, a Leap motion sensor affixed to the phone in the latter case), as well as 3D marks distributed in space to interact with. Both projects demonstrate their respective techniques with abstract 3D volumes of virtual representations of real objects, though these volumes or objects could just as well be points in a 3D scatterplot, data glyphs in a 3D space-time cube, or other manifestations of volumetric data.

New mobile devices. Finally, we consider the potential of new and forthcoming mobile devices and their implications for interactive visualization design. This list includes wearable devices other than smartwatches: pendants, belts, e-textile garments, temporary tattoos featuring integrated circuits, and on-skin projection devices. Previously underutilized components of wearable devices may also be exploited, such as how Klamka et al. [63] created a smartwatch strap with a flexible e-ink display. These and other devices may have varying degrees of display resolution and sensing capabilities for detecting interactions.

Though we did not discuss head-mounted augmented reality devices in our overview, as Chapter 4 discusses augmented reality and 3D data in greater detail, it is nevertheless worth noting the capabilities of next-generation displays such as with the HoloLens 2 [75] and the Magic Leap One [72] and how mobile and wearable devices might be used in concert with them. For instance, Büschel et al. [23] demonstrated how a mobile phone instrumented with additional tracking sensors could serve as a precise panning and zooming tool for navigating 3D volumes. Work by Langner et al. [69] extended the VisTiles approach [67] by combining mobile devices with head-mounted augmented reality, thereby augmenting visualization views with additional 2D and 3D information around and above displays. Wearable input devices could also be used to manipulate content shown in head-mounted augmented reality, such as ARCord [62], in which a lapel-mounted strap serves as a way of specifying a value along a single continuous dimension by pinching and sliding up or down the strap.

Handheld devices with semi-transparent displays may also invite novel interactions for visualization; consider Lucid Touch [125], in which one interacts with the underside of the device and thereby avoids the problem of fingers occluding content. Finally, new flexible handheld display devices (e.g., [47]) may provide new input channels for interaction, such as squeezing, twisting, and stretching. Foldable mobile phones such as Samsung Galaxy Fold [99], Samsung Galaxy Z Flip [100], Huawei Mate X [50], Motorola Razr [81], and Microsoft Surface Duo [78] may provide opportunities for multi-view visualization applications, or they may be ideal for scrollytelling-based presentations that juxtapose text and visualization content.

3.4 SUMMARY

The world has been captivated by the prospect of mobile interactive technology for the better part of the last century. From science fiction films to expositions that envision the future of work and leisure [83], we have been captivated by the prospect of performing an increasingly diverse set of tasks from a mobile or wearable device. The emergence of interactive data visualization over the past three decades has both amplified and shaped this captivation, prompting us to question how we can interact with data in new contexts. In parallel, mobile device display sizes have grown and support an array of multi-point touch interactions, while both processor capabilities and display resolutions have improved to the point where it has become possible to visualize large and complex datasets from a mobile device.

There are still challenges with respect to responsive design (as summarized in Chapter 2), the legibility of text elements, and both the specificity and discoverability of interactions across modalities. However, we are nevertheless witnessing an increasing number of interactive visualization applications intended for mobile devices, as well as an increasing number of responsive and interactive visualizations embedded in websites. The breadth of application areas and data types, spanning both work and leisure, is both staggering and inspiring. Visualization and human-computer interaction researchers also continue to test the boundaries of interacting with visual representations of data on mobile devices.

In this chapter, we have put forward a summary of this research to date, one classified according to the possible interaction modalities, namely touch interaction, spatial interaction, and voice interaction. In focusing primarily on mobile phone and tablet devices, we acknowledge a need for further examination of interaction with visualization on watches and wearable devices. In the coming years, we expect innovation along these modalities to continue, along with a further blending of multimodal interaction for visualization on mobile devices. New modalities may yet emerge. We are also excited by the prospect of seeding mobile visualization research with recent advances in mobile human-computer interaction research, in which we will collectively ask how the addition of data and visual mappings modulate these interaction techniques. In particular, we are excited by the prospect of visualizing data in mobile and head-mounted augmented reality; much of this data is inherently spatial, situated, and often three-dimensional, which is the topic of the next chapter.

REFERENCES

[1] Aigner, W., Miksch, S., Schumann, H., and Tominski, C. *Visualization of Time-Oriented Data*. Springer, 2011. DOI: 10.1007/978-0-85729-079-3. URL: http://www.timeviz.net (cited on page 81).

[2] Aisch, G. *Data Visualization and the News*. Information+ Conference presentation. https://vimeo.com/182590214. 2016. URL: https://vimeo.com/182590214 (cited on page 68).

[3] Aisch, G., Cox, A., and Quealy, K. *You Draw It: How Family Income Predicts Children's College Chance*. May 2015. URL: http://nyti.ms/1ezbuWY (cited on page 69).

[4] Antoine, A., Malacria, S., and Casiez, G. "ForceEdge: Controlling Autoscroll on Both Desktop and Mobile Computers Using the Force". In: *Proceedings of the Conference on Human Factors in Computing Systems (CHI)*. 2017. DOI: 10.1145/3025453.3025605 (cited on page 80).

[5] Apple. *iPad Pro*. 2020. URL: https://apple.com/ipad-pro/ (cited on page 71).

[6] ASICS Digital, Inc. *Runkeeper*. 2020. URL: https://runkeeper.com/ (cited on page 87).

[7] Badam, S. K. and Elmqvist, N. "Visfer: Camera-Based Visual Data Transfer for Cross-Device Visualization". In: *Information Visualization* 18.1 (2019). **Open Access version:** https://karthikbadam.github.io/assets/data/visfer.pdf. DOI: 10.1177/1473871617725907 (cited on pages 72, 86, 87).

[8] Bae, J., Setlur, V., and Watson, B. "GraphTiles: A Visual Interface Supporting Browsing and Imprecise Mobile Search". In: *Proceedings of the Conference on Human Computer Interaction with Mobile Devices and Services (MobileHCI)*. ACM, 2015, pp. 63–70. DOI: 10.1145/2785830.2785872 (cited on pages 72, 79).

[9] Bae, J., Setlur, V., and Watson, B. *GraphTiles: Visualizing Graphs on Mobile Devices*. Tech. rep. North Carolina State University. Dept. of Computer Science, 2013. URL: https://tinyurl.com/graphtilesTR (cited on page 79).

[10] Bartlett, J. F., Brakmo, L. S., Farkas, K. I., Hamburgen, W. R., Mann, T., Viredaz, M. A., Waldspurger, C. A., and Wallach, D. A. *The Itsy Pocket Computer*. Tech. rep. Research report 2000/6. Compaq Western Research Laboratory, 2000. URL: https://tinyurl.com/bartlett2000 (cited on page 89).

[11] Bau, O. and Mackay, W. E. "OctoPocus: A Dynamic Guide for Learning Gesture-Based Command Sets". In: *Proceedings of the Conference on User Interface, Software, and Technology (UIST)*. Monterey, CA, USA: ACM, 2008, pp. 37–46. DOI: 10.1145/1449715.1449724. URL: http://doi.acm.org/10.1145/1449715.1449724 (cited on page 85).

[12]   Baur, D. and Goddemeyer, D. *Subspotting: Mapping Available Cell Phone Reception on the New York Subway.* Information+ conference presentation, Video. 2016. URL: `https://vimeo.com/181724718` (cited on pages 72, 88).

[13]   Baur, D., Lee, B., and Carpendale, S. "TouchWave: Kinetic Multi-Touch Manipulation for Hierarchical Stacked Graphs". In: *Proceedings of the Conference on Interactive Tabletops and Surfaces (ITS).* **Open Access version:** `https://innovis.cpsc.ucalgary.ca/innovis/uploads/Publications/Publications/Baur2012ITS.pdf`. New York, NY, USA: ACM, 2012, pp. 255–264. DOI: `10.1145/2396636.2396675` (cited on pages 72, 75).

[14]   Baur, D. and Stefaner, M. *Everything Except the Chart: Responsiveness + Mobile Support.* IEEE Visualization Tutorial; slides: `http://webvis-do.minik.us/#/responsiveness`. 2018. URL: `http://webvis-do.minik.us/%5C#/responsiveness` (cited on pages 68, 73).

[15]   Bergé, L.-P., Serrano, M., Perelman, G., and Dubois, E. "Exploring Smartphone-Based Interaction With Overview+ Detail Interfaces on 3D Public Displays". In: *Proceedings of the Conference on Human Computer Interaction with Mobile Devices and Services (MobileHCI).* ACM, 2014, pp. 125–134. DOI: `10.1145/2628363.2628374` (cited on page 92).

[16]   Besançon, L., Issartel, P., Ammi, M., and Isenberg, T. "Hybrid Tactile/Tangible Interaction for 3D Data Exploration". In: *Transactions on Visualization and Computer Graphics (TVCG)* 23.1 (Jan. 2017). **Open Access version:** `https://hal.inria.fr/hal-01372922`, pp. 881–890. DOI: `10.1109/TVCG.2016.2599217` (cited on page 92).

[17]   Blumenstein, K., Niederer, C., Wagner, M., Schmiedl, G., Rind, A., and Aigner, W. "Evaluating Information Visualization on Mobile Devices: Gaps and Challenges in the Empirical Evaluation Design Space". In: *Proceedings of the Workshop on BEyond Time and Errors: Novel Evaluation Methods for Information Visualization (BELIV).* **Open Access version:** `http://mc.fhstp.ac.at/sites/default/files/publications/postprint-id11.pdf`. ACM, 2016, pp. 125–132. DOI: `10.1145/2993901.2993906` (cited on page 91).

[18]   Bolt, R. A. "'Put-That-There' Voice and Gesture at the Graphics Interface". In: *Proceedings of the Conference on Computer graphics and Interactive Techniques (SIGGRAPH).* ACM, 1980, pp. 262–270. DOI: `10.1145/800250.807503` (cited on page 89).

[19]   Boy, G. A. *Tangible Interactive Systems: Grasping the Real World With Computers.* Springer, 2016. DOI: `10.1007/978-3-319-30270-6` (cited on page 82).

[20]   Brehmer, M., Lee, B., Isenberg, P., and Choe, E. "Visualizing Ranges Over Time on Mobile Phones: A Task-Based Crowdsourced Evaluation". In: *Transactions on Visualization and Computer Graphics (TVCG)* 25.1 (Jan. 2019). **Open Access version:** `https://hal.inria.fr/hal-01857469`, pp. 619–629. DOI: `10.1109/TVCG.2018.2865234` (cited on pages 72, 80, 91).

[21] Brehmer, M. and Munzner, T. "A Multi-Level Typology of Abstract Visualization Tasks". In: *Transactions on Visualization and Computer Graphics (TVCG)* 19.12 (Dec. 2013). **Open Access version:** http://www.cs.ubc.ca/labs/imager/tr/2013/MultiLevelTaskTypology/, pp. 2376–2385. DOI: 10.1109/TVCG.2013.124 (cited on page 69).

[22] Buering, T., Gerken, J., and Reiterer, H. "User Interaction With Scatterplots on Small Screens - A Comparative Evaluation of Geometric-Semantic Zoom and Fisheye Distortion". In: *Transactions on Visualization and Computer Graphics (TVCG)* 12.5 (Sept. 2006), pp. 829–836. DOI: 10.1109/TVCG.2006.187. URL: https://doi.org/10.1109/TVCG.2006.187 (cited on page 71).

[23] Büschel, W., Mitschick, A., Meyer, T., and Dachselt, R. "Investigating Smartphone-Based Pan and Zoom in 3D Data Spaces in Augmented Reality". In: *Proceedings of the Conference on Human Computer Interaction with Mobile Devices and Services (MobileHCI)*. **Open Access version:** https://imld.de/cnt/uploads/mobilehci2019_bueschel.pdf. ACM, 2019. DOI: 10.1145/3338286.3340113 (cited on page 95).

[24] Chan, L., Müller, S., Roudaut, A., and Baudisch, P. "CapStones and ZebraWidgets: Sensing Stacks of Building Blocks, Dials and Sliders on Capacitive Touch Screens". In: *Proceedings of the Conference on Human Factors in Computing Systems (CHI)*. ACM, 2012, pp. 2189–2192. DOI: 10.1145/2207676.2208371 (cited on page 82).

[25] Chang, J. C., Hahn, N., and Kittur, A. "Supporting Mobile Sensemaking Through Intentionally Uncertain Highlighting". In: *Proceedings of the Conference on User Interface, Software, and Technology (UIST)*. ACM, 2016, pp. 61–68. DOI: 10.1145/2984511.2984538 (cited on page 80).

[26] Chen, Y., Barlowe, S., and Yang, J. "Click2Annotate: Automated Insight Externalization With Rich Semantics". In: *Proceedings of the Symposium on Visual Analytics Science and Technology (VAST)*. IEEE, 2010, pp. 155–162. DOI: 10.1109/VAST.2010.5652885 (cited on page 78).

[27] Chen, Z., Su, Y., Wang, Y., Wang, Q., Qu, H., and Wu, Y. "Marvist: Authoring Glyph-Based Visualization in Mobile Augmented Reality". In: *Transactions on Visualization and Computer Graphics (TVCG)* 26.8 (Aug. 2020). **Open Access version:** https://chenzhutian.org/projects/2018_marvist/paper.pdf, pp. 2645–2658. DOI: 10.1109/TVCG.2019.2892415 (cited on pages 72, 86, 88, 93).

[28] Choe, E. K., Lee, B., and Hwang, S.-W. "Personal Data Exploration With Speech on Mobile Devices". In: *Proceedings of the AVI Workshop on Multimodal Interaction for Data Visualization*. **Open Access version:** https://multimodalvis.github.io/papers/AVI_2018_paper_159.pdf. 2018 (cited on page 89).

[29] Corsten, C., Voelker, S., Link, A., and Borchers, J. "Use the Force Picker, Luke: Space-Efficient Value Input on Force-Sensitive Mobile Touchscreens". In: *Proceedings of the Conference on Human Factors in Computing Systems (CHI)*. ACM, 2018, pp. 1–12. DOI: 10.1145/3173574.3174235 (cited on page 80).

[30] Da Lozzo, G., Di Battista, G., and Ingrassia, F. "Drawing Graphs on a Smartphone". In: *Proceedings of the Symposium on Graph Drawing (GD)*. Springer, 2010, pp. 153–164. DOI: 10.1007/978-3-642-18469-7_14 (cited on page 71).

[31] Dachselt, R. and Buchholz, R. "Natural Throw and Tilt Interaction Between Mobile Phones and Distant Displays". In: *Extended Abstracts of the Conference on Human Factors in Computing System (CHI)*. **Open Access version:** https://imld.de/cnt/uploads/2009-CHI_Throw-Tilt.pdf. ACM, 2009, pp. 3253–3258. DOI: 10.1145/1520340.1520467 (cited on page 85).

[32] Dimara, E. and Perin, C. "What Is Interaction for Data Visualization?" In: *Transactions on Visualization and Computer Graphics (TVCG)* 26.1 (2020). **Open Access version:** https://hal.archives-ouvertes.fr/hal-02197062, pp. 119–129. DOI: 10.1109/TVCG.2019.2934283 (cited on page 70).

[33] Drewes, H., De Luca, A., and Schmidt, A. "Eye-Gaze Interaction for Mobile Phones". In: *Proceedings of the Conference on Mobile Technology, Applications, and Systems (Mobility)*. ACM, 2007, pp. 364–371. DOI: 10.1145/1378063.1378122 (cited on page 94).

[34] Drucker, S. M., Fisher, D., Sadana, R., Herron, J., and schraefel m. c. "TouchViz: A Case Study Comparing Two Interfaces for Data Analytics on Tablets". In: *Proceedings of the Conference on Human Factors in Computing Systems (CHI)*. **Open Access version:** http://citeseerx.ist.psu.edu/viewdoc/summary?doi=10.1.1.362.7241. New York: ACM, 2013, pp. 2301–2310. DOI: 10.1145/2470654.2481318 (cited on pages 72, 75, 76, 91).

[35] Ebert, A., Weber, C., Cernea, D., and Petsch, S. "TangibleRings: Nestable Circular Tangibles". In: *Extended Abstracts of the Conference on Human Factors in Computing System (CHI)*. ACM, 2013, pp. 1617–1622. DOI: 10.1145/2468356.2468645 (cited on page 82).

[36] Eichmann, P., Edge, D., Evans, N., Lee, B., Brehmer, M., and White, C. "Orchard: Exploring Multivariate Heterogeneous Networks on Mobile Phones". In: *Computer Graphics Forum* 39.3 (2020), pp. 115–126. DOI: 10.1111/cgf.13967 (cited on pages 72, 79).

[37] Fitbit. *Fitbit*. 2020. URL: https://www.fitbit.com/ (cited on page 87).

[38] Frisch, M., Heydekorn, J., and Dachselt, R. "Investigating Multi-Touch and Pen Gestures for Diagram Editing on Interactive Surfaces". In: *Proceedings of the Conference on Interactive Tabletops and Surfaces (ITS)*. ITS '09. **Open Access version:** https://imld.de/cnt/uploads/2009-ITS-DiagramGestures.pdf. Banff, Alberta, Canada: ACM, 2009, pp. 149–156. DOI: 10.1145/1731903.

1731933. URL: http://doi.acm.org/10.1145/1731903.1731933 (cited on pages 73, 77).

[39] Games, P. S. and Joshi, A. "An Evaluation-Guided Approach for Effective Data Visualization on Tablets". In: *Proceedings of the Electronic Imaging Symposium on Visualization and Data Analysis (VDA)*. Vol. 9397. **Open Access version:** https://www.cs.usfca.edu/~apjoshi/papers/evaluation-guidelines_vda2015.pdf. International Society for Optics and Photonics, 2015, p. 939704. DOI: 10.1117/12.2076523 (cited on page 91).

[40] GestureWorks ®. *Gesture Library (© Attribution Sharealike)*. 2018. URL: https://gestureworks.com/ (cited on pages 79, 80).

[41] Gladisch, S., Kister, U., Tominski, C., Dachselt, R., and Schumann, H. *Mapping Tasks to Interactions for Graph Exploration and Graph Editing on Interactive Surfaces*. Tech. rep. arXiv:1504.07844 [cs.HC]. **Open Access version:** https://imld.de/cnt/uploads/Gladisch15MappingTasks.pdf. CoRR, 2015. URL: https://arxiv.org/abs/1504.07844 (cited on pages 74, 92).

[42] Goguey, A., Malacria, S., and Gutwin, C. "Improving Discoverability and Expert Performance in Force-Sensitive Text Selection for Touch Devices With Mode Gauges". In: *Proceedings of the Conference on Human Factors in Computing Systems (CHI)*. ACM, 2018. DOI: 10.1145/3173574.3174051 (cited on page 80).

[43] Hao, J. and Zhang, K. "A Mobile Interface for Hierarchical Information Visualization and Navigation". In: *Proceedings of the International Symposium on Consumer Electronics (ICSE)*. IEEE, 2007, pp. 1–7. DOI: 10.1109/ISCE.2007.4382214 (cited on page 71).

[44] Heer, J. and Shneiderman, B. "Interactive Dynamics for Visual Analysis". In: *Queue* 10.2 (2012). DOI: 10.1145/2133416.2146416 (cited on page 69).

[45] Hinckley, K., Heo, S., Pahud, M., Holz, C., Benko, H., Sellen, A., Banks, R., O'Hara, K., Smyth, G., and Buxton, W. "Pre-Touch Sensing for Mobile Interaction". In: *Proceedings of the Conference on Human Factors in Computing Systems (CHI)*. ACM, 2016, pp. 2869–2881. DOI: 10.1145/2858036.2858095 (cited on page 95).

[46] Hinckley, K., Yatani, K., Pahud, M., Coddington, N., Rodenhouse, J., Wilson, A., Benko, H., and Buxton, B. "Pen + Touch = New Tools". In: *Proceedings of the Conference on User Interface, Software, and Technology (UIST)*. New York, New York, USA: ACM, 2010, pp. 27–36. DOI: 10.1145/1866029.1866036. URL: http://doi.acm.org/10.1145/1866029.1866036 (cited on page 95).

[47] Holman, D., Burstyn, J., Brotman, R., Younkin, A., and Vertegaal, R. "Flexkit: A Rapid Prototyping Platform for Flexible Displays". In: *Adjust Proceedings of the Symposium on User Interface Software and Technology (UIST)*. ACM, 2013, pp. 17–18. DOI: 10.1145/2508468.2514934 (cited on page 96).

[48] Horak, T., Badam, S. K., Elmqvist, N., and Dachselt, R. "When David Meets Goliath: Combining Smartwatches With a Large Vertical Display for Visual Data Exploration". In: *Proceedings of the Conference on Human Factors in Computing Systems (CHI)*. **Open Access version:** `http://users.umiacs.umd.edu/~elm/projects/david-goliath/david-goliath.pdf`. Montreal QC, Canada: ACM, 2018, 19:1–19:13. DOI: `10.1145/3173574.3173593`. URL: `http://doi.acm.org/10.1145/3173574.3173593` (cited on page 94).

[49] Horak, T., Mathisen, A., Klokmose, C. N., Dachselt, R., and Elmqvist, N. "Vistribute: Distributing Interactive Visualizations in Dynamic Multi-Device Setups". In: *Proceedings of the Conference on Human Factors in Computing Systems (CHI)*. **Open Access version:** `https://imld.de/cnt/uploads/Horak-Vistribute-CHI2019.pdf`. ACM, 2019, 616:1–616:13. DOI: `10.1145/3290605.3300846` (cited on pages 92, 93).

[50] Huawei. *Mate X*. 2020. URL: `https://tinyurl.com/huaweimate` (cited on page 96).

[51] Huot, S. and Lecolinet, E. "Focus + Context Visualization Techniques for Displaying Large Lists With Multiple Points of Interest on Small Tactile Screens". In: *Proceedings of the Conference on Human-Computer Interaction (INTERACT)*. Springer, 2007, pp. 219–233. DOI: `10.1007/978-3-540-74800-7_18` (cited on page 71).

[52] Isenberg, P., Fisher, D., Morris, M. R., Inkpen, K., and Czerwinski, M. "An Exploratory Study of Co-Located Collaborative Visual Analytics Around a Tabletop Display". In: *Proceedings of the Symposium on Visual Analytics Science and Technology (VAST)*. **Open Access version:** `https://hal.inria.fr/inria-00587236`. IEEE, 2010, pp. 179–186. DOI: `10.1109/VAST.2010.5652880` (cited on page 73).

[53] Isenberg, T. and Hancock, M. "Gestures vs. Postures: 'Gestural' Touch Interaction in 3D Environments". In: *Proceedings of the CHI Workshop on The 3rd Dimension of CHI: Touching and Designing 3D User Interfaces (3DCHI)*. **Open Access version:** `https://hal.inria.fr/hal-00781237`. 2012, pp. 53–61 (cited on page 74).

[54] Jansen, Y. and Dragicevic, P. "An Interaction Model for Visualizations Beyond the Desktop". In: *Transactions on Visualization and Computer Graphics (TVCG)* 19.12 (Dec. 2013), pp. 2396–2405. DOI: `10.1109/TVCG.2013.134` (cited on page 70).

[55] Jansen, Y., Dragicevic, P., Isenberg, P., Alexander, J., Karnik, A., Kildal, J., Subramanian, S., and Hornbæk, K. "Opportunities and Challenges for Data Physicalization". In: *Proceedings of the Conference on Human Factors in Computing Systems (CHI)*. CHI '15. **Open Access version:** `https://hal.inria.fr/hal-01120152`. Seoul, Republic of Korea: ACM, 2015, pp. 3227–3236. DOI: `10.1145/2702123.2702180` (cited on page 82).

[56] Jo, J., L'Yi, S., Lee, B., and Seo, J. "TouchPivot: Blending WIMP & Post-Wimp Interfaces for Data Exploration on Tablet Devices". In: *Proceedings of the Conference on Human Factors in Computing Systems (CHI)*. **Open Access version:** `https://www.microsoft.com/en-us/research/wp-content/uploads/2017/02/TouchPivot-CHI2017.pdf`. New York: ACM, 2017, pp. 2660–2671. DOI: `10.1145/3025453.3025752` (cited on pages 72, 77, 78, 81).

[57] Karstens, B., Kreuseler, M., and Schumann, H. "Visualization of Complex Structures on Mobile Handhelds". In: *Proceedings of the Workshop on Mobile Computing (IMC)*. 2003. URL: `https://tinyurl.com/karstens2003` (cited on page 71).

[58] Khamis, M., Alt, F., and Bulling, A. "The Past, Present, and Future of Gaze-Enabled Handheld Mobile Devices: Survey and Lessons Learned". In: *Proceedings of the Conference on Human Computer Interaction with Mobile Devices and Services (MobileHCI)*. ACM, 2018, 38:1–38:17. DOI: `10.1145/3229434.3229452` (cited on page 94).

[59] Kim, Y.-H., Jeon, J. H., Lee, B., Choe, E. K., and Seo, J. "OmniTrack: A Flexible Self-Tracking Approach Leveraging Semi-Automated Tracking". In: *Proceedings of the ACM on Interactive, Mobile, Wearable and Ubiquitous Technologies (IMWUT)* 1.3 (Sept. 2017). **Open Access version:** `https://omnitrack.github.io/assets/files/IMWUT-2017-Kim-OmniTrack.pdf`. DOI: `10.1145/3130930` (cited on page 93).

[60] Kim, Y.-H., Lee, B., Srinivasan, A., and Choe, E. K. "Data@Hand: Fostering Visual Exploration of Personal Data on Smartphones Leveraging Speech and Touch Interaction". In: *Proceedings of the Conference on Human Factors in Computing Systems (CHI)*. **Open Access version:** `https://arxiv.org/abs/2101.06283`. ACM, 2021. DOI: `10.1145/3411764.3445421` (cited on page 89).

[61] Kister, U., Klamka, K., Tominski, C., and Dachselt, R. "GRASP: Combining Spatially-Aware Mobile Devices and a Display Wall for Graph Visualization and Interaction". In: *Computer Graphics Forum* 36.3 (June 2017). **Open Access version:** `https://mt.inf.tu-dresden.de/cnt/uploads/Kister_GraSp_EuroVis17.pdf`, pp. 503–514. DOI: `10.1111/cgf.13206` (cited on pages 72, 83, 84, 92).

[62] Klamka, K. and Dachselt, R. "ARCord: Visually Augmented Interactive Cords for Mobile Interaction". In: *Extended Abstracts of the Conference on Human Factors in Computing System (CHI)*. **Open Access version:** `https://imld.de/cnt/uploads/klamka2018_arcord.pdf`. ACM, 2018, pp. 1–6. DOI: `10.1145/3170427.3188456` (cited on page 95).

[63] Klamka, K., Horak, T., and Dachselt, R. "Watch+Strap: Extending Smart-watches With Interactive StrapDisplays". In: *Proceedings of the Conference on Human Factors in Computing Systems (CHI)*. CHI '20. **Open Access version:** `https://dl.acm.org/doi/10.1145/3313831.3376199`. New York,

NY, USA: ACM, 2020, pp. 1–15. DOI: 10.1145/3313831.3376199 (cited on page 95).

[64] Kurosawa, H., Sakamoto, D., and Ono, T. "MyoTilt: A Target Selection Method for Smartwatches Using the Tilting Operation and Electromyography". In: *Proceedings of the Conference on Human Computer Interaction with Mobile Devices and Services (MobileHCI)*. ACM, 2018. DOI: 10.1145/3229434. 3229457 (cited on page 94).

[65] Langner, R. and Dachselt, R. "Towards Visual Data Exploration at Wall-Sized Displays by Combining Physical Navigation With Spatially-Aware Devices". In: *Poster Proceedings of the Conference on Visualization (VIS)*. **Open Access version:** https://imld.de/cnt/uploads/Langner-2018_PhysNav-SpatialMobiles_InfoVis2018-Poster.pdf. 2018 (cited on page 92).

[66] Langner, R., Horak, T., and Dachselt, R. "Information Visualizations With Mobile Devices: Three Promising Aspects". In: *Proceedings of the Workshop on Data Exploration for Interactive Surfaces (DEXIS)*. **Open Access version:** https://imld.de/cnt/uploads/Langner_Infovis-with-mobiles_DEXIS-15.pdf. 2015. URL: https://tinyurl.com/langner2015 (cited on page 90).

[67] Langner, R., Horak, T., and Dachselt, R. "VisTiles: Coordinating and Combining Co-Located Mobile Devices for Visual Data Exploration". In: *Transactions on Visualization and Computer Graphics (TVCG)* 24.1 (Jan. 2018). **Open Access version:** https://imld.de/cnt/uploads/Langner_VisTiles_InfoVis17.pdf, pp. 626–636. DOI: 10.1109/TVCG.2017.2744019 (cited on pages 72, 84, 85, 93, 95).

[68] Langner, R., Kister, U., and Dachselt, R. "Multiple Coordinated Views at Large Displays for Multiple Users: Empirical Findings on User Behavior, Movements, and Distances". In: *Transactions on Visualization and Computer Graphics (TVCG)* 25.1 (2018). **Open Access version:** https://imld.de/cnt/uploads/Langner-2018_MCV-LargeDisplays_InfoVis2018.pdf, pp. 608–618. DOI: 10.1109/TVCG.2018.2865235 (cited on page 92).

[69] Langner, R., Satkowski, M., Büschel, W., and Dachselt, R. "MARVIS: Combining Mobile Devices and Augmented Reality for Visual Data Analysis". In: *Proceedings of the ACM Conference on Human Factors in Computing Systems (CHI)*. **Open Access version:** https://imld.de/cnt/uploads/Langner-2021_MARVIS_author-version.pdf. ACM, 2021. DOI: 10.1145/3411764. 3445593 (cited on page 95).

[70] Lee, B., Choe, E. K., Isenberg, P., Marriott, K., and Stasko, J. "Reaching Broader Audiences With Data Visualization". In: *Computer Graphics and Applications (CG&A)* 40.2 (Mar. 2020). **Open Access version:** https://hal.inria.fr/hal-02459678, pp. 82–90. DOI: 10.1109/MCG.2020.2968244 (cited on page 89).

[71] Lee, B., Isenberg, P., Henry Riche, N., and Carpendale, S. "Beyond Mouse and Keyboard: Expanding Design Considerations for Information Visualization Interactions". In: *Transactions on Visualization and Computer Graphics (TVCG)* 18.12 (Dec. 2012), pp. 2689–2698. DOI: 10.1109/TVCG.2012.204 (cited on page 70).

[72] Magic Leap. *Magic Leap 1*. 2020. URL: https://www.magicleap.com/magic-leap-1 (cited on page 95).

[73] Maher, M. L. and Lee, L. "Designing for Gesture and Tangible Interaction". In: *Synthesis Lectures on Human-Centered Informatics* 10.2 (2017). DOI: 10.2200/S00758ED1V01Y201702HCI036 (cited on page 82).

[74] Méndez, G. G., Nacenta, M. A., and Vandenheste, S. "iVoLVER: Interactive Visual Language for Visualization Extraction and Reconstruction". In: *Proceedings of the Conference on Human Factors in Computing Systems (CHI)*. CHI '16. Santa Clara, California, USA: ACM, 2016, pp. 4073–4085. DOI: 10.1145/2858036.2858435. URL: http://doi.acm.org/10.1145/2858036.2858435 (cited on page 93).

[75] Microsoft. *HoloLens 2*. 2020. URL: https://www.microsoft.com/hololens/ (cited on page 95).

[76] Microsoft. *Power BI Mobile*. 2020. URL: https://powerbi.microsoft.com/mobile/ (cited on page 73).

[77] Microsoft. *Surface*. 2020. URL: https://www.microsoft.com/surface (cited on page 71).

[78] Microsoft. *Surface Duo*. 2020. URL: https://tinyurl.com/surface-duo (cited on page 96).

[79] Microstrategy. *Microstrategy Mobility*. 2020. URL: https://www.microstrategy.com/product/mobile (cited on page 73).

[80] Moscovich, T. and Hughes, J. F. "Navigating Documents With the Virtual Scroll Ring". In: *Proceedings of the Conference on User Interface, Software, and Technology (UIST)*. ACM, 2004, pp. 57–60. DOI: 10.1145/1029632.1029642 (cited on page 91).

[81] Motorola. *Razr*. 2020. URL: https://tinyurl.com/motorolafoldrazr (cited on page 96).

[82] Nguyen, F., Shrestha, S., Germuska, J., Kim, Y.-S., and Hullman, J. "Belief-Driven Data Journalism". In: *Computation + Journalism Symposium* (2019). URL: https://tinyurl.com/nguyenbelief2019 (cited on page 69).

[83] Noessel, C. and Shedroff, N. *Make It So: Interaction Design Lessons From Science Fiction*. Rosenfeld Media, 2012 (cited on page 96).

[84] North, C., Dwyer, T., Lee, B., Fisher, D., Isenberg, P., Robertson, G., and Inkpen, K. "Understanding Multi-Touch Manipulation for Surface Computing". In: *Proceedings of the Conference on Human-Computer Interaction (INTERACT)*. INTERACT '09. Uppsala, Sweden: Springer, 2009, pp. 236–249. DOI: 10.1007/978-3-642-03658-3_31. URL: http://dx.doi.org/10.1007/978-3-642-03658-3_31 (cited on page 73).

[85] OECD. *OECD Regional Well-Being*. 2018. URL: http://oecdregionalwellbeing.org/ (cited on page 88).

[86] Offenhuber, D. "Data by Proxy — Material Traces as Autographic Visualizations". In: *Transactions on Visualization and Computer Graphics (TVCG)* 26.1 (2019), pp. 98–108. DOI: 10.1109/TVCG.2019.2934788 (cited on page 93).

[87] Pelurson, S. and Nigay, L. "Bimanual Input for Multiscale Navigation With Pressure and Touch Gestures". In: *Proceedings of the Conference on Multimodal Interaction (ICMI)*. ACM, 2016, pp. 145–152. DOI: 10.1145/2993148.2993152 (cited on page 80).

[88] Pfeuffer, K., Hinckley, K., Pahud, M., and Buxton, B. "Thumb + Pen Interaction on Tablets". In: *Proceedings of the Conference on Human Factors in Computing Systems (CHI)*. ACM, 2017, pp. 3254–3266. DOI: 10.1145/3025453.3025567 (cited on page 94).

[89] Plank, T., Jetter, H.-C., Rädle, R., Klokmose, C. N., Luger, T., and Reiterer, H. "Is Two Enough?! Studying Benefits, Barriers, and Biases of Multi-Tablet Use for Collaborative Visualization". In: *Proceedings of the Conference on Human Factors in Computing Systems (CHI)*. **Open Access version:** https://kops.uni-konstanz.de/handle/123456789/42030. Denver, Colorado, USA: ACM, 2017, pp. 4548–4560. DOI: 10.1145/3025453.3025537 (cited on page 92).

[90] Qian, J., Ma, J., Li, X., Attal, B., Lai, H., Tompkin, J., Hughes, J. F., and Huang, J. "Portal-ble: Intuitive Free-hand Manipulation in Unbounded Smartphone-based Augmented Reality". In: *Proceedings of the Conference on User Interface, Software, and Technology (UIST)*. ACM, 2019, pp. 133–145. DOI: 10.1145/3332165.3347904 (cited on pages 87, 95).

[91] Qlik. *Qlik Sense*. 2020. URL: https://www.qlik.com/us/products/qlik-sense (cited on page 73).

[92] Ren, D., Brehmer, M., Lee, B., Höllerer, T., and Choe, E. K. "ChartAccent: Annotation for Data-Driven Storytelling". In: *Proceedings of the Pacific Visualization Symposium (PacificVis)*. IEEE, 2017, pp. 230–239. DOI: 10.1109/PACIFICVIS.2017.8031599 (cited on page 78).

[93] Roberts, J. C., Ritsos, P. D., Badam, S. K., Brodbeck, D., Kennedy, J., and Elmqvist, N. "Visualization Beyond the Desktop–The Next Big Thing". In: *Computer Graphics and Applications (CG&A)* 34.6 (Nov. 2014), pp. 26–34. DOI: 10.1109/MCG.2014.82 (cited on page 70).

[94]   Ros, I. and Bocoup. *MobileVis: Examples Tagged With "Responsive"*. 2014. URL: http://mobilev.is/tag/19 (cited on page 73).

[95]   Rzeszotarski, J. M. and Kittur, A. "Kinetica: Naturalistic Multi-Touch Data Visualization". In: *Proceedings of the Conference on Human Factors in Computing Systems (CHI)*. Toronto, Ontario, Canada: ACM, 2014, pp. 897–906. DOI: 10.1145/2556288.2557231. URL: http://doi.acm.org/10.1145/2556288.2557231 (cited on pages 72, 73, 76).

[96]   Sadana, R. and Stasko, J. "Designing and Implementing an Interactive Scatterplot Visualization for a Tablet Computer". In: *Proceedings of the Conference on Advanced Visual Interfaces (AVI)*. **Open Access version:** http://citeseerx.ist.psu.edu/viewdoc/summary?doi=10.1.1.473.6882. New York, NY, USA: ACM, 2014, pp. 265–272. DOI: 10.1145/2598153.2598163 (cited on pages 72, 73, 76, 77).

[97]   Sadana, R. and Stasko, J. "Designing Multiple Coordinated Visualizations for Tablets". In: *Computer Graphics Forum* 35.3 (June 2016). **Open Access version:** https://www.cc.gatech.edu/~stasko/papers/eurovis16-mcv.pdf, pp. 261–270. DOI: 10.1111/cgf.12902 (cited on pages 72, 76, 77).

[98]   Sadana, R. and Stasko, J. "Expanding Selection for Information Visualization Systems on Tablet Devices". In: *Proceedings of the Conference on Interactive Surfaces and Spaces (ISS)*. **Open Access version:** https://www.cc.gatech.edu/~john.stasko/papers/iss16-selection.pdf. ACM, 2016, pp. 149–158. DOI: 10.1145/2992154.2992157 (cited on pages 72, 76, 77, 81, 95).

[99]   Samsung. *Galaxy Fold*. 2020. URL: https://tinyurl.com/samsungfold (cited on page 96).

[100] Samsung. *Galaxy Z Flip*. Product. 2020. URL: https://www.samsung.com/us/mobile/galaxy-z-flip/ (cited on page 96).

[101] Schwab, M., Hao, S., Vitek, O., Tompkin, J., Huang, J., and Borkin, M. A. "Evaluating Pan and Zoom Timelines and Sliders". In: *Proceedings of the Conference on Human Factors in Computing Systems (CHI)*. ACM, 2019, 556:1–556:12. DOI: 10.1145/3290605.3300786 (cited on pages 72, 81, 82, 91).

[102] Sedig, K. and Parsons, P. "Interaction Design for Complex Cognitive Activities with Visual Representations: A Pattern-Based Approach". In: *Transactions on Human-Computer Interaction (THCI)* 5.2 (June 2013), pp. 84–133. URL: http://aisel.aisnet.org/thci/vol5/iss2/1 (cited on page 69).

[103] Seyed, T., Yang, X.-D., and Vogel, D. "Doppio: A Reconfigurable Dual-Face Smartwatch for Tangible Interaction". In: *Proceedings of the Conference on Human Factors in Computing Systems (CHI)*. ACM, 2016, pp. 4675–4686. DOI: 10.1145/2858036.2858256 (cited on page 94).

[104] Smith, G. M. and schraefel m. c. "The Radial Scroll Tool: Scrolling Support for Stylus-Or Touch-Based Document Navigation". In: *Proceedings of the Conference on User Interface, Software, and Technology (UIST)*. ACM, 2004, pp. 53–56. DOI: 10.1145/1029632.1029641 (cited on page 91).

[105] Spindler, M., Martsch, M., and Dachselt, R. "Going Beyond the Surface: Studying Multi-Layer Interaction Above the Tabletop". In: *Proceedings of the Conference on Human Factors in Computing Systems (CHI)*. **Open Access version:** `https://imld.de/cnt/uploads/2012/12/2012-CHI-HeightStudy. pdf`. ACM, 2012, pp. 1277–1286. DOI: `10.1145/2207676.2208583` (cited on page 83).

[106] Spindler, M., Schuessler, M., Martsch, M., and Dachselt, R. "Pinch-Drag-Flick vs. Spatial Input: Rethinking Zoom & Pan on Mobile Displays". In: *Proceedings of the Conference on Human Factors in Computing Systems (CHI)*. CHI '14. **Open Access version:** `https://imld.de/cnt/uploads/paper425-Pinch-Drag-Flick-vs.-Spatial-Input.pdf`. Toronto, Ontario, Canada: ACM, 2014, pp. 1113–1122. DOI: `10.1145/2556288.2557028`. URL: `https://doi.org/10.1145/2556288.2557028` (cited on page 82).

[107] Spindler, M., Tominski, C., Schumann, H., and Dachselt, R. "Tangible Views for Information Visualization". In: *Proceedings of the Conference on Interactive Tabletops and Surfaces (ITS)*. **Open Access version:** `https://imld.de/cnt/uploads/2010-ITS-TangibleViews.pdf`. ACM, 2010, pp. 157–166. DOI: `10.1145/1936652.1936684` (cited on pages 72, 83, 85).

[108] Srinivasan, A., Lee, B., Riche, N. H., Drucker, S. M., and Hinckley, K. "InChorus: Designing Consistent Multimodal Interactions for Data Visualization on Tablet Devices". In: *Proceedings of the Conference on Human Factors in Computing Systems (CHI)*. **Open Access version:** `https://arxiv.org/abs/2001.06423`. New York: ACM, 2020, 653:1–653:13. DOI: `10.1145/3313831.3376782` (cited on pages 72, 89, 90, 92).

[109] Srinivasan, A., Lee, B., and Stasko, J. "Facilitating Spreadsheet Manipulation on Mobile Devices Leveraging Speech". In: *Proceedings of the CHI Workshop on Data Visualization on Mobile Devices*. **Open Access version:** `https://tinyurl.com/srinivasan2018`. 2018 (cited on page 89).

[110] Strava. *Strava.* 2020. URL: `https://www.strava.com/` (cited on page 87).

[111] Subramonyam, H. and Adar, E. "SmartCues: A Multitouch Query Approach for Details-On-Demand Through Dynamically Computed Overlays". In: *Transactions on Visualization and Computer Graphics (TVCG)* 25.1 (Jan. 2018). **Open Access version:** `http://haridecoded.com/images/papers/smartcues. pdf`, pp. 597–607. DOI: `10.1109/TVCG.2018.2865231` (cited on pages 72, 78).

[112] Subramonyam, H., Drucker, S. M., and Adar, E. "Affinity Lens: Data-Assisted Affinity Diagramming With Augmented Reality". In: *Proceedings of the Conference on Human Factors in Computing Systems (CHI)*. ACM, 2019. DOI: `10.1145/3290605.3300628` (cited on pages 72, 86, 87).

[113] Tableau. *Tableau Launches Vizable, a Breakthrough Mobile App for Data Exploration.* 2015. URL: `https://tinyurl.com/vizable2015` (cited on page 93).

[114] Tableau. *Tableau Mobile.* 2020. URL: `https://www.tableau.com/products/mobile` (cited on page 73).

[115] Thoughtspot. *Thoughtspot Mobile*. 2020. URL: https://www.thoughtspot.com/mobile (cited on page 73).

[116] Tominski, C. *Interaction for Visualization*. Synthesis Lectures on Visualization 3. Morgan & Claypool, 2015. DOI: 10.2200/S00651ED1V01Y201506VIS003 (cited on page 70).

[117] Tominski, C. and Schumann, H. *Interactive Visual Data Analysis*. A K Peters Visualization Series. A K Peters/CRC Press, 2020. DOI: 10.1201/9781315152707. URL: https://ivda-book.de (cited on pages 70, 83).

[118] Tse, A. *Why We Are Doing Fewer Interactives*. Malofiej conference presentation; slides. 2016. URL: https://tinyurl.com/tse-malofiej (cited on page 68).

[119] Vallandingham, J. *So You Think You Can Scroll*. OpenVisConf presentation; video. 2015. URL: https://youtu.be/fYQGgaE_b4I (cited on page 68).

[120] Voida, S., Tobiasz, M., Stromer, J., Isenberg, P., and Carpendale, S. "Getting Practical With Interactive Tabletop Displays: Designing for Dense Data, "Fat Fingers," Diverse Interactions, and Face-To-Face Collaboration". In: *Proceedings of the Conference on Interactive Tabletops and Surfaces (ITS)*. ITS '09. Banff, Alberta, Canada: ACM, 2009, pp. 109–116. DOI: 10.1145/1731903.1731926. URL: http://doi.acm.org/10.1145/1731903.1731926 (cited on page 92).

[121] Von Zadow, U., Büschel, W., Langner, R., and Dachselt, R. "Sleed: Using a Sleeve Display to Interact with Touch-Sensitive Display Walls". In: *Proceedings of the Conference on Interactive Tabletops and Surfaces (ITS)*. **Open Access version:** https://imld.de/cnt/uploads/p129-von-zadow.pdf. ACM, 2014, pp. 129–138. DOI: 10.1145/2669485.2669507 (cited on page 94).

[122] Wacker, P., Nowak, O., Voelker, S., and Borchers, J. "ARPen: Mid-Air Object Manipulation Techniques for a Bimanual AR System With Pen & Smartphone". In: *Proceedings of the Conference on Human Factors in Computing Systems (CHI)*. ACM, 2019. DOI: 10.1145/3290605.3300849 (cited on pages 87, 95).

[123] Wang, X., Besançon, L., Ammi, M., and Isenberg, T. "Augmenting Tactile 3D Data Navigation With Pressure Sensing". In: *Computer Graphics Forum* 38.3 (June 2019). **Open Access version:** https://hal.inria.fr/hal-02091999, pp. 635–647. DOI: 10.1111/cgf.13716 (cited on pages 72, 80, 81).

[124] Whitlock, M., Wu, K., and Szafir, D. A. "Designing for Mobile and Immersive Visual Analytics in the Field". In: *Transactions on Visualization and Computer Graphics (TVCG)* 26.1 (Jan. 2020). **Open Access version:** https://arxiv.org/abs/1908.00680, pp. 503–513. DOI: 10.1109/TVCG.2019.2934282 (cited on pages 69, 72, 88, 89).

[125] Wigdor, D., Forlines, C., Baudisch, P., Barnwell, J., and Shen, C. "Lucid Touch: A See-Through Mobile Device". In: *Proceedings of the Conference on User Interface, Software, and Technology (UIST)*. ACM, 2007, pp. 269–278. DOI: 10.1145/1294211.1294259 (cited on page 96).

[126]   Wolf, K. and Henze, N. "Comparing Pointing Techniques for Grasping Hands on Tablets". In: *Proceedings of the Conference on Human Computer Interaction with Mobile Devices and Services (MobileHCI)*. ACM, 2014, pp. 53–62. DOI: 10.1145/2628363.2628371 (cited on page 94).

[127]   Xia, H., Grossman, T., and Fitzmaurice, G. "NanoStylus: Enhancing Input on Ultra-Small Displays With a Finger-Mounted Stylus". In: *Proceedings of the Conference on User Interface, Software, and Technology (UIST)*. ACM, 2015, pp. 447–456. DOI: 10.1145/2807442.2807500 (cited on page 94).

[128]   Yi, J. S., Kang, Y. a., and Stasko, J. "Toward a Deeper Understanding of the Role of Interaction in Information Visualization". In: *Transactions on Visualization and Computer Graphics (TVCG)* 13.6 (2007). **Open Access version:** https://www.cc.gatech.edu/~john.stasko/papers/infovis07-interaction.pdf, pp. 1224–1231. DOI: 10.1109/TVCG.2007.70515 (cited on page 69).

[129]   Zhang, Y., Buxton, W., Hinckley, K., Pahud, M., Holz, C., Xia, H., Laput, G., McGuffin, M., Tu, X., Mittereder, A., and Su, F. "Sensing Posture-Aware Pen+Touch Interaction on Tablets". In: *Proceedings of the Conference on Human Factors in Computing Systems (CHI)*. ACM, 2019, 55:1–55:14. DOI: 10.1145/3290605.3300285 (cited on page 95).

CHAPTER 4

3D Mobile Data Visualization

Lonni Besançon

Linköping University, Sweden

Wolfgang Aigner

St. Pölten University of Applied Sciences, Austria

Magdalena Boucher

St. Pölten University of Applied Sciences, Austria

Tim Dwyer

Monash University, Australia

Tobias Isenberg

Université Paris-Saclay, CNRS, Inria, LISN, France

CONTENTS

W E survey the space of three-dimensional mobile visualizations, that is, 3D abstract or spatial data on mobile 2D displays, or mobile head-mount augmented- and virtual-reality displays. As a playful "case study" we use a scenario from the film "*Aliens*," in which a mobile, small-screen visualization device is used to track the movements of enemy aliens around a group of space marines. In this scenario, the marines are overrun by aliens in the ceiling, as their device fails to show them the

DOI: 10.1201/9781003090823-4

height dimension of the space around them. We use this example to illustrate how different mobile and 3D interaction techniques could have prevented the misunderstanding in the movie, using both hypothetical descriptions of the improved movie action and a scientific discussion of these scenarios and their implications.

4.1 INTRODUCTION

It could be argued that we live in "Flatland" [1] because we are typically confined to the surface of the planet. Many of our interactions with the world are largely two-dimensional: we move and navigate on a largely two-dimensional plane (considering typical scales), when we place physical items they rest on 2D surfaces, and we read and write text on 2D canvases (i. e., paper), just to name a few examples. Nonetheless, there are certain situations and scales when we have to embrace 3D space. For example, people who go scuba diving suddenly find themselves in a truly three-dimensional world. Similarly, airplane pilots also face the challenge of having to navigate 3D space while surgeons and mechanical engineers also work with 3D structures. With respect to the subject of this book's focus of mobile visualization, there are numerous domains in which the produced data has an inherent mapping to 3D space. While these may be considered to be niche applications within the space of visualization applications (i. e., since a typical person is less likely to encounter them), the ability to explore certain datasets in their native 3D space is essential to a sizable number of experts. Some example data domains where 3D spatial structure is important include:

medical applications where data needs to be represented and understood within the 3D context of the human body;

biological and chemical applications for which the scale can be very small, at the cellular or the atomic level;

engineering applications where the underlying 3D structure comes, e. g., from a building information model (BIM) or computer aided design (CAD), Figure 4.1;

geography or geology where the structure is the earth's crust or some other aspect of the physical world, Figure 4.2;

astronomy or astrophysics applications where the structure extends beyond the world to the various scales of space.

In this chapter we explore how mobile computing and display technologies, existing and emerging, can be used to explore such data particularly taking advantage of these devices to provide a live window onto these 3D structures. For this purpose we take a rather broad view of what it means to have a *mobile* visualization, embracing aspects of being able to move the displays, move our heads with head-mounted equipment or even with respect to static stereoscopic screens, and if the 3D visualization subject moves in space with respect to a screen (also see the discussion on the definition of mobile visualization in Chapter 1). However, first we motivate the discussion considering both the need for, but also the challenges facing 3D mobile data visualization.

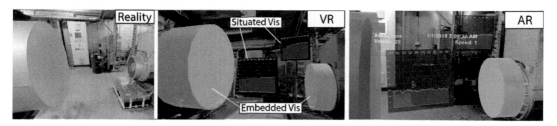

Figure 4.1 Integration of time-series (in this case energy consumption by HVAC systems), and CAD model data into a physical building with both VR and AR views to support different scenarios. Images taken with the Corsican Twin system [69].

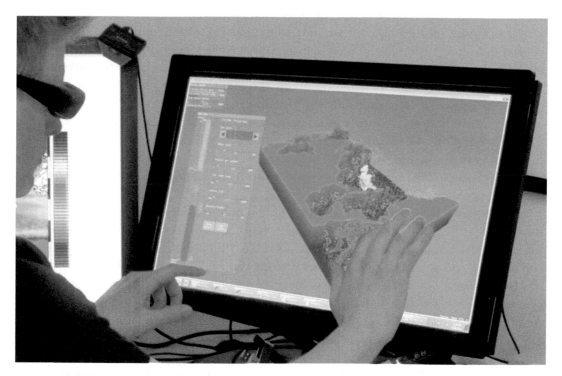

Figure 4.2 Example of a non-mobile ocean flow visualization supported by multi-touch interaction in 3D rendering [17]. *Image © Thomas Butkiewicz, used with permission.*

4.2 NEED FOR 3D MOBILE DATA VISUALIZATION

In Section 4.6 we introduce a design space for 3D mobile data visualization which considers "3D-ness" across three perspectives: *data*, *device*, and *representation*. We define these perspectives more formally in that section, but it is already useful to consider the examples of domain specific data above in these terms in order to identify opportunities for 3D mobile visualization.

Medical imaging—such as CT scans or X-rays—gives rise to 3D volumetric data. An opportunity for augmented reality is to provide a doctor with a view of this volumetric imaging 'spatially-anchored' in the context of the patient's body. For example, to precisely locate a foreign body or tumor and potentially to guide surgery. In such a scenario, a hands-free device such as a headset, is desirable to leave the surgeon's hands free to operate.

Electron microscopy or simulation gives rise to volumetric data of biological or chemical substances and processes. However, they are not typically anchored in a useful spatial context. Here, virtual reality (VR)—decoupled from the viewer's surrounds—might be a more appropriate medium for visualization.

The engineering applications examples we mentioned may be spatially anchored, for example in built infrastructure. It may be useful for site workers to visualize this in-situ with AR, or it may be more useful in a design context, or in the case where the engineer needs to view the model in miniature, to explore this visualization in virtual reality, from the safety of an office for instance.

Geography and geology are similar to engineering, in that the geo-spatially anchored data may need to be viewed in context when the viewer is on site, or in isolation when it needs to be considered holistically. The same thing applies to astronomy: a casual viewer may want information about the night sky as they look at it, while an astronomer may be interested in galaxy scale visualization.

To summarize, some data scenarios are best understood in a situated way, that means we see the visualization at the location to which it refers. If the reference location is in the world, we define such data as being *geo-spatially anchored*. In the medical example, the reference space against which the data is *spatially anchored* is the patient's body.

Seeing data in its spatial context is not the only reason why mobile visualization devices capable of 3D are useful. Engineers may need to look up the CAD model for an entire site while out of the office. A portable VR capable device would be helpful in this scenario to enable data exploration on the go.

Increasingly, dedicated immersive devices become available that were specifically created to be used in a mobile fashion. At the consumer end, Google Cardboard[1] pioneered the notion of a simple holder and lenses to turn a modern smartphone into a VR headset. For professionals, commercial AR systems like Microsoft HoloLens are fully self-contained computing devices with dedicated graphics and computer vision hardware to provide stable augmented reality data overlays. These devices represent opportunities for new applications for 3D mobile data visualization that will permeate the way we work or potentially, our personal lives, as discussed in Section 4.9.

4.3 PROGRESS TOWARD 3D MOBILE DATA VISUALIZATION: A MOVING TARGET

At the time of writing, mixed-reality technology has been under development in research labs for a long time. The term was coined in 1994 by Milgram and Kishino [58] to describe multisensory blending along a continuum between virtuality and reality. In recent years advances in the underlying technologies (such as display resolution, graphics rendering capability, tracking, but also optics) have made wearable headset

---

[1]https://arvr.google.com/cardboard/, accessed January, 2021

technology seem tantalizingly close to commercialization. A number of very highly touted startup companies have delivered products (e. g., Meta[2], Daqri[3]) but have ultimately failed to recoup on very significant startup funding, due to a number of factors. Mixed reality (MR) encompasses a broad range of technological solutions with heterogeneous levels of development or commercial success: VR has, for instance, attracted more attention, and achieved more technological advances and commercialization (e. g., Oculus Rift[4]) than AR. Technology immaturity still remains a significant challenge across the mixed reality continuum: headsets remain cumbersome, much less powerful than desktop computing environments, and aspects like field of view, natural hand gesture and voice interaction have remained disappointing even in recent devices. These remaining problems, it seems, still require significant research and development.

Despite the technical challenges facing practical deployment of MR into real-world applications, there are still some organizations with very deep pockets pushing the technology forward. Close to deployment but still ironing out problems, the US military has probably the most sophisticated AR system in the F-35 plane's Helmet Mounted Display System (HMDS) [64]. The HMDS uses the significant computing and sensor resources of the plane to give the pilot a seamless view of important information around the plane, such as the positions of targets, even *through* the opaque floor and walls of the cockpit. Microsoft and the US Army have signed a very significant contract to adapt its Hololens headset technology to a device incorporated into soldiers' helmets [36]. Similar in intent to the F-35 HMDS, this project aims to provide situational awareness to soldiers in the field via mixed-reality. However, since such a headset needs self-contained computing resources and may need to operate in more challenging environments, this project is further from practical deployment.

4.4 MOTIVATING USE CASE

There is a strong tradition of Human-Computer Interaction researchers taking inspiration from science fiction. A recent survey [42] found 137 references to science fiction by 83 papers from the ACM CHI conference's proceedings to 2017. It is also not without precedent for information visualization researchers to cite science fiction as a source of inspiration. For example, Elmqvist et al. [29] cite the film Iron Man 2 as an example of fluid interaction for immersive data analytics. In the Iron Man universe, holographic imagery blends seamlessly into the characters' world and effortless interaction with that imagery using "magical" technology enables impressive data analytics to relentlessly drive Tony Stark's genius-level insights. Such depictions of mixed-reality go well beyond the limitations of current technology. They are closer to virtual-reality pioneer Ivan Sutherland's [83] 1965 concept of an "Ultimate Display" (one which makes the virtual and real indistinguishable). This was a thought experiment on the theoretical possibilities of the technology, rather than something we might critically analyze and practically learn from in terms of usability.

---

[2]https://en.wikipedia.org/wiki/Meta_(company), accessed January, 2021
[3]https://en.wikipedia.org/wiki/Daqri, accessed January, 2021
[4]https://en.wikipedia.org/wiki/Oculus_Rift, accessed April, 2021

While fun and inspiring to watch, it is difficult to relate such fanciful scenes as those of films like Iron Man[5] back to what might be realistically achievable for mobile data visualization with foreseeable technology. We therefore take a slightly different approach. We introduce our discussion in this chapter with a look at an older science fiction film that posits a mobile data visualization scenario. It is interesting in that the film's vision predates the current wave of mixed-reality technology and related enthusiasm. In fact, the "future technology" depicted looks rather achievable—even primitive—compared to mobile-screened devices now in everyday use. Arguably, it presents an industrial, in-the-field, use-case not too dissimilar to those likely being considered by Microsoft and the US Army. After describing the scene as it was originally presented using technology that we might now consider mainstream, we ask the question: with mixed-reality 3D data visualization, would this scene have played out differently?

4.4.1   An Example: *Aliens*

The film *Aliens* was released in 1986. Depicting a rescue mission by a team of "colonial marines" of a human colony in distress on an alien planet, it is clearly futuristic. Yet its depiction of technology is a product of its time. The scene we focus on begins at 98 minutes and 25 seconds into the film.[6] A team of marines led by Corporal Hicks and accompanied by a level-headed civilian (Ripley) has already survived terrifying encounters with the Alien "Xenomorph" creatures. They are in the process of barricading themselves into a room, PFC Vasquez welding the door shut to keep the creatures at bay. Key to the scene is a piece of mobile data visualization technology being wielded by PFC Hudson, a "tracker" which uses ultrasound to detect motion nearby.[7] The source of motion is depicted in a top-down radial display on a small 2D screen on a handheld device.

The scene is depicted in Figure 4.3. The synopsis is as follows [21]:

HUDSON: Twelve meters. Man, this is a big #@$%ing signal. Ten meters.

RIPLEY: They're right on us. Vasquez, how you doing?

Vasquez is heedlessly showering herself with molten metal as she welds the door shut. Working like a demon.

HUDSON: Nine meters. Eight.

RIPLEY: Can't be. That's inside the room!

HUDSON: It's readin' right. Look!

Ripley fiddles with her tracker, adjusting the tuning.

---

[5]Star Trek's holodeck is also a classically cited mixed-reality "MacGuffin" (the movie trope of an artifact that exists just to drive the plot), e.g., [54]. Arguably, the Holodeck has inspired a great deal of mixed-reality research and created resonance for technologies like CAVE.

[6]*Aliens*Ceiling Scene on YouTube: https://www.youtube.com/watch?v=1bqSgvEZNtY, accessed January, 2021

[7]The M314 Motion Tracker: https://avp.fandom.com/wiki/M314_Motion_Tracker, accessed January, 2021

Figure 4.3 A high-consequence failure of a mobile visualization device to correctly convey the 3D structure of data—from the film *Aliens. Image © Magdalena Boucher.*

HICKS: Well you're not reading it right!

HUDSON: Six meters. Five. What the #@...

He looks at Ripley. It dawns on both of them at the same time. She feels a cold premonitory dread as she angles her tracker upward to the ceiling, almost overhead. The tone gets louder.

Hicks climbs onto a file cabinet and raises a panel of acoustic drop-ceiling. He shines his light inside.

At this point the team discovers that they have been overrun by the alien swarm which advanced through the ceiling. Lacking a representation of the third, vertical dimension their 2D device gave them no forewarning. They make a frantic retreat and several lives are lost in gruesome fashion.

4.4.2 Analysis of the Example: Different Kinds of Mobility

The example mentioned above led to human casualties in the movie because the situation at hand was actually quite complex and the visualization of the data not particularly suited for it. Several components contribute to the complexity of the situation.

The first challenge is that the data to be visualized—the positions of the incoming aliens—is inherently three-dimensional and needs to be mapped appropriately to be understood correctly. The visualization of spatial 3D data has unique challenges due to problems such as occlusion [75] (in particular on classical, non-stereoscopic displays) or the need for appropriate interaction techniques that may or may not mimic real-world interactions [4, 9, 82, 90]. This first challenge can be addressed by using 3D rendering together with suitable stereoscopic display hardware to create environments like those we are used to in our daily lives.

A second challenge in our motivational scenario is the issue of *mobility*: many things are happening and can happen at the same time yet at different places, and the visual representation should be updated to account for the movements of all the actors in the scene. The first actors are the moving aliens whose positions need to be updated. Nothing there is particularly challenging as long as the employed sensors track the aliens precisely and responsively. Nonetheless, the positioning of the visual representation might have to be adjusted accordingly as well, which begs the question of whether the (stereoscopically shown) visual representation itself is mobile or not: it can change its position with respect to the mobile device/display and to the world itself. The second set of actors are the humans and the devices they are holding or wearing. They too are mobile in 3D space and the representation should account for this mobility.

Overall, we can then distinguish different types of mobility with respect to the viewer, the display, and the visual representation to characterize different mobile 3D visualizations (see also Chapter 1):

- *mobility of the user*: the user can be mobile or (more or less) static in the 3D world as well as with respect to the device providing the visualization,

- *mobility of the display device*: the display itself may be static with respect to the world reference frame or with respect to the user('s vision), and

- *mobility of the visual representation*: the visual representation can be fixed or mobile with respect to the 3D world or the device that displays the visualization.

Characterizing 3D mobile visualizations with these dimensions facilitates understanding what kind of information is available at what moment as well as how to interact with the visualization in order to obtain more insights.

4.5 CHALLENGES OF 3D MOBILE DATA VISUALIZATION

While Section 4.1 outlines opportunities for 3D mobile visualization and promises the imminent availability of devices capable of realising these opportunities, many challenges remain which may impede the uptake of this technology in many situations. Some of these challenges are directly visible in our motivating example. Nonetheless, these challenges represent opportunities for researchers to make impactful contributions to the field. We now detail some of these challenges.

A new interaction paradigm. One obvious challenge is that mobile 3D computing environments offer very different modes of both display and interaction to traditional desktop computing environments. Thus, much of what human-computer interaction researchers have learned about desktop computer interaction since the 1960s may need to be reassessed or reinvented to support natural immersive interaction. In more recent times, touch-computing has been studied extensively as phones and tablets have become many peoples' primary digital devices. While 3D interaction techniques on mobile devices have been extensively studied (see, e. g., existing surveys of 3D interaction or selection techniques [2, 40]) to select and manipulate pre-defined objects, these techniques are unlikely to translate to 3D data visualization scenarios in which datasets do not present such pre-defined features or structures (see [11]). Similarly, interaction with data visualizations has now been extensively explored in all of these contexts, but similar effort may be required to realize natural and effective data visualization in immersive environments [11, 13]. A survey of many relevant interaction techniques for 3D mobile data visualization can be found in the report from Besançon et al. [11] who classify approaches based on the visualization tasks they help achieve, the interaction paradigm used and the supported output devices. Finally, if we want to use 3D data visualization in a mobile context with limited resources, we need ways to transition from traditional desktop/workstation-based data analysis/data storage to a mobile analysis/data access, and back [91, 92].

Integrating data and environment views. In general, a lot of the scenarios for mobile data visualization considered in this book involve devices being carried through the world, and the particular location of the device in the world is important context for the visualization. The location of the device and other objects or data in the 3D world around the device are therefore important pieces of context which must be accurately displayed to the user. There are many ways in which this kind of spatio-data coordination can be achieved, including ways that developments in technology, such as spatial tracking and immersive displays, are only now making viable. Devices like smartphones have long had location services which are adequate for applications requiring knowledge of the position of the device to tens of meters. Examples of such applications include turn-by-turn navigation, or the kind of *in-situ* geographic or geological survey data visualization scenarios described above. But devices which can use, for example, on-board cameras to locate themselves to centimeter accuracy are a much more recent development. Commercial software development kits providing accurate 3D location services based on camera, accelerometer and compass sensors in commodity phone and tablet devices started appearing about 2009 [47]. Such accurate positioning in all three spatial dimensions, as well as accurate orientation tracking, makes the above-mentioned "window on the world" data overlay for handheld devices scenario a possibility. It also enables wearable headset devices to more seamlessly introduce data overlays onto the wearer's field of view. Whether with headsets or handheld devices, such overlay of virtual data onto the world, is referred to as *Augmented Reality* (AR). As headsets improve and provide more seamless mixing of the virtual and real worlds the term *Mixed-Reality* (MR) is becoming more common.

Another challenge implicit in many of the example domains above is integrating visual overlays with the environment [71]. For example, for handheld AR the screen of the device may function as a window onto the world that overlays the physical world as the user moves the device in front of their field of view. The handset obstructs their actual view of the environment, but lowering the device easily allows the viewer to recover an unobstructed view. Headset AR provides a similar "data window" on the world, but with the additional challenge that the user cannot so easily remove the display from their field of view. We cannot control the environment. We cannot ensure that it is a safe place to stop and explore data. How can we show information and data without obstructing people's vision or distracting them from avoiding running into static obstacles or dodging objects moving toward them in the environment? We must design displays that can adapt, for example, placing data graphics to one side of important objects or against blank areas of the scene.

Physical scale. The scale of the underlying spatial data may be significant when considering applications of mobile data visualization. This is because the scale of the data being similar to, or radically different from the scale of the display of the device being used to visualize that data, may have significant implications on how the device can be used to explore the data. The engineering example above highlights this challenge. How do we view a CAD model that is bigger than the room in which an engineer is standing? How do we reconcile an overview of the whole building site with detail at the location that the worker is examining? If the geo-spatial data needs to be presented in the context of a map of a large area around the user (as perhaps may be used by a geologist in a field survey) then it may be important to represent the device's location relative to the map. At the extreme scales of atomic or astronomical data, the representation must be much more decoupled from physical space and the spatial mapping may be more abstract for convenience.

Computational and hardware challenges. Apart from the physical scale of data, another type of scalability issue is the computing challenge of dealing with very large (as in quantity) data. Many 3D volumetric datasets are huge: scaling cubicly with the dimensions of the volume under consideration. There is both an algorithmic challenge in dealing with such data efficiently, but also a hardware challenge. Mobile devices are limited in their computational, visual, and power/battery fidelity compared to 3D rendering workstations. The massive market for smartphones has been a strong driver of steady improvement against these limitations, but further innovation is needed. For visualization, improved display technology is critical. A research challenge for immersive displays is providing true depth of field. For example, the so-called *vergence problem* causes discomfort when a headset display presents an entire scene in focus, rather than allowing the wearer to naturally focus their eyes on objects at different depths. Experimental "light-field displays" use multi-layer LCD screens to render true depth of field [41], but these have yet to be successfully deployed beyond laboratories.

Abstract versus spatial data and spatio-data coordination. Three-dimensional structures can also be important to represent data that does not have a physical spatialization. Examples of such *abstract* or *non-spatial* data visualization include visualizing changes in any two-dimensional dataset over time. Such time-dependent 3D data visualizations are typically called "space-time cubes" [3]. An example of a space-time cube representation of abstract data might be a visualization of stock trade price versus volume over time. 3D abstract data visualization is also applicable when the relationships between any three quantitative, ordinal or categorical dimensions need to be viewed equally against each other. In these scenarios, the mapping of the data to space around the user of the mobile data visualization may be arbitrary or metaphorical, but doing so may make sense if it provides a natural way—using the capabilities of the mobile data visualization device—to explore that data. Following Cordeil et al. [26] we refer to this mapping of the data visualization space to the space of interaction around the user as *spatio-data coordination*.

Co-located collaborative contexts. While immersive co-located collaborative scenarios of immersive visualizations are very promising [53] and used for other purposes such as design work (e. g., [65]), a survey of collaborative work in augmented reality [74] has highlighted that only very little work has considered such scenarios and its challenges. Yet, some interesting problems should be studied in that context: how to distinguish between public and private view points (especially when using a separate device as interaction proxy, e. g., [73]), how to best convey collaborator internal state and private or public interaction, or how to handle undo/redo actions on the publicly shared views are fundamental issues that have not yet been addressed for immersive collaborative visualization contexts.

Human and organizational barriers to adoption. Not all barriers to practical use-cases for mixed reality are technological. There are also significant organizational and environmental concerns that may impede adoption of mixed-reality technologies into work-place scenarios. Masood and Eggar [56] develop a model designed to help predict success of AR applications given particular challenges in a given scenario. However, many of the concerns outlined in this model, technological, organizational or environmental, are becoming more understood and most can be reasonably expected to be overcome in the medium term—though whether this happens in five years or 20 years is still difficult to predict. The point is that understanding the full potential of mixed-reality, and the kind of impact it may be able to achieve for applications like data visualization, remains a speculative activity.

The playful speculations we engaged in through Section 4.4 and some of the challenges we have just explored help set the agenda for a more traditional survey of techniques and applications for 3D mobile data visualization, as well as some theoretical contributions in the form of a design space for 3D mobile data visualization.

4.6 A DESIGN SPACE FOR 3D MOBILE DATA VISUALIZATION

In order to provide a more systematic view of 3D mobile data visualization, we consider relevant aspects from three main perspectives: data, device, and representation (see Figure 4.4 for an overview of the design space).

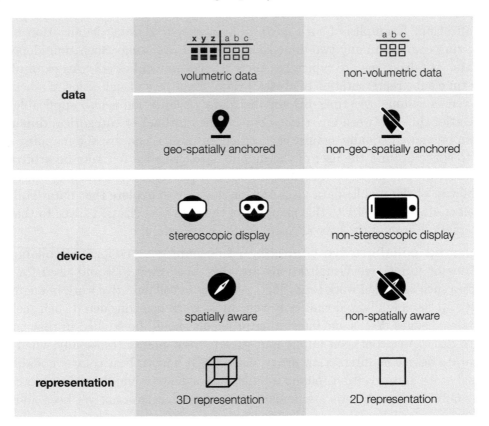

Figure 4.4 Design space of 3D mobile data visualization. In this chapter, we focus on the aspects marked in yellow (left column). *Image courtesy of Wolfgang Aigner* ©①.

Data. Obviously, when talking about data visualization, data is the basis for all further considerations. Different types of data lend itself to different visualization techniques for their graphical representation. Therefore, different kinds of data and their characteristics are considered in visualization in general [60, 85]. In the context of 3D mobile data visualization, two relevant aspects come to play. First, we can distinguish whether the data itself encodes 3D geometry (*volumetric data* that is inherently spatial such as the construction plan for a wind turbine) or not (*non-volumetric data* such as wind measurements). Second, data might be directly related to 3D space or not. An example for *geo-spatially anchored* data are wind measurements at different geo-spatial positions, areas, or volumes. *Non-geo-spatially anchored* data lack such a positional relation and are more abstract, as for example stock market data. For spatially anchored data we consider both, data connected to absolute positions in 3D space (**geo**-spatial anchoring, e. g., the mentioned wind data) as well as data connected to relative positions in 3D space (spatial anchoring, e. g., medical 3D scans related to certain body parts of a patient).

Device.   From a device perspective, we can differentiate between *stereoscopic display* where a true 3D impression can be created for the human user and *non-stereoscopic display* where only 2D projections can be rendered. Typical examples for stereoscopic displays are VR headsets like the Oculus Quest or HTC Vive, AR headsets like Microsoft Hololens or Magic Leap, but also CAVEs or shutter glasses used in 3D movie theaters. Besides that, non-stereoscopic displays are also relevant in the context of 3D mobile data visualization. Examples are tablets and smartphones but also smartglasses like Google Glass or Epson Moverio. In addition to stereoscopy, spatial awareness is a relevant aspect to consider. *Spatially aware* devices are able to relate their display to the 3D space around them. For instance, AR devices, like the Hololens, include different kinds of sensors to recognize its surroundings and can attach a virtual item to a wall or physical object in the field of view. *Non-spatially aware* devices lack this capability and are thus more detached from the real-world physical context. Note that devices for all four possible combinations of stereoscopy and spatial awareness exist and both stereoscopic and non-stereoscopic displays might be spatially aware. For example, while a smartphone (handheld AR) might be spatially aware, a VR headset like the HTC Vive might not be.

Representation.   Independently from the stereoscopic ability of devices, visualization methods can either employ three-dimensional or two-dimensional visual primitives. *3D representation* uses 3D geometric objects, e. g., for volume visualization or in a 3D bar chart. *2D representation* applies 2D shapes such as points, lines, or areas, e. g., for drawing a treemap or regular bar chart.

Focusing on the perspectives presented above allows us to emphasize the aspects that are most relevant to 3D mobile data visualization. Specifically, we unpacked the aspect of "3D" which is multi-faceted and might be related to data, the device, or the representation. With the presented design space, we have a tool that lets us describe what needs to be taken into account more precisely, characterize available approaches more systematically, and point out challenges and areas that need further research.

We consider methods, technologies, and techniques relevant for 3D mobile data visualization if at least one (and often more) of its aspects fall into a category of the left (yellow) column (see Figure 4.4). Bear in mind that most of the theoretically possible combinations of the five mentioned design aspects make sense and can be found in concrete examples. This leads to a wide variety of possible approaches and clearly shows the complexity of the topic. To structure our chapter, we have identified the most relevant configurations of the mentioned design space aspects. In the following sections, we provide an overview of the available approaches and discuss their specifics.

4.7 EXPLORATION OF RELEVANT CONFIGURATIONS OF OUR DESIGN SPACE

In this section we explore relevant applications of the design space we previously explored. We focus particularly on configurations that align with our definition of 3D mobile data visualization in this chapter, in other words approaches that satisfy at least one of the following: the data is volumetric, the data is geo-spatially anchored, the display is stereoscopic, the display is spatially aware, the representation of the data is 3D (see Figure 4.4). We structure this exploration into two main categories by data and display type: Volumetric data on non-stereoscopic displays (Section 4.7.1); Volumetric data on stereoscopic displays (Section 4.7.2); and Non-volumetric data on stereoscopic displays (Section 4.7.3).

4.7.1 Volumetric Data on Non-Stereoscopic Displays

Classical non-stereoscopic displays (for instance desktop monitors, mobile phones, or tablets) can represent volumetric data using a projected 3D representation. Popular 3D-based applications such as Fusion 360 from Autodesk,[8] or VTK with Kiwiviewer[9] have mobile versions of their 3D tools. In addition, platforms such as Unity[10] or the Unreal Engine[11] also made development of 3D applications on mobile devices easier in the last couple of years.

Classical 3D representation on non-stereoscopic mobile devices

Apart from the popular CAD softwares on mobile devices, mobile applications have also been developed to tackle the needs of researchers working with volumetric data. Kitware has made their famous visualization tool VTK available and running on mobile devices[12] to support analysis of scientific and medical data on the go.

A lot of past research has focused on the challenges to provide interactive 3D rendering of scientific data on mobile devices, which have a much lower processing

---

[8]https://www.autodesk.com/products/fusion-360/blog/fusion-360-mobile-ios-android/, accessed January, 2021

[9]https://www.kitware.com/kiwiviewer/, accessed January, 2021

[10]https://unity.com/, accessed January, 2021

[11]https://www.unrealengine.com/en-US/, accessed January, 2021

[12]https://vtk.org/Wiki/VES, accessed January, 2021

power than classical desktop stations, through specific rendering algorithms and techniques (e. g., [62, 63, 72]) while other approaches focused on the possibility of offload the processing/rendering to servers and directly stream from them (e. g., [22, 34, 67]).

Providing interactive 3D representations on mobile devices helps leverage the benefits of these devices within the workflow of domain experts. For instance, 3D representations on tablets or phones can be helpful for medical experts to rapidly select deep brain stimulation settings (e. g., [19]) or easily integrate in the workflow of other researchers (e. g., [8]).

In these classical examples of mobile, volumetric data visualization on mobile devices, users are usually static with respect to the device and the visual representation is static in the 3D reference frame (non-spatially aware). However, users can move around without affecting the visual representation and bring the devices with them. The initial *Aliens* example we studied is a specific example of such visualization but is augmented here with 3D rendering capabilities and interaction. In most cases, such 3D mobile visualization is used in order to benefit from the familiarity that users have with handheld devices such as phones or tablets. This means that most interaction with 3D representations is achieved through 2D touch input on the screen which can be difficult to translate into 3D interactions. Currently, there is no standard way of interacting with 3D representations using touch input [9]. Recent work has investigated the possibility to augment 2D touch input with pressure sensing in order to facilitate mapping to 3D manipulations [90] showing the benefits of such hybrid interactions, but such interaction mappings are still not common for regular users.

Coming back to our *Aliens* motivating example, we could easily imagine that the mobile device the team is using could display a proper 3D rendering of the vessel that would show the 3D positioning of the aliens. We could envision that casualties could have, therefore, been avoided. However, one also has to consider in this case that the marines would have had to identify on which floor the aliens were which might have been difficult on a full model of the ship they are in. This would have therefore required interaction to navigate the model and identify the precise location of their enemies, which, with only 2D touch input could have taken a long time [9].

The *Aliens* scenario might have been slightly better when considering spatially-aware devices. With spatially-aware devices, users can directly manipulate the device in order to interact with the 3D data projected on the screen. In this case, the mobile device acts as a tangible interface and users are able to manipulate the visualized data [8, 32, 76], manipulate a cutting plane to understand the internal structure of the data [8, 23, 77, 78], perform 3D selections and annotations [10, 23], or manipulate specific tools to better understand the data [8]. In most cases, tangible interaction is combined with the touch screen to provide hybrid interactions. If we consider the marines scenario, such hybrid interaction can potentially help navigate through the different levels of the 3D model of the spaceship in order to identify more quickly where the aliens are which might have saved the marines.

Fishtank VR

A first exception to the classical 3D projection on a non-stereoscopic display is the one of Fishtank VR applications [59, 93], see Figure 4.5. They provide head-coupled perspective projected stereo imaging on a rather small display that is fixed at a specific location. Recent examples of this are portable devices like the *Cubee* [80], its variations (e.g., [33, 79]) and other fishtank devices (e.g., [51]). Other fishtank shapes have also been investigated (e.g., polyhedric or spheric screens [5, 6, 35, 84]). Moving the device around does not have any impact on the visualized world, but the user can look at virtual information from different angles and thus leverage the shape of the device. For this, the user is tracked in order to adjust the view and give them an illusion of looking at 3D objects or data. The user is therefore mobile while the device and the visual representation are static in the 3D world.

Figure 4.5 Examples of fishtank VR devices. On the left, a 5-face p-cubee [79], on the right an AR simulation of an interactive cubee [37]. *Left image courtesy of Ian Stavness* ⓒⓘ*, right image from [37] © IEEE 2014, used with permission.*

Coming back to the *Aliens* scenario, we can easily imagine that such a device would have been useful in order to get a perception of real 3D locations without the use for headset or stereoscopic rendering. However, the location would only be perceptible by one user at a time and might require them to position themselves awkwardly such that they might not be in the best posture to defend themselves. In addition to these limitations, the one marine who would have had access to the information would have needed to then transmit the information to the others, probably wasting precious time when facing an alien invasion. Nonetheless, one can argue that their odds would already have been greater than in the movie.

Handheld AR

A second exception lies in handheld augmented reality [45, 25, 88, 89, 97], see Figure 4.6. Here, we make use of the handheld device as if it was see-through. The idea is to use the device's camera in order to mirror the real-world behind it and add 3D virtual information on top of it on the screen. In this case the display is mobile in the 3D world while the user is mostly static. The visual representation can either be fixed or mobile: it can on the one hand follow the device's movement and always be visible to the users (non-spatially aware) or stay at a fixed position in order to

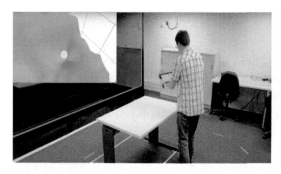

Figure 4.6 Examples of handheld AR devices used for visualization purposes. On the left, a tablet's spatial movements are tracked to interact with 3D visualization [15], on the right, the tablet or the tangible stylus are used to slice through a volumetric dataset [38]. *Left image courtesy of and Wolfgang Büschel* ⓒⓘ, *right image courtesy of and CC-BY Issartel et al.*

reflect the "real" position of the data/object in the 3D world (spatially aware). In practice, these solutions rely often on optical markers tracked by the device's camera in order to allow data manipulation and exploration [15, 38, 66] although commercial markerless solutions have also been developed, e. g., IKEA Place.[13] Finally, the cubee example mentioned in Section 4.7.1 has also been envisioned as an interactive and spatially-aware handheld VR/AR device [37] displaying data based on its location and allowing users to interact with and select virtual data and objects.

In our *Aliens* scenario, handheld AR devices are an improvement over the static fishtank VR devices. The display being mobile, interactive and potentially spatially-aware removes the problem of awkward positioning. However, the real 3D location of the aliens is still only correct for one user. The odds of all marines surviving the aliens are therefore much higher although the device still needs to be held and might therefore hinder the marine's access to their rifle. The two limitations of this solutions can actually be solved by stereoscopic rendering which we investigate next.

4.7.2 Volumetric Data on Stereoscopic Displays

Due to the nature of the data, stereoscopic rendering is often considered to mean that one visualizes data in a "volumetric" way. The data is not projected onto a 2D screen anymore, but instead can be perceived directly in 3D. Early work on stereoscopic rendering (e. g., [28, 43]) demonstrated the benefits of immersion for volumetric data analysis and understanding. Different environments and devices can realize stereoscopic rendering such as CAVEs (e. g., [28]), stereoscopic screens (e. g., [52]), stereoscopic glasses, or headsets (e. g., [14, 50, 61, 92]). Depending on the envisioned solution, users are more or less constrained in their movements in the real

---

[13]https://apps.apple.com/us/app/ikea-place/id1279244498, accessed January, 2021

world. For example, on the one hand, headsets provide a high degree of flexibility and can, therefore, be particularly interesting for understanding the spatial arrangement of data. Yet, they currently provide a limited field of view. On the other hand, CAVEs, allow users to be immersed in data [70] but do not provide mobility and are rather complicated to set up [7]. The mobility of the spatial representation is also something that has to be considered with stereoscopic rendering: The displayed data can remain static with respect to the user's field of view (non-spatially-aware setting; mobile with respect to the world reference frame). It can also remain static with respect to the world reference frame (spatially-aware setting; mobile in the user's field of view reference frame). In the first case, the virtual position of the data might not reflect its real physical position (if the data are related to real objects or processes) but will provide users with information regardless of their position. In the second case, if the data related to real objects or processes, its virtual position will reflect its real position but users will have to actively navigate the real world in order to see the visual representation of the data.

Modern head-mounted display devices make rendering 3D data in a stereoscopic context a relatively mainstream proposition. It has thus become fairly common activity to provide immersive walk-throughs of architectural and engineering plans. For instance, professional solutions allow clients of architects to explore, walk through, and analyze the results of architectural designs in VR (e. g., Enscape[14] or theViewer[15]). AR in particular is starting to be used in manufacturing to guide workers in assembly tasks [57]. Thanks to computer vision and marker based positioning, overlays can be accurately placed on surfaces to show workers precisely where components should be placed (spatially aware). Both VR and AR are starting to have significant roles in industrial training scenarios.

Stereoscopic rendering can also be coupled with regular displays. Some researchers created Hybrid Virtual Environments (e. g., [50, 73, 91, 92]) that combine several output devices together (and often also several input devices) to benefit from the advantages of immersion and the traditional 2D analysis tools available on classical devices, see Figure 4.7.

In our *Aliens* scenario, having access to stereoscopic and spatially aware renderings could have proven to be extremely useful to the marines. If we consider that the visualization was designed to follow the positions of the aliens, the marines could have easily identified the data points representing the creatures but would have had to pay attention to check in every direction until they actually found out their physical location. The virtual overlay might have made aiming at the invaders slightly more difficult but casualties could have probably been avoided.

---

[14]https://enscape3d.com/features/architectural-virtual-reality/, accessed January 2021

[15]https://theviewer.co/home, accessed January 2021

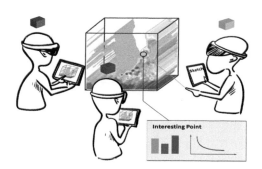

Figure 4.7 On the left, combining a laptop with traditional visualization tools and a Hololens for particle physics visualization [92], and, on the right, using a tablet as a visualization and interaction proxy in AR co-located collaborative analysis [73]. *Image from [92] © ACM, image from [73] © Mickael Sereno, Lonni Besançon, and Tobias Isenberg, both used with permission.*

4.7.3   Non-Volumetric Data on Stereoscopic Displays

In this section, we focus on non-volumetric data that do not encode 3D geometry by itself. Albeit such data might not seem to lend itself well to be represented by a 3D visualization, such presentations can be beneficial to the user (e. g., [12]). Particularly in traditional information visualization research, which focuses on 2D representation on non-stereoscopic displays, 3D representations are viewed very critically due to perceptual issues that make perception and interaction more difficult than with 2D representations [60]. Main issues put forward in this regard are depth perception and occlusion. However, when mobile, stereoscopic displays are being used, these disadvantages can be mitigated and further opportunities can be harnessed which cannot be provided in 2D representations [12, 55]. First, depth perception taps into our experience of perceiving the real world around us, where we are constantly taking depth into account through stereoscopic vision. Second, with the mobility of stereoscopic displays (e. g., HMDs) occlusions can be untangled more directly and intuitively by moving in space. Third, co-located collaboration is easier, as physical space can act as common shared display space within which analytical tasks can be performed. And fourth, in case of AR, (objects in) physical space around the viewer can be used as concrete external anchors for information to enhance cognitive processing [49]. This means that, albeit the data itself might not be geo-spatially anchored, it can still be virtually attached to physical objects for spatially aware displays.

Based on the kind of immersive technology used, available methods can be grouped into spatially aware and non-spatially aware approaches. An example for non-spatially aware approaches is the work of Cordeil et al. [27] who developed a system called *ImAxes* to interactively construct axes-based 3D visualizations in VR. Axes can be combined and configured by the end users to create novel visualizations (see Figure 4.8)

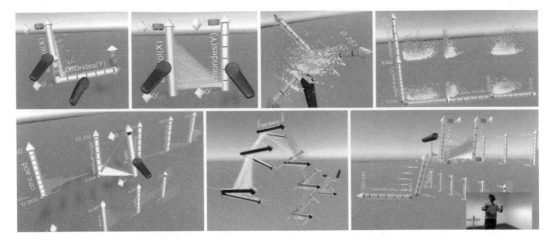

Figure 4.8 ImAxes: Visualizations built with ImAxes by end users in VR [27]. *Image courtesy of and © Tim Dwyer, used with permission.*

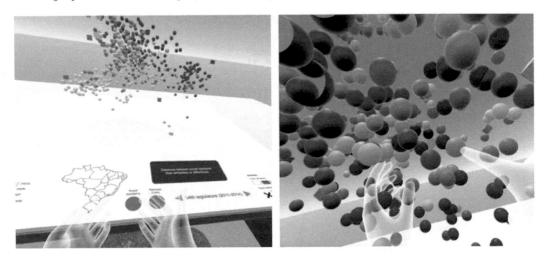

Figure 4.9 VirtualDesk: Projected multidimensional data are shown as 3D point clouds. *Images © 2019 IEEE, reprinted, with permission, from [31].*

in the form of coordinated 3D charts. In addition to the work on the design, interaction with, and authoring of data visualization techniques in VR, the topics of storytelling and effects of immersion are highly relevant due to the special characteristics of such immersive environments. In this context, Ivanov et al. [39] present a quite different approach of a VR-based immersive visualization environment with a focus on storytelling and emotional immersion. In their work, metaphor graphics and unit visualizations are used to communicate engaging experiences into statistics of mass shooting victims for example. Avatars represent humans and users can interact with these avatars directly to get personalized stories from the avatars.

In addition to the fully virtual experiences discussed above, Filho et al. [31] introduce the *VirtualDesk*, a VR-based display and interaction metaphor that interweaves VR and physical space. The user sits at a desk wearing a VR HMD and is thus also able to benefit from tangible feedback of the real table (see Figure 4.9).

Going one step further, the physical environment around a user might not only be used to provide haptic feedback and foster situatedness, but also visually, i.e., reality and virtual visualization environments can be interwoven in form of augmented and mixed reality approaches. In their work on AR graph visualization, Büschel et al. [16] display abstract, 3D node-link diagrams in the context of real physical space. The main contribution of their work was an empirical study to compare different options for edge styles. For collaboratively analyzing multi-dimensional data, Butscher et al. [18] developed *ART* (Augmented Reality above the Tabletop) that shows a 3D parallel coordinates visualization anchored on a tabletop (see Figure 4.10).

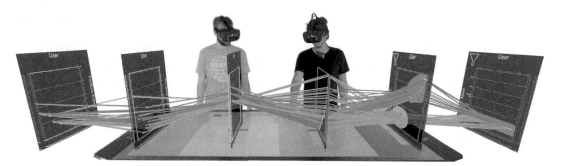

Figure 4.10 ART: Augmented Reality above the Tabletop—a 3D parallel coordinate plot that utilizes 2D scatterplots instead of 1D axes to collaboratively explore multi-dimensional data [18]. *Image © Simon Butscher, Sebastian Hubenschmid, Jens Müller, Johannes Fuchs, and Harald Reiterer, used with permission.*

An even more concrete approach of combining physical space and visual representations has been put forward by Chen et al. [24]. MARVisT is an authoring system for glyph-based visualization in mobile AR. Figure 4.11 shows an example of placing stacks of virtual sugar cubes next to drinks the data is related to. In contrast to most of the approaches presented so far, that focus on visual data exploration, MARVisT has a strong authoring component that allows for the creation of visual representation in an immersive environment. Another approach combines mobile devices and AR headsets to augment 2D mobile visualizations with 3D components on and around the devices [46].

In the *Aliens* scenario, we could imagine abstract representations of captured data about the intruders or about their own resources being shown right next to stereoscopic views of 3D data, allowing the defenders to quickly switch between the two views without the need to refer to external, stationary screens. They could thus keep their focus on the aliens and, with head-worn display equipment, even have access to their weapons.

Geo-spatially anchored data on spatially aware devices

For many data-driven tasks, like repairing a manufacturing machine or conducting a site visit to understand the existing conditions of a physical site, visualizing data in its original environmental context brings benefits to fulfil the task. Visualization methods that deal with linking of data to their origin are also referred to as "situated

Figure 4.11 MARVisT, a Glyph-based AR representation of the sugar content of drinks that places stacks of virtual sugar cubes next to drinks the data is related to. *Image © 2019 IEEE, reprinted, with permission from [24].*

Figure 4.12 SiteLens: Non-stereoscopic display of air quality measurements (non-volumetric, geo-spatially anchored data) using 3D representations in an outdoor environment [94]. *Image © Sean White, used with permission.*

visualization" [96]. Related to our design space, we are focusing on geo-spatially anchored data in this section.

For connecting the representation to the physical context, the approaches presented are usually spatially aware. Such overlays of virtual elements on top of the physical environment can however be challenging. First of all, the visuals should not occlude real-world elements. Several parameters therefore have to be taken into account: the size of the visuals, their positions, and their transparency. Then, the design of the visual should be compact and complementary to the real world so that it would not stand out too much and potentially take away the users' attention constantly. Finally, visuals should be properly linked to objects in the virtual world in order to give each visual representation the necessary context [68].

A further aspect related to visual perception is the use of text, for example to label axes or items of the visual representations. In their recent study, Kruijff et al. [44] investigated different aspects of label design on search performance and noticeability in two experiments. One of their findings was that noticeability of motion differs between optical and video see-through displays, but using blue coloration is most noticeable in both.

In contrast to most of the work presented in the previous section that was targeting indoor use cases, the approaches presented in this section mostly concern outdoor use cases. A classic example of applying this approach is SiteLens by White and Feiner [94]. In their work, air quality measurements (non-volumetric, geo-spatially anchored data) are represented on a PDA (non-stereoscopic, spatially aware display) using 3D representation (see Figure 4.12).

The *FieldView* system, introduced by Whitlock et al. [95], brings together 2D mobile visualization on a non-stereoscopic device (smartphone, tablet) with a 3D representation on stereoscopic displays (AR headsets). Figure 4.13 shows three

Figure 4.13 FieldView: Stereoscopic display of non-volumetric data using 3D represen-tations. © 2020 IEEE. Reprinted, with permission, from [95].

visualizations of the system *FieldView* using 3D representations of non-volumetric data. However, note that Figure 4.13 is an example of a non-spatially aware display albeit the data is geo-spatially anchored. In addition, the system is also capable of visualizing individual measurements in a spatially aware, stereoscopic representation, i. e., the visual elements representing measurements are positioned where they have been measured in real space.

2D representation on a stereoscopic display

Until now we have focused on employing the capability of stereoscopic environments to faithfully render data in 3D. What seems to be somewhat counter-intuitive is to use 2D representations in a stereoscopic context. Yet, there are also compelling use cases for this approach. First, stereoscopic displays like VR and AR headsets are capable of rendering 2D imagery on panels in the environment. This is particularly interesting when users cannot access classical workstations or analysis tools that Hybrid Virtual Environments (HVEs) usually provide. It becomes necessary when the data visualization supports work in a spatial context; for instance, workers have to repair or assemble in-situ within physical environments that cannot accommodate HVEs or when 2D visual representation have to be overlaid directly on physical elements. With this, workers wearing headsets can perform conventional 2D data visualization activities in unconventional environments. HYDROSYS [87] is an example of 2D representations in a spatially aware device. It overlays environmental monitoring data that is geo-spatially anchored over the real-world physical location of the measurement (see Figure 4.14). Extensions of this approach with area-based visual representations overlaid over the ground can be found in [86].

4.8 LESSONS LEARNED: COULD THE MARINES BE SAVED?

In the previous section, we have explored different ways to visualize 3D data with mobile devices and, for each configuration, we revisited our motivating example—the *Aliens* scenario. As simple as it seems, this scenario highlights some of the challenges that we have detailed in Section 4.5.

Being able to accurately visualize the 3D data of the aliens' position is of utmost importance to the survival of the marines. All investigated configurations can provide this, each of them with specific limitations which should be weighed based on the final

rendered data   video image

rendered data registered
over video image

Figure 4.14 HYDROSYS: a project for on-site environmental monitoring that uses spatially aware 2D representations to display geo-spatially anchored data over a physical location [87]. *Image © Eduardo Veas, used with permission.*

use-case. Non-stereoscopic screens require us to design specific interaction mechanisms to allow the marines to easily navigate through the 2D slices of the representation of their spaceship. Spatially-aware handheld solutions are cumbersome and not ideal for collaborative analysis of data. Spatially-aware headsets leave the hands of users free but the virtual overlay can hide other relevant information. Eventually, the choice of a configuration over another will depend on the context and use-case. In the specific context of the *Aliens* scenario, mixed-reality headsets would probably be better suited for the marines. We therefore propose and illustrate (see Figure 4.15) a revised scenario in which the headsets are incorporated into the marines' helmets. Here is the synopsis:

HICKS: Seal the door, hurry!

As in the original scenario, the team begins to barricade by welding the doors shut. However, now as soon the Aliens pass over the doors through the ceiling the marines become aware of the problem due to the signal from the tracker being directly overlaid on their helmet visors. They see the position of the aliens precisely in the context of the facility through a World-In-Miniature (WIM) view [81], they are also able to look up and see the Aliens approaching directly over the doors through an in-situ "x-ray vision" AR overlay.

HICKS: It's no use, they're coming through the ceiling.

Hudson and Vasquez begin accurately firing at the Aliens through the ceiling using this feature of their headsets, holding the advance at bay. Meanwhile, Ripley and Hicks continue using their shared WIM view of the facility plan to plot an escape route.

RIPLEY: We can get out this way!

Upon reaching safety, the marines are breathless and shaking with adrenaline.

Figure 4.15 Reimagined scenario. *Image © Magdalena Boucher.*

HICKS: Are we all good?

HUDSON: I think so...

Hicks uses an AR small multiples view [48] of his team's vital statistics to confirm their status.

HICKS: We've used quite a bit of ammo, but other than that, we're good.

As his pulse rate returns to normal, Hudson's attention wanders from immediate concerns, to his next priority, life after The Corp. He begins to perform some abstract data visualization, browsing an immersive representation of actors and the films in which they appear on IMDB. He finds that Bill Paxton (not to be confused with proponent of sketching for user experience design, Bill Buxton [20]) appears in multiple films with Sigourney Weaver in the Aliens' franchise.

HUDSON: Hey, since I survived that last scene, I get to appear with you in four sequels!

RIPLEY: Your 3D AR Vis is breaking the fourth wall.

Fin.

In this revisited scenario, beyond the relatively simple task of locating the aliens, other challenges that we mentioned in Section 4.5 are also highlighted. Two of the marines collaborated to find an escape route, further highlighting the need to study co-located collaborative analysis and natural interactions techniques for immersive content. We can observe in this revised scenario that the model of spaceship is probably scaled from the first panel to the second one: to locate the aliens, the model is represented at scale and highlights the enemy's positions whereas when the marines are trying to plan an escape route, the model is scaled down to allow an overview of the spaceship. During all of this, it is obvious that the visual overlay provided by the headset should also be properly integrated with the marines' environment and not hinder their perception of critical objects, people, or aliens.

4.9 CONCLUSION

In this chapter, we have discussed scenarios that one might characterize as niche, workplace and domain specific examples. It therefore seems reasonable to wonder whether 3D mobile data visualization will become ubiquitous and, if so, when?

There is an argument that situated data visusalization can be useful in many real-world situations. While many of the examples above come from technical domains (e. g., engineering), the utility of receiving information about any object in the world that you look at, in the form of banners or other visual overlays hovering directly around that object, that may be transformational to engineers operating complex equipment, can be beneficial to people in their day-to-day lives also.

An obvious (but futuristic) example is technology supporting the party trick of low-key headsets (or implants?) reminding the wearer of the name of every person they encounter in a busy room, whether they have met them before or not. Names are just the beginning, with a lot of information already available in social-media services. Consider the implications for social engineering of reminding the wearer of their personal connection to every person they meet, or their tertiary connection via their social network. The physical world that we walk through can be overlaid with a "web" of connections that were previously invisible to show connections between people or objects, physically present or virtual. Managing the complexity of such virtual link overlays is a research challenge in itself [68].

Apart from social encounters 3D mobile visualization can usefully support people in their encounters with inanimate or electronic objects in their environment, just as it can support a facilities manager in a machine room. In the shopping center, people regularly are called upon to make complex purchasing decisions based upon all kinds of information that is not made obvious by a product's packaging. Examples include relating nutritional information to one's own dietary requirements, or the ethical or sustainability concerns related to a product that will certainly not be advertised by the manufacturer [30]. Some of these things can be achieved with today's handheld devices, for example with apps that can search for information about products based on images of their barcodes or packaging. However, hands-free, spatially aware headsets offer convenience as well as seamless, unobtrusive use that make them very attractive.

If 3D data visualization can assist or guide during design or engineering tasks, it is easy to imagine 3D mobile data visualization being used in situations where users' awareness and need for spatially-anchored information is crucial: driving while getting directions for instance. The superimposition of directions on the road and information that is necessary to safely drive a vehicle (other vehicle's speed or potential danger on the road) would be helpful in this task. Geo-spatially-anchored information would also help avoid the recurring last minute realization that, as a driver, we are in the wrong lane for a specific turn, or could help warn us about potential dead-angle dangers and therefore, not unlike our Alien scenario, potentially save lives. However, specific interaction techniques would have to be designed to best assist drivers whose hands are already taken by the car they are driving.

These scenarios quickly become data visualization challenges with a mix of complex abstract, quantitative and spatial information requiring effective representation in the space around the wearer of the device and the things they are looking at. While some of them seem far in the future, we already possess most of the technology to start solving the specific challenges they offer. One might therefore claim that 3D mobile data visualization will be ubiquitous, but the "when" is up to our ability to overcome remaining technological, social and organizational barriers to adoption.

REFERENCES

[1] Abbott, E. A. *Flatland: A Romance of Many Dimensions*. **Open Access version:** https://en.wikisource.org/wiki/Flatland_(first_edition). London: Seeley & Co., 1884 (cited on page 112).

[2] Argelaguet, F. and Andujar, C. "A Survey of 3D Object Selection Techniques for Virtual Environments". In: *Computers & Graphics* 37.3 (May 2013). **Open**

Access version: https://hal.inria.fr/hal-00907787, pp. 121–136. DOI: 10.1016/j.cag.2012.12.003 (cited on page 119).

[3] Bach, B., Dragicevic, P., Archambault, D., Hurter, C., and Carpendale, S. "A Review of Temporal Data Visualizations Based on Space-Time Cube Operations". In: *State of the Art Reports of the European Conference on Visualization (EuroVis)*. **Open Access version:** https://hal.inria.fr/hal-01006140. Goslar, Germany: Eurographics, June 2014, pp. 23–41. DOI: 10.2312/eurovisstar.20141171 (cited on page 121).

[4] Bach, B., Sicat, R., Beyer, J., Cordeil, M., and Pfister, H. "The Hologram in My Hand: How Effective Is Interactive Exploration of 3D Visualizations in Immersive Tangible Augmented Reality?" In: *Transactions on Visualization and Computer Graphics (TVCG)* 24.1 (Jan. 2018). **Open Access version:** https://www.pure.ed.ac.uk/ws/files/42969387/Bach2018holostudy.pdf, pp. 457–467. DOI: 10.1109/TVCG.2017.2745941 (cited on page 118).

[5] Berard, F. and Louis, T. "The Object Inside: Assessing 3D Examination With a Spherical Handheld Perspective-Corrected Display". In: *Proceedings of the Conference on Human Factors in Computing Systems (CHI)*. **Open Access version:** https://hal.archives-ouvertes.fr/hal-02954820. Denver, Colorado, USA: ACM, 2017, pp. 4396–4404. DOI: 10.1145/3025453.3025806 (cited on page 126).

[6] Bérard, F. and Louis, T. "A Low-Latency, High-Precision Handheld Perspective Corrected Display". In: *Adjust Proceedings of the Symposium on Mixed and Augmented Reality (ISMAR)*. **Open Access version:** https://hal.archives-ouvertes.fr/hal-02954796. Los Alamitos: IEEE, 2018, pp. 397–398. DOI: 10.1109/ISMAR-Adjunct.2018.00114 (cited on page 126).

[7] Besançon, L. "An Interaction Continuum for 3D Dataset Visualization". **Open Access version:** https://tel.archives-ouvertes.fr/tel-01684210. Theses. Université Paris-Saclay, Dec. 2017 (cited on page 128).

[8] Besançon, L., Issartel, P., Ammi, M., and Isenberg, T. "Hybrid Tactile/Tangible Interaction for 3D Data Exploration". In: *Transactions on Visualization and Computer Graphics (TVCG)* 23.1 (Jan. 2017). **Open Access version:** https://hal.inria.fr/hal-01372922, pp. 881–890. DOI: 10.1109/TVCG.2016.2599217 (cited on page 125).

[9] Besançon, L., Issartel, P., Ammi, M., and Isenberg, T. "Mouse, Tactile, and Tangible Input for 3D Manipulation". In: *Proceedings of the Conference on Human Factors in Computing Systems (CHI)*. **Open Access version:** https://hal.inria.fr/hal-01436206. New York: ACM, May 2017, pp. 4727–4740. DOI: 10.1145/3025453.3025863 (cited on pages 118, 125).

[10] Besançon, L., Sereno, M., Yu, L., Ammi, M., and Isenberg, T. "Hybrid Touch/Tangible Spatial 3D Data Selection". In: *Computer Graphics Forum* 38.3 (June 2019). **Open Access version:** https://hal.inria.fr/hal-02079308, pp. 553–567. DOI: 10.1111/cgf.13710 (cited on page 125).

[11] Besançon, L., Ynnerman, A., Keefe, D. F., Yu, L., and Isenberg, T. "The State of the Art of Spatial Interfaces for 3D Visualization". In: *Computer Graphics Forum* (2021). In press. **Open Access version:** `https://hal.inria.fr/hal-03012861`. DOI: `10.1111/cgf.14189` (cited on page 119).

[12] Brath, R. "3D InfoVis Is Here to Stay: Deal With It". In: *Proceedings of the IEEE VIS Workshop on 3DVis (3DVis)*. Los Alamitos: IEEE, 2014, pp. 25–31. DOI: `10.1109/3DVis.2014.7160096` (cited on page 129).

[13] Büschel, W., Chen, J., Dachselt, R., Drucker, S., Dwyer, T., Görg, C., Isenberg, T., Kerren, A., North, C., and Stuerzlinger, W. "Interaction for Immersive Analytics". In: *Immersive Analytics*. **Open Access version:** `https://hal.inria.fr/hal-01907526`. Berlin, Heidelberg: Springer, 2018, pp. 95–138. DOI: `10.1007/978-3-030-01388-2_4` (cited on page 119).

[14] Büschel, W., Lehmann, A., and Dachselt, R. "MIRIA: A Mixed Reality Toolkit for the In-Situ Visualization and Analysis of Spatio-Temporal Interaction Data". In: *Proceedings of the ACM Conference on Human Factors in Computing Systems (CHI)*. **Open Access version:** `https://imld.de/cnt/uploads/MIRIA_Author_Version.pdf`. ACM, 2021. DOI: `10.1145/3411764.3445651` (cited on page 127).

[15] Büschel, W., Reipschläger, P., Langner, R., and Dachselt, R. "Investigating the Use of Spatial Interaction for 3D Data Visualization on Mobile Devices". In: *Proceedings of the Conference on Interactive Surfaces and Spaces (ISS)*. **Open Access version:** `https://mt.inf.tu-dresden.de/cnt/uploads/iss2017-3dvis-paper.pdf`. Brighton, United Kingdom: ACM, 2017, pp. 62–71. DOI: `10.1145/3132272.3134125` (cited on page 127).

[16] Büschel, W., Vogt, S., and Dachselt, R. "Augmented Reality Graph Visualizations". In: *Computer Graphics and Applications (CG&A)* 39.3 (May 2019). **Open Access version:** `https://imld.de/cnt/uploads/bueschel_cga2019.pdf`, pp. 29–40. DOI: `10.1109/MCG.2019.2897927` (cited on page 131).

[17] Butkiewicz, T. and Ware, C. "Multi-Touch 3D Exploratory Analysis of Ocean Flow Models". In: *Proceedings of the OCEANS conference*. **Open Access version:** `https://scholars.unh.edu/ccom/808/`. Los Alamitos: IEEE, Sept. 2011, pp. 746–755. DOI: `10.23919/OCEANS.2011.6107079` (cited on page 113).

[18] Butscher, S., Hubenschmid, S., Müller, J., Fuchs, J., and Reiterer, H. "Clusters, Trends, and Outliers: How Immersive Technologies Can Facilitate the Collaborative Analysis of Multidimensional Data". In: *Proceedings of the Conference on Human Factors in Computing Systems (CHI)*. **Open Access version:** `https://kops.uni-konstanz.de/handle/123456789/43062`. New York: ACM, 2018, 90:1–90:12. DOI: `10.1145/3173574.3173664` (cited on page 131).

[19] Butson, C. R., Tamm, G., Jain, S., Fogal, T., and Krüger, J. "Evaluation of Interactive Visualization on Mobile Computing Platforms for Selection of Deep Brain Stimulation Parameters". In: *Transactions on Visualization and Computer Graphics (TVCG)* 19.1 (Jan. 2013). **Open Access version:**

http://europepmc.org/articles/pmc3686862, pp. 108–117. DOI: 10.1109/TVCG.2012.92 (cited on page 125).

[20] Buxton, B. *Sketching User Experiences: Getting the Design Right and the Right Design*. Morgan Kaufmann, 2010. DOI: 10.1016/B978-012374037-3/50043-2 (cited on page 136).

[21] Cameron, J. *Aliens*. Accessed March 3, 2020. 1985. URL: http://www.dailyscript.com/scripts/Aliens_James_Cameron_May_28_1985_first_draft.html (cited on page 116).

[22] Campoalegre, L., Brunet, P., and Navazo, I. "Interactive Visualization of Medical Volume Models in Mobile Devices". In: *Personal and Ubiquitous Computing* 17.7 (Oct. 2013), pp. 1503–1514. DOI: 10.1007/s00779-012-0596-0 (cited on page 125).

[23] Cassinelli, A. and Ishikawa, M. "Volume Slicing Display". In: *Proceedings of SIGGRAPH ASIA Art Gallery & Emerging Technologies*. **Open Access version:** https://www.researchgate.net/publication/220720976. ACM, 2009, p. 88. DOI: 10.1145/1665137.1665207 (cited on page 125).

[24] Chen, Z., Su, Y., Wang, Y., Wang, Q., Qu, H., and Wu, Y. "Marvist: Authoring Glyph-Based Visualization in Mobile Augmented Reality". In: *Transactions on Visualization and Computer Graphics (TVCG)* 26.8 (Aug. 2020). **Open Access version:** https://chenzhutian.org/projects/2018_marvist/paper.pdf, pp. 2645–2658. DOI: 10.1109/TVCG.2019.2892415 (cited on pages 131, 132).

[25] Čopič Pucihar, K., Coulton, P., and Alexander, J. "The Use of Surrounding Visual Context in Handheld AR: Device vs. User Perspective Rendering". In: *Proceedings of the Conference on Human Factors in Computing Systems (CHI)*. **Open Access version:** https://www.researchgate.net/publication/266655447. Toronto, Ontario, Canada: ACM, 2014, pp. 197–206. DOI: 10.1145/2556288.2557125 (cited on page 126).

[26] Cordeil, M., Bach, B., Li, Y., Wilson, E., and Dwyer, T. "A Design Space for Spatio-Data Coordination: Tangible Interaction Devices for Immersive Information Visualisation". In: *Proceedings of the Pacific Visualization Symposium (PacificVis)*. **Open Access version:** https://www.research.ed.ac.uk/portal/files/36905895/bb.pdf. Los Alamitos: IEEE, 2017, pp. 46–50. DOI: 10.1109/PACIFICVIS.2017.8031578 (cited on page 121).

[27] Cordeil, M., Cunningham, A., Dwyer, T., Thomas, B. H., and Marriott, K. "ImAxes: Immersive Axes as Embodied Affordances for Interactive Multivariate Data Visualisation". In: *Proceedings of the Conference on User Interface, Software, and Technology (UIST)*. **Open Access version:** https://ialab.it.monash.edu/~dwyer/papers/imaxes.pdf. New York: ACM, 2017, pp. 71–83. DOI: 10.1145/3126594.3126613 (cited on pages 129, 130).

[28] Cruz-Neira, C., Sandin, D. J., DeFanti, T. A., Kenyon, R. V., and Hart, J. C. "The CAVE: Audio Visual Experience Automatic Virtual Environment". In: *Communications of the ACM* 35.6 (June 1992). **Open Access version:** https://www.researchgate.net/publication/242619900, pp. 64–72. DOI: 10.1145/129888.129892. URL: https://doi.org/10.1145/129888.129892 (cited on page 127).

[29] Elmqvist, N., Moere, A. V., Jetter, H.-C., Cernea, D., Reiterer, H., and Jankun-Kelly, T. J. "Fluid Interaction for Information Visualization". In: *Information Visualization* 10.4 (2011). **Open Access version:** https://kops.uni-konstanz.de/handle/123456789/18146, pp. 327–340. DOI: 10.1177/1473871611413180 (cited on page 115).

[30] ElSayed, N. A. M., Thomas, B. H., Marriott, K., Piantadosi, J., and Smith, R. T. "Situated Analytics: Demonstrating Immersive Analytical Tools With Augmented Reality". In: *Journal of Visual Languages and Computing* 36 (2016). **Open Access version:** https://www.researchgate.net/publication/305486262, pp. 13–23. DOI: 10.1016/j.jvlc.2016.07.006 (cited on page 137).

[31] Filho, J. A. W., Freitas, C. M. D. S., and Nedel, L. "Comfortable Immersive Analytics With the VirtualDesk Metaphor". In: *Computer Graphics and Applications (CG&A)* 39.3 (May 2019), pp. 41–53. DOI: 10.1109/MCG.2019.2898856 (cited on page 130).

[32] Forbes, A. G., Fast, T., and Höllerer, T. "The Natural Materials Browser: Using a Tablet Interface for Exploring Volumetric Materials Science Datasets". In: *Poster Proceedings of the Conference on Visualization (VIS)*. **Open Access version:** http://citeseerx.ist.psu.edu/viewdoc/summary?doi=10.1.1.638.6788. 2013 (cited on page 125).

[33] Grubert, J. and Kranz, M. "MpCubee: Towards a Mobile Perspective Cubic Display Using Mobile Phones". In: *Proceedings of the Conference on Virtual Reality and 3D User Interfaces (VR)*. **Open Access version:** https://www.mixedrealitylab.de/paper/2017-vr/2017_ieee_vr_demo_mpcubee.pdf. Los Alamitos: IEEE, 2017, pp. 459–460. DOI: 10.1109/VR.2017.7892378 (cited on page 126).

[34] Gutenko, I., Petkov, K., Papadopoulos, C., Zhao, X., Park, J. H., Kaufman, A., and Cha, R. "Remote Volume Rendering Pipeline for mHealth Applications". In: *Proceedings of Medical Imaging*. Vol. 9039. International Society for Optics and Photonics, 2014, pp. 12–18. DOI: 10.1117/12.2043946 (cited on page 125).

[35] Harish, P. and Narayanan, P. J. "Designing Perspectively Correct Multiplanar Displays". In: *Transactions on Visualization and Computer Graphics (TVCG)* 19.3 (Mar. 2013). **Open Access version:** https://europepmc.org/article/MED/22689080, pp. 407–419. DOI: 10.1109/TVCG.2012.135 (cited on page 126).

[36] Haselton, T. *How the Army Plans to Use Microsoft's High-Tech HoloLens Goggles on the Battlefield.* Accessed March 3, 2020. 2019. URL: `https://www.cnbc.com/2019/04/06/microsoft-hololens-2-army-plans-to-customize-as-ivas.html` (cited on page 115).

[37] Issartel, P., Besançon, L., Isenberg, T., and Ammi, M. "A Tangible Volume for Portable 3D Interaction". In: *Adjust Proceedings of the Symposium on Mixed and Augmented Reality (ISMAR).* **Open Access version:** `https://hal.inria.fr/hal-01423533`. Los Alamitos: IEEE, 2016, pp. 215–220. DOI: `10.1109/ISMAR-Adjunct.2016.0079` (cited on pages 126, 127).

[38] Issartel, P., Guéniat, F., and Ammi, M. "Slicing Techniques for Handheld Augmented Reality". In: *Proceedings of the Symosium on 3D User Interfaces (3DUI).* **Open Access version:** `https://hal.archives-ouvertes.fr/hal-00992132`. Los Alamitos: IEEE, 2014, pp. 39–42. DOI: `10.1109/3DUI.2014.6798839` (cited on page 127).

[39] Ivanov, A., Danyluk, K., Jacob, C., and Willett, W. "A Walk Among the Data". In: *Computer Graphics and Applications (CG&A)* 39.3 (May 2019), pp. 19–28. DOI: `10.1109/MCG.2019.2898941` (cited on page 130).

[40] Jankowski, J. and Hachet, M. "A Survey of Interaction Techniques for Interactive 3D Environments". In: *Eurographics State of the Art Reports.* **Open Access version:** `https://hal.inria.fr/hal-00789413`. Goslar, Germany: Eurographics, 2013, pp. 65–93. DOI: `10.2312/conf/EG2013/stars/065-093` (cited on page 119).

[41] Jones, A., McDowall, I., Yamada, H., Bolas, M., and Debevec, P. "Rendering for an Interactive 360° Light Field Display". In: *Transactions on Graphics (TOG)* 26.3 (July 2007). **Open Access version:** `http://citeseerx.ist.psu.edu/viewdoc/summary?doi=10.1.1.685.3118`, 40:1–40:10. DOI: `10.1145/1275808.1276427` (cited on page 121).

[42] Jordan, P., Mubin, O., Obaid, M., and Silva, P. A. "Exploring the Referral and Usage of Science Fiction in HCI Literature". In: *Proceedings of the Conference on Design, User Experience and Usability (DUXU).* **Open Access version:** `https://arxiv.org/abs/1803.08395`. Berlin, Heidelberg: Springer, 2018, pp. 19–38. DOI: `10.1007/978-3-319-91803-7_2` (cited on page 115).

[43] Krüger, W. and Fröhlich, B. "The Responsive Workbench". In: *Computer Graphics and Applications (CG&A)* 14.3 (May 1994), pp. 12–15. DOI: `10.1109/38.279036` (cited on page 127).

[44] Kruijff, E., Orlosky, J., Kishishita, N., Trepkowski, C., and Kiyokawa, K. "The Influence of Label Design on Search Performance and Noticeability in Wide Field of View Augmented Reality Displays". In: *Transactions on Visualization and Computer Graphics (TVCG)* 25.9 (Sept. 2019). **Open Access version:** `https://www.researchgate.net/publication/326306721`, pp. 2821–2837. DOI: `10.1109/TVCG.2018.2854737` (cited on page 132).

[45] Kurkovsky, S., Koshy, R., Novak, V., and Szul, P. "Current Issues in Handheld Augmented Reality". In: *Proceedings of the Conference on Convergence Information Technology (ICCIT)*. **Open Access version:** https://www.researchgate.net/publication/261468696. IEEE, June 2012, pp. 68–72. DOI: 10.1109/ICCITechnol.2012.6285844 (cited on page 126).

[46] Langner, R., Satkowski, M., Büschel, W., and Dachselt, R. "MARVIS: Combining Mobile Devices and Augmented Reality for Visual Data Analysis". In: *Proceedings of the ACM Conference on Human Factors in Computing Systems (CHI)*. **Open Access version:** https://imld.de/cnt/uploads/Langner-2021_MARVIS_author-version.pdf. ACM, 2021. DOI: 10.1145/3411764.3445593 (cited on page 131).

[47] Layar. *Layar About Page*. Accessed March 3, 2020. URL: https://www.layar.com/about/ (cited on page 120).

[48] Liu, J., Prouzeau, A., Ens, B., and Dwyer, T. "Design and Evaluation of Interactive Small Multiples Data Visualisation in Immersive Spaces". In: *Proceedings of the Conference on Virtual Reality and 3D User Interfaces (VR)*. **Open Access version:** https://ialab.it.monash.edu/~dwyer/papers/ImmersiveSmallMultiples.pdf. Los Alamitos: IEEE, 2020, pp. 588–597. DOI: 10.1109/VR46266.2020.00081 (cited on page 136).

[49] Liu, Z. and Stasko, J. T. "Mental Models, Visual Reasoning and Interaction in Information Visualization: A Top-Down Perspective". In: *Transactions on Visualization and Computer Graphics (TVCG)* 16.6 (Nov. 2010). **Open Access version:** https://www.cc.gatech.edu/~john.stasko/papers/infovis10-model.pdf, pp. 999–1008. DOI: 10.1109/TVCG.2010.177 (cited on page 129).

[50] López, D., Oehlberg, L., Doger, C., and Isenberg, T. "Towards an Understanding of Mobile Touch Navigation in a Stereoscopic Viewing Environment for 3D Data Exploration". In: *Transactions on Visualization and Computer Graphics (TVCG)* 22.5 (May 2016). **Open Access version:** https://hal.inria.fr/hal-01174618, pp. 1616–1629. DOI: 10.1109/TVCG.2015.2440233 (cited on pages 127, 128).

[51] Lopez-Gulliver, R., Yoshida, S., Yano, S., and Inoue, N. "gCubik: Real-Time Integral Image Rendering for a Cubic 3D Display". In: *Proceedings of SIG-GRAPH ASIA Art Gallery & Emerging Technologies*. New Orleans, Louisiana: ACM, 2009, 11:1. DOI: 10.1145/1597956.1597967. URL: https://doi.org/10.1145/1597956.1597967 (cited on page 126).

[52] Mandalika, V. B. H., Chernoglazov, A. I., Billinghurst, M., Bartneck, C., Hurrell, M. A., de Ruiter, N., Butler, A. P. H., and Butler, P. H. "A Hybrid 2D/3D User Interface for Radiological Diagnosis". In: *Journal of Digital Imaging* 31.1 (Feb. 2018). **Open Access version:** https://hdl.handle.net/10092/18234, pp. 56–73. DOI: 10.1007/s10278-017-0002-6 (cited on page 127).

[53] Marai, G. E., Forbes, A. G., and Johnson, A. "Interdisciplinary Immersive Analytics at the Electronic Visualization Laboratory: Lessons Learned and Upcoming Challenges". In: *Proceedings of the Workshop on Immersive Analytics (IA)*. **Open Access version:** `https://www.evl.uic.edu/aej/papers/2016_IEEE_VR_IA.pdf`. Los Alamitos: IEEE, 2016, pp. 54–59. DOI: `10.1109/IMMERSIVE.2016.7932384` (cited on page 121).

[54] Marks, S., Estevez, J. E., and Connor, A. M. "Towards the Holodeck: Fully Immersive Virtual Reality Visualisation of Scientific and Engineering Data". In: *Proceedings of the Conference on Image and Vision Computing New Zealand (IVCNZ)*. **Open Access version:** `https://arxiv.org/abs/1604.05797`. New York: ACM, 2014, pp. 42–47. DOI: `10.1145/2683405.2683424` (cited on page 116).

[55] Marriott, K., Schreiber, F., Dwyer, T., Klein, K., Riche, N. H., Itoh, T., Stuerzlinger, W., and Thomas, B. H., eds. *Immersive Analytics*. en. Cham, Switzerland: Springer, 2018. DOI: `10.1007/978-3-030-01388-2`. URL: `https://www.springer.com/gp/book/9783030013875` (visited on 03/13/2020) (cited on page 129).

[56] Masood, T. and Egger, J. "Augmented Reality in Support of Industry 4.0—Implementation Challenges and Success Factors". In: *Robotics and Computer-Integrated Manufacturing* 58 (Aug. 2019). **Open Access version:** `https://strathprints.strath.ac.uk/74481/`, pp. 181–195. DOI: `10.1016/j.rcim.2019.02.003` (cited on page 121).

[57] Maw, I. *How Lockheed Martin Is Using Augmented Reality in Aerospace Manufacturing*. 2019 (accessed March 3, 2020). URL: `https://www.engineering.com/story/how-lockheed-martin-is-using-augmented-reality-in-aerospace-manufacturing` (cited on page 128).

[58] Milgram, P. and Kishino, F. "A Taxonomy of Mixed Reality Visual Displays". In: *Transactions on Information and Systems* 77.12 (1994). **Open Access version:** `https://www.researchgate.net/publication/231514051`, pp. 1321–1329 (cited on page 114).

[59] Mulder, J. D. and van Liere, R. "Enhancing Fish Tank VR". In: *Proceedings of the Conference on Virtual Reality and 3D User Interfaces (VR)*. **Open Access version:** `https://www.researchgate.net/publication/2857656`. Los Alamitos: IEEE, 2000, pp. 91–98. DOI: `10.1109/VR.2000.840486` (cited on page 126).

[60] Munzner, T. *Visualization Analysis and Design*. A K Peters Visualization Series. A K Peters/CRC Press, 2014. DOI: `10.1201/b17511` (cited on pages 122, 129).

[61] Nagao, K., Ye, Y., Wang, C., Fujishiro, I., and Ma, K.-L. "Enabling Interactive Scientific Data Visualization and Analysis With See-Through HMDs and a Large Tiled Display". In: *Proceedings of the Workshop on Immersive Analytics (IA)*. Los Alamitos: IEEE, 2016, pp. 1–6. DOI: `10.1109/IMMERSIVE.2016.7932374` (cited on page 127).

[62] Noguera, J. and Jiménez, J.-R. "Visualization of Very Large 3D Volumes on Mobile Devices and WebGL". In: *Proceedings of the Conference on Computer Graphics, Visualization and Computer Vision (WSCG)*. **Open Access version:** https://www.researchgate.net/publication/267203117. Plzen, Czech Republic: University of West Bohemia, Jan. 2012, pp. 105–112 (cited on page 125).

[63] Noguera, J. M. and Jimenez, J. R. "Mobile Volume Rendering: Past, Present and Future". In: *Transactions on Visualization and Computer Graphics (TVCG)* 22.2 (Feb. 2015), pp. 1164–1178. DOI: 10.1109/TVCG.2015.2430343 (cited on page 125).

[64] Norman, P. *Pentagon Gets a Fix for F-35 Bug in $400,000 Pilot Helmets.* 2019 (accessed March 3, 2020). URL: https://www.bloomberg.com/news/articles/2019-11-10/pentagon-gets-a-fix-for-f-35-bug-in-400-000-pilot-helmets (cited on page 115).

[65] Ong, S. and Shen, Y. "A Mixed Reality Environment for Collaborative Product Design and Development". In: *CIRP Annals* 58.1 (2009), pp. 139–142. DOI: 10.1016/j.cirp.2009.03.020 (cited on page 121).

[66] Pahud, M., Ofek, E., Riche, N. H., Hurter, C., and Grubert, J. "Mobiles as Portals for Interacting With Virtual Data Visualizations". In: *Proceedings of the CHI Workshop on Data Visualization on Mobile Devices*. **Open Access version:** https://hal.archives-ouvertes.fr/hal-01767415. 2018 (cited on page 127).

[67] Park, S., Kim, W., and Ihm, I. "Mobile Collaborative Medical Display System". In: *Computer Methods and Programs in Biomedicine* 89.3 (Mar. 2008), pp. 248–260. DOI: 10.1016/j.cmpb.2007.11.012 (cited on page 125).

[68] Prouzeau, A., Lhuillier, A., Ens, B., Weiskopf, D., and Dwyer, T. "Visual Link Routing in Immersive Visualisations". In: *Proceedings of the Conference on Interactive Surfaces and Spaces (ISS)*. **Open Access version:** https://ialab.it.monash.edu/~dwyer/papers/VisualLinks.pdf. New York: ACM, 2019, pp. 241–253. DOI: 10.1145/3343055.3359709 (cited on pages 132, 137).

[69] Prouzeau, A., Wang, Y., Ens, B., Willett, W., and Dwyer, T. "Corsican Twin: Authoring in Situ Augmented Reality Visualisations in Virtual Reality". In: *Proceedings of the Conference on Advanced Visual Interfaces (AVI)*. **Open Access version:** https://hal.archives-ouvertes.fr/hal-02614521. New York: ACM, 2020, 11:1–11:9. DOI: 10.1145/3399715.3399743 (cited on page 113).

[70] Raja, D., Bowman, D., Lucas, J., and North, C. "Exploring the Benefits of Immersion in Abstract Information Visualization". In: *Proceedings of the Immersive Projection Technology Workshop*. **Open Access version:** https://www.researchgate.net/publication/228854652. 2004, pp. 61–69 (cited on page 128).

[71] Satkowski, M. and Dachselt, R. "Investigating the Impact of Real-World Environments on the Perception of 2D Visualizations in Augmented Reality". In: *Proceedings of the ACM Conference on Human Factors in Computing Systems (CHI)*. **Open Access version:** `https://imld.de/cnt/uploads/Satkowski-2021_AR-Vis-Perception_author-version.pdf`. ACM, 2021. DOI: `10.1145/3411764.3445330` (cited on page 120).

[72] Schiewe, A., Anstoots, M., and Krüger, J. "State of the Art in Mobile Volume Rendering on iOS Devices". In: *State of the Art Reports of the European Conference on Visualization (EuroVis)*. **Open Access version:** `http://hpc.uni-due.de/publications/2015/Schiewe_2015_SOTA.pdf`. Goslar, Germany: Eurographics, 2015, pp. 139–143. DOI: `10.2312/eurovisshort.20151139` (cited on page 125).

[73] Sereno, M., Besançon, L., and Isenberg, T. "Supporting Volumetric Data Visualization and Analysis by Combining Augmented Reality Visuals With Multi-Touch Input". In: *Poster Proceedings of the European Conference on Visualization (EuroVis)*. **Open Access version:** `https://hal.inria.fr/hal-02123904`. Eurographics, 2019, pp. 21–23 (cited on pages 121, 128, 129).

[74] Sereno, M., Wang, X., Besançon, L., McGuffin, M. J., and Isenberg, T. "Collaborative Work in Augmented Reality: A Survey". In: *Transactions on Visualization and Computer Graphics (TVCG)* (2021). **Open Access version:** `https://hal.inria.fr/hal-02971697`. DOI: `10.1109/TVCG.2020.3032761` (cited on page 121).

[75] Shneiderman, B. "The Eyes Have It: A Task by Data Type Taxonomy for Information Visualizations". In: *Proceedings of the Symposium on Visual Languages (VL)*. **Open Access version:** `http://hdl.handle.net/1903/466`. Los Alamitos: IEEE, 1996, pp. 336–343. DOI: `10.1109/VL.1996.545307` (cited on page 118).

[76] Sollich, H., von Zadow, U., Pietzsch, T., Tomancak, P., and Dachselt, R. "Exploring Time-Dependent Scientific Data Using Spatially Aware Mobiles and Large Displays". In: *Proceedings of the Conference on Interactive Surfaces and Spaces (ISS)*. **Open Access version:** `https://imld.de/cnt/uploads/biovis.pdf`. Niagara Falls, Ontario, Canada: ACM, 2016, pp. 349–354. DOI: `10.1145/2992154.2996779` (cited on page 125).

[77] Song, P., Goh, W. B., Fu, C.-W., Meng, Q., and Heng, P.-A. "WYSIWYF: Exploring and Annotating Volume Data With a Tangible Handheld Device". In: *Proceedings of the Conference on Human Factors in Computing Systems (CHI)*. **Open Access version:** `https://www.researchgate.net/publication/221518364`. New York: ACM, 2011, pp. 1333–1342. DOI: `10.1145/1978942.1979140` (cited on page 125).

[78] Spindler, M., Büschel, W., and Dachselt, R. "Use Your Head: Tangible Windows for 3D Information Spaces in a Tabletop Environment". In: *Proceedings of the Conference on Interactive Tabletops and Surfaces (ITS)*. **Open Access**

version: https://www.researchgate.net/publication/235664025. Cambridge, Massachusetts, USA: ACM, 2012, pp. 245–254. DOI: 10.1145/2396636.2396674 (cited on page 125).

[79] Stavness, I., Lam, B., and Fels, S. "PCubee: A Perspective-Corrected Handheld Cubic Display". In: *Proceedings of the Conference on Human Factors in Computing Systems (CHI)*. **Open Access version:** https://www.researchgate.net/publication/221517816. Atlanta, Georgia, USA: ACM, 2010, pp. 1381–1390. DOI: 10.1145/1753326.1753535 (cited on page 126).

[80] Stavness, I., Vogt, F., and Fels, S. "Cubee: A Cubic 3D Display for Physics-Based Interaction". In: *Proceedings of SIGGRAPH Sketches*. **Open Access version:** https://www.researchgate.net/publication/228880058. New York: ACM, 2006, p. 165. DOI: 10.1145/1179849.1180055 (cited on page 126).

[81] Stoakley, R., Conway, M. J., and Pausch, R. "Virtual Reality on a WIM: Interactive Worlds in Miniature". In: *Proceedings of the Conference on Human Factors in Computing Systems (CHI)*. **Open Access version:** https://www.researchgate.net/publication/2598327. Denver, Colorado, USA: ACM, 1995, pp. 265–272. DOI: 10.1145/223904.223938 (cited on page 134).

[82] Sun, J., Stuerzlinger, W., and Riecke, B. E. "Comparing Input Methods and Cursors for 3D Positioning With Head-Mounted Displays". In: *Proceedings of the Symposium on Applied Perception (SAP)*. Vancouver, British Columbia, Canada: ACM, 2018, 8:1–8:8. DOI: 10.1145/3225153.3225167 (cited on page 118).

[83] Sutherland, E. I. "The Ultimate Display". In: *Proceedings of IFIP Congress*. **Open Access version:** http://citeseer.ist.psu.edu/viewdoc/summary?doi=10.1.1.136.3720. London: Macmillan, 1965, pp. 506–508 (cited on page 115).

[84] Teubl, F., Kurashima, C. S., Cabral, M. C., de Deus Lopes, R., Anacleto, J. C., Zuffo, M. K., and Fels, S. "Spheree: An Interactive Perspective-Corrected Spherical 3D Display". In: *Proceedings of the 3DTV-Conference: The True Vision - Capture, Transmission and Display of 3D Video (3DTV-CON)*. **Open Access version:** https://www.researchgate.net/publication/264000785. Los Alamitos: IEEE, 2014, pp. 225–228. DOI: 10.1109/3DTV.2014.6874768 (cited on page 126).

[85] Tominski, C. and Schumann, H. *Interactive Visual Data Analysis*. A K Peters Visualization Series. A K Peters/CRC Press, 2020. DOI: 10.1201/9781315152707. URL: https://ivda-book.de (cited on page 122).

[86] Veas, E., Grasset, R., Ferencik, I., Grünewald, T., and Schmalstieg, D. "Mobile Augmented Reality for Environmental Monitoring". In: *Personal and Ubiquitous Computing* 17.7 (Oct. 2013). **Open Access version:** https://www.researchgate.net/publication/231538113, pp. 1515–1531. DOI: 10.1007/s00779-012-0597-z. (Visited on 05/31/2020) (cited on page 133).

[87] Veas, E. E., Kruijff, E. P. C., and Mendez, E. "HYDROSYS - First Approaches Towards On-Site Monitoring and Management With Handhelds". In: *Proceedings of the European Conference Towards eEnvironment.* **Open Access version:** https://www.researchgate.net/publication/228816223. 2009, pp. 511–518 (cited on pages 133, 134).

[88] Wagner, D. and Schmalstieg, D. "Handheld Augmented Reality Displays". In: *Proceedings of the Conference on Virtual Reality and 3D User Interfaces (VR).* Los Alamitos: IEEE, 2006, pp. 321–321. DOI: 10.1109/VR.2006.67 (cited on page 126).

[89] Wagner, D., Schmalstieg, D., and Billinghurst, M. "Handheld AR for Collaborative Edutainment". In: *Proceedings of the Conference on Artificial Reality and Telexistence (ICAT).* Edited by Pan, Z., Cheok, A., Haller, M., Lau, R. W. H., Saito, H., and Liang, R. **Open Access version:** http://hdl.handle.net/10092/2341. Berlin, Heidelberg: Springer, 2006, pp. 85–96. DOI: 10.1007/11941354_10 (cited on page 126).

[90] Wang, X., Besançon, L., Ammi, M., and Isenberg, T. "Augmenting Tactile 3D Data Navigation With Pressure Sensing". In: *Computer Graphics Forum* 38.3 (June 2019). **Open Access version:** https://hal.inria.fr/hal-02091999, pp. 635–647. DOI: 10.1111/cgf.13716 (cited on pages 118, 125).

[91] Wang, X., Besançon, L., Guéniat, F., Sereno, M., Ammi, M., and Isenberg, T. "A Vision of Bringing Immersive Visualization to Scientific Workflows". In: *Proceedings of the CHI Workshop on Immersive Analytics.* **Open Access version:** https://hal.inria.fr/hal-02053969. 2019 (cited on pages 119, 128).

[92] Wang, X., Besançon, L., Rousseau, D., Sereno, M., Ammi, M., and Isenberg, T. "Towards an Understanding of Augmented Reality Extensions for Existing 3D Data Analysis Tools". In: *Proceedings of the Conference on Human Factors in Computing Systems (CHI).* **Open Access version:** https://hal.inria.fr/hal-02442690. New York: ACM, 2020, 528:1–528:13. DOI: 10.1145/3313831.3376657 (cited on pages 119, 127–129).

[93] Ware, C., Arthur, K., and Booth, K. S. "Fish Tank Virtual Reality". In: *Proceedings of the Conference on Human Factors in Computing Systems (CHI).* **Open Access version:** https://www.researchgate.net/publication/221517266. New York: ACM, 1993, pp. 37–42. DOI: 10.1145/169059.169066. URL: https://doi.org/10.1145/169059.169066 (cited on page 126).

[94] White, S. and Feiner, S. "SiteLens: Situated Visualization Techniques for Urban Site Visits". In: *Proceedings of the Conference on Human Factors in Computing Systems (CHI).* New York, NY, USA: ACM, 2009, pp. 1117–1120 (cited on page 132).

[95] Whitlock, M., Wu, K., and Szafir, D. A. "Designing for Mobile and Immersive Visual Analytics in the Field". In: *Transactions on Visualization and Computer Graphics (TVCG)* 26.1 (Jan. 2020). **Open Access version:** https://arxiv.

org/abs/1908.00680, pp. 503–513. DOI: 10.1109/TVCG.2019.2934282 (cited on pages 132, 133).

[96] Willett, W., Jansen, Y., and Dragicevic, P. "Embedded Data Representations". In: *Transactions on Visualization and Computer Graphics (TVCG)* 23.1 (Jan. 2017). **Open Access version:** https://hal.inria.fr/hal-01377901, pp. 461–470. DOI: 10.1109/TVCG.2016.2598608 (cited on page 132).

[97] Yin, J., Fu, C., Zhang, X., and Liu, T. "Precise Target Selection Techniques in Handheld Augmented Reality Interfaces". In: *Access* 7 (2019), pp. 17663–17674. DOI: 10.1109/ACCESS.2019.2895219 (cited on page 126).

CHAPTER 5

Characterizing Glanceable Visualizations: From Perception to Behavior Change

Tanja Blascheck

University of Stuttgart, Germany

Frank Bentley

Yahoo, USA

Eun Kyoung Choe

University of Maryland, College Park, USA

Tom Horak

Technische Universität Dresden, Germany

Petra Isenberg

Université Paris-Saclay, CNRS, Inria, LISN, France

CONTENTS

DOI: 10.1201/9781003090823-5

W E detail and illustrate glanceability as a crucial requirement for several types of mobile visualizations. For example, in a difficult terrain, a runner can only check a smartwatch for elevation or heart rate data for a few hundred milliseconds before the eyes need to refocus on the trail ahead. Such quick information needs differ from those in traditional visualizations that are meant for deep analysis and interaction with possibly large and complex datasets. Visualizations designed for quick information needs are described under a variety of terms in the literature such as glanceable visualizations, glanceable displays, peripheral displays, ambient visualizations, or sometimes as forms of casual visualizations. To clarify how glanceability is used in the field of Visualization, we discuss these related terms with respect to visualization concepts, drawing from not only Visualization but also, Vision Sciences, Human-Computer Interaction, and Ubiquitous Computing, revealing how the use of the term *glanceable* differs in these communities. Drawing from these different perspectives, we discuss specific values for glanceable mobile visualizations: presence and accessibility, simplicity and understandability, as well as suitability and purposefulness. Based on these values, we explore different evaluation methodologies, ranging from lab studies, to online experiments, to evaluation in the field and conclude with a discussion of open challenges in the design of future glanceable mobile visualizations.

5.1 INTRODUCTION AND CONTEXT

Anne is on her way out of the house. While brushing her teeth she turns on her smartphone's screen and glances at the weather widget to decide if she needs a raincoat today. In the car she turns on her smartphone's GPS navigation system and gets going. While driving she looks at the screen for traffic updates. At work she attends a meeting but frequently checks her smartphone's notification light to see if she received an important message she has been expecting. During her lunch break she goes running and, while moving, glances at her smartwatch to see which distance she has already covered and whether her current pace is in-line with her training goal.

The purpose of this chapter is to take a deeper look at the topic of glanceable visualizations integrating knowledge from multiple domains: the Vision Sciences, Visualization, Human-Computer Interaction, and Ubiquitous Computing. With this deeper look we want to establish a source of references and inspiration for more research in this important research direction. In the context of this chapter we refer to a "visualization" as a mapping from data to a visual representation. The Vision Sciences often researches simple data mappings while the Visualization community is often interested in establishing combinations of complex multi-encodings. A "visualization" in Ubiquitous Computing research does not need to be a graph or proportional drawing of data, it can take the form of a moving object (such as the movement of a dangling string, or changing fountain height), an abstraction (such as a garden representing physical activity), or a change in color could indicate a change in data.

As can be seen in the mock-scenario above, mobile devices and their visualizations are often needed as part of tasks with quick information needs. These quick information needs require someone to switch attention from a primary task to briefly attend to an information display as input on how to further continue with the primary task. For example, for someone driving to work, paying attention to the road is a primary task. Yet, sometimes quick glances to the car's GPS are necessary. The longer these glances are, the longer the primary task is disrupted resulting in potentially severe consequences.

In the scenario above, Ann performs her secondary tasks with different mobile devices—her smartphone and smartwatch. These mobile devices are often used on-the-go making it desirable that a person can perceive visualizations depicted on them at a glance. This new context leads to new challenges that traditional visualizations were not designed for; for example, not only the limited availability of time for inspection (usually just a few seconds or less), the context of use while in locomotion, the different focus of attention (as a secondary task) but also the smaller device size especially for smartwatches. Therefore, a new research challenge we call *glanceable visualizations* has evolved in recent years. Interestingly, despite the importance of glanceable visualizations we still know little about how to best design and evaluate visualizations for quick information needs.

5.2   PERSPECTIVES ON GLANCEABILITY

Several research fields have created and studied displays that are meant to be looked at only for a short amount of time. Within each of these disciplines, different terms and time frames have emerged for referring to these types of displays and the types of interactions that people have with them: from the Vision Sciences, which investigate the temporal limits of vision, to Visualization, which is regularly concerned with instant perception of data characteristics, to the field of Ubiquitous Computing, in which researchers use glanceable visualizations to provoke awareness and behavior change. In addition, the goals and implementations of glanceable visualizations, as well as the methods for evaluating their success vary in these domains. Visualization focuses on promoting insights and understanding from datasets with research ranging from low-level perception of specific data encodings, such as length of lines versus area size, to more encompassing notions of higher-level thinking with visualization. Glanceable visualizations have so far received little attention in the Visualization community with much of its history having been focused on work-related in-depth data analysis. In the Ubiquitous Computing domain the availability and understanding of information is considered a prerequisite. Here, research specifically focuses on the effect of technology on people's awareness, decision making, or behaviors.

Due to these different goals, we found a range of time scales researchers consider in these domains. Figure 5.1 shows these time scales: the Vision Science literature

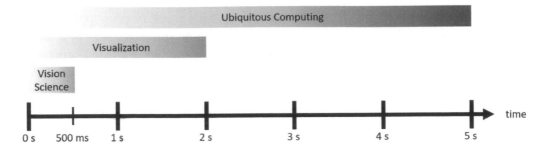

Figure 5.1 Different time scales of glanceability depending on the domain: Vision Science (50–500 ms), Visualization, and Ubiquitous Computing (500 ms–5 s).

mentions time scales between 50 and 500 milliseconds [31], whereas the Visualization literature has been using the term *glance* for viewing times of up to 2 seconds [9]. The field of Ubiquitous Computing, as first envisioned by Weiser [56], saw computing existing in the world. As people went about their days, they would notice information ambiently displayed in the environment, understand the implications for their own actions, and act on it. This process of noticing information, understanding it, and acting on it, can take up to five seconds [26] and acting on this information can lead to short-term changes in behavior (e.g., pulling into a parking spot that has a green light) or long-term ones (e.g., increasing daily step count as a result of a wrist-worn visualization). In the following sections, we discuss where these different time scales come from based on related work that defines typical types, tasks, and goals of each individual domain.

5.2.1 Glanceability in Vision Science

Questions regarding a *glance* or the temporal limits of human vision—"the timescale on which the machinery of perception operates" [31]—drive research in the Vision Sciences, and researchers have invested careers conducting experiments to answer theses questions.

Holcombe [31] summarizes the results of these experiments and concludes that there are two groups of temporal limits of vision: fast and slow visual judgments. However, this phenomenon does not mean that we see quickly, but means that we "see things that occupy fast timescales." The first group consists of visual judgments that occur with up to 50 Hz (20 ms), such as flicker perception, perception of motion direction, or certain color perception. The second, slow group, concerns rates from 10 Hz (50 ms) up to around 3 Hz (166 ms) and consists of visual judgments such as the detection of changes in speed, direction of moving objects or word perception.

Some past work has offered insight on how the notion of attention relates to quick perception of stimuli. Rapid and parallel low-level visual processes (also referred to as pre-attentive processing) of unique visual properties (e.g., color hue, length, size, curvature) lead to a "pop out" effect. People can detect targets, boundaries, or regions as well as count and estimate the number of elements [29]. These capabilities allow people to rapidly detect whether an orange circle is present among many blue circles (cf. Figure 5.2a). Some of these visual properties are asymmetric. For example, people cannot quickly find a horizontal line among sloped lines (cf. Figure 5.2b), while they can find a sloped line among horizontal lines (cf. Figure 5.2c). Seminal work by Treisman et al. [53, 54, 55] studied these unique visual properties. Treisman and Gelade [55] described a feature integration theory, in which simple basic features (i.e., feature maps) allow parallel processing in an early stage of visual processing. If multiple of these features are present in a stimulus at the same time, conjunction or serial search is needed (e.g., detection of an orange circle in a group of orange squares and blue circles, cf. Figure 5.2d). However, some conjunction tasks involving motion, depth, color, and orientation have been shown to be processed in parallel [59] (cf. Figure 5.2e).

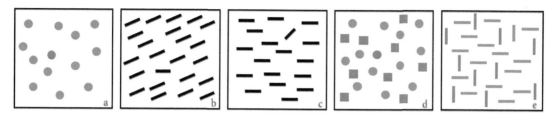

Figure 5.2 Parallel and serial processing of stimuli. (a) An orange circle amongst blue circles can be quickly detected. (b) A horizontal line amongst sloped lines cannot be quickly detected, while (c) a sloped line amongst horizontal lines can. (d) An orange circle amongst orange squares and blue circles cannot be rapidly processed, while (e) a vertical blue line amongst horizontal blue lines and orange vertical lines can.

Several experiments by Biederman et al. [5, 6, 7, 8] also gave evidence that humans are able to digest the schema of a scene based on a single glance at it. Others have similarly studied *gist perception* to understand to which extent people can see basic information quickly, often in a single fixation. Summarizing past work in this area Jahanian et al. [34] note that people can, in viewing times of 100–300 ms, identify the category of a natural scene, say whether an object is present in an image, distinguish cities, and see colors or textures. Jahanian et al. [34] also showed that participants could perceive the category of a website within 120 ms and detect certain elements on the website.

5.2.2 Glanceability in Visualization

From these vision experiments we can learn that humans are able to perform specific detection tasks quickly. However, why is this important for mobile devices? In several studies, researchers found out that a large amount of usage sessions on smartphones and smartwatches only lasted several seconds [3, 20], much longer than the timespans considered at a glance in the Vision Sciences, but still short enough to ask oneself how much information a person can perceive and act on.

Therefore, it is interesting to find out how much information can be conveyed using visualizations within such short glances, especially when trying to communicate data for quick information needs. For defining what glanceability in the Visualization domain means, we first have to understand the context such visualizations are used in. The ubiquity of smartphones and smartwatches has made it obvious that the use of visualization is not restricted to the office anymore. Visualizations are nowadays present everywhere, at home, in the office, and outside, and they can show all kinds of work-related or personal data. Traditional visualizations in the office or at home are typically used as a primary task to fulfill an information need such as finding out which activities are risky during a pandemic and planning a safe exercise routine. On mobile devices, however, reading a visualization is often not the primary task anymore. For example, a person might be running outside and while running they quickly check their fitness bracelet to get information about their current heart rate or speed. These two examples show, not only, differences in the amount of potential attention to and engagement with a visualization, but the different usage time scales. In the mobile example, a runner only shortly focuses on a glanceable visualization on their smartwatch to see their step count, whereas with a traditional visualization a person spends more time to investigate and understand a visualization depicting information about a complex problem, such as, for example, the current data available on the Corona Virus.

This notion of using visualizations to quickly communicate data has in the past been considered in the context of ambient (non-mobile) visualizations. In this context, researchers were interested in how to integrate more data into ones' life without disrupting a person's primary task. Miller and Stasko [40] called this *peripheral awareness information*: "data that is not absolutely essential to people and their work or tasks." In an attempt to summarize and define what ambient versus peripheral information systems are, Pousman and Stasko [43] investigated the related work and provided a definition as well as taxonomy for ambient information visualizations. In a later paper, Pousman et al. [44] go one step further and define *casual information visualization*, with ambient information systems belonging to this new group of information visualization systems. However, specific viewing timespans and how much information people could retain during quick glances at ambient displays was not the focus of dedicated visualization studies.

More recently, researchers in the Human-Computer Interaction and Visualization communities worked on ways to help people better collect personal data and gain personal insights. Called *Personal Informatics*, this field of research deals with understanding people's data tracking needs and usage to design and develop novel self-tracking technologies for a variety of contexts (e.g., food, sleep, productivity, physical activity). This field shares with the Visualization community the goal of making it easy for people to better understand their own data and communicate personal insights, which often are captured on mobile devices due to their omnipresent nature and powerful sensing capabilities. As such, researchers have been examining how to design effective glanceable visualizations that convey personal data on mobile devices especially for lay individuals.

In the mobile visualization context, researchers have recently started to study exact thresholds of glanceability for different chart types. Blascheck et al. [9] found that a simple data comparison task, which required participants to quickly identify the larger of two marks in a bar, donut, and radial chart, can be performed within less than 300 ms for donut and bar charts (cf. Figure 5.3). Neshati et al. [41] investigated different compression types for line charts on smartwatches. Their main focus was not to find a minimal threshold for completion time, but they did record the response time per task. For tasks involving the comparison of line chart start and endpoints the response times were in a range of 2000–3000 ms but included the time to enter an answer on the keyboard.

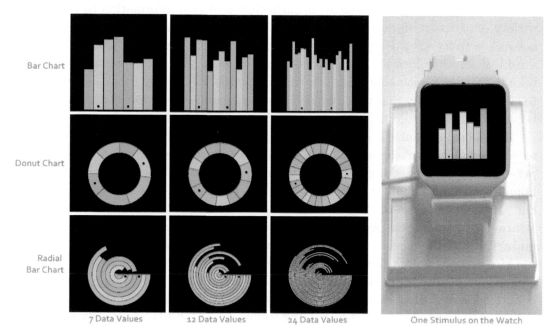

Figure 5.3 Stimuli (left) and smartwatch (right) used in a lab-study to assess glanceability of different visualizations for simple data comparison task on a smartwatch. *Image © 2019 IEEE. Reprinted, with permission, from [9].*

In summary, dedicated research on minimal perception times for visualizations on mobile devices is still in its beginning. Few studies have been carried out and this is a vast area to explore further and for which to develop dedicated design guidelines.

5.2.3 Glanceability in Ubiquitous Computing

Since its inception, the field of Ubiquitous Computing has been interested in systems that present information as a part of a person's environment. Visualization are often meant to be sensed in the periphery of one's environment. In 1996, Mark Weiser and John Seely Brown at Xerox PARC [57] described the periphery as "what we are attuned to without attending to explicitly" and the goal of the peripheral displays they created was to allow people to have a subconscious awareness of a variety of information and to move particular pieces of information from the periphery to the center of their attention and back again when that information was particularly salient and relevant. They described this *calm* technology as allowing people to be aware of many things without overburdening them with needing to explicitly attend to differences in graphs or data tables to gain information.

This vision was extended by Hiroshi Ishii's group at the MIT Media Lab, using the term *ambient displays*, in 1998 [58]. They defined these new types of displays as systems in which "information is moved off the screen into the physical environment, manifesting itself as subtle changes in form, movement, sound, color, smell, temperature, or light" [58].

These two projects kicked off decades of research and commercial products focused on creating peripheral or ambient displays that provided information to people in a variety of abstract ways. Early systems in this space allowed people to learn about network activity via a dangling string (and decide when to print) [57], to hear ambient sound of another location [58], to have an umbrella that glows when you need to take it [45], or to see a glowing orb that indicates when your friends are watching television [28]. Many examples of this type of research can be found in David Rose's book, Enchanted Objects [49].

Peripheral or ambient displays typically have a goal of guiding behavior leading to focused behavior change. The first goal of one of these displays is to make a person aware of something—that it will rain [45], that their partner is on their way home from work [36], that they are behind on their step count for the day [17], etc. Once a person is aware of this information, the goal is that they then are able to make a targeted behavior change given that new data. For example, they might take the umbrella with them, start preparing dinner, or go for a walk in the cases mentioned.

Most notably, with these types of systems a person should not have to explicitly look at and attend to the display. However, this information should be something that is noticed as a part of living one's ordinary life and traversing the spaces where one lives and works, with changes in lighting, color, sound, or smell naturally translating into gained awareness.

Many times, these visualizations end up being quite abstract. For example, the InfoCanvas system [52] allowed graphics that conveyed information to be placed onto a framed photo. Fogarty et al.'s [21] Kadinsky system generated even more artistic representations of data made for a digital canvas. In these systems, it is often not efficiency or accuracy of conveying data that is the most important but rather the experience of living with these data displays for extended periods of time and their utility in daily life that is the most important aspect to measure.

While peripheral or ambient displays are meant to catch a person's attention from the periphery, a new field of *glanceable* displays has emerged with a goal of providing information quickly to a person who has chosen to give the display their explicit attention for a brief amount of time. These systems have used a variety of techniques to display information in a rapidly understandable fashion. In the Ubiquitous Computing domain, these displays most commonly borrowed abstractions from ambient devices, but adapted the lessons learned from physical devices for use on a screen [38]. Color, icons, graphical representations, or changes in size were used to convey information at a glance.

The key difference between a peripheral or ambient display and a glanceable one is a person's attention. With glanceable visualizations, a person intentionally looks at the screen to receive information, instead of it being delivered without explicit attention in the periphery. This makes glanceable visualizations a more purposeful instrument, much like a pilot checking an instrument panel to make sure nothing has gone wrong.

Matthews et al. [39] explored many types of glanceable displays in detail, defining several key terms. While the actual time looking at a display may be small (on average 34 ms in their work), the *peripheral processing time* that it took a person to understand and internalize what they saw often took as much as two seconds (mean = 1,931 ms). They also found that text was the "fastest and most accurate to interpret" representation, compared to a variety of abstractions (note that Plaue et al. [42] find that graphical abstractions are more salient to remember later on). Because the goal is to inspire behavior change, time for contemplation and internalization of the results is critical for people to decide on a change to their actions.

5.2.4 Summary

These past sections have shown that there are contrasting perspectives what *glanceable* means across disciplines and Figure 5.1 shows this continuum of time scales the different disciplines consider a *glance*. This reflects the differing goals of research projects within these research communities.

As discussed in the previous paragraphs, Vision Science looks at temporal time scales of 50 Hz—500 ms to be considered a glance. The Visualization community, which often takes inspiration from Vision Science has been considering similar times closer to the upper end of those looked at in Vision Science [9]. In Visualization, the goal is typically to identify differences in data values in artificially created scenes, for example, asking people to determine if one bar is bigger or smaller than another. So far, research on glanceable visualizations has not considered people's understanding of what the data represents and what it implies. Therefore, it has often only been the time needed for perception that is measured, not time to understand the data and especially not for realizing implications to one's life. These questions, are however interesting to Visualization researchers and here the community begins to intersect with Ubiquitous Computing. The Ubiquitous Computing literature often has the goal of understanding how various visualizations affect people's awareness, decision making, or behavior and if people can understand the data within a visualization and what that means for their lives. Therefore, this literature often considers viewing interactions up to five seconds or more as glanceable [26], as this includes the time that a person takes to process this information in their brain and understand if there is any behavior that should be changed. Therefore, for the remainder of this chapter, when we refer to a glanceable visualization we take a broad view and use viewing times between 20 ms and 5 s to describe a *glance*, depending on the goal of a person.

5.3 CHARACTERISTICS OF GLANCEABLE VISUALIZATIONS

As the previous section has shown, the different communities have different takes on what *glanceability* means. Here, we move away from trying to understand glanceability in terms of perception times and instead try to summarize the characteristics that could make visualizations glanceable. Specifically, we see three categories of characteristics:

First, the visualizations and their hosting displays must be visible to one or more people or be able to attract their attention, i. e., they are *present & accessible*. Second, people must be able to process the shown visualization at a glance, therefore, a visualization must be designed with *simplicity & understandability* in mind. Finally, glanceable visualizations are meant to support people in everyday life by informing short-term decisions or enabling long-term behavior changes. In consequence, it is important to reflect about the *suitability & purpose* of a glanceable visualization for a given goal of a person.

5.3.1 Presence and Access

The main goal for glanceable visualizations is to quickly provide information to an individual when the person switches their attention to it, either on purpose or based on peripheral stimuli. Therefore, the represented content must be present and accessible, or in other words, ready to be consumed. As a precondition for presence and access, the display or device should be placed in a way that only a minimal eye movement is required to glance at the content. Consider a smartphone lying on a table or mounted in a car: here, the person can quickly look at the device without any further movements or interactions. In contrast, when the smartphone is in a pocket and must be taken out first, a primary task might get too interrupted for the device to be considered glanceable. In contrast, smartwatches or fitness trackers require a small arm rotation to look at the display, but this movement only takes up a minimal amount of time and effort. These minimal body movements, rotating wrist or head, are a simplistic, natural type of interaction and differ from the typical conception of *interaction* in the Visualization or Human-Computer Interaction domain, for example, as a sequence of mouse or touch events. As such, the context of use of a display can have a large impact on whether or not it can adequately host glanceable visualizations.

For the visualizations themselves, interactions should be short-term and most often passive [51, p.141]. People should not be required to select, activate, or manipulate shown content but to primarily look at it. However, to enable looking, deliberate movements to see the content might be involved, such as rotating the wrist with a smartwatch, looking up at a public display, or fixating a certain area of the phone.

For the activities that involve quick information needs, explicitly glancing at a visualization can be considered as a part of a persons' primary task, for example, confirming the current pace while running, looking at turn-by-turn instructions while driving, or checking the progress toward a daily goal. In most cases, one specific piece of information is of interest and looked at, however, other information might be shown as well, for example, running distance, surroundings during navigation, or progresses toward additional goals. People can still perceive these additional information peripherally and incorporate them for spontaneous change of plans.

As an example encapsulating the characteristics of presence and access to content, consider the setup presented by Klamka et al. [37]. The authors proposed to extend smartwatches with interactive wrist bands that come with embedded displays (Figure 5.4). Such a setup improves the glanceability of smartwatches further, as the inward facing strap band is visible without rotating the arm. The authors propose to use this

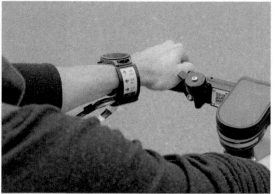

Figure 5.4 Smartwatch with additional displays embedded in the straps [37]; a person can glance at these displays without additional movements or interactions. *Images © 2020 Tom Horak and Konstantin Klamka*

display area, for example, to show core information while running but also to show text-based notifications. The first example represents a case, in which the glanceable visualization supports a primary task, while the notifications are an example of a peripheral display. In both cases the information is provided in an unobtrusive way with only minimal eye movements being required to consume it. It is, therefore, present at an instance and easily accessible to the wearer.

5.3.2 Simplicity and Understandability

Another important characteristic of glanceable visualizations is the ease at which they are able to be processed. Glanceable visualizations should favor simple representations and understandability without requiring much (or any) learning. This touches on knowledge coming from Perception and Visualization research: Which chart, or representation in general, can be efficiently read? What color schemes are more effective? Which visual attributes are perceived without focused attention? For most glanceable visualizations the underlying data is likely simple (e.g., dates with a low number of attributes, a few data points), so simple chart types should be considered. These can comprise, for example, bar charts, line charts, pie charts, or donut charts, but their use should be carefully considered. Existing research on micro or word-sized visualizations [4, 25, 33] (Figure 5.5a) as well as glyph representations [10, 23] can provide further insights in how to visualize data in a compact way. Past research has shown that there might be considerable time differences with which certain tasks can be performed [9] and considerable differences in the general public's ability to understand basic charts [24].

In this context, it should also be considered *whether* a chart is required at all. In the context of running, displaying the values as numbers is currently the default case and text can be read quickly by most people. Having numbers, a runner can see the specific values and does not have to mentally map a mark to a value. Another example is the Whereabouts Clock by Sellen et al. [50] and Brown et al. [15]. As

(a)   (b)

Figure 5.5 Glanceable visualizations often feature a rather simple appearance. (a) Examples of micro visualizations as found on smartwatch faces [33]. (b) Illustration of the Whereabouts Clock as proposed by Brown et al. [15].

illustrated in Figure 5.5b, the abstract locations (e.g., at home, at school, at the office) of family members are shown on a circular interface. The different locations are colored, circular segments, into which small avatars for each person are placed in. While no exact mapping is done, it is straightforward to understand the encoded information, that is, where a person currently is located. In contrast, displaying the location on a map would add more detail, but would also make it more difficult to extract the relevant information. Such simplifications and suitable abstractions are especially important as visualization literacy cannot be taken for granted [12, 13, 24]. In general, the understandability of specific representations or concepts is driven by the familiarity of a person with these or similar ones.

5.3.3 Suitability and Purpose

Glanceable visualizations should consider specific tasks that an individual wants to accomplish. For example, the goal can be as specific as acquiring a certain piece of information or more vague like informing a decision: Should I run faster or slower? Should I take the stairs or the elevators? Should I do some stretches in the next minutes? As a result, the chosen representation must be suitable to actually inform these tasks by providing a fitting data encoding.

For example, Amini et al. [1] conducted a design elicitation, during which designers had to provide sketches for different insight types within a smartwatch fitness application. These types comprised single values, multiple values, goal-based, comparison (other), comparison (multiple), and motivational. For goal-based insights, the proposed designs used chart-based representations showing the progress toward a goal, while for motivational insights (e.g., 5 min to go) designers relied more heavily on metaphors such as trophies or cupcakes as waiting rewards. The representations provided in Figure 5.6 are illustrating some instances of the possible designs. The exploration of Amini et al. [1] clearly indicates the dimensions of the available design space for mobile visualizations and that for a specific design the expected usage context and user goals have to be carefully considered to provide a suitable visualization. Notably,

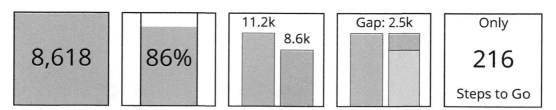

Figure 5.6 Example representations for visualizing progress toward a goal; inspired by design explorations of Amini et al. [1]. How well a specific design is suited depends on the current usage context.

which visualization design is most suited can also change within the same general context. For example, for a progress toward a goal the difference between 54 and 55% is not as relevant to a person as the difference between 99 and 100%. In consequence, this could mean that values are shown in a compact format by default, for example, *8.6k steps*, but when getting closer to a specific goal or simply a round number, the value is shown in full length (*8,618 steps*) to emphasize this small gap. By explicitly emphasizing these important differences, the visualization can better serve its purpose of motivating people in reaching their goals.

This purpose of glanceable visualizations becomes even more important when considering long term behavior changes. Representations made for this context must provide a certain appeal to be revisited over and over again. On the one hand, appeal could come from indicators that the person is making progress toward a given goal, and on the other hand from an aesthetic design that pleases the viewer. For the daily question of taking the stairs or the elevator, Rogers et al. [48] proposed an ambient installation in an office building consisting of blinking lights in the floor directing people toward the stairs, a physical presentation indicating how often people took the stairs or the elevator, and a large display with pie charts visualizing the ratio of the last days. This simple but aesthetic design caused discussions between passing persons but also seemed to lead to an increased stair usage.

As an example for a strong usage of metaphors for communicating progress, the UbiGreen tracking tool [22] encodes the weekly transportation habits of a person, and how environmentally friendly they are, as a blooming tree or a growing polar ecosystem. Because the representation is placed as an animated background screen on the mobile device, people can check the status anytime and perceive their current state; further, a rewarding detail is added to the scenery if a certain goal is reached at the end of the week. The metaphor of a growing plant (see Figure 5.7) or ecosystem also addresses an aesthetic aspiration by providing a natural looking scene instead of a technical appearance; however, this notion of aesthetics is likely to vary between different target groups and contexts.

5.3.4 Summary

In summary, the provided examples show that the suitability and purpose of glanceable visualizations are strongly related to simplicity and aesthetics. By providing a pleasing and easy-to-understand representation, chances are higher that people will keep

Figure 5.7 An example of a glanceable visualization on smartwatch's watch face. In this watch face app called "Sprout," the growth of the plants is mapped to the user's step count. The plants reset daily.

consuming a visualization and, consequently, may be better supported in reaching their long term goals. However, it is important to note that just because information is presented in an easy to perceive manner in the right place at the right time, it does not mean that people will necessarily act on it. The literature is full of examples of failed systems [38], in which people did not desire to change their behavior, found maintenance of devices or sensors not to be worth the effort, or did not find value in the data collected. No matter how compelling the visualization, people might still want to eat their pizza, drive their car, or do other actions that are not in their long-term best interest.

For all these characteristics, it is challenging to assess if a mobile visualization adequately satisfied its goals, especially as knowledge from multiple research disciplines is involved and comes to play. At the same time, the Visualization, Human-Computer Interaction, and Ubiquitous Computing communities have established approaches of how to evaluate various aspects of visualizations, which we discuss in the next section.

5.4 EVALUATION OF GLANCEABLE VISUALIZATIONS

In a systematic review of 581 visualization research papers, researchers [32] found that a visualization's effectiveness is predominantly measured by resulting images and algorithmic performance. Only recently has there been a steady increase in human subjects studies, in which researchers measure experience (e.g., reporting feedback from experts) and performance (e.g., time, error, cognitive workload). However, these traditional ways of evaluating visualizations may not be enough to capture all of the key values and uniqueness that glanceable visualizations offer, which we mentioned in the earlier sections. Glanceable visualizations are meaningfully *lived with* rather than *used* [27], and present new challenges to evaluation methods. As described in Section 5.3.1, the nature of the interaction is brief, hence the information conveyed via glanceable visualizations should be perceived in a quick and effective manner. Moreover, to evaluate simplicity and understandability of glanceable visualizations as mentioned in Section 5.3.2, we need methods that can capture people's level of comprehension, ideally with realistic datasets. Suitability and purpose (see Section 5.3.3) could be meaningfully captured in-situ over a prolonged period of time. In this section, we review how researchers have evaluated glanceable visualizations in prior work, discuss what challenges they present, and offer recommendations on evaluation methods and metrics to be used for a variety of goals. We note that in Chapter 6, broader goals and methods beyond measuring and evaluating glanceability are discussed.

5.4.1 Evaluations in the Lab

In evaluating glanceable visualization, it is critical to measure the glanceability of the visualization—defined as "how quickly and easily feedback is able to convey information after one pays attention" [18]. As such, glanceability can be measured with traditional metrics such as time and accuracy through an in-lab study. Blascheck et al. [9] conducted two perception studies to assess how quickly people can perform a simple data comparison task for small-scale visualizations on a smartwatch. To evaluate glanceability, the authors designed a simple data comparison task and calculated a reading time threshold for each chart type by data size condition (cf. Figure 5.3). They found that on a smartwatch, data can be read for up to 24 data values for bar and donut charts within less than 300 ms (donut: 216 ms, bar: 285 ms). The radial chart on average had times larger than 500 ms. This study indicates that when it comes to a data comparison task, these visualizations were glanceable, although different charts offered different efficacy of glanceability. These perception studies use domain-agnostic data and do not consider people's ability to comprehend the data—that is, people can answer a question without having to understand the meaning of the data or data encoding. In Blascheck et al.'s work, the study was conducted in a lab setting, in which a smartwatch was positioned in a fixed setting and participants were not distracted with other activities. While such a setup is far from people's real-world experience with glanceable visualizations, lab studies can be a first step in determining and measuring the glanceability of visualizations in the most strict sense, as the glanceability can only be diminished in a real-world environment, in which people are exposed to a variety of distractions (e.g., light, noise, movement, and other activities).

5.4.2 Online Experiments

Glanceable visualizations can also be evaluated through online experiments, although the goal may be to evaluate glanceability as well as other aspects of glanceable visualization. Mechanical Turk or Prolific could be used as an online experiment platform to test graphical perception experiments, exemplified by Heer and Bostock [30]. Such crowdsourced perception experiments make it possible to recruit a large number of participants within a short time period with relatively less amount of money [11].

Going beyond testing graphical perception, online experiments can be useful in capturing other proxy measures such as behavioral intention. For example,

Choe et al.'s [16] study on examining the effect of different types of framing (i.e., valence, presentation type, data unit) on people's perceived behavioral intention, the researchers measured self-efficacy, a strong predictor of behavior change and maintenance [2], as an outcome variable (cf. Figure 5.8). In Kay et al.'s [35] study on evaluating uncertainty visualizations for transit predictions, the researchers measured how precisely and confidently participants extract probability information. In online experiments, researchers typically pose a hypothetical scenario (e.g., imagine you are receiving the following step count feedback on a weekday at 4:30 pm [16]; suppose you are waiting for a bus and must decide if you have enough time to get coffee before the bus arrives based on the visualization [35]). They then show a visualization or stimulus, and ask questions related to variables of interest. Similar to evaluations in the lab, a tutorial precedes the actual tasks. To ensure response quality, it is highly recommended to embed attention checks (or *gotcha*) questions to filter out participants who did not pay attention to the study materials or follow study instructions.

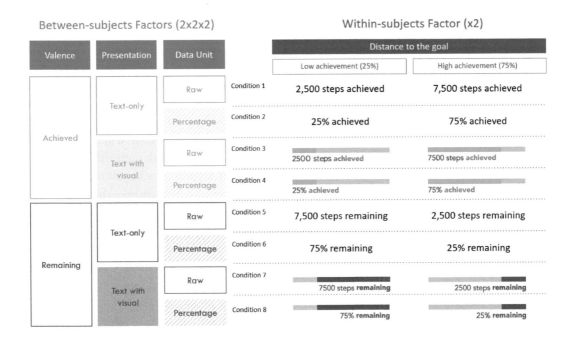

Figure 5.8 An example of a mixed-methods study evaluating 16 different glanceable visualization stimuli in an online experiment [16]. Between-subjects factors were *valence*, *presentation*, and *data unit*, each of which with two levels (hence 8 conditions). Within-subjects factor was distance to the goal with two level, with the low level of goal achievement at 25% and high level of goal achievement at 75%. Participants were shown each visual stimulus with a scenario and asked to report their level of self-efficacy.

Although not all glanceable visualizations are mobile-specific, online experiments can be done exclusively on mobile devices when necessary, enabling participants to use their own mobile device in their natural environment. Such decisions and online experiments at large necessarily involve a trade-off between the control over potential confounds (e.g., device type, device resolution, display brightness, ambient lighting condition) and external validity (see Section 5.3. in Brehmer et al. [14] for more in-depth discussion on this topic.) Furthermore, it is hard to measure exact and trustworthy task completion times when it is unclear how or if participants were distracted from the task. Despite the trade-offs, online experiments are useful evaluation methods that can complement in-lab evaluations. It is particularly useful when researchers want to compare several visualization candidates through an experiment design (e.g., between-subjects study) with relatively low cost.

5.4.3   Evaluations in the Field

Through in-lab studies and online experiments, researchers can assess the effectiveness that glanceable visualizations provide, such as glanceability, perceived simplicity, and behavioral intention. However, these studies are not enough to capture other unique values of glanceable visualizations such as suitability, purposefulness, and short- and long-term effects on people's behaviors. It is also common for glanceable visualizations to support or accompany other tasks (e.g., catching a bus, driving a car), and therefore, the evaluations should ideally be situated for ecological validity. Moreover, glanceable visualizations are meant to be embedded in our everyday lives, and even worn on our body. Therefore, subjective metrics, such as calmness (in terms of interaction and timing; see Riekki et al. [46] for an overview of the framework), aesthetics [27, 43, 47], and expressiveness [27] may also be considered, along with more utilitarian metrics such as data insights gained over time and their effects on people, for example, behavior change. Because these metrics can be measured through a prolonged and situated experience, researchers have conducted evaluations in the wild to capture these unique values.

One of the seminal works in glanceable visualization in the Ubiquitous Computing domain is UbiFit Garden by Consolvo et al. [17, 19]. In this work, the authors displayed an abstract depiction of people's physical activity using the garden metaphor on their smartphone's background screen. The goal of this work was to encourage people's physical activity through enhancing their awareness of their current state. One of the design goals of UbiFit Garden was to communicate a person's physical activities and goal attainment using a non-literal, aesthetic image. The display was shown on the background screen as a subtle reminder whenever a person unlocks their smartphone. To evaluate UbiFit Garden, the authors first conducted a 3-week field trial, which was aimed to examine people's reactions to activity inference and the overall concept [17]. This study was followed by a 3-month deployment study, which was aimed to systematically examine the effectiveness of glanceable visualizations on people's awareness and actual behavior [19]. Such a stepwise evaluation approach is particularly useful in understanding a technology's impact on people's actual behaviors.

5.4.4 Summary

In this section, we described types of evaluation studies conducted to study specific characteristics of glanceable visualizations. Evaluations in the lab affords assessing minimal timespans needed to perform a task in ideal settings. In particular, this is useful when actual display conditions such as the size of the displayed data items or viewing angles need to be controlled. Online experiments reach a wider audience and collect data on questions that focus on accuracy or subjective experiences related to aesthetics or the simplicity of findings. Field studies in general yield higher ecological validity, and such methods are particularly useful in the case of longer-term behavior related research, or examining glanceable visualizations in the real context of use (e.g., interacting with visualizations while moving) in diverse environments (e.g., factoring in light and noise condition). While in this chapter we described evaluation methods for glanceable visualizations, many of the methods are suitable for evaluating mobile visualizations at large. Chapter 6 offers a general evaluation framework to cover more diverse mobile visualization contexts.

5.5 DISCUSSION AND FUTURE CHALLENGES

Different communities have been studying glanceable visualizations, and they have developed different perspectives of glanceable visualizations. Unifying these perspectives and goals from the different domains is impossible, however, showing the different time scales of glanceability can help researchers position their work. At the same time, such a unified overview can help to communicate the ideas of glanceable visualizations to practitioners and help to bring them to real-world applications and the people using them.

If we take the ideas of glanceable visualization one step further, we can imagine scenarios in which people are not only checking their devices for quick information needs, but they are surrounded by (augmented) glanceable visualizations, as for example, in Hyper Reality (http://hyper-reality.co/), requiring them not only to digest the information they are seeing at a glance but also to decide which information is currently relevant for their task at all, and in an extreme scenario ignoring the ads and suggestions continuously displayed. Now, more than ever, design guidelines for good and useful glanceable visualizations are needed.

One dimension we have not discussed in this chapter is the complexity and quantity of data to display. Creating glanceable visualizations of complex or a large amount of data is not always possible (or not even appropriate) as they may not be properly visualized with simple representations. It is also unclear how to embed glanceable visualizations in more elaborate application contexts. For instance, most glanceable visualizations we discussed so far require passive interactions (see Section 5.3.1). However, as not all data can be depicted so that it can be perceived at a glance, suitable interaction mechanisms become necessary for gaining further insights. Therefore, a next logical step is to explore ways to efficiently interact with (complex) mobile visualizations so that only quick glances are required to see where to interact and to perceive the feedback of an interaction. Further, with the advent of novel device classes such as head-mounted AR displays and related visions of the future such as situated, embedded, and immersive visualizations, there is a growing need for concepts on how glanceable content can be provided as well as be made interactive within such environments. For now, we refer the interested reader to Chapter 3 for more information on interaction on mobile devices and to Chapter 9 for a discussion on future visualization environments.

The types of evaluations discussed above have different ranges in the level of ecological validity. Although lab experiments give complete control to the study designer, they have little ecological validity, whereas online experiments give up some part of the control but have more ecological validity. Evaluations in the field are usually the experiments with least control but they have the most ecological validity. Therefore, a designer has to choose between the level of control and the level of ecological validity when conducting experiments. However, as one of the main usage contexts of glanceable visualizations is their use *on-the-go*, both lab experiments as well as evaluations in the field are necessary to fully evaluate a novel glanceable visualization.

5.6 CONCLUSION

In this chapter, we have discussed glanceable mobile visualizations and the quick information needs that fuel the design of such visualizations. We have looked at the time scales of glanceability in the Vision Sciences, the Visualization domain, and the Ubiquitous Computing community as well as the goals and tasks each domain investigates. In addition, we briefly touched on the history of glanceable (mobile) visualization, which stems from ambient and peripheral devices that research has studied since the 1990s and the current trend in developing visualizations that are often small in form factor and focused on for only a short period of time. Based on the perspectives, we have suggested core values for glanceability—presence and access, simplicity and understandability, and suitability and purpose. These core values form useful design considerations and can help to specify how glanceable visualizations might be studied for not only efficiency and accuracy, but also for evaluating aesthetics, and understanding potential behavior change. Even though research concerned with glanceable visualization has been around for over 30 years, with the onset of new mobile devices, new research questions have and are emerging, offering exciting research futures to explore.

REFERENCES

[1] Amini, F., Hasan, K., Bunt, A., and Irani, P. "Data Representations for In-Situ Exploration of Health and Fitness Data". In: *Proceedings of the Conference on Pervasive Computing Technologies for Healthcare (PervasiveHealth)*. ACM, 2017, pp. 163–172 (cited on pages 162, 163).

[2] Bandura, A. "Perceived Self-Efficacy in the Exercise of Control Over AIDS Infection". In: *Evaluation and Program Planning* 13.1 (1990), pp. 9–17 (cited on page 166).

[3] Banovic, N., Brant, C., Mankoff, J., and Dey, A. "ProactiveTasks: The Short of Mobile Device Use Sessions". In: *Proceedings of the Conference on Human Computer Interaction with Mobile Devices and Services (MobileHCI)*. ACM, 2014, pp. 243–252 (cited on page 155).

[4] Beck, F. and Weiskopf, D. "Word-Sized Graphics for Scientific Texts". In: *Transactions on Visualization and Computer Graphics (TVCG)* 23.6 (2017), pp. 1576–1587. DOI: 10.1109/tvcg.2017.2674958 (cited on page 161).

[5] Biederman, I. "On Processing Information From a Glance at a Scene: Some Implications for a Syntax and Semantics of Visual Processing". In: *Proceedings of the SIGGRAPH Workshop on User-Oriented Design of Interactive Graphics Systems*. ACM, 1976, pp. 75–88 (cited on page 155).

[6] Biederman, I. "Perceiving Real-World Scenes". In: *Science* 177.4043 (1972), pp. 77–80 (cited on page 155).

[7] Biederman, I., Glass, A., and Stacy, W. "Searching for Objects in Real-World Scenes". In: *Journal of Experimental Psychology* 97.1 (1973), pp. 22–27 (cited on page 155).

[8] Biederman, I., Rabinowitz, J., Glass, A., and Stacy, W. "On the Information Extracted From a Glance at a Scene". In: *Journal of Experimental Psychology* 103.3 (1974), pp. 597–600 (cited on page 155).

[9] Blascheck, T., Besançon, L., Bezerianos, A., Lee, B., and Isenberg, P. "Glanceable Visualization: Studies of Data Comparison Performance on Smartwatches". In: *Transactions on Visualization and Computer Graphics (TVCG)* 25.1 (Jan. 2018). **Open Access version:** https://hal.inria.fr/hal-01851306, pp. 630–640. DOI: 10.1109/TVCG.2018.2865142 (cited on pages 154, 156, 157, 159, 161, 165).

[10] Borgo, R., Kehrer, J., Chung, D., Maguire, E., Laramee, R., Hauser, H., Ward, M., and Chen, M. "Glyph-based Visualization: Foundations, Design Guidelines, Techniques and Applications". In: *Eurographics State of the Art Reports*. Eurographics, 2013, pp. 39–63. DOI: 10.2312/conf/EG2013/stars/039-063 (cited on page 161).

[11] Borgo, R., Micallef, L., Bach, B., McGee, F., and Lee, B. "Information visualization evaluation using crowdsourcing". In: *Computer Graphics Forum*. Vol. 37. 3. Wiley Online Library. 2018, pp. 573–595 (cited on page 165).

[12] Börner, K., Maltese, A., Balliet, R. N., and Heimlich, J. "Investigating Aspects of Data Visualization Literacy Using 20 Information Visualizations and 273 Science Museum Visitors". In: *Information Visualization* 15.3 (2015), pp. 198–213 (cited on page 162).

[13] Boy, J., Rensink, R. A., Bertini, E., and Fekete, J.-D. "A Principled Way of Assessing Visualization Literacy". In: *Transactions on Visualization and Computer Graphics (TVCG)* 20.12 (Dec. 2014), pp. 1963–1972. DOI: 10.1109/TVCG.2014.2346984 (cited on page 162).

[14] Brehmer, M., Lee, B., Isenberg, P., and Choe, E. "A Comparative Evaluation of Animation and Small Multiples for Trend Visualization on Mobile Phones". In: *Transactions on Visualization and Computer Graphics (TVCG)* 26.1 (2020). **Open Access version:** https://hal.inria.fr/hal-02317687, pp. 364–374. DOI: 10.1109/TVCG.2019.2934397 (cited on page 167).

[15] Brown, B., Taylor, A., Izadi, S., Sellen, A., Kaye, J., and Eardley, R. "Locating Family Values: A Field Trial of the Whereabouts Clock". In: *Proceedings of the Conference on Ubiquitous Computing (Ubicomp)*. Springer, 2007, pp. 354–371 (cited on pages 161, 162).

[16] Choe, E. K., Lee, B., Munson, S., Pratt, W., and Kientz, J. "Persuasive Performance Feedback: The Effect of Framing on Self-Efficacy". In: *American Medical Informatics Association Annual Symposium Proceedings.* **Open Access version:** https://www.ncbi.nlm.nih.gov/pmc/articles/PMC3900219/. American Medical Informatics Association, 2013, pp. 825–833 (cited on page 166).

[17] Consolvo, S., Klasnja, P., McDonald, D., Avrahami, D., Froehlich, J., LeGrand, L., Libby, R., Mosher, K., and Landay, J. "Flowers or a Robot Army? Encouraging Awareness & Activity With Personal, Mobile Displays". In: *Proceedings of the Conference on Ubiquitous Computing (Ubicomp)*. ACM, 2008, pp. 54–63 (cited on pages 158, 167).

[18] Consolvo, S., Klasnja, P., McDonald, D., and Landay, J. "Designing for Healthy Lifestyles: Design Considerations for Mobile Technologies to Encourage Consumer Health and Wellness". In: *Foundations and Trends® in Human-Computer Interaction* 6.3–4 (2014), pp. 167–315 (cited on page 165).

[19] Consolvo, S., Libby, R., Smith, I., Landay, J., McDonald, D., Toscos, T., Chen, M., Froehlich, J., Harrison, B., Klasnja, P., LaMarca, A., and LeGrand, L. "Activity Sensing in the Wild: A Field Trial of Ubifit Garden". In: *Proceedings of the Conference on Human Factors in Computing Systems (CHI)*. ACM, 2008, pp. 1797–1806. DOI: 10.1145/1357054.1357335 (cited on page 167).

[20] Ferreira, D., Goncalves, J., Kostakos, V., Barkhuus, L., and Dey, A. "Contextual Experience Sampling of Mobile Application Micro-Usage". In: *Proceedings of the Conference on Human Computer Interaction with Mobile Devices and Services (MobileHCI)*. ACM, 2014, pp. 91–100 (cited on page 155).

[21] Fogarty, J., Forlizzi, J., and Hudson, S. "Aesthetic Information Collages: Generating Decorative Displays That Contain Information". In: *Proceedings of the Conference on User Interface, Software, and Technology (UIST)*. ACM, 2001, pp. 141–150 (cited on page 158).

[22] Froehlich, J., Dillahunt, T., Klasnja, P., Mankoff, J., Consolvo, S., Harrison, B., and Landay, J. A. "UbiGreen: Investigating a Mobile Tool for Tracking and Supporting Green Transportation Habits". In: *Proceedings of the Conference on Human Factors in Computing Systems (CHI)*. CHI '09. Boston, MA, USA: ACM, 2009, pp. 1043–1052. DOI: 10.1145/1518701.1518861. URL: https://doi.org/10.1145/1518701.1518861 (cited on page 163).

[23] Fuchs, J., Isenberg, P., Bezerianos, A., and Keim, D. "A Systematic Review of Experimental Studies on Data Glyphs". In: *Transactions on Visualization and Computer Graphics (TVCG)* 23.7 (2017). **Open Access version:** `https://hal.inria.fr/hal-01378429`, pp. 1863–1879. DOI: `10.1109/tvcg.2016.2549018` (cited on page 161).

[24] Galesic, M. and Garcia-Retamero, R. "Graph Literacy: A Cross-Cultural Comparison". In: *Medical Decision Making* 31.3 (2011), pp. 444–457 (cited on pages 161, 162).

[25] Goffin, P., Boy, J., Willett, W., and Isenberg, P. "An Exploratory Study of Word-Scale Graphics in Data-Rich Text Documents". In: *Transactions on Visualization and Computer Graphics (TVCG)* 23.10 (2017). **Open Access version:** `https://hal.inria.fr/hal-01389998`, pp. 2275–2287. DOI: `10.1109/tvcg.2016.2618797` (cited on page 161).

[26] Gouveia, R., Pereira, F., Caraban, A., Munson, S., and Karapanos, E. "You Have 5 Seconds: Designing Glanceable Feedback for Physical Activity Trackers". In: *Adjunct Proceedings of the Conference on Pervasive and Ubiquitous Computing and Proceedings of the Symposium on Wearable Computers.* ACM, 2015, pp. 643–647 (cited on pages 154, 159).

[27] Hallnäs, L. and Redström, J. "From Use to Presence: On the Expressions and Aesthetics of Everyday Computational Things". In: *Transactions on Computer-Human Interaction (TOCHI)* 9.2 (2002), pp. 106–124 (cited on pages 164, 167).

[28] Harboe, G., Metcalf, C., Bentley, F., Tullio, J., Massey, N., and Romano, G. "Ambient Social TV: Drawing People Into a Shared Experience". In: *Proceedings of the Conference on Human Factors in Computing Systems (CHI).* ACM, 2008, pp. 1–10. DOI: `10.1145/1357054.1357056` (cited on page 158).

[29] Healey, C. and Enns, J. "Attention and visual memory in visualization and computer graphics". In: *IEEE transactions on visualization and computer graphics* 18.7 (2011), pp. 1170–1188 (cited on page 154).

[30] Heer, J. and Bostock, M. "Crowdsourcing Graphical Perception: Using Mechanical Turk to Assess Visualization Design". In: *Proceedings of the Conference on Human Factors in Computing Systems (CHI).* ACM, 2010, pp. 203–212 (cited on page 165).

[31] Holcombe, A. "Seeing Slow and Seeing Fast: Two Limits on Perception". In: *Trends in Cognitive Sciences* 13.5 (2009), pp. 216–221 (cited on page 154).

[32] Isenberg, T., Isenberg, P., Chen, J., Sedlmair, M., and Möller, T. "A systematic review on the practice of evaluating visualization". In: *IEEE Transactions on Visualization and Computer Graphics* 19.12 (2013), pp. 2818–2827 (cited on page 164).

[33] Islam, A., Bezerianos, A., Lee, B., Blascheck, T., and Isenberg, P. "Visualizing Information on Watch Faces: A Survey With Smartwatch Users". In: *Short Paper Proceedings of the Conference on Visualization (VIS)*. **Open Access version:** https://hal.inria.fr/hal-03005319. Los Alamitos: IEEE, Oct. 2020. DOI: 10.1109/VIS47514.2020.00038 (cited on pages 161, 162).

[34] Jahanian, A., Keshvari, S., and Rosenholtz, R. "Web Pages: What Can You See in a Single Fixation?" In: *Cognitive Research: Principles and Implications* 3.14 (2018), pp. 1–15 (cited on page 155).

[35] Kay, M., Kola, T., Hullman, J., and Munson, S. "When (Ish) Is My Bus? User-Centered Visualizations of Uncertainty in Everyday, Mobile Predictive Systems". In: *Proceedings of the Conference on Human Factors in Computing Systems (CHI)*. ACM, 2016, pp. 5092–5103 (cited on page 166).

[36] Kaye, J., Levitt, M., Nevins, J., Golden, J., and Schmidt, V. "Communicating Intimacy One Bit at a Time". In: *Extended Abstracts of the Conference on Human Factors in Computing System (CHI)*. ACM, 2005, pp. 1529–1532 (cited on page 158).

[37] Klamka, K., Horak, T., and Dachselt, R. "Watch+Strap: Extending Smart-watches With Interactive StrapDisplays". In: *Proceedings of the Conference on Human Factors in Computing Systems (CHI)*. CHI '20. **Open Access version:** https://dl.acm.org/doi/10.1145/3313831.3376199. New York, NY, USA: ACM, 2020, pp. 1–15. DOI: 10.1145/3313831.3376199 (cited on pages 160, 161).

[38] Lazar, A., Koehler, C., Tanenbaum, J., and Nguyen, D. "Why We Use and Abandon Smart Devices". In: *Proceedings of the Joint Conference on Pervasive and Ubiquitous Computing (Ubicomp)*. ACM, 2015, pp. 635–646 (cited on pages 158, 164).

[39] Matthews, T., Blais, D., Shick, A., Mankoff, J., Forlizzi, J., Rohrbach, S., and Klatzky, R. *Evaluating Glanceable Visuals for Multitasking*. Tech. rep. UC Berkeley, 2006 (cited on page 159).

[40] Miller, T. and Stasko, J. "The InfoCanvas: Information Conveyance Through Personalized, Expressive Art". In: *Extended Abstracts of the Conference on Human Factors in Computing System (CHI)*. **Open Access version:** https://www.cc.gatech.edu/~john.stasko/papers/chi01.pdf. ACM, 2001, pp. 305–306. DOI: https://doi.org/10.1145/634067.634248 (cited on page 156).

[41] Neshati, A., Sakamoto, Y., Leboe-McGowan, L. C., Leboe-McGowan, J., Serrano, M., and Irani, P. "G-Sparks: Glanceable Sparklines on Smartwatches". In: *Proceedings of the Graphics Interface Conference (GI)*. **Open Access version:** https://doi.org/10.20380/GI2019.23. Kingston, Canada: Canadian Human-Computer Communications Society, 2019. DOI: 10.20380/GI2019.23 (cited on page 157).

[42] Plaue, C. M., Miller, T., and Stasko, J. *Is a Picture Worth a Thousand Words? An Evaluation of Information Awareness Displays.* Tech. rep. 1853/52. **Open Access version:** http://hdl.handle.net/1853/52. Georgia Institute of Technology, 2004 (cited on page 159).

[43] Pousman, Z. and Stasko, J. "A Taxonomy of Ambient Information Systems: Four Patterns of Design". In: *Proceedings of the Conference on Advanced Visual Interfaces (AVI).* **Open Access version:** https://www.cc.gatech.edu/~john.stasko/papers/avi06.pdf. ACM, 2006, pp. 67–74. DOI: https://doi.org/10.1145/1133265.1133277 (cited on pages 156, 167).

[44] Pousman, Z., Stasko, J., and Mateas, M. "Casual Information Visualization: Depictions of Data in Everyday Life". In: *Transactions on Visualization and Computer Graphics (TVCG)* 13.6 (2007). **Open Access version:** https://www.cc.gatech.edu/~john.stasko/papers/infovis07-casual.pdf, pp. 1145–1152. DOI: 10.1109/TVCG.2007.70541 (cited on page 156).

[45] Resner, B., Gandhi, P., Negroponte, N., Dredge, R., and Rose, D. "Weather Forecasting Umbrella". US Patent App. 11/699,314. Nov. 2007. URL: http://appft.uspto.gov/netacgi/nph-Parser?Sect1=PTO1&Sect2=HITOFF&p=1&u=/netahtml/PTO/srchnum.html&r=1&f=G&l=50&d=PG01&s1=20070256716.PGNR. (cited on page 158).

[46] Riekki, J., Isomursu, P., and Isomursu, M. "Evaluating the Calmness of Ubiquitous Applications". In: *International Conference on Product Focused Software Process Improvement (PROFES).* Springer, 2004, pp. 105–119 (cited on page 167).

[47] Rodgers, J. "Residential Resource Use Feedback: Exploring Ambient and Artistic Approaches". PhD thesis. Communication, Art & Technology: School of Interactive Arts and Technology, 2011 (cited on page 167).

[48] Rogers, Y., Hazlewood, W., Marshall, P., Dalton, N., and Hertrich, S. "Ambient Influence: Can Twinkly Lights Lure and Abstract Representations Trigger Behavioral Change?" In: *Proceedings of the Conference on Ubiquitous Computing (Ubicomp).* ACM, 2010, pp. 261–270 (cited on page 163).

[49] Rose, D. *Enchanted Objects: Design, Human Desire, and the Internet of Things.* Simon and Schuster, 2014 (cited on page 158).

[50] Sellen, A., Eardley, R., Izadi, S., and Harper, R. "The Whereabouts Clock: Early Testing of a Situated Awareness Device". In: *Extended Abstracts of the Conference on Human Factors in Computing System (CHI).* ACM, 2006, pp. 1307–1312 (cited on page 161).

[51] Spence, R. *Information visualization.* 2nd. Springer, 2007 (cited on page 160).

[52] Stasko, J., Miller, T., Pousman, Z., Plaue, C., and Ullah, O. "Personalized Peripheral Information Awareness Through Information Art". In: *Proceedings of the Conference on Ubiquitous Computing (Ubicomp).* **Open Access version:** https://www.cc.gatech.edu/~john.stasko/papers/ubicomp04.pdf.

Springer, 2004, pp. 18–35. DOI: 10.1007/978-3-540-30119-6_2 (cited on page 158).

[53] Treisman, A. "Preattentive processing in vision". In: *Computer vision, graphics, and image processing* 31.2 (1985), pp. 156–177 (cited on page 155).

[54] Treisman, A. and Gormican, S. "Feature analysis in early vision: evidence from search asymmetries." In: *Psychological review* 95.1 (1988), p. 15 (cited on page 155).

[55] Treisman, A. M. and Gelade, G. "A feature-integration theory of attention". In: *Cognitive psychology* 12.1 (1980), pp. 97–136 (cited on page 155).

[56] Weiser, M. "The Computer for the 21st Century". In: *Scientific American* 265.3 (1991), pp. 94–105 (cited on page 154).

[57] Weiser, M. and Brown, J. S. "Designing Calm Technology". In: *POWERGRID International* 1.1 (1996), pp. 75–85 (cited on pages 157, 158).

[58] Wisneski, C., Ishii, H., Dahley, A., Gorbet, M., Brave, S., Ullmer, B., and Yarin, P. "Ambient Displays: Turning Architectural Space Into an Interface Between People and Digital Information". In: *Proceedings of the Workshop on Cooperative Buildings (CoBuild)*. Springer, 1998, pp. 22–32 (cited on page 158).

[59] Wolfe, J. M. "Guided search 2.0 a revised model of visual search". In: *Psychonomic bulletin & review* 1.2 (1994), pp. 202–238 (cited on page 155).

CHAPTER 6

Evaluating Mobile Visualizations

Frank Bentley

Yahoo, USA

Eun Kyoung Choe

University of Maryland, College Park, USA

Lena Mamykina

Columbia University, USA

John Stasko

Georgia Institute of Technology, USA

Pourang Irani

University of Manitoba, Canada

CONTENTS

Evaluation is important for data visualization because it can help us to understand whether a system is achieving its intended goals and how well (or not) it is doing so. The evaluation of mobile visualizations builds upon research and knowledge gained from data visualization broadly, but it provides an additional set of challenges. There are many reasons to evaluate mobile visualizations with people, including potential end users and experts. However, depending on the research questions that one wants to answer and the intended audience, different methods are needed. In the mobile information visualization domain, there is a broad continuum of research questions that can be answered by an evaluation study. Some goals include validating rapid perception of differences in data, while others focus on examining the long-term use of visualizations and whether seeing a visualization over months leads to their intended impact on users. Very different methods, time scales of research, and participant recruitment strategies are needed depending on the questions that one wants to answer. This chapter will explore the literature, discussing a variety of goals and evaluation approaches, highlighting best practices and making recommendations for future approaches to evaluating mobile visualizations.

6.1 INTRODUCTION

Evaluation is a vitally important yet extremely challenging aspect of data visualization [18, 70]. Visualization developers often want to compare their approach to that of others, or they may simply want to assess if their approach is achieving its intended goals. Visualization researchers have drawn from all that has been learned about evaluation from fields such as Human-Computer Interaction (HCI), Psychology, and others. Data visualization offers its own unique set of challenges, however, with many involving the difficulty of evaluating the utility of a visualization. Mobile visualization presents even more challenges including the purpose and context of use, diversity of potential users, and variety of display devices, to name just a few.

As discussed in Chapter 1, mobile data visualizations are developed for many different purposes, and researchers from many disciplines design and create mobile data visualizations. Whether they are interested in measuring human perception of differences in information presentation, trying to visualize a dataset in a new way to derive insights, or trying to create successful long term behavior change in a diverse set of users, researchers often have vastly different goals when setting out on a new visualization project.

Perhaps in part due to the different disciplines of researchers involved in creating mobile visualizations, a common set of best practices for their evaluation has not emerged. Researchers from the InfoVis, Mobile HCI, and Ubiquitous Computing communities, respectively, have traditionally used different sets of methods with different sets of research participants to evaluate their work. If one is only concerned about human perceptions of differences, long-term, longitudinal studies are not needed, and a short in-lab study can often suffice. However, behavior change is a long process that can take months (or even years) to measure, and therefore needs long-term studies with participants that carefully match the broader population to determine a system's effectiveness in real world conditions. Chapter 5 of this book further explores this continuum from perception to behavior change.

The domain of mobile devices brings new challenges to evaluating information visualizations. Mobile devices are more commonly used in the background throughout the day, in short bursts of activity, compared to longer and more purposeful interactions with desktop systems. Mobile devices also have a broad range of device characteristics, with differing screen sizes, resolutions, brightness levels, and other technical aspects that can alter a user's ability to perceive differences in a visualization. Ultra-small mobile devices, such as smartwatches, impose even greater constraints. The places where users choose to engage with mobile visualizations are also quite varied. Some might be used in bright sunlight while running, on a bumpy public bus, or while one's hands are full with other objects. These constraints mean that traditional, lab-based evaluation while seated at a desk with standard lighting conditions, are increasingly not appropriate methods to evaluate these systems that will be used in different situations and settings outside of an office.

Mobile devices are also ubiquitous in today's world. Therefore mobile visualizations often have an audience of the general public, over earlier work in the information visualization domain that was often focused on domain experts or other more highly educated individuals. When deploying systems to the general population, it is important to remember that a significant proportion of adults (studies have identified 41% of Americans as well as 44% of Germans [39]) have low graph literacy skills in understanding very simple bar and pie charts, and two-thirds of American adults do not have a bachelor's degree [17]. Therefore, with any visualization that one wishes the general public to use, it is important to recruit participants that match that broader population. Evaluations with college students or staff will lead to skewed results of use and understanding of data compared to a general population.

Furthermore, like the people using mobile devices, the devices themselves are quite diverse. Mobile displays vary in size, form factor, resolution, and input capabilities, as well as other characteristics. For example, many older mobile devices do not have the high-definition displays and the pixel scaling ratios of newer models, and thus cannot display visualizations at a comparable level of detail. Many people, especially those in developing countries, are using older phones as well as basic feature phones with smaller screens and limited touch capabilities. Addressing this diversity of devices in evaluations is important.

The remainder of this chapter will discuss existing best practices for evaluating visualizations, discuss our method for discovering and exploring different goals for evaluation, and then will explore best practices for each of these goals in turn. While there are obvious overlaps to the evaluation methods covered in Chapter 5, we cover goals and evaluation methods for mobile visualizations more broadly, going beyond what are necessary for glanceable visualizations. We will conclude with a discussion about the current state of mobile visualization evaluation and open areas of research in this domain.

6.2 BACKGROUND

The HCI community has made great strides toward effectively evaluating the usability of software systems. Techniques for determining whether a person can effectively use a piece of software are now commonplace and employed widely throughout the information technology community. Recent books about HCI lay out both methods and best practices for conducting such evaluations [60, 67].

The field of data visualization has leveraged much of that knowledge, but it also introduces some new challenges. One of the primary challenges in evaluating visualizations is the importance of determining a system's utility. While usability is often the evaluation focus of HCI, utility goes beyond it and toward the effective and beneficial application of the software for achieving greater goals. Specifically within the visualization domain, utility involves interpretation of visual representations of data for better understanding of the data and use in subsequent sensemaking and decision-making. Is a visualization helping viewers understand the depicted data better? Can viewers then make better decisions based on the improved data understanding? What kind of reaction, reflection, or memory does the visualization spur?

Plaisant [70] identifies the key challenges in evaluating visualizations and explains why this process is so difficult. Example issues that she calls out are the need for longer term assessments, for ways to judge whether a visualization can answer questions that a person does not know they have, and for methods to identify beneficial discoveries or general awareness facilitated by a visualization. She calls for more repositories of example data and tasks, as well as case studies and success stories.

Carpendale builds upon those thoughts and provides an in-depth tutorial of visualization evaluation methods and challenges [18]. She states that three key features are desirable to evaluation: generalizability, precision, and realism. She then describes a variety of quantitative and qualitative methods that visualization evaluators could utilize, explaining the methodological details, challenges, and threats to validity that each face. Ultimately, her goal is to provide guidance to others for choosing an evaluation approach.

When determining which evaluation method to use, fundamentally, one must first determine the ultimate goal of the evaluation. For example, is the goal to determine whether a person can accurately interpret what they see, or possibly it is to determine whether the visualization provides a greater understanding of the underlying data thus assisting subsequent decision-making. Depending on the objective of the evaluation, a variety of metrics may be appropriate to achieve that goal. Determining what to measure is one of the fundamental steps of any evaluation process. Of course, the next question is how to measure it. A wide variety of evaluation techniques have been proposed, with each providing specific benefits and challenges.

One of the most common evaluation approaches for visualizations is a controlled experiment. Study participants are given a series of benchmark tasks to perform while using a visualization. In some cases, multiple visualizations may be employed in a comparative study seeking to understand how they perform against each other. Potential metrics for this type of evaluation are the task success rate, time to completion, and number of errors made. These types of studies and their metrics are typically more quantitative in nature, and are viewed as being more objective. However, while these studies provide a large degree of *internal validity*, meaning that they can be replicated in the same exact lab conditions, they often lack *external validity*, meaning that they often cannot be replicated in real world situations with real devices and diverse people out in their natural contexts and activities.

Other forms of evaluation are much more observational and interpretive in nature. These types of studies usually seek *ecological validity* and thus emphasize observation of a visualization's use and application in realistic environments and scenarios. Frequently, these types of evaluations involve significant interaction with users of the visualization including interviews and capturing use over time. These types of evaluations are much more qualitative in nature and seek to accurately interpret and understand people's use of and opinions about the visualizations. However, these studies can also capture objective measures related to behavior change over time in order to augment the more qualitative data from interviews and diaries.

Shneiderman and Plaisant advocated for these more observational and interpretive methods, arguing that short-term lab-based studies simply will not be sufficient for evaluating visualizations. The researchers specifically articulate the need and motivations for longer-term studies of deployed visualization use [84]. They introduce the Multi-dimensional In-depth Long-term Case (MILC) methodology that is more like a case study, examining in-depth usage of a visualization by a few individuals. This type of evaluation has gained increasing traction within the visualization community.

Another form of evaluation does not involve studies with sets of target audience, but instead employs expert reviews of a software system. The Insight-based evaluation methodology is a hybrid form of a controlled experiment and an expert review. It attempts to quantify the number of insights generated in the use of a visualization [81]. Evaluation participants, who must be at least knowledgeable in the domain of the data being presented, use different visualizations while the evaluators count and measure information such as the time to reach the first insight, count of insights, and domain value of the insights. Although it is conceptually appealing, this technique is quite methodologically challenging to implement.

More recently, Wall et al. proposed the ICE-T evaluation methodology that provides a heuristic-based discount evaluation approach [88], a form of expert review. The technique employs a hierarchy of evaluation heuristics under four primary components: insight, confidence, essence, and time. Evaluators who bring knowledge of data visualization rate a system on each of the heuristics, ultimately producing a score for the visualization that estimates its value and utility for helping to understand the underlying data. The technique is designed to be fast and easy to deploy, not requiring interactions with potential users.

More recently, researchers have begun to look beyond performance-based metrics such as a visualization's usability and utility [80, 89]. Alternative metrics such as the memorability of a visualization or the engagement, and the enjoyment it provides, also may be important.

Lam et al. conducted a meta-study of information visualization evaluations, drawing from 361 academic papers discussing some type of visualization evaluation [58]. The researchers identified seven primary evaluation scenarios under two high-level goals: understanding data analysis and understanding visualizations. For each of the seven categories, they then describe its goals and outputs, evaluation questions, methods, and list examples. Isenberg et al. subsequently expanded this review to other subareas of visualization [47]. The authors reported that measuring visualization system's resulting images and its algorithmic performance has been the most predominant evaluation methods, and only recently, there has been a steady increase in evaluation methods that include participants.

Moving beyond work in Data Visualization, the Ubiquitous Computing and Mobile HCI communities also have developed a large set of methods for use in evaluating the use of technology in the wild. The goals of many of these studies have been to understand how technology is adopted into everyday life and how people alter their behavior when given a new system. Many of these studies therefore employ short and long-term field study methods, where participants interact with a system throughout their own daily life as they see fit, and the evaluation is meant to measure their understanding of the data collected, specific changes to behavior that have been made, or to understand if enough data can be collected at high quality to make a system feasible for use in the world.

Diary Studies [68] are frequently used to understand specific actions that people take in a system over time when interacting with a system naturally outside of controlled lab conditions. Participants can leave voicemail entries, complete paper worksheets, or online surveys to leave details of specific interactions that they had with the system close to the time of usage, while memories are still fresh. Diaries are often combined with Experience Sampling Method (ESM) [3, 30], where an application prompts a participant for feedback about their experiences at random times throughout the day or after specific events take place (e.g., after logging food in a diet tracking application). Both of these methods are particularly important for studying the use of mobile systems, as interactions take place in the world over time and are not directly observable by researchers. Gathering data about a person's experience as close as possible to the interaction helps to improve the accuracy of the data collected as experiences are recent and not recalled weeks or months later in an interview. A thorough review of both of these methods can be found in Consolvo et al.'s Mobile User Research book [26].

Other field study methods can involve Contextual Inquiry [46], where researchers travel to locations where participants typically engage in an activity and study existing practices or the use of a new system within that context. This method can help researchers to understand environmental variables (e.g., noise, light, distractions, network conditions) that can impact use of a system in real world contexts.

Finally, often researchers need to conduct a formal experimental study to validate that a design meets a specific objective. Whether this is a classic A/B test, first explored by Google in 2000, where a random sample of users get one experience and the rest get a control, or a more complex experimental design [44], experiments can prove that a given experience can change a user's behavior in a statistically measurable way. Often, this is required for field studies of behavior change systems in order to prove that they perform better than existing approaches or interview-based methods without a system in place.

Overall, these varied methods have been applied to a wide range of systems by researchers working in several adjacent disciplines. However, what was lacking in the community was a more systematic investigation of how these methods could be used in the evaluation of mobile visualizations in particular. The remainder of the chapter will explore this topic.

6.3 METHOD

We conducted a literature review through searching on Google Scholar and the ACM Digital library to identify papers that include a visualization on a mobile device and were evaluated directly with end users in some way. This search included both directed search for papers that we were familiar with as long-time researchers in the field, branching off from those papers based on citations, and more general searches of the databases for keywords related to mobile visualizations. We also looked through proceedings of recent Ubicomp/IMWUT, Mobile HCI, CHI, and InfoVis conferences.

In total, we reviewed 31 papers that met our criteria and represented a wide range of systems from each of the research communities that create and evaluate mobile visualizations. For each paper that we found, we identified the evaluation method used as well as the primary goal of the evaluation (e.g., perception, usability, behavior change). These codes for the primary goal evolved as we examined additional papers until we arrived at the set of six that are explored in the next section.

We further examined papers in each of the goal areas to identify common methods and best practices for research that can answer a variety of types of research questions. For example, very different methods are required if one wants to see if participants can perceive a difference between two bars compared to one that is trying to quantify behavior changes that participants make over a 90-day period as a result of having a particular visualization in their lives.

The following sections will introduce the framework of six evaluation goals for studying mobile visualization systems and then will explore each goal in additional detail, covering the methods and typical study designs used when faced with each evaluation goal.

6.4 FRAMEWORK

After reviewing the literature using the method above, we settled on six goals for conducting evaluations of mobile visualizations. These goals, as shown in Table 6.1, form a rough hierarchy, whereby questions at the top of the list should be explored before answering more involved questions below.

Perception: At its simplest, the most basic goal of evaluating a visualization is to see if a participant can perceive it. Can they recognize what is shown and differences between data representations? For example, one might want to know if a participant can tell that one slice of a circular graph is larger than another.

Usability: The next goal is to see if a participant can interact with the visualization and if the visualization is usable. For example, can a participant navigate to the correct data, filter it in meaningful ways, and understand the various controls and UI elements of the visualization? It is important to understand if a visualization is usable before going through the effort of running a feasibility study, as quick design iterations can improve the interaction and increase the likelihood that users will stick with the system long enough to capture the data needed to support long term goals.

Feasibility: Mobile visualizations often are powered with data that is collected out in the world, often on mobile devices themselves. The next goal is to evaluate

TABLE 6.1 The six goals for evaluating mobile visualizations with example projects highlighting the methods used to evaluate systems for each of the goals.

Goals of Evaluation	Examples
Perception (Can the user recognize what is shown in the visualization?)	SmartWatch Vis [9], Residential Energy Use [74], Ambient Phone [82]
Usability (Can the user interact with the visualization and understand its controls?)	Google Maps [73], Minimap [76], VisTiles [59], User Interactions with Scatterplots [15]
Feasibility (Can the data be collected/cleaned to power this visualization?)	OmniTrack [54], Mobile Health Mashups Pilot [85], Patterns of Everyday Life [29]
Understanding (Can a user understand the state of the data and what it represents?)	Whereabouts Clock [14], Motion Presence [8], GSparks [64], inAir [53], Ranges over Time [12], Animation vs. Small Multiple [11], GlucOracle [31], When(ish) is My Bus [52]
Reflection and Insights (Can a user learn new things from the visualization?)	TummyTrials [50], Lullaby [51], SleepTight [22], Tangere [77], Pass the Ball [75], VisualizedSelf [24], Orchard [33]
Behavior Change (Can the user change their behavior given accurate interpretations of the visualization?)	Health Mashups [7], UbiFit [28], UbiGreen [38], Fish'n'Steps [61], How to Nudge InSitu [48], BeWell [16], Glanceable Feedback for Physical Activity Tracker [41], WaterJewel [37], Persuasive Performance Feedback [23]

if a visualization is feasible. Can the appropriate amount and accuracy of data be collected to lead to meaningful experiences? These types of evaluations might have a participant collect data for several weeks, and then see what could be populated into their visualization to see if real-world data collection can power the design.

Understanding: The final three goals of mobile evaluation involve participants being able to take meaning away from the visualization. The most basic of these goals involves understanding the real-world meaning behind what they are seeing. Where the basic goal of perception is typically agnostic of the data (e.g., bar 1 is longer than bar 2), this goal involves understanding what the data actually means (e.g., you walked a little more on Tuesday compared to Wednesday).

Reflection and Insights: Moving beyond understanding comes reflection and data insights. Here, the goal is to see if participants can go beyond the data itself to uncover something more complex about their lives or the underlying data. For example, a participant might see that every Sunday he walks less than other days of the week, or that a particular variable is trending up or down over time.

Behavior Change: Finally, the most complex goal is understanding if participants are changing their behavior based on the visualization. In these evaluations, participants often live with a design in their life for weeks or months, and the goal is to see if the visualization leads them to change behaviors—to walk more, drink less, find a faster route through traffic, etc.

These six goals are not always explored in isolation. As we will discuss with the examples in the next section, often a project will span several goals—for example, exploring perception and understanding together, or data insights and behavior change together. However they do build on each other. If a given system does not meet the goals on the top of the list, then it will be very difficult to meet the more complex goals below. For example, if a person cannot perceive a difference or understand the data, it is quite unlikely that they can produce accurate data insights or change their behavior based on a trustworthy interpretation of the data.

6.5 EVALUATION METHODS

We will now move through Table 6.1, exploring example research projects as case studies under each evaluation goal as well as best practices for choosing methods, research participants, durations of studies, and evaluation metrics for each category.

6.5.1 Perception

One of the more fundamental criteria of a good visual display is whether it is perceptually legible. Activating the appropriate perceptual mechanisms is vital to identifying key aspects of a graph or a visualization. As such, designers can guide their choices based on low-level visual processing of the information display [90]. The perceptibility of visual information on mobile, often smaller displays, is distinct from our understanding of guidelines for presenting graphs on paper, or even on a fixed desktop screen. Often, visual content is consumed while moving or on-the-go and this alone can generate significant variability in terms of screen glare and color disturbance, as much data has to be compressed on a smaller display. Further, these visualizations frequently accommodate a primary task the user may be engaged with, such as jogging, and therefore users can possibly be less attentive to the display, making the need for fast and accurate perception of the data critical. The smaller display or displays of varying form-factors and resolutions further exacerbate the designer's task for identifying the optimal rules under which to display data. Under these constraints it is evident that a first stage that involves assessing the perceptual limits or perceptibility of a design is necessary for suitable mobile information displays.

Perceptual assessments were initially popular when mobile visual displays were primarily geared at showing spatial information, such as points-of-interest on a map [21]. For such a problem, choosing any non-trivial display can often result in portraying far too much in a small display region. A common approach involves filtering the data and navigating to elements of interest. However, this does not eliminate the necessity to visually parse through content, as it is cognitively demanding to pan and zoom through a display [15], but further also forces users to lose the global context when inspecting details. The small display in such types of datasets also results in placing content outside the display's viewport, also commonly referred to as off-screen content. Techniques such as Halos [4] resolve this concern by placing concentric circles centered at the off-screen points-of-interest. Furthermore, the Wedge [42] relies on the Gestalt principle of amodal completion [34] by providing a small section of the visible arc, along with two 'legs' that would form a triangle, with the tip placed at the off-screen object location. In validating their visualizations, the researchers resorted to asking participants to provide their best estimate of the off-screen target locations, but on an emulated mobile device presented on a desktop. While mobile emulation can assess the perceptual limits of such techniques, it lacks the degree of ecological validity needed to fully capture visualization when viewed on an actual mobile device. Furthermore, such perceptual tasks do not capture on-the-go contexts, as the targets were placed in static positions. To offer a more ecologically valid task, Gustafson and Irani [43] made the points-of-interest 'disappear' as would be common when the user would move through an environment. Their evaluation was also carried out on a mobile emulation, lacking the rigour needed to fully gauge the ability to quickly glance and perceive the visual changes on the screen.

While such earlier perceptual evaluations were geared at understanding the effectiveness of the visualizations, current interest for displaying content on mobile devices has predominantly focused toward the evaluation of data charts [10]. Graphs, including line graphs, bar charts and even pie or donut graphs, have gained recent popularity for their ability to scale in size while still preserving a general sense of the content. These are often displayed on very small smartwatch displays, for the general consumer interested in taking a peek at their heart rate or other measurable biometrics, often produced by the worn device. They are not spatially constrained, as with points-of-interest on a map, but yet have to portray as accurately as possible the underlying dataset. Producing generic guidelines for displaying content suitably on such small devices is challenging, as smartwatches are extremely limited in terms of pixel resolution. Yet, these visual displays need to be sufficiently glanceable (to enable quick perception of the key graph content). Furthermore, smartwatches being either circular or rectilinear add additional perceptual constraints on how best to present the graph [64].

Inspiration can be drawn from a wide number of visualization techniques that have been designed and proposed and that could be suitable for small screens. For example, that specifically compress data pixels along a given axis (usually the y-axis) have be adapted to displaying charts on small screens.

Drawing inspiration from techniques such as HorizonGraphs [79] and SparkLines [87], Neshati et al. introduced G-Sparks [64] that compresses the visual pixels to present as much as possible on a small screen. Their evaluations were carried out directly on a smartwatch display, thus offering a more ecological valid baseline for future designs. Similarly, Blascheck et al. performed a perceptual study that asked participants to compare data points from three chart types, on a smartwatch display, while seated a fixed distance away from the device [9]. The researchers sought to find out how quickly people can perform a very basic task—to ultimately understand whether certain charts might be useful in situations where people can only quickly glance at a watch (e.g., while doing sports, driving, etc.). Their results suggested that Bar and Donut charts performed similarly while Radial Bar charts performed the worst. They provide guidelines on the glanceability of such graphs for small displays.

Pushing the tradition of graphical perception experiments further, Brehmer et al. conducted a series of crowdsourced experiments on participants' mobile devices [12, 11]. They demonstrated that it is feasible to directly deploy experimental software on participants' mobile devices to run controlled experiments and to collect measures such as task completion time, error, and subjective feedback. To identify effective ways to present ranges over time on small displays, the researchers compared two visual encodings for time-oriented data—linear layout vs. radial layout, while also varying the data granularity, data sources, and task types [12]. In a later study, the researchers conducted a comparative evaluation of animation and small multiples for trend visualization on mobile devices [11]. In both studies, the research team leveraged Amazon Mechanical Turk (AMT), a popular crowdsource platform, to recruit about 100 participants. To ensure instruction compliance and data quality, various techniques (e.g., minimum instruction reading time, interruption monitoring) were embedded in the experimental platform. Participants recruited via AMT were in a range of physical settings using a diversity of devices, ideally being more reflective of when and where they would use their mobile device, with no physical presence of an observer watching them. Such a method comes with a loss in consistency, and like college student participants, crowdworkers constitute a specific demographic that may not be representative of the intended target population for the visualization. However, with quality control measures in place, mobile visualization evaluation applications deployed via crowdsourcing platforms have the edge in its capability to recruit many participants within a short time period.

Previously proposed studies evaluating the visual efficacy of common graphs on small displays often limit the assessment, for practical reasons, to only a few conditions. Namely, tasks given to participants require a comparison among different points, such as identifying the minimum or maximum within the graph, detecting the slope direction, or differences among points [9]. Such tasks have been commonly used for assessing the legibility of data graphs on typical displays. Furthermore, current devices are equipped with legacy visual designs, such as bar or line graphs. However, it is unclear whether these are also the best suited for tasks needed by participants wearing small displays. Amini et al. [1] sought to identify what may be common tasks participants could benefit from in mobile conditions, and how to support these visually. The authors collected such tasks from those already equipped with a smartwatch and asked designers to produce suitable visual presentations. Very few among these were considered standard among the visualizations used on such small displays. This exercise thus leads to rethinking our approach to evaluating visual designs, by first developing an initial understanding of commonly needed tasks, and then adapting our presentation to these.

6.5.2 Usability

As the mobile phone has become the de facto platform for people to access information, conducting usability evaluations in a mobile environment has become common as well. Usability evaluation is a critical step to ensure that the user interface designed for a mobile environment functions as we expect and meets the requirements of the end users. Tasks for mobile usability studies deal with *why* and *how* people interact with information on the screen, as well as *what* people enter [13]. In a traditional usability study, researchers measure how effectively or efficiently a system supports people's tasks, typically in a controlled lab setting [32]. Usability is measured through success rate (whether participants can perform the task at all), task completion time, error rate, and participant's subjective satisfaction [65]. Collecting such measures will help companies, researchers, or developers assess their original design in comparison to a redesign or a competitor' product, and help improve the design of the interface iteratively.

In comparison to evaluating desktop-based applications, usability testing for mobile is different in three aspects. First, special equipment (e.g., document camera, webcam) and software may be required to record the mobile screen, which would allow real-time projection and monitoring of the mobile screen. Sometimes, mobile (e.g., Eyezag [36]) and head-mounted (e.g., Tobii Pro [72]) eye-tracking devices are used to capture people's natural viewing behavior or "areas of interest." Incorporating eye-tracking in a usability evaluation, researchers can capture a comprehensive picture of people's experience with a mobile user interface, as in the case of Cheng et al.'s usability study, which was aimed to evaluate people's mobile browsing and searching behaviors on a mobile device [20].

Second, as mobile devices are used across a broad range of places and contexts (e.g., in the car, on the street, standing or walking), creating a realistic mobility testing environment with high ecological validity may be necessary. To create such usability testing environments, researchers have created simulated walking conditions using a treadmill (e.g., [62, 2]) or conducted studies on a closed course (e.g., hallway) (e.g., [63]). Notably, Kane et al. created a "Walking user interfaces" (WUIs) that adapt their layout (e.g., button sizes) when the participant is moving [49]). WUIs were evaluated in an outdoor public open plaza where other people besides the participant were frequently standing, walking, and interacting with one another. Hincapié-Ramos and Irani also designed WUIs, which provide safety visual cues of obstacles to prevent collision for those who use mobile phones while walking [45]. To evaluate the system in a realistic setting, participants were asked to walk down the university cafeteria where an "actor" was present to provoke potential collisions (e.g., cut the participants' path orthogonally) [45].

A third aspect of interest in mobile usability studies is the additional focus of the assessment—the different interaction repertoire available on or with mobile devices that are not available in desktop solutions. Such interactions include cross-device interaction techniques leveraging spatially-aware mobile devices to counteract the limited screen space of single mobile device [59]. In Langner et al.'s work, a preliminary usability testing was performed to get quick feedback on the key interaction concepts and workflow before they built the final prototype [59].

The number of participants recruited in these mobile usability studies are similar to that of typical usability study counterparts, ranging from 10 to 30 participants. Sometimes, mobile usability study can be done completely remotely on the participant's phone. In such a case, detailed logging or installing software (e.g., TeamViewer) to project participants' mobile screen is necessary to capture their behaviors.

Evaluating usability will always be an important step toward designing novel visualization systems. Using creative methods like the ones we mentioned above will particularly be helpful in situating and capturing people's realistic mobile experience with smartphones and smartwatches, providing us with useful insights that might have not been possible from employing traditional usability testing methods.

6.5.3 Feasibility

When developing a new visualization technique, or applying an established one to a new domain or means of data collection, evaluating if you can feasibly collect the amount and quality of data that you need to power the visualization is often necessary. Mobile visualizations add to this need since the data that powers the visualization is often collected from the phone or physical environment over time and can often be spotty or inaccurate due to the nature of consumer-grade mobile sensors. There are several aspects that researchers need to address when checking for the feasibility of a mobile visualization. These include compliance rates, retrieving data from sensors in real world situations, and data quality.

If a system involves participants needing to manually log or upload data, understanding the compliance rate is critical to understand if it will provide enough data, and that the data is not biased to particular days or times of day. For example, if participants only provide data in the evenings, it might not represent their behaviors throughout the day. Or if participants do not engage in providing data on weekends, key aspects of their lives may be left out. It is also important to ensure that you can collect enough data to power your visualization. If you need 100 data points, how long will it take participants to provide that many? What attrition might occur due to fatigue or lack of benefits until enough data is provided?

When evaluating a system that collects sensed data (e.g., heart rate, location), understanding the error rates, sampling frequencies, and battery impact to the device might be necessary in order to understand if a given visualization is feasible. Mobile sensors, such as location, often have error margins associated with them. Location in particular can have several hundreds of meters of error when indoors or when using network-based location technologies when saving power. Using GPS frequently could drain a participant's battery. Other sensors, such as pedometers might have greater than 20% error [86], or participants might not wear them every day or for every activity [27]. Feasibility evaluations can help researchers to understand the data that particular sensors can provide in real-world situations.

Since most visualizations require a certain amount or quality of data to function, it is critical to understand if your system will provide appropriate data before continuing on with a longer and likely more expensive field evaluation, for example those in the behavior change section below. It is also critical to be able to show or mimic realistic data when performing studies of visualization understanding (in the following subsection). Presenting participants with overly idealistic data will not lead to valid conclusions about how your system will function in the wild with real data.

Several methods can be used to check the feasibility of a visualization, mostly depending on where the data is coming from. If the data is coming from end users, these studies typically include pilot field studies where a small group of participants, typically around 10 to 15, interact with your system for a few weeks. It is important that these participants are representative of your target user base (e.g., in terms of education, data and smartphone literacy, age, physical abilities). If you are aiming for mass-market adoption, ensuring that 2/3 of your participants do not have a college degree is important, as well as age, gender, and racial balancing to match the broader population as closely as you can, as any of these demographic or cultural factors might impact compliance rates and overall data quality.

An example of a feasibility study is the pilot for the Health Mashups project [85]. In this study, ten participants used a system to collect data about their wellbeing from a variety of sensors for a 4-week baseline and 4-week study period. The goal was to understand if participants would provide enough data for statistically significant correlations to be made between streams of data, for example being able to tell a participant that they walk less on hot days or that they gain weight on Sundays. A reasonable amount of data was received from automatic tracking sources such as the Fitbit for step count and the scale for weight, however the researchers discovered that participants were not providing enough samples of manually logged data such as food intake or mood. As a result, a new mechanism was designed using silent push notifications for reminding participants to log these [6], which led to a significant increase in logging in the full study [7]. Without this feasibility study and resulting design change, time and money would have been wasted in running a larger and longer behavior change focused study, as enough data would not have been provided for these key aspects of wellbeing. This highlights the importance of checking more basic goals in the framework before moving on to the more complex goals.

In Omnitrack [54], researchers explored how a flexible, personalized tracking platform can support people's diverse tracking goals. Using OmniTrack, participants created their own tracking systems for a wide variety of goals (from tracking beer drinking to quality of sleep) and used the trackers during the two-week field study. The field study showed the feasibility of a personalized tracking approach in terms of compliance and the amount of data collected. Correia et al. [29], in another example of an evaluation to measure feasibility, had participants use a location-capturing app for four days, and then looked to see if the data was sufficient to power their visualization showing patterns of everyday life.

Whitlock et al. [91] illustrated another way to assess a visualization's feasibility, among other measures. The researchers developed a visual analytics system, deployed on mobile devices, to assist with data gathering in the field in domains such as earth science and emergency response. They used a form of expert review to evaluate their prototype. More specifically, they demonstrated the system to ten field analysts and had each work through example tasks and scenarios. Finally, the researchers conducted in-depth interviews with each analyst to gauge their response to and opinions about the system.

These examples highlight the need to ensure that mobile systems can capture enough data with high enough accuracy in order to power a particular mobile visualization. Ensuring the users or the device can, in typical use, provide meaningful amounts of data is critical before moving on to later, more complex goals. Most importantly, this step gives researchers an idea of the amount of data needed to power the system, such that later evaluations can be designed around typical data that the system would provide, and not idealistic designs that might be more precise or contain more data than the system would produce when running in the wild with a diverse population of users in everyday conditions.

6.5.4 Understanding

After knowing that gathering the data for a given visualization is feasible, it is then necessary to know if users can understand the data presented within that visualization. Beyond just perceiving differences in bars or data (e.g., the bar on the right is smaller than the one on the left), these evaluations seek to understand if typical users can understand what the data actually means (e.g., I walked fewer steps today compared to yesterday) for realistic data sets with data density similar to what was shown to be feasible.

Often, studies with these goals will deploy a combination of in-lab or online evaluation and short-term field studies with the goal of understanding how participants perceive the data that is shown. Can they answer specific questions about the data itself after seeing the visualization? Do they understand the meaning of the various bars or charts present in the visualization? Again, in these types of studies, it is important that the participants who participate are representative of your target user base. If you intend to release your system to the general public, that means that two-thirds of your participants should not have college degrees and they should span a wide range of ages and ethnic backgrounds. Since a significant proportion of adults cannot interpret a standard time-series graph [39], it is critical to get a sample of participants that matches the broader population for solutions intended to be used outside of elite circles of trained and data-literate professionals. As Peck et al. [69] show that including rural participants and those of varying educational and political backgrounds can yield diverse reactions to understanding and engaging with visualizations.

Simple studies can involve in-lab study or online studies that ask participants to onboard to a system via a natural means (e.g., downloading and installing an app, signing up on a website) and then looking at a visualization in the context of that experience and explaining what it is showing. Thereafter, specific pointed questions might be asked to ensure that participants understand what they are seeing. These types of studies can often be conducted with a few dozen diverse participants from outside of an academic environment.

On the other end of study complexity, systems can be deployed in the lives of users, and interviews can be conducted after a participant engages with a system for several days or weeks. This might be necessary if the data that is collected needs to be related to a user's life, such as with health data such as step counts. Participants should be able to understand what a visualization says about their own life and activities, which might be easier than looking at abstract data in a lab setting that is not related to their own experience.

Examples of these types of studies include "When(ish) is my bus" [52], where participants saw a probabilistic distribution of bus arrival times. In this study, participants were asked real-world questions such as if they had enough time to get a coffee before the bus was likely to arrive, rating the chance that the bus would show up within the next 10 minutes. The researchers had 500 participants view this visualization online and respond to these questions about data understanding. Consolvo et al. [28] explored the understandability of their Ubifit Garden visualization, prior to a larger field study focused on behavior change, through an online survey with 75 diverse participants.

Another example of this style of testing is the evaluation conducted for the Tangere visualization system [78] running on iPad tablets. Tangere supported up to three simultaneous views of scatterplot, barchart, and line graph visualizations. In this evaluation [77], participants received a set of 12 tasks (questions to answer) about a beverage sales data set. What was unique about this evaluation was that it was a "discoverability-focused" study. The researchers argued that for mobile interfaces running on a tablet, most people would not spend time working through tutorials and user manuals. Instead, they would simply open the interface and start working. Thus, the researchers followed a protocol just like that—participants only had a very short exposure to the system interface before attempting the tasks. Ultimately, the study provided significant qualitative data about the discoverability, learnability, and usability of interface gestures in terms of supporting how data was understood, as well as insights about the design of specific interactive operations.

The evaluation of Tangere utilized minimal onboarding, instead focusing on discoverability. Brehmer et al. have conducted studies in which they introduced participants to a visualization with incremental tutorials and asked screening questions to assess whether the participants understood how to read the visualization before proceeding with the experimental tasks [12, 11]. Onboarding user interfaces and tutorial tasks are common in (mobile) games, and it is worth considering how visualization designers evaluate comparable aspects of mobile apps that feature visualization.

Studies focused on measuring user understanding can also include exploring how users understand limitations or missing data for responsive visualizations. As discussed in Chapter 2, the responsiveness of a mobile visualization is its ability to adapt to different screen sizes and configurations. Responsive visualization design strategies include reducing the amount of data to show, aggregation, and changing the encoding. The designers of a mobile visualization may wonder whether a user on a mobile interface that omits key data points comes to the same understanding of the data as a user who views that same dataset on a desktop interface. But how should one evaluate the responsiveness of visualization? An evaluation strategy could involve quantifying the difference in the amount of information conveyed by visualization on a larger display and the amount of information conveyed on a mobile display. An example of this type of study is Schwab et al.'s evaluation of pan and zoom timelines and sliders in which they experimentally compare interaction alternatives on both desktop and mobile platforms [83].

The trickiest thing to get right with these types of studies is the research protocol. Making sure that questions are not leading, represent real world scenarios, and do not give away answers to future questions is key. The When(ish) is my bus study was a good example of this, asking real world questions about having enough time to get a coffee instead of priming users to understand that the visualization was showing variance in arrival time or giving hints about what either axis represented. Thinking about what you want the user to be able to accomplish with the visualization and ask about those real world goals instead of focusing on specifics of the visualization itself can ensure that you are measuring true user understanding of the visualization and not their ability to follow researcher directions.

6.5.5 Reflection and Insights

The utility of visualizations is greater than a mere conveyance of data. As shown in Table 6.1, many of the visualizations are designed to aid in awareness, decision making, or behavior change for the general audiences. Just because people can "comprehend" visualization does not necessarily mean that they can act on it. Visualizations may facilitate such transition from comprehension to action by supporting people to reflect on the data and generate insights from it. As such, we can assess visualizations' effectiveness by measuring its ability to support the process of self-reflection [24] and insight generation [66].

Visualization systems' capability to facilitate self-reflection has been studied in the personal data visualization contexts, in which people interact with the data about themselves, often with mobile and wearable devices. In prior works, researchers conceptualized different types of self-reflection (e.g., reflection-in-action vs. reflection-on-action [71]) and employed a variety of approaches to facilitate self-reflection, the outcome of which is personal insights. For example, Choe et al. designed a visual data exploration platform called Visualized Self that integrates personal data from multiple sources and promotes self-reflection [24]. Through an in-lab, think-aloud study, the researchers identified common personal insight types (e.g., external context, confirmation, contradiction, comparison, value judgment) people generated from interacting with Visualized Self. In Karkar et al.'s work, the authors proposed a framework for self-experimentation and designed a mobile application that provides personal insights on triggers for irritable bowel syndrome (IBS) [50]. In the same domain of providing individualized insights for IBS patients, Chung et al. explored the use of lightweight food diaries, which helped both patients and experts develop individualized, actionable plans and strategies [25]. In all of the works above, people's active involvement in data collection and exploration were essential in promoting self-reflection, which led to personalized insights.

In the visualization community, North suggested "insight-based evaluation" as a practical alternative to traditional evaluation methods (e.g., usability test, controlled experiment) [66]. Insight-based evaluation aims to directly capture insight while preserving the positive aspects of the traditional evaluation methods: participants are given initial questions, but they are encouraged to freely explore the data going beyond the initial question until they feel that they have learned everything from a given dataset. During this task, participants—typically domain experts—verbalize their findings, which are later segmented as an insight occurrence and coded based on a variety of metrics, such as insight category, complexity, time to generate, and errors. Insight-based evaluation is in general more time consuming than traditional experiments for both evaluators and participants. However, it can provide rich understanding on visualization's effectiveness in helping people generate insights.

While there is no seminal example of insight-based evaluation of mobile visualization, we believe such a method can be particularly helpful in evaluating domain-specific mobile information visualization targeting a specific group (e.g., patients, domain experts), or when there is no reasonable and fair counterpart to compare against the mobile device. For example, in evaluating personal informatics applications, we can tag insight-based evaluation onto a field deployment study, especially during the exit interview by asking what new insights the tool has enabled people to generate. In this way, participants can share new insights they gained throughout interacting with the new tool over a prolonged period, which can subsequently be analyzed based on the meaningful criteria for the domain.

6.5.6 Behavior Change

As with many interactive computing systems, the ultimate goal of many mobile visualizations is to assist people in achieving some goals through action. These goals and actions can vary greatly depending on the focus and purpose of the visualization. As a result, studies that focus on evaluating the impact of mobile visualizations on people's actions vary in their characteristics. There are a number of considerations that often influence the design of evaluation studies that focus on influencing people's action.

Depending on the type of action the visualizations aim to support, the timeframe of an evaluation study may vary from short-term to longitudinal. For example, for visualizations that aim to influence purchasing behaviors that are often made in the moment, evaluation studies could examine the immediate impact of visualization on individuals' purchasing choice. Following this idea, Kalnikaite et al. evaluated the impact of lambent devices that deliver salient information while shopping on individuals' purchases [48]; while this study included two separate shopping trips, the researchers captured each purchasing decision made while using the visualization. However, studies that focus on changing lifestyle behaviors and habits require considerably longer timeframes, on the order of months, as lifestyle behaviors change slowly. This applies, for example, to visualizations that target health behaviors, such as sleep, exercise, or diet. The evaluation study by King et al. [55] examined the impact of mobile visualizations on individuals exercise and sleep pattern in a study that included a 3-week run-in period and 8-week evaluation period.

Another important consideration is the setting in which the study is conducted. To a large degree, studies that aim to examine the impact of mobile visualizations on actions, choices, and behaviors are conducted in naturalistic settings and in the context where such decisions are typically made [19]. This approach allows researchers to minimize the impact of laboratory settings and argue for ecological validity of their findings. While, arguably, it is possible to evaluate such impact in controlled settings, the ecological validity of such studies will be limited.

In some cases, achievement of goals can be measured with standardized and validated questionnaires, which could be deployed at the baseline and upon completion of the study. For example, if users' goals include changes in psycho-social characteristics, such as self-efficacy, or changes in opinions and perceptions, such as satisfaction, there exist multiple validated questionnaires for measuring these outcomes in a reliable and consistent manner. However, oftentimes, for studies that target changes in users' behaviors, it becomes necessary to capture these target behaviors and objectively assess individuals' achievement of their goals. Gouveia et al. [40] evaluated the impact of a glanceable display of physical activity on individuals' achievement of personal activity goals as measured by the number of steps captured in a 28-day study.

In cases when researchers wish to evaluate the ability of visualization to influence users' behaviors, it is important to use a study design that allows one to differentiate between the impact of the visualization from other factors, for example from a simple influence of participating in a research study. In these cases, it often becomes necessary to introduce a control group, in which participants are exposed to all the other aspects of being in the study, but are not exposed to the mobile visualization under evaluation. Furthermore, randomizing participants into a control group and an experimental group helps to minimize potential differences between groups due to other factors, such as age, gender, or experience with technology. These study designs are typically called between-subject studies. An alternative approach allows researchers to use a single group, but randomize participants into receiving or not receiving an intervention, at different times, and comparing participants behaviors with and without the intervention [57]. These designs are often called micro-randomization. While these designs are not common for evaluating mobile visualizations, they are often used to evaluate other types of mobile technologies for behavior change. While not all evaluation studies rely on a comparison with a control group, simpler one-group pre-post study designs provide less reliable results.

Finally, another critical consideration is the strength of evidence needed to support researchers' claims, which determines the scale of the study and the rigor with which it was conducted. If the main goal of the researchers is to assert whether the visualization can have the intended impact in a limited setting and under a certain set of conditions, they may be able to support these claims with a small study. The majority of studies of mobile visualizations we reviewed would fall into this category. However, stronger claims that may suggest that such visualizations are ready for wide-scale dissemination and adoption require larger-scale studies with tests of statistical significance of their results, and analysis of statistical power.

Of all the evaluation studies reviewed in this chapter, these studies are typically the most challenging and expensive to conduct. They require full implementation of the mobile visualization in a robust enough way to be used by multiple individuals over extended periods of time. Furthermore, they may require additional development costs if researchers wish to isolate the impact of the visualization itself from the impact of the application that hosts the visualization. In this case, the researchers may need two versions of the application, one with the visualization and one without. However, these types of evaluation studies also provide the most direct evidence as to the ability of mobile visualizations to achieve their intended purpose and help their users achieve their goals. At the same time, we urge researchers and practitioners to not jump into a study to assess a system's impact on behavior change. As we discussed in Section 6.4, even though the system's ultimate goal is to demonstrate behavior change in the long term, if a given system does not meet the basic goals, such as perception, usability, and feasibility, it will be very difficult to meet the more complex goals such as behavior change. Klasnja et al. also discuss the importance of separating these different goals for different stages of design and indicate that HCI contributions should focus on efficacy evaluations that are tailored to a specific behavior change technique because results from such studies can provide in-depth insights on *why* and **how** a certain design decision works [56].

6.6 DISCUSSION

In this chapter, we have reviewed a rich spectrum of goals for evaluating mobile visualizations that come from multiple academic disciplines. Each of these approaches can solve specific needs and research questions that projects may have in various states of their development. As more basic goals need to be met before more complex goals can be tackled, we hope that this review can encourage researchers to adapt methods from adjacent disciplines to move evaluation beyond one specific goal to explore more complex goals along the spectrum.

We have explored the new constraints that mobile brings to the evaluation of visualizations, including issues with data capture in the wild and the wide variety of different handsets that users might have (and their differences in screen resolution, size, brightness, default font size, and other device or user setting characteristics) that can add complexity to establishing validity of results for real-world situations.

In addition, when translating to mobile use by everyday people, some aspects of evaluation may need to be simplified from studies focused on desktop or large display-based visualizations aimed at professionals. Tasks such as identifying the extreme values (e.g., max, min) and trends are perhaps not the most important things to understand about a visualization in a mobile application intended for the mass-market. Instead, tasks for mobile visualization are more personal and about users being able to understand what the visualization means for their life over understanding raw numbers, identifying trends, or statistics.

We hope that researchers will use our framework and progression of goals in order to better align their evaluation with the stage of their research. By answering more basic questions first such as perception and feasibility, researchers can fail faster and earlier in the process by understanding basic deficiencies in design before progressing to longer multi-week field studies. This framework can also help researchers to better tailor research methods to the specific stage of their development and types of research questions that they seek to answer.

Finally, there are new considerations to take into account when conducting mobile visualization research. The first is the participants that you choose to recruit. For example, if your design is meant to be used by wider populations, ensuring that your participants have a variety of educational backgrounds and that they are varied in age and are gender-balanced can help ensure that your design can be used by all. Whereas traditional visualization evaluations typically employ targeted recruiting (e.g., those with a certain level of visualization literacy, college/graduate students, data analysts), recruiting a broader spectrum of user groups may be important for evaluating mobile applications that convey quantitative information pertaining to weather, news, personal health, finance, and other topics of pertinence to the wider population.

Second, there may be additional safety and human subjects considerations to take into account. If you are collecting data over multiple weeks from a user's own handset, laws such as GDPR [35] and CCPA [5] might apply. You may need to make sure data is anonymized and encrypted in transit and stored in a safe location with limited access. The data you are collecting might also be sensitive, potentially including health or location data of the user. Participants' physical safety may be another concern if you are having them use your design while walking or exercising.

However, regardless of these potential difficulties, we would like to stress that real world conditions are so different from a lab, and that learnings from evaluation in real contexts are so important that giving up the control of a lab experiment is often the best course. Having real users engage with a visualization using their own data in their own settings on their own devices can show you if your visualization is valid for real people in the world, which is much more powerful than stating that it only works in a very controlled lab setting for a very biased subset of the population.

We hope that this framework of six evaluation goals can help researchers to pick the best methods for their goals, and to answer research questions related to goals in a logical order as their project progresses.

REFERENCES

[1] Amini, F., Hasan, K., Bunt, A., and Irani, P. "Data Representations for In-Situ Exploration of Health and Fitness Data". In: *Proceedings of the Conference on Pervasive Computing Technologies for Healthcare (PervasiveHealth)*. ACM, 2017, pp. 163–172 (cited on page 187).

[2] Barnard, L., Yi, J. S., Jacko, J. A., and Sears, A. "Capturing the Effects of Context on Human Performance in Mobile Computing Systems". In: *Personal and Ubiquitous Computing* 11.2 (2007), pp. 81–96 (cited on page 188).

[3] Barrett, L. F. and Barrett, D. J. "An Introduction to Computerized Experience Sampling in Psychology". In: *Social Science Computer Review* 19.2 (2001), pp. 175–185 (cited on page 182).

[4]   Baudisch, P. and Rosenholtz, R. "Halo: A Technique for Visualizing Off-Screen Objects". In: *Proceedings of the Conference on Human Factors in Computing Systems (CHI)*. **Open Access version:** https://www.researchgate.net/ publication/2557993_Halo_a_Technique_for_Visualizing_Off-Screen_ Locations. ACM, 2003, pp. 481–488. DOI: 10.1145/642611.642695 (cited on page 186).

[5]   Becerra, X. *California Consumer Privacy Act (CCPA)*. Website. Accessed: 2020-03-17. 2019. URL: https://oag.ca.gov/privacy/ccpa (cited on page 197).

[6]   Bentley, F. and Tollmar, K. "The Power of Mobile Notifications to Increase Wellbeing Logging Behavior". In: *Proceedings of the Conference on Human Factors in Computing Systems (CHI)*. CHI '13. Paris, France: ACM, 2013, pp. 1095–1098. DOI: 10.1145/2470654.2466140. URL: https://doi.org/10. 1145/2470654.2466140 (cited on page 190).

[7]   Bentley, F., Tollmar, K., Stephenson, P., Levy, L., Jones, B., Robertson, S., Price, E., Catrambone, R., and Wilson, J. "Health Mashups: Presenting Statistical Patterns Between Wellbeing Data and Context in Natural Language to Promote Behavior Change". In: *Transactions on Computer-Human Interaction (TOCHI)* 20.5 (Nov. 2013). DOI: 10.1145/2503823 (cited on pages 184, 190).

[8]   Bentley, F. R. and Metcalf, C. J. "Sharing Motion Information With Close Family and Friends". In: *Proceedings of the Conference on Human Factors in Computing Systems (CHI)*. CHI '07. San Jose, California, USA: ACM, 2007, pp. 1361–1370. DOI: 10.1145/1240624.1240831. URL: https://doi.org/10. 1145/1240624.1240831 (cited on page 184).

[9]   Blascheck, T., Besançon, L., Bezerianos, A., Lee, B., and Isenberg, P. "Glanceable Visualization: Studies of Data Comparison Performance on Smartwatches". In: *Transactions on Visualization and Computer Graphics (TVCG)* 25.1 (Jan. 2018). **Open Access version:** https://hal.inria.fr/hal-01851306, pp. 630–640. DOI: 10.1109/TVCG.2018.2865142 (cited on pages 184, 186, 187).

[10]   Blumenstein, K., Niederer, C., Wagner, M., Schmiedl, G., Rind, A., and Aigner, W. "Evaluating Information Visualization on Mobile Devices: Gaps and Challenges in the Empirical Evaluation Design Space". In: *Proceedings of the Workshop on BEyond Time and Errors: Novel Evaluation Methods for Information Visualization (BELIV)*. **Open Access version:** http://mc. fhstp.ac.at/sites/default/files/publications/postprint-id11.pdf. ACM, 2016, pp. 125–132. DOI: 10.1145/2993901.2993906 (cited on page 186).

[11]   Brehmer, M., Lee, B., Isenberg, P., and Choe, E. "A Comparative Evaluation of Animation and Small Multiples for Trend Visualization on Mobile Phones". In: *Transactions on Visualization and Computer Graphics (TVCG)* 26.1 (2020). **Open Access version:** https://hal.inria.fr/hal-02317687, pp. 364–374. DOI: 10.1109/TVCG.2019.2934397 (cited on pages 184, 187, 192).

[12] Brehmer, M., Lee, B., Isenberg, P., and Choe, E. "Visualizing Ranges Over Time on Mobile Phones: A Task-Based Crowdsourced Evaluation". In: *Transactions on Visualization and Computer Graphics (TVCG)* 25.1 (Jan. 2019). **Open Access version:** https://hal.inria.fr/hal-01857469, pp. 619–629. DOI: 10.1109/TVCG.2018.2865234 (cited on pages 184, 187, 192).

[13] Brehmer, M. and Munzner, T. "A Multi-Level Typology of Abstract Visualization Tasks". In: *Transactions on Visualization and Computer Graphics (TVCG)* 19.12 (Dec. 2013). **Open Access version:** http://www.cs.ubc.ca/labs/imager/tr/2013/MultiLevelTaskTypology/, pp. 2376–2385. DOI: 10.1109/TVCG.2013.124 (cited on page 188).

[14] Brown, B., Taylor, A. S., Izadi, S., Sellen, A., Kaye, J. ", and Eardley, R. "Locating Family Values: A Field Trial of the Whereabouts Clock". In: *Proceedings of the Conference on Ubiquitous Computing (Ubicomp)*. UbiComp '07. Innsbruck, Austria: Springer, 2007, pp. 354–371. DOI: 10.5555/1771592.1771613 (cited on page 184).

[15] Buering, T., Gerken, J., and Reiterer, H. "User Interaction With Scatterplots on Small Screens - A Comparative Evaluation of Geometric-Semantic Zoom and Fisheye Distortion". In: *Transactions on Visualization and Computer Graphics (TVCG)* 12.5 (Sept. 2006), pp. 829–836. DOI: 10.1109/TVCG.2006.187. URL: https://doi.org/10.1109/TVCG.2006.187 (cited on pages 184, 185).

[16] Buman, M. P., Epstein, D. R., Gutierrez, M., Herb, C., Hollingshead, K., Huberty, J. L., Hekler, E. B., Vega-López, S., Ohri-Vachaspati, P., Hekler, A. C., and Baldwin, C. M. "BeWell24: Development and Process Evaluation of a Smartphone "App" to Improve Sleep, Sedentary, and Active Behaviors in US Veterans With Increased Metabolic Risk". In: *Translational Behavioral Medicine* 6.3 (Nov. 2015), pp. 438–448. DOI: 10.1007/s13142-015-0359-3 (cited on page 184).

[17] Bureau, U. S. C. *Educational Attainment in the United States: 2018*. https://www.census.gov/data/tables/2018/demo/education-attainment/cps-detailed-tables.html. Accessed: 2020-03-17. 2019 (cited on page 179).

[18] Carpendale, S. "Evaluating Information Visualizations". In: *Information Visualization: Human-Centered Issues and Perspectives*. Edited by Kerren, A., Stasko, J. T., Fekete, J.-D., and North, C. Berlin, Heidelberg: Springer, 2008, pp. 19–45 (cited on pages 178, 180).

[19] Carter, S., Mankoff, J., Klemmer, S. R., and Matthews, T. "Exiting the Cleanroom: On Ecological Validity and Ubiquitous Computing". In: *Human-Computer Interaction* 23.1 (2008), pp. 47–99 (cited on page 195).

[20] Cheng, S. "The Research Framework of Eye-Tracking Based Mobile Device Usability Evaluation". In: *Proceedings of the Workshop on Pervasive Eye Tracking & Mobile Eye-Based Interaction (PETMEI)*. ACM, 2011, pp. 21–26. DOI: 10.1145/2029956.2029964 (cited on page 188).

[21] Chittaro, L. "Visualizing Information on Mobile Devices". In: *Computer* 39.3 (Mar. 2006). **Open Access version:** http://hcilab.uniud.it/images/ stories / publications / 2006 – 03 / VisualizingInformationMobile _ IEEECOMPUTER . pdf, pp. 40–45. DOI: 10 . 1109 / MC . 2006 . 109 (cited on page 185).

[22] Choe, E. K., Lee, B., Kay, M., Pratt, W., and Kientz, J. A. "SleepTight: Low-Burden, Self-Monitoring Technology for Capturing and Reflecting on Sleep Behaviors". In: *Proceedings of the Joint Conference on Pervasive and Ubiquitous Computing (Ubicomp)*. UbiComp '15. Osaka, Japan: ACM, 2015, pp. 121–132. DOI: 10.1145/2750858.2804266. URL: https://doi.org/10. 1145/2750858.2804266 (cited on page 184).

[23] Choe, E. K., Lee, B., Munson, S., Pratt, W., and Kientz, J. "Persuasive Performance Feedback: The Effect of Framing on Self-Efficacy". In: *American Medical Informatics Association Annual Symposium Proceedings*. **Open Access version:** https://www.ncbi.nlm.nih.gov/pmc/articles/PMC3900219/. American Medical Informatics Association, 2013, pp. 825–833 (cited on page 184).

[24] Choe, E. K., Lee, B., Zhu, H., Riche, N. H., and Baur, D. "Understanding Self-Reflection: How People Reflect on Personal Data Through Visual Data Exploration". In: *Proceedings of the Conference on Pervasive Computing Technologies for Healthcare (PervasiveHealth)*. ACM, 2017, pp. 173–182. DOI: 10.1145/3154862.3154881 (cited on pages 184, 193).

[25] Chung, C.-F., Wang, Q., Schroeder, J., Cole, A., Zia, J., Fogarty, J., and Munson, S. A. "Identifying and Planning for Individualized Change: Patient-Provider Collaboration Using Lightweight Food Diaries in Healthy Eating and Irritable Bowel Syndrome". In: *Proceedings of the ACM on Interactive, Mobile, Wearable and Ubiquitous Technologies (IMWUT)* 3.1 (2019), pp. 1–27 (cited on page 193).

[26] Consolvo, S., Bentley, F. R., Hekler, E. B., and Phatak, S. S. *Mobile User Research: A Practical Guide*. Morgan & Claypool, 2017. DOI: 10 . 2200 / S00763ED1V01Y201703MPC012 (cited on page 182).

[27] Consolvo, S., Everitt, K., Smith, I., and Landay, J. A. "Design Requirements for Technologies That Encourage Physical Activity". In: *Proceedings of the Conference on Human Factors in Computing Systems (CHI)*. CHI '06. Montréal, Québec, Canada: ACM, 2006, pp. 457–466. DOI: 10.1145/1124772.1124840. URL: https://doi.org/10.1145/1124772.1124840 (cited on page 189).

[28] Consolvo, S., Libby, R., Smith, I., Landay, J., McDonald, D., Toscos, T., Chen, M., Froehlich, J., Harrison, B., Klasnja, P., LaMarca, A., and LeGrand, L. "Activity Sensing in the Wild: A Field Trial of Ubifit Garden". In: *Proceedings of the Conference on Human Factors in Computing Systems (CHI)*. ACM, 2008, pp. 1797–1806. DOI: 10.1145/1357054.1357335 (cited on pages 184, 192).

[29] Correia, N., Rodrigues, A., Amorim, T., Hawkey, J., and Oliveira, S. "A Mobile System to Visualize Patterns of Everyday Life". In: *Proceedings of the Symposium on Ambient Intelligence*. Springer, 2011, pp. 241–245 (cited on pages 184, 190).

[30] Csikszentmihalyi, M. and Larson, R. "Validity and Reliability of the Experience-Sampling Method". In: *Flow and the Foundations of Positive Psychology: The Collected Works of Mihaly Csikszentmihalyi*. Dordrecht: Springer, 1987, pp. 35–54. DOI: 10.1007/978-94-017-9088-8_3. URL: https://doi.org/10.1007/978-94-017-9088-8_3 (cited on page 182).

[31] Desai, P. M., Levine, M. E., Albers, D. J., and Mamykina, L. "Pictures Worth a Thousand Words: Reflections on Visualizing Personal Blood Glucose Forecasts for Individuals With Type 2 Diabetes". In: *Proceedings of the Conference on Human Factors in Computing Systems (CHI)*. CHI '18. Montreal QC, Canada: ACM, 2018. DOI: 10.1145/3173574.3174112. URL: https://doi.org/10.1145/3173574.3174112 (cited on page 184).

[32] Dix, A., Dix, A. J., Finlay, J., Abowd, G. D., and Beale, R. *Human-Computer Interaction*. Pearson Education, 2003 (cited on page 188).

[33] Eichmann, P., Edge, D., Evans, N., Lee, B., Brehmer, M., and White, C. "Orchard: Exploring Multivariate Heterogeneous Networks on Mobile Phones". In: *Computer Graphics Forum* 39.3 (2020), pp. 115–126. DOI: 10.1111/cgf.13967 (cited on page 184).

[34] Elder, J. and Zucker, S. "The Effect of Contour Closure on the Rapid Discrimination of Two-Dimensional Shapes". In: *Vision Research* 33.7 (1993), pp. 981–991 (cited on page 186).

[35] European Commission. *EU Data Protection Rules*. Law. Accessed: 2020-03-17. 2018. URL: https://ec.europa.eu/info/priorities/justice-and-fundamental-rights/data-protection/2018-reform-eu-data-protection-rules/eu-data-protection-rules_en (cited on page 197).

[36] Eyezag. *Eye Tracking on Mobile Devices*. Website. Accessed 2020-03-17. URL: https://eyezag.com/eye-tracking/mobile/ (cited on page 188).

[37] Fortmann, J., Cobus, V., Heuten, W., and Boll, S. "WaterJewel: Design and Evaluation of a Bracelet to Promote a Better Drinking Behaviour". In: *Proceedings of the Conference on Mobile and Ubiquitous Multimedia (MUM)*. MUM '14. Melbourne, Victoria, Australia: ACM, 2014, pp. 58–67. DOI: 10.1145/2677972.2677976 (cited on page 184).

[38] Froehlich, J., Dillahunt, T., Klasnja, P., Mankoff, J., Consolvo, S., Harrison, B., and Landay, J. A. "UbiGreen: Investigating a Mobile Tool for Tracking and Supporting Green Transportation Habits". In: *Proceedings of the Conference on Human Factors in Computing Systems (CHI)*. CHI '09. Boston, MA, USA: ACM, 2009, pp. 1043–1052. DOI: 10.1145/1518701.1518861. URL: https://doi.org/10.1145/1518701.1518861 (cited on page 184).

[39]   Galesic, M. and Garcia-Retamero, R. "Graph Literacy: A Cross-Cultural Comparison". In: *Medical Decision Making* 31.3 (2011), pp. 444–457 (cited on pages 179, 191).

[40]   Gouveia, R., Pereira, F., Karapanos, E., Munson, S., and Hassenzahl, M. "Exploring the Design Space of Glanceable Feedback for Physical Activity Trackers". In: *Proceedings of the Joint Conference on Pervasive and Ubiquitous Computing (Ubicomp)*. ACM, 2016, pp. 144–155 (cited on page 195).

[41]   Gouveia, R., Pereira, F., Karapanos, E., Munson, S. A., and Hassenzahl, M. "Exploring the Design Space of Glanceable Feedback for Physical Activity Trackers". In: *Proceedings of the Joint Conference on Pervasive and Ubiquitous Computing (Ubicomp)*. UbiComp '16. Heidelberg, Germany: ACM, 2016, pp. 144–155. DOI: 10.1145/2971648.2971754 (cited on page 184).

[42]   Gustafson, S., Baudisch, P., Gutwin, C., and Irani, P. "Wedge: Clutter-Free Visualization of Off-Screen Locations". In: *Proceedings of the Conference on Human Factors in Computing Systems (CHI)*. ACM, 2008, pp. 787–796 (cited on page 186).

[43]   Gustafson, S. G. and Irani, P. P. "Comparing Visualizations for Tracking Off-Screen Moving Targets". In: *Extended Abstracts of the Conference on Human Factors in Computing System (CHI)*. ACM, 2007, pp. 2399–2404 (cited on page 186).

[44]   Hekler, E. B., Klasnja, P., Froehlich, J. E., and Buman, M. P. "Mind the Theoretical Gap: Interpreting, Using, and Developing Behavioral Theory in HCI Research". In: *Proceedings of the Conference on Human Factors in Computing Systems (CHI)*. CHI '13. Paris, France: ACM, 2013, pp. 3307–3316. DOI: 10.1145/2470654.2466452. URL: https://doi.org/10.1145/2470654.2466452 (cited on page 182).

[45]   Hincapié-Ramos, J. D. and Irani, P. "CrashAlert: Enhancing Peripheral Alertness for Eyes-Busy Mobile Interaction While Walking". In: *Proceedings of the Conference on Human Factors in Computing Systems (CHI)*. ACM, 2013, pp. 3385–3388. DOI: 10.1145/2470654.2466463 (cited on page 188).

[46]   Holtzblatt, K. and Beyer, H. *Contextual Design: Defining Customer-Centered Systems*. Elsevier, 1997 (cited on page 182).

[47]   Isenberg, T., Isenberg, P., Chen, J., Sedlmair, M., and Möller, T. "A Systematic Review on the Practice of Evaluating Visualization". In: *Transactions on Visualization and Computer Graphics (TVCG)* 19.12 (2013). **Open Access version:** https://hal.inria.fr/hal-00846775, pp. 2818–2827. DOI: 10.1109/TVCG.2013.126 (cited on page 181).

[48]   Kalnikaite, V., Rogers, Y., Bird, J., Villar, N., Bachour, K., Payne, S., Todd, P. M., Schöning, J., Krüger, A., and Kreitmayer, S. "How to Nudge in Situ: Designing Lambent Devices to Deliver Salient Information in Supermarkets". In: *Proceedings of the Conference on Ubiquitous Computing (Ubicomp)*. UbiComp

'11. Beijing, China: ACM, 2011, pp. 11–20. DOI: 10.1145/2030112.2030115 (cited on pages 184, 194).

[49] Kane, S. K., Wobbrock, J. O., and Smith, I. E. "Getting Off the Treadmill: Evaluating Walking User Interfaces for Mobile Devices in Public Spaces". In: *Proceedings of the Conference on Human Computer Interaction with Mobile Devices and Services (MobileHCI)*. ACM, 2008, pp. 109–118 (cited on page 188).

[50] Karkar, R., Schroeder, J., Epstein, D. A., Pina, L. R., Scofield, J., Fogarty, J., Kientz, J. A., Munson, S. A., Vilardaga, R., and Zia, J. "TummyTrials: A Feasibility Study of Using Self-Experimentation to Detect Individualized Food Triggers". In: *Proceedings of the Conference on Human Factors in Computing Systems (CHI)*. **Open Access version:** https://depstein.net/assets/pubs/rkarkar_chi17.pdf. Denver, Colorado, USA: ACM, 2017, pp. 6850–6863. DOI: 10.1145/3025453.3025480 (cited on pages 184, 193).

[51] Kay, M., Choe, E. K., Shepherd, J., Greenstein, B., Watson, N., Consolvo, S., and Kientz, J. A. "Lullaby: A Capture & Access System for Understanding the Sleep Environment". In: *Proceedings of the Conference on Ubiquitous Computing (Ubicomp)*. UbiComp '12. **Open Access version:** https://www.researchgate.net/publication/261849983. Pittsburgh, Pennsylvania: ACM, 2012, pp. 226–234. DOI: 10.1145/2370216.2370253 (cited on page 184).

[52] Kay, M., Kola, T., Hullman, J. R., and Munson, S. A. "When (Ish) Is My Bus? User-Centered Visualizations of Uncertainty in Everyday, Mobile Predictive Systems". In: *Proceedings of the Conference on Human Factors in Computing Systems (CHI)*. CHI '16. San Jose, California, USA: ACM, 2016, pp. 5092–5103. DOI: 10.1145/2858036.2858558. URL: https://doi.org/10.1145/2858036.2858558 (cited on pages 184, 192).

[53] Kim, S. and Paulos, E. "InAir: Measuring and Visualizing Indoor Air Quality". In: *Proceedings of the Conference on Ubiquitous Computing (Ubicomp)*. UbiComp '09. Orlando, Florida, USA: ACM, 2009, pp. 81–84. DOI: 10.1145/1620545.1620557. URL: https://doi.org/10.1145/1620545.1620557 (cited on page 184).

[54] Kim, Y.-H., Jeon, J. H., Lee, B., Choe, E. K., and Seo, J. "OmniTrack: A Flexible Self-Tracking Approach Leveraging Semi-Automated Tracking". In: *Proceedings of the ACM on Interactive, Mobile, Wearable and Ubiquitous Technologies (IMWUT)* 1.3 (Sept. 2017). **Open Access version:** https://omnitrack.github.io/assets/files/IMWUT-2017-Kim-OmniTrack.pdf. DOI: 10.1145/3130930 (cited on pages 184, 190).

[55] King, A. C., Hekler, E. B., Grieco, L. A., Winter, S. J., Sheats, J. L., Buman, M. P., Banerjee, B., Robinson, T. N., and Cirimele, J. "Harnessing Different Motivational Frames via Mobile Phones to Promote Daily Physical Activity and Reduce Sedentary Behavior in Aging Adults". In: *PLOS ONE* 8.4 (2013), e62613 (cited on page 194).

[56] Klasnja, P., Consolvo, S., and Pratt, W. "How to Evaluate Technologies for Health Behavior Change in HCI Research". In: *Proceedings of the Conference on Human Factors in Computing Systems (CHI)*. CHI '11. Vancouver, BC, Canada: ACM, 2011, pp. 3063–3072. DOI: 10.1145/1978942.1979396 (cited on page 196).

[57] Klasnja, P., Smith, S., Seewald, N. J., Lee, A., Hall, K., Luers, B., Hekler, E. B., and Murphy, S. A. "Efficacy of Contextually Tailored Suggestions for Physical Activity: A Micro-Randomized Optimization Trial of HeartSteps". In: *Annals of Behavioral Medicine* 53.6 (2019), pp. 573–582 (cited on page 195).

[58] Lam, H., Bertini, E., Isenberg, P., Plaisant, C., and Carpendale, S. "Empirical Studies in Information Visualization: Seven Scenarios". In: *Transactions on Visualization and Computer Graphics (TVCG)* 18.9 (Sept. 2012). **Open Access version:** https://hal.inria.fr/hal-00932606, pp. 1520–1536. DOI: 10.1109/TVCG.2011.279 (cited on page 181).

[59] Langner, R., Horak, T., and Dachselt, R. "VisTiles: Coordinating and Combining Co-Located Mobile Devices for Visual Data Exploration". In: *Transactions on Visualization and Computer Graphics (TVCG)* 24.1 (Jan. 2018). **Open Access version:** https://imld.de/cnt/uploads/Langner_VisTiles_InfoVis17.pdf, pp. 626–636. DOI: 10.1109/TVCG.2017.2744019 (cited on pages 184, 188, 189).

[60] Lazar, J., Feng, J., and Hochheiser, H. *Research Methods in Human-Computer Interaction.* Morgan Kaufmann, 2017 (cited on page 179).

[61] Lin, J. J., Mamykina, L., Lindtner, S., Delajoux, G., and Strub, H. B. "Fish'n'Steps: Encouraging Physical Activity With an Interactive Computer Game". In: *Proceedings of the Conference on Ubiquitous Computing (Ubicomp)*. Edited by Dourish, P. and Friday, A. Berlin, Heidelberg: Springer, 2006, pp. 261–278. DOI: 10.1007/11853565_16 (cited on page 184).

[62] Lin, M., Goldman, R., Price, K. J., Sears, A., and Jacko, J. "How Do People Tap When Walking? An Empirical Investigation of Nomadic Data Entry". In: *International Journal of Human-Computer Studies* 65.9 (2007), pp. 759–769 (cited on page 188).

[63] Mizobuchi, S., Chignell, M., and Newton, D. "Mobile Text Entry: Relationship Between Walking Speed and Text Input Task Difficulty". In: *Proceedings of the Conference on Human Computer Interaction with Mobile Devices and Services (MobileHCI)*. ACM, 2005, pp. 122–128 (cited on page 188).

[64] Neshati, A., Sakamoto, Y., Leboe-McGowan, L. C., Leboe-McGowan, J., Serrano, M., and Irani, P. "G-Sparks: Glanceable Sparklines on Smartwatches". In: *Proceedings of the Graphics Interface Conference (GI)*. **Open Access version:** https://doi.org/10.20380/GI2019.23. Kingston, Canada: Canadian Human-Computer Communications Society, 2019. DOI: 10.20380/GI2019.23 (cited on pages 184, 186).

[65] Nielsen, J. *Usability Metrics.* https : / / www . nngroup . com / articles / usability-metrics/. Accessed: 2020-03-17. 2001 (cited on page 188).

[66] North, C. "Toward Measuring Visualization Insight". In: *Computer Graphics and Applications (CG&A)* 26.3 (May 2006), pp. 6–9. DOI: 10.1109/MCG.2006.70. URL: http://dx.doi.org/10.1109/MCG.2006.70 (cited on pages 193, 194).

[67] Olson, J. S. and Kellogg, W. A. *Ways of Knowing in HCI.* Springer, 2014 (cited on page 179).

[68] Palen, L. and Salzman, M. "Voice-Mail Diary Studies for Naturalistic Data Capture Under Mobile Conditions". In: *Proceedings of the Conference on Computer Supported Cooperative Work (CSCW).* CSCW '02. New Orleans, Louisiana, USA: ACM, 2002, pp. 87–95. DOI: 10.1145/587078.587092. URL: https://doi.org/10.1145/587078.587092 (cited on page 182).

[69] Peck, E. M., Ayuso, S. E., and El-Etr, O. "Data Is Personal: Attitudes and Perceptions of Data Visualization in Rural Pennsylvania". In: *Proceedings of the Conference on Human Factors in Computing Systems (CHI).* CHI '19. Glasgow, Scotland Uk: ACM, 2019. DOI: 10.1145/3290605.3300474. URL: https://doi.org/10.1145/3290605.3300474 (cited on page 191).

[70] Plaisant, C. "The Challenge of Information Visualization Evaluation". In: *Proceedings of the Conference on Advanced Visual Interfaces (AVI).* AVI '04. Gallipoli, Italy: ACM, 2004, pp. 109–116. DOI: 10.1145/989863.989880. URL: http://doi.acm.org/10.1145/989863.989880 (cited on pages 178, 180).

[71] Ploderer, B., Reitberger, W., Oinas-Kukkonen, H., and van Gemert-Pijnen, J. "Social Interaction and Reflection for Behaviour Change". In: *Personal and Ubiquitous Computing* 18 (2014), pp. 1667–1676. DOI: 10.1007/s00779-014-0779-y (cited on page 193).

[72] Pro, T. *Tobii Pro Glasses 2.* Product. Accessed 2020-03-17. URL: https ://www.tobiipro.com/product-listing/tobii-pro-glasses-2/ (cited on page 188).

[73] Riegelsberger, J. and Nakhimovsky, Y. "Seeing the Bigger Picture: A Multi-Method Field Trial of Google Maps for Mobile". In: *Extended Abstracts of the Conference on Human Factors in Computing System (CHI).* CHI EA '08. Florence, Italy: ACM, 2008, pp. 2221–2228. DOI: 10.1145/1358628.1358655. URL: https://doi.org/10.1145/1358628.1358655 (cited on page 184).

[74] Rodgers, J. and Bartram, L. "Exploring Ambient and Artistic Visualization for Residential Energy Use Feedback". In: *Transactions on Visualization and Computer Graphics (TVCG)* 17.12 (Dec. 2011), pp. 2489–2497. DOI: 10.1109/TVCG.2011.196 (cited on page 184).

[75]   Rooksby, J., Rost, M., Morrison, A., and Chalmers, M. "Pass the Ball: Enforced Turn-Taking in Activity Tracking". In: *Proceedings of the Conference on Human Factors in Computing Systems (CHI)*. CHI '15. Seoul, Republic of Korea: ACM, 2015, pp. 2417–2426. DOI: 10.1145/2702123.2702577. URL: https://doi.org/10.1145/2702123.2702577 (cited on page 184).

[76]   Roto, V., Popescu, A., Koivisto, A., and Vartiainen, E. "Minimap: A Web Page Visualization Method for Mobile Phones". In: *Proceedings of the Conference on Human Factors in Computing Systems (CHI)*. CHI '06. Montréal, Québec, Canada: ACM, 2006, pp. 35–44. DOI: 10.1145/1124772.1124779. URL: https://doi.org/10.1145/1124772.1124779 (cited on page 184).

[77]   Sadana, R., Agnihotri, M., and Stasko, J. *Touching Data: A Discoverability-Based Evaluation of a Visualization Interface for Tablet Computers*. ArXiv preprint 1806.06084. **Open Access version:** https://arxiv.org/abs/1806.06084. ArXiV, Aug. 2018 (cited on pages 184, 192).

[78]   Sadana, R. and Stasko, J. "Designing Multiple Coordinated Visualizations for Tablets". In: *Computer Graphics Forum* 35.3 (June 2016). **Open Access version:** https://www.cc.gatech.edu/~stasko/papers/eurovis16-mcv.pdf, pp. 261–270. DOI: 10.1111/cgf.12902 (cited on page 192).

[79]   Saito, T., Miyamura, H. N., Yamamoto, M., Saito, H., Hoshiya, Y., and Kaseda, T. "Two-Tone Pseudo Coloring: Compact Visualization for One-Dimensional Data". In: *Proceedings of the Symposium on Information Visualization (InfoVis)*. IEEE, 2005, pp. 173–180 (cited on page 186).

[80]   Saket, B., Endert, A., and Stasko, J. "Beyond Usability and Performance: A Review of User Experience-Focused Evaluations in Visualization". In: *Proceedings of the Workshop on BEyond Time and Errors: Novel Evaluation Methods for Information Visualization (BELIV)*. BELIV '16. **Open Access version:** https://www.cc.gatech.edu/~john.stasko/papers/beliv16-ux.pdf. 2016, pp. 133–142. DOI: 10.1145/2993901.2993903 (cited on page 181).

[81]   Saraiya, P., North, C., and Duca, K. "An Insight-Based Methodology for Evaluating Bioinformatics Visualizations". In: *Transactions on Visualization and Computer Graphics (TVCG)* 11.4 (2005), pp. 443–456 (cited on page 181).

[82]   Schmidt, A., Holleis, P., Häkkilä, J., Rukzio, E., and Atterer, R. "Mobile Phones as Tool to Increase Communication and Location Awareness of Users". In: *Proceedings of the Conference on Human Computer Interaction with Mobile Devices and Services (MobileHCI)*. Mobility '06. Bangkok, Thailand: ACM, 2006, 21–es. DOI: 10.1145/1292331.1292355. URL: https://doi.org/10.1145/1292331.1292355 (cited on page 184).

[83]   Schwab, M., Hao, S., Vitek, O., Tompkin, J., Huang, J., and Borkin, M. A. "Evaluating Pan and Zoom Timelines and Sliders". In: *Proceedings of the Conference on Human Factors in Computing Systems (CHI)*. ACM, 2019, pp. 1–12 (cited on page 193).

[84] Shneiderman, B. and Plaisant, C. "Strategies for Evaluating Information Visualization Tools: Multi-Dimensional In-Depth Long-Term Case Studies". In: *Proceedings of the Workshop on BEyond Time and Errors: Novel Evaluation Methods for Information Visualization (BELIV)*. BELIV '06. New York, NY, USA: ACM, 2006, pp. 1–7. DOI: 10.1145/1168149.1168158. URL: http://doi.acm.org/10.1145/1168149.1168158 (cited on page 181).

[85] Tollmar, K., Bentley, F., and Viedma, C. "Mobile Health Mashups: Making Sense of Multiple Streams of Wellbeing and Contextual Data for Presentation on a Mobile Device". In: *Proceedings of the Conference on Pervasive Computing Technologies for Healthcare (PervasiveHealth)*. IEEE, 2012, pp. 65–72. DOI: 10.4108/icst.pervasivehealth.2012.248698 (cited on pages 184, 190).

[86] Tudor-Locke, C., Sisson, S. B., Lee, S. M., Craig, C. L., Plotnikoff, R. C., and Bauman, A. "Evaluation of Quality of Commercial Pedometers". In: *Canadian Journal of Public Health/Revue Canadienne de Sante'e Publique* 97 (2006), S10–S15 (cited on page 189).

[87] Tufte, E. R. *Beautiful Evidence*. Graphics Press, 2006 (cited on page 186).

[88] Wall, E., Agnihotri, M., Matzen, L., Divis, K., Haass, M., Endert, A., and Stasko, J. "A Heuristic Approach to Value-Driven Evaluation of Visualizations". In: *Transactions on Visualization and Computer Graphics (TVCG)* 25.1 (Jan. 2019). **Open Access version:** https://www.cc.gatech.edu/~john.stasko/papers/infovis18-icet.pdf, pp. 491–500. DOI: 10.1109/TVCG.2018.2865146 (cited on page 181).

[89] Wang, Y., Segal, A., Klatzky, R., Keefe, D. F., Isenberg, P., Hurtienne, J., Hornecker, E., Dwyer, T., and Barrass, S. "An Emotional Response to the Value of Visualization". In: *Computer Graphics and Applications (CG&A)* 39.5 (2019), pp. 8–17 (cited on page 181).

[90] Ware, C. *Information Visualization: Perception for Design*. English. 3rd. Morgan Kaufmann, 2012 (cited on page 185).

[91] Whitlock, M., Wu, K., and Szafir, D. A. "Designing for Mobile and Immersive Visual Analytics in the Field". In: *Transactions on Visualization and Computer Graphics (TVCG)* 26.1 (Jan. 2020). **Open Access version:** https://arxiv.org/abs/1908.00680, pp. 503–513. DOI: 10.1109/TVCG.2019.2934282 (cited on page 190).

CHAPTER 7

Challenges in Everyday Use of Mobile Visualizations

Daniel A. Epstein
University of California, Irvine, USA

Tanja Blascheck
University of Stuttgart, Germany

Sheelagh Carpendale
Simon Fraser University, Canada

Raimund Dachselt
Technische Universität Dresden, Germany

Jo Vermeulen
Aarhus University, Denmark & Autodesk Research, Canada

CONTENTS

As visualizations become more widely incorporated into mobile devices such as phones, smartwatches, or fitness bracelets, they become more ingrained in everyday life. The contexts in which they are used introduce a range of challenges caused by the small form factor, screen space, temporal limits of viewing, and increased

DOI: 10.1201/9781003090823-7

integration of personal data. In this chapter, we illustrate challenges resulting from the everyday use of mobile visualizations in three categories: logistical challenges relating to situated use, privacy challenges involved with potential data disclosures, and ethical challenges surrounding increased access and decreased evidence. In spite of these challenges, introducing visualizations in everyday life can lead to positive experiences viewing and reflecting on data in their natural contexts. Using scenarios to depict use opportunities, we introduce a set of considerations for designers and researchers looking to develop mobile visualizations for everyday contexts.

7.1 INTRODUCTION

As will be discussed in Chapter 9, the increasingly ubiquitous nature of mobile visualizations introduces a variety of contexts and circumstances which influence how people interact with the visualizations and derive value from them. While early visualization work envisioned controlled environments viewed by a relatively homogeneous group of experts, the move towards Casual Information Visualization [51] and Narrative Visualization [55] highlights the ongoing increase in access and circumstances. The evolution into Mobile Visualization even further increases access and circumstances, as illustrated by examples of mobile visualization shown in Chapter 1. We would now expect people to encounter and interact with visualizations as they are living their lives.

The move toward increased use of visualization in everyday life caused by mobile visualization introduces significant benefits and opportunities. Mobile visualizations offer the ability to review and react to data in the circumstances people need to make informed decisions, such as learning about bus arrival times when waiting [35] or about nutrition when choosing what to eat [11]. They also increase access to visualizations, as mobile devices are the only resource that many adults have for accessing information online. People often interact with mobile visualizations in the presence of others, introducing opportunities for people to share knowledge they have gained about themselves or the world.

However, the integration of mobile visualization into everyday life also introduces significant challenges. Today, people view and interact with visualization environments that are often removed from the context from which they were created. Visualizations of personal data are often expected to be private, however, the contexts in which they are viewed undermine that expectation. For example, someone is commuting on a bus, and looking at personal data, while the person behind them might be shoulder surfing and following along. The devices and modalities people use to view these visualizations can limit people's ability to make sense of or interact with their data. Due to limited screen space, data may be only partially represented, aggregated, or specific aspects of the data might be highlighted. People also use mobile visualization with quick interactions, while on the go, or to pass time while waiting in queue (see Chapter 5 on details about glanceability of mobile visualizations). As a result, the assumptions we make about careful analysis or consideration of visualized data are unlikely to hold up for many people in many circumstances.

In this chapter, we unpack some of the everyday challenges people currently encounter or may encounter when interacting with mobile visualizations in their everyday lives. We discuss challenges under three categories: (1) *logistical challenges*, relating to certain interactions or observations becoming more challenging or impossible in mobile visualization; (2) *privacy challenges*, caused by the social circumstances where mobile visualizations are often viewed; and (3) *ethical challenges*, impacted by more frequent access to visualizations by more people at the mercy of what visualization designers create. For each category, we introduce scenarios to illustrate key challenges and discuss potential considerations those challenges illustrate for visualization practitioners and researchers.

Our chapter primarily focuses on current and near-term mobile visualizations to allow us to understand the challenges involved with integration into everyday life. Future mobile visualizations, such as those discussed in Chapter 8 could introduce further everyday challenges. We also focus on the challenges caused by viewing and interacting with visualizations, ignoring technical challenges around data leakage or theft caused by deeper entanglement of data, often personal data, with devices people are using in everyday life. Finally, we acknowledge that mobile visualizations introduce additional sociocultural and societal challenges, such as datafication [24] and using visualizations of data to reinforce societal health ideals [43].

7.2 EVERYDAY INTERACTION CHALLENGES OF MOBILE VISUALIZATIONS

Mobile visualization provides increased opportunity for viewing and interacting with visualizations in the context under which the data is collected or can be used to inform decisions. But the form factors that mobile visualizations are viewed on can lead to more frequent or unintended viewing of visualizations than in desktop environments, which can cause challenging or even stressful interactions.

7.2.1 From Being Informed to Information Overload

Data is becoming increasingly collected digitally,[1] driven by the ubiquity of mobile devices and proliferation of smartwatches and fitness bracelets that allow people to track themselves constantly. The research literature often refers to this phenomenon as the Quantified Self [43] or personal informatics [42], with people reflecting on data collected about themselves for self-knowledge or self-understanding.

As displays proliferate beyond desktop computers, visualizations will become even more ubiquitous. We often think of visualizations in terms of opportunities for smartwatches, fitness bands, mobile phones, data jewelry, and augmented clothing, but also e-ink displays, billboards, drones, and robots are and will be used in the future to depict data in the form of visualizations. This increase in available information as well as the number of different channels and the often historical or contradictory information can help people to be more informed, but also lead to information overload.

---

[1]https://www.statista.com/chart/17723/the-data-created-last-year-is-equal-to/

Scenarios

Unimportant weather information. Thomas is going to meet up with friends. He recently installed a new weather app so he can check if he needs to take an umbrella or not. He is about to leave the house and wants to quickly check his new app to find the weather forecast for the next couple of hours. When he opens his new app he is confronted with a complicated looking interface, depicting all kinds of environment related data, such as the current threat of pollen, the current UV index (UVI), an air quality index (AQI) representing air pollution, the temperature, current weather, the moon phase and wind speed (cf. Figure 7.1) all shown with different colorful visualizations. Although he knows where the forecast is located on the watch face and can quickly see that it will rain today, he is reminded that most of the information is irrelevant to him most of the time. He is frustrated that he cannot customize the interface to his needs, highlighting other information or more prominently displaying the forecast.

Figure 7.1 An example of app showing different kinds of environmental information using different types of visualizations and different color scales. The visualization's complexity can lead to information overload for a person looking to answer a specific question, such as whether or not it is currently raining.

Hyper reality visualization. Decades from now, Sara is leaving the house to go grocery shopping after a busy day at work. Her augmented reality headset shows her world as a hyper reality[2] and she is exposed to advertisements, information about her surroundings, gamified performance scores, and suggestions on how to improve herself. She hops on the bus, eager to use her headset to help her formulate a shopping list as she travels. While in transit, her headset displays visualizations relevant to the buildings she's passing. As she looks out the bus window at a gas station, the headset shows a line graph highlighting how the price of gas has reached an all-time low. Glancing nextdoor at a phone store, Sara sees a bar chart advertising a 20% reduction in phone plan rates, personalized to her current phone plan. Distracted by

---

[2]http://hyper-reality.co/

this information and the use of visualizations to make persuasive arguments, Sara arrives at her bus stop having not written her shopping list.

Problem Description

Advances in personal sensing and capabilities of mobile devices have increased the amount of data people are able to collect about themselves for self-reflection. For example, the Android platform offers 13 different sensor types[3] that a mobile phone or smartwatch can use, such as accelerometer, temperature, gravity, gyroscope, light, acceleration, pressure, and proximity. People are also increasingly using these devices to manually journal their daily activities and experiences, such as what they eat and how they are feeling. Therefore, people can nowadays not only track where they are, but they can now track many different aspects of their lives from sleep duration and quality, to calorie and water intake, step count, distance walked, floors climbed, heart rate, electrocardiography, and much more. These high volumes of collected data can be visualized and shown to people for self improvement, for example, leading to healthier and more active lives.

Modern watch faces nowadays depict this collected personal information together with the time. For example, a person using an Apple Watch can choose between many watch faces[4] that can depict up to eight different data types at the same time. Although, people usually learn where which type of data is located and can quickly glance at the relevant information they are interested in, often such interfaces cannot be customized as described in the scenario above. For example, the way a data type is represented—often step count is depicted as a number with an icon—cannot be chosen. In some cases, interfaces do not allow people to choose which data types are presented at all. This lack of customization can lead to people being frustrated or ultimately stopping to use an interface.

In addition to the amount of data one device collect, the ubiquity of devices (e.g., billboards, data jewelry, ambient clothing, robots) visualizing data can lead to an increase of channels to receive information and thus cause distractions. Although such ubiquitous devices can help people to make informed decisions and live healthier lives, having many visualizations around oneself can distract people from their current task or make it difficult to determine what data to focus on.

Potential Considerations

Allowing customization. Most watches enable people to customize the layout of their watchfaces choosing which data types to represent and how prominently to present them. Other devices often enable similar customizations, such as allowing people to select modules with visualizations for the homescreens of their mobile phones. The inclusion or exclusion of visualization modules may be helpful to reduce distractions or allow people to better match their homescreens to their intended goals, such as by enlarging visualizations with the data they are primarily interested in.

---

[3] https://developer.android.com/guide/topics/sensors/sensors_overview
[4] https://support.apple.com/guide/watch/apde9218b440/watchos

However, relatively fewer devices and tools support customization of the construction of the visualizations themselves. Gouveia et al. [31] suggest that tools offer multiple or customizable encodings, to allow people to choose a visualization which represents their personality. As one example, Kim et al.'s [36] DataSelfie contributes techniques for allowing people to customize visual mappings of their self-tracked data either automatically or manually.

Visualizing sparingly and at-a-glance. It is worth considering whether the displayed content benefits from being a visualization or being visualized. Text, icons, or other less cognitively-demanding representations are often sufficient for showing many kinds of data. For example, many fitness bracelets show the collected data as numbers with icons to represent the data type, which is sufficient if a person wants to see how many steps they have taken today [15].

The usage context of mobile visualizations is often different from traditional visualization on desktops or other large displays. Mobile visualizations are viewed while in motion, and the devices they are visualized on are mostly used to satisfy quick information needs. Visualizations either are not needed or can be designed in a way that makes them easy to comprehend even when focusing only for a few seconds at it. For a detailed discussion on glanceable mobile visualizations, we refer to Chapter 5.

7.2.2 Fewer Opportunities for Interaction

We mostly use mobile devices for passive consumption of information and media, and value the possibility of interacting with data while on the go without the need for external input devices. It can be helpful to interact with a map visualization, a stock chart, or personal health data while on the go with a few touch gestures. However, not having keyboard or precise mouse input available in mobile settings also significantly reduces the possible interactions. While the limited output capability of mobile devices (i.e., their reduced screen estate) seems immediately obvious in the context of visualization, its influence is perhaps less clear for interaction and its implications. Although the resolution and pixel density of mobile devices and smartwatches might be high, the smaller physical dimensions introduce dilemmas for designers of interactive visualizations. Being able to show less information than on desktop computers requires adapting well-known interaction techniques such as distributing the information onto multiple coordinated views [54], zoomable interfaces, overview and detail approaches, and focus+context techniques [32, 14]. However, all these solutions require extensive interaction like flipping through pages, scrolling, zooming and panning, scaling lenses, filtering, brushing data, etc., which in turn are harder to accomplish on mobile devices due to the lack of precise pointing as well as limited input space and lack of haptic feedback, especially for multitouch input.

Of course, not all mobile visualizations require the same level of interaction. The scenarios described in this chapter range in scope from passive consumption of glanceable visualizations (e.g., detailed weather information) to simple and shorter interaction with less complex information (e.g., personal fitness data) up to more direct and involved interaction with more complicated data (e.g., comparison of several stock quotes for making investment decisions). With increasing interaction complexity, mobile devices are less suited for some tasks, especially under time pressure and in in-the-wild situations, as the following scenarios further exemplify.

Scenarios

Wrong choice caused by inaccurate touch. Alicia is a government researcher who analyzes patterns of disease spread over time. Sitting in the bus on her way back home, she received an urgent email from a news reporter asking whether this year's seasonal flu is spreading more rapidly than last year's. For that, she opens a chart of this year's cases and zooms to the the current time span using two fingers. This is necessary, because the display is too small to show her the entire disease spread at once. While she is opening last year's chart in a different view below for comparison, she has to leave the bus, but wants to quickly finish her action. Due to the shaking of the mobile phone while getting off the bus and the inaccuracy in touch interaction, she accidentally chooses the wrong time span in the zoom view provided by the app. Because the curves look similar to her, she does not realize that she is comparing disease spread at different levels of time granularity; this year's chart shows days while last year's shows weeks. Still on her walk home she decides to call the reporter and state there is no cause for concern.

Inconvenient to impossible interaction. Fred is in his mid-fifties and loves to go running regularly to stay healthy and reduce weight. He uses a running app on his smartwatch, which also provides a desktop version he uses on his computer at home. To track his progress over time, he loves to use the time-oriented charts on his desktop app which require mouse interactions to understand how the length, duration, heart rate, pulse, etc., have changed over time. While again going running on a sunny day, he gets ambitious and tries to set a new record on his usual track. He, therefore, looks at his watch to request data on previous runs, but struggles with the bright sunlight and reflections on the watch surface. In his attempt to request the speed distribution along the track for his best attempt so far, he misses touching the tiny data mark he intended to click on and gets the wrong details shown. When he tries to overcome the problem by using the digital crown, his sweaty fingers prevent an easy selection of the correct data set. Having to interrupt his run and eventually missing his ambitious daily goal makes him angry.

Too cool to be controlled reliably. Mercedes is a young fashion aficionado and bought herself the latest interactive wearable: a touch-enabled jacket based on smart e-textiles. The cloth includes interesting woven-in displays which allow her to communicate either her mood or any personal information to others by means of some simple multi-color segment displays. She can control this information not only using her connected smartphone, but also via touch- and pressure-sensitive areas on the sleeve and cuff. Before going out in the evening, she has agreed with her close friends on a visual code to represent the number of compliments and/or drinks they each receive in the club. Using her smartphone app, she loads the initial design to the segment displays on her jacket and is now able to increase or decrease numbers by pressing the respective textile touch-buttons on her sleeve. Later in the evening, she forgets to switch to the passive mode which should prevent involuntary input. While dancing, she touches other dancers with her sleeves, who accidentally change her e-textile displays several times. She does not notice, but wonders about the comments of a group of people making fun of her and the rapidly changing light ("like Christmas tree lighting") and later on about the laughter of her friends who comment on her rather unrealistic numbers accidentally shown on her jacket. Mercedes feels slightly embarrassed on what she thought would be a cool dernier cri accessory.

Problem Description

These scenarios exemplify how input challenges on mobile devices and wearables can impact visualization interactivity. The output space is often insufficient to show and compare data for longer time periods at once. Further details of visualized data sets, like a previous run, may need to be explicitly requested on mobile devices because they might not fit on the screen alongside other visualizations. Even the rather simple interactions mentioned in the examples highlight some of the interaction limits of mobile visualizations. There exists a trade-off on mobile devices between the advice to show less data at once (cf. Section 7.2.1) and the additional interaction required by this reduction. This is even amplified if people desire supporting more advanced exploration, comparison, and filtering tasks on mobile devices.

Many visualization tasks require interaction such as a pinch to zoom in on an information space, dragging to move a visualization lens, or just a simple tap for requesting details for a data mark. The opportunities for interaction are, however, limited on mobile devices (cf. Chapter 3). Issues like the fat finger problem on small touchscreens [4, 57], limited input precision, missing hover state, or missing implicit mode switches (like pressing a mouse button and dragging on desktop computers) severely reduce the interaction repertoire well-known from desktop solutions. Therefore, it is important to decouple interaction steps and apply them one after the other.

On the one hand, mobile devices are the only way of accessing data for many people worldwide with limited or no access to different computing devices. With this in mind, the example of numerous complex interactive dashboards showing important information about the COVID-19 pandemic, most of which are almost challenging to be seen or interacted with on smaller devices, is a cautionary tale. Therefore, interfaces should be as simple as possible for everyday people, and visualization designers should neither assume sophisticated devices nor specialized knowledge and skills of their users. On the other hand, people also have expectations from using high-bandwidth desktop applications, which they might want to transfer to the mobile world. These constraints require careful balance.

Looking into the future of mobile visualization head-mounted displays or interactive wearables (e.g., clothing-based displays described in [18]) have the great advantage of overcoming the boundaries of the flat and stiff screens of today's mobile devices. They also offer ability to integrate visualizations naturally into the environment or relate them to our bodies. Such novel devices lose the comfort and familiarity of established input methods, and interaction can be severely constrained. However, more natural means of (perhaps casually) interacting with mobile data visualizations open up new opportunities. Hand gestures in mid-air or gentle touches and movements on personal clothes like in the Mercedes' scenario can be subtle means of interacting with visualizations. However, more advanced or complex interactions may not be not well-supported with such techniques, if they are possible at all. In addition, the involuntary activation like in Mercedes' case or the possible embarrassment of performing mid-air gestures in certain environments are novel problems designers need to be aware of, which might prevent social acceptance and widespread use.

People typically have limited interaction time with mobile devices, which is another important problem pertaining to all mobile devices and scenarios. Like in the first two scenarios, people often do not have the time to leverage more complex interactions with visualizations while on the go, and the display surface for interaction might be moving or shaking. Touch interaction as the dominant way of using mobile devices, while per se already less accurate, becomes even more problematic on small *moving* surfaces. For example, selecting items in a scatterplot might cause severe problems on a smartphone and potentially lead to subsequent errors or wrong decisions. This is less noteworthy for tablets and larger devices.

Design Considerations

The aforementioned problems related to interaction with mobile visualizations are being examined not only in research, but also by mobile device manufacturers, because companies are interested in selling their mobile units along with well-designed and usable apps. However, while interface guidelines like Apple's Human Interface Guidelines for iOS and WatchOS [5] address mobile interface design in detail, there exist only few recommendations for mobile visualizations—beyond simple charts—yet. In the following, some thoughts and recommendations are outlined with regard to limited opportunities for interacting with mobile visualizations.

Considering adapting existing visualization solutions. When transforming desktop visualization solutions to mobile devices, it should be considered how to adapt both the visualization views *and* the interaction, as well as how the two interplay. This often means reducing complexity and capabilities that cannot be achieved on smaller mobile devices such as brushing and linking in multiple coordinated views. For other techniques like zoomable interfaces or focus+context techniques, mobile variants have been developed [9, 10, 50]. Because the mobile phone is the primary means of information access for many people, carefully adapting visualizations to mobile devices also with regard to interaction becomes crucial.

Reducing interaction complexity. Connected to the previous recommendation, mobile visualizations should ideally rely on interactions that people already use on mobile devices for other applications. Avoiding complex gestures, bimanual interaction, asymmetric interaction techniques, or incomprehensible mode switches can help remedy this. High dexterity should not be required and may not be possible in on-the-go mobile contexts, in which it is hard to hold the device in a stable manner. When designing for lay people, a pitfall could be designing for the lowest common denominator. Instead, providing alternative techniques or introducing advanced techniques for experts could

---

[5]https://developer.apple.com/design/human-interface-guidelines/

be a viable solution like known from traditional computers, for which one size also does not fit all.

Considering novel interaction principles. Another solution is to provide novel interaction capabilities which go beyond what has been known from the desktop computer or is currently used on larger mobile devices like tablets. These might include pure software solutions. Examples for this are popular text entry methods like SwiftKey, based on the ShapeWriter and SHARK approaches [61], or the pointing technique Shift [60]—in which a callout shows a copy of the mobile screen area occluded by the finger and places it in a non-occluded location. These are just inspiring examples for approaches to overcome the fat finger problem, for example, by means of gesture-based shortcuts for interacting with visualizations.

Novel interaction techniques could also be designed, which might employ different sensing technology beyond multitouch. Examples for the latter are back-of-device interaction approaches (e.g., Vogel et al. [60]) or physical input sensors like digital crowns or rotatable bezels on current smartwatches. While rarely being used in current mobile visualizations, more physical approaches like squeezing or bending a mobile phone [30] could provide interesting means of data exploration. Multimodal approaches can also become interesting solutions, like physical smartwatch interaction combined with additional touch-enabled wristbands [39], the combination of touch and spatial movements [50, 58] or the usage of speech in combination with touch [38, 59]. However, though promising, such solutions might contradict with the previous design consideration.

Towards mobile visualization guidelines. The already-existing guidelines of mobile device manufacturers on how to design mobile apps could be further extended to include recommendations on mobile visualization and interaction. Guidelines on chart design could, for example, be incorporated into Apple's HealthKit Human Interface Guidelines.[6] While interaction standards for working with mobile visualizations will be difficult to establish (if at all), such guidelines might help ensuring consistency across visualizations. Perceptual studies on mobile visualizations (e.g., Blascheck et al. [6]) can help lay the foundations for and expand these design considerations.

7.3 EVERYDAY PRIVACY CHALLENGES OF MOBILE VISUALIZATIONS

Being able to access visualizations on more displays, from public displays to phones or watches, naturally has implications when personal data is being visualized. One clear upside is that visualizations can be shared for sensemaking or reporting of information. However, visualizations being more available naturally open up access opportunities for people other than the intended party or parties, whether accidental or intentional.

7.3.1 Violating Privacy Expectations

When people are using mobile devices to visualize and review data about themselves, such as data sensed about them or from personal accounts, they might assume that

---

[6]https://developer.apple.com/design/human-interface-guidelines/carekit/overview/views/

they are the only ones who are able to view the data. However, the personal and social contexts under which mobile visualizations are used can challenge this assumption.

Scenarios

Shoulder surfing. Jackson is an executive at a pharmaceutical company, and he recently started using a financial planning app to manage his children's inheritances. While Jackson commutes home by train after a long and tiring day at work, he receives a notification about some changes his financial planner made, which prompts him to check his app. The graph breaking down how his earnings are getting divided draws the attention of the passenger next to him, who strikes up a conversation and asks for career advice. Although there is no further fallout, Jackson wonders whether future passerbys might see him as a potential target for identity theft.

Unwanted advertisement. Natalie and her partner are trying to have a child, and have been using an app to monitor and review her basal body temperature and potential conception windows. At lunch, she goes out for a hilly run with a coworker at her small company. After the run, Natalie and her coworker use their smartwatches to compare how the elevation impacted each of their heart rates. Natalie scrolls slightly too far, revealing a graph of her temperature readings to her coworker and prompting an awkward discussion about the impact of a potential pregnancy on the long-term goals of the company.

Problem Description

The varied circumstances in which data is viewed can lead to many positive sharing circumstances, but also unintentional disclosures. Compared to desktop environments, the portability and convenience of mobile visualizations make people more likely look at visualizations in the presence of others. As a plus, this can promote shared reviewing and reflecting on visualized information. For example, prior work has highlighted opportunities for shared sensemaking around visualized patient data in hospitals and other clinical settings [13, 44, 45]. Although there remain many interaction and sociotechnical challenges (e.g., collaborative browsing, finding time to look at data during a clinical consultation), mobile visualization increases opportunities for patients to collaboratively review data with their healthcare providers.

As the scenarios illustrate, the ease of bringing up visualizations in daily life can also lead to less positive disclosures. Peeking at a person's screen on a bus or a train, whether intentional or not, is prevalent in today's society. This experience is common in more private spaces as well, such as seeing what a colleague is doing on their phone during a meeting. We often hold interpretability and glanceability as ideals in the design of visualizations, but these principles can also enable others around us to easily perceive and interpret the data.

Prior work has shown that people express concern about how mobile visualizations can accidentally disclose their personal data in social settings. For example, people frequently use mobile apps to keep track of and visualize where they are in their menstrual cycle (cf. Figure 7.2 left). These mobile apps often have obvious names (e.g., Period Tracker) or use gendered color schemes (e.g., pink, cf. Figure 7.2 right),

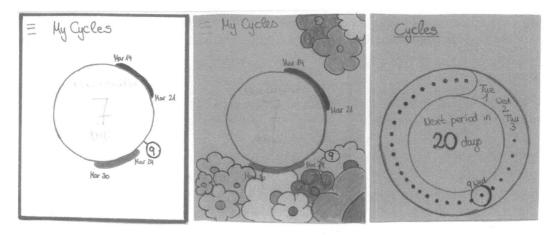

Figure 7.2 Left and Middle: Some apps include the ability to adjust the app's theme to use more neutral colors. However, rarely is the visualization itself adjustable. Right: Gendered color draws attention to menstrual cycle information.

Figure 7.3 Gardy [31] represented progress toward physical activity goals as growth in a garden. *Republished with permission of the ACM, from [31]; permission conveyed through Copyright Clearance Center, Inc.*

drawing attention to data that people might view as sensitive. People describe taking precautionary measures to avoid disclosure, such as by changing the app's default color scheme or avoiding use of the app in public spaces [23].

In another example, Gouveia et al. [31] explored design opportunities for representing physical activity on the home screen of a smartwatch. One of their design approaches, Gardy (cf. Figure 7.3), implemented an abstract representation of physical activity as flowers growing in a garden. In their field deployment of the interface, some participants appreciated how the abstract display instigated rewarding conversations with children and their parents who happened to see their watch. However, other participants felt the display was too vibrant, fearing that it would invite unwanted attention or would result in others judging their interests and goals. They instead chose to hide the display in public. Overall, Gardy was the least preferred and least motivating of the different interfaces considered in their study.

Related literature often exposes these risks in explicit data sharing scenarios, such as disclosing physical activity or location. These overt disclosures of information can lead to exposing more information than a person is comfortable sharing. For example, Epstein et al. [22] describe scenarios for what sharing fine-grained physical activity data (e.g., minute- or hour-level) could expose in an effort to examine how aggregating, truncating, or manipulating the data could help avoid these risks. They describe a scenario in which an employee decides to go for a run in the middle of the workday, but worries that sharing his run on a social media web site on which he is friends with his co-workers might reflect poorly on his work performance. These same challenges persist in-person as well when others nearby have the opportunity to look at a person's data.

Design Considerations

As the field continues to explore ideas around glanceable displays, this risk of unexpected or unwanted viewers increases. Unfortunately, potential strategies for addressing these unwanted views are often directly in tension with the benefits people derive from the visualizations being ubiquitous.

Making visualizations abstract. Abstract visualizations of data, such as in Gardy or in UbiFit Garden [16], are typically used to provide metaphors to motivate further behavioral change. However, they have the additional advantage of not being easily read or interpreted for people not privy to the encoding scheme, such as that the presence of a butterfly in the abstract display represents goal achievement [15].

However, as Gouveia et al. [31] point out, the public nature of these abstract visualizations need to align with people's self-presentation desires. As discussed in Section 7.2.1, customization can enable people to choose how bold they want to display what they are visualizing, responding to their personal perspectives on privacy and the sensitivity of the data being visualized.

Ensuring viewing intentionality. To preserve privacy, a system can aim to better understand who is looking at the visualization and assess whether their access to it is reasonable or expected. One strategy would be to ensure that a person is comfortable with their current surroundings prior to displaying a visualization. For example, people could configure visualizations of information they find sensitive behind confirmation screens or passwords, rather than prominently displaying when an app is first opened or a device is first glanced at.

However, this strategy comes into tension with principles around supporting glanceability and passive pick-up of information. For example, much of the value people find in seeing their physical activity data visualized on a phone or watch involves being able to quickly check in on how they are doing relative to their goals. When that information is displayed on a phone or watch home screen, it promotes quick check-ins even when the device is being viewed for other reasons (e.g., seeing step activity while responding to a notification). However, it also provides frequent opportunities for passersby to see and interpret that data.

Measures taken to protect privacy in mobile visualizations have the potential to challenge other aspects of usability or utility. When deciding what privacy measures, if any, to put into place, designers of mobile visualizations should consider the sensitivity of the data displayed and the circumstances under which it will often be viewed.

7.4 EVERYDAY ETHICAL CHALLENGES OF MOBILE VISUALIZATIONS

The visualization research community is increasingly aware of changing issues with regards to people, data, and visualization. For example, Dörk et al. [20] discussed ethics in the context of data representation for *Critical Information Visualization*. Kong et al. [40] have pointed out how even the words we choose to entitle a visualization with may change its interpretation. Correll [17] broadened this discussion to include more ethical dimensions to consider, including whose data is being incorporated into data sources and the rhetorical impact of visualizations.

For many people, mobile devices are the primary or only means of accessing online content. A Pew study in the United States shows that smartphone ownership exceeds desktop, laptop, and tablet ownership, particularly among people with lower levels of education, incomes, and those who do not have internet connections at home[7]. In studying visualization attitudes by primarily low-income individuals living in rural Pennsylvania, Peck et al. [49] argue that visualization has the opportunity to make data more accessible and democratic. However, the individuals most at risk may not have access to displays any larger than mobile devices, and therefore not facilitate deep exploration of data.

7.4.1 Low Visualization Literacy

Visualization literacy has been a longstanding focus of study and concern in the visualization community [7, 8]. We illustrate a few potential challenges which can arise from a lack of visualization literacy in mobile contexts.

Scenarios

Misleading climate impact. Tonya is browsing Facebook, and quickly scrolls past an ad with the caption "CLIMATE CHANGE IS A HOAX." The ad shows a relatively flat line of average yearly temperature from 1900 to present in her native city, citing data from a National Weather Service report. Puzzled, Tonya scrolls back up to the ad to look at it further. Remembering what she learned about visualization from high school, she goes to check the chart axes, noticing that there is no label on the Y-axis. She suspects if you were to calculate the bounds, they would be from $-1000°$F to $1000°$F. She reports the ad and returns to looking at her friend's pets.

Interpretable metaphors. Oliver was recently diagnosed with Type 1 Diabetes, and his doctor suggested using a mobile app to help him monitor his glucose level. The app includes a few different line, area, and bar charts for monitoring glucose. While the app looks sophisticated, he isn't able to make sense of the graphs, and instead

---

[7]https://www.pewresearch.org/internet/fact-sheet/mobile/

guesses when he should be taking insulin. After explaining this confusion in his next visit, Oliver's doctor recommends a different app which uses a hot-air balloon hovering at different levels (too high, too low, just right) to indicate glucose levels and whether to take more insulin. Oliver finds the balloon much easier to understand than the graph, and uses the new app to better manage his diabetes.

Problem Description

There are numerous examples of articles and advertisements leveraging misleading visualization strategies just like what Tonya experienced, from promoting the competitiveness of political campaigns to raise interest and donations[8] to aiming to suggest a stronger impact of governmental policies than reality.[9] In these cases, the designer often aims to use the visualization to convey objectivity in order to persuade people toward their cause [17].

While Tonya is careful to investigate and question the data being visualized and the sources of information, the mobile nature of the visualization makes the kind of misleading content present in the scenario more problematic. Although Tonya looked back to consider and reflect on the visualization, people's tendency toward quick interactions with mobile visualizations suggests that many others would not, though they may still interpret the overall message. The limited screen space also potentially enables the visualization designer to take shortcuts they otherwise would not have, choosing not to label axes or cite data sources to reduce data-ink and make the trend being visualized more immediately comprehensible.

While a mobile visualization might enable someone to monitor and address chronic conditions as they go about their daily life, Oliver's example highlights that for many, the graphs are not interpretable and may lead people to discount the advice they give. Research literature have suggested that visual metaphors can be used to educate people about graph interpretability alongside disseminating health information [19, 52].

Tonya's and Oliver's examples sit in a context where developing curricula around visualization comprehension is an ongoing goal and area for improvement. Challenges around visualization literacy are more societal than related to the design of visualizations, and thus have an impact on people's ability to interpret traditional desktop visualizations as well as mobile ones. However, the increased access to visualizations via mobile devices, particularly among people who may not have had as many educational opportunities, makes more people susceptible to the rhetoric surrounding the mobile visualization rather than critical examination of the data being shown.

Design Considerations

Creating Visualizations Responsibly. Ultimately, the decision around what to visualize and how relies on creators being benevolent and advocating for truth. Correll argues

---

[8]https://www.washingtonpost.com/graphics/politics/2016-election/trump-charts/
[9]https://www.independent.co.uk/news/health/coronavirus-charts-trump-axios-interview-cases-deaths-us-tests-data-a9652631.html

that visualization designers have a moral obligation to challenge unethical uses of data visualization [17]. This obligation is particularly important in mobile contexts, where quick interactions lead people to be more reliant on the gestalt of a visualization or rhetoric surrounding it, and when viewed by people who may not be predisposed to put the visualization under as much scrutiny. The constraints of mobile visualization put people more at the mercy of the designer's assumptions around data literacy and their desires for what information they choose to convey on a small screen with limited interaction potential.

Improving Education. At a societal level, there continues to be a need to study and improve how we teach data visualization concepts to enable more people to critically consider the data being visualized and their sources. Mobile data visualization only increases the need for further work on improving visualization education and literacy.

Pertaining to the design of mobile visualizations, designers can consider whether there are ways to incorporate teaching visualization principles into the design of mobile tools. Past work has highlighted how rhetorical descriptions can be made based on the data to aid people in interpreting it [5, 21]. Such descriptions could further connect back to the mobile visualization to teach people how to interpret similar visualizations in the future. Additionally, mobile platforms where visualizations are often shared could flag misleading or untrustworthy visualizations similar to other misinformation content.

7.4.2 Limited Resources Lead to Missing Context

Although desktop visualizations might enable interactive exploration or questioning the data being presented, quick interactions and limited screen real estate also introduce challenges surrounding interpreting data when missing context. The limited resources of mobile devices (e.g., display space, interaction capabilities, processing power) and their use on the go with typically limited duration of interaction [33] mean that people are more at the mercy of the visualization designer to avoid misleading or misinforming them about the data that is being visualized. Due to the limited display space, it is common practice to only show certain aspects of the data. However, it is often unclear to a person how the choice of what data to show has been made, and people tend to lack options to control or configure which data attributes are visualized and how.

Scenarios

Incomplete Jobs Report. Horace is reading a news article on his phone with the latest unemployment numbers in his country. The article presents a graph showing that unemployment has decreased by about 1% each month over the past 6 months, suggesting a strong economy. Because the graph is relatively small, it does not show the impact of a global crisis which occurred 8 months earlier, resulting in an unemployment spike 3x the improvement of the last 6 months. While Horace is well aware of the global crisis, the graph and article's focus on improvement leads him to think that the economy is already back on track.

Case Numbers. Estelle is a ranch owner in a geographically-small, low-population, rural county in Texas in the United States. In the midst of the global COVID-19 pandemic, Estelle uses her phone to look at an interactive national map of case counts colored on a gradient, zooming in on Texas. She cannot locate her county due to its size, and it does not appear near the top on the nearby table highlighting what counties have the most cases, like Dallas County (Dallas) and Harris County (Houston). She instead finds a few larger, neighboring counties on the map and table, noting that they are colored "green" and have only a few daily cases. She decides to proceed to hold a 300-person wedding for a local couple on her ranch, only later learning that cases in her county were actually quite high at the time. However, this fact was not visible on the map due to the size of her county, nor the table due to the focus on raw case counts versus per-capita.

Problem Description

Similar to the previous scenarios, Horace and Estelle's experiences highlight that the limited space for displaying and interacting with visualizations on mobile devices put people more at the mercy of the visualization designer's choices, whether those choices are intentional or not. For Horace, the missing contextual information leads him to make inaccurate assumptions about the state of the economy, while Estelle's case points to a reasonable, but inaccurate assumptions in the absence of being able to find her county and a less desirable method of aggregating data.

In desktop environments, a well-intentioned visualization designer might implement a jobs report as interactive to enable a person to better understand the full context. For many desktop visualization tasks, a person may also spend more time researching the topic, such as looking up alternate data sources. But the barriers to doing further research on mobile devices, and challenges creating effective interactions (see section 7.2.2), again leave people reliant on the visualization designer. Estelle's case highlights that even a well-intentioned visualization designer can make choices which mislead people about risks when limited by the mobile context.

Visualizations are often simplified for mobile consumption and, as a result, have to aggregate or leave out certain parts of the data (see also discussions on responsive visualization in Chapter 2). An important issue with incomplete information—and particularly visualizations that leave out information about uncertainty—is that these may lead to more misinterpretations and may cast doubt on the credibility of the data and its sources. For instance, during the COVID-19 pandemic, there were many discussions on social media about the inherent uncertainty in certain measures such as the number of new cases compared to the number of deaths. When mobile visualizations on such a high-profile and heavily debated topic lack nuances on how new cases are influenced by changing testing strategies or how the number of deaths may lag behind new case numbers, it could lead to mistrust in the institutions that release the data.

With the rise of misinformation and conspiracy theories on social media, people may be compelled to believe that these visualizations were deliberately designed to hide this uncertainty. When viewing visualizations on a desktop, it is more possible to provide additional details such as links to additional sources, elaborate details on the data collection methodology, further explanations and additional aspects of the data in the visualization. On a desktop, a person may be more likely to open multiple browser tabs and follow hyperlinks to find additional background information, or even compare visualizations side by side. With the majority of people consuming their news—and the accompanying data visualizations—on mobile devices, simplified mobile visualizations combined with the increasing spread of misinformation could lead to mistrust in scientific institutions and governments.

Design Considerations

Both scenarios again highlight the importance of responsible visualization creation and improving education around interpreting visualizations. They additionally highlight a need to imagine the audience and emphasize uncertainty when appropriate.

Imagining the Audience. Getting feedback from people who might potentially use a visualization is central to visualization design principles. Estelle's case points out a need to ensure that visualizations are not only speaking to the largest audiences, but can also answer the questions of smaller or less-privileged groups. Estelle's example points out that mobile visualizations can strengthen the correlation between size and importance often made in visualizations, particularly when they aim to reflect real-world characteristics like maps. Ensuring that potential use cases like Estelle's are considered in the design of visualizations can help increase the utility for a broader group of people, and serve as a model for creating more equitable visualizations.

Supporting exploration and interaction. As previously discussed, limited real-estate and interaction techniques make supporting exploration of data a challenge. But when possible, it should be considered whether designs can support people in exploring data beyond what the visualization designer chose to present, such as through a details on demand paradigm[56]. While doing so can be difficult from an interaction design perspective, it can help alleviate limitations of missing context. Cross-device interactions can assist by extending the screen space on which a visualization can be interacted with, and thus supporting further context. Figure 7.4 demonstrates some cross-device interaction examples from past literature.

  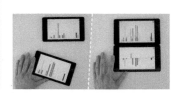

Figure 7.4 Left and Middle: Vistribute by Horak et al. [34]. Right: Vistiles by Langner et al. [41]. All images show cross-device interaction between visualizations. *Figures courtesy of Tom Horak, used with permission.*

Emphasizing Uncertainty. Given the increased reliance on choices made by designers in mobile visualization contexts, it is worth considering whether a mobile visualization can present when measures are uncertain, and how they are uncertain. Kay et al.'s approach [35] to displaying uncertainty around traffic prediction could serve as one model, using potential outcomes to help people understand a potential data distribution.

7.4.3 Persuasive Mobile Visualizations Can Foster Behavior Change, But Not Always for the Better

With persuasive technologies, it is possible to influence people's behavior and to change their attitude. Increasingly, computer technologies are being used to support this [25, 26, 47]. As described as far back as 2007 [27], mobile devices have become a powerful channel for digital persuasion. Only in recent years have researchers started to investigate, how visualization can contribute to influencing people or in making a message more persuasive. The power of persuasive visualization [48] can be particularly unleashed on mobile devices, which people have on them almost every day, in almost any environment.

Like with any persuasive technology, persuasive visualizations can function as a tool (e.g., supporting peoples' goals), medium (e.g., creating persuasive experiences), or social actor (e.g., creating social relationships) [25]. Many modern health or fitness apps, for example, have the functional role of a *tool*, because they support the people's ability to follow a goal they want to achieve. People might want to walk 10,000 steps, get 2 hours of REM sleep, get 30 minutes of activity, drink at least 3 liters of water, etc. to live a better and healthier life. Visualizations can also work as a *medium* if they facilitate data-driven *persuasive storytelling* [53]. If they, for example, include characters (animals, cartoon figures, avatars), they might even take over the role of a *social actor* and companion.

Therefore, the spectrum ranges from rather ambient or casual information visualizations [51] triggering or nudging people to sophisticated analysis tools monitoring personal behavior. Regarding the scope of change, there is a range from personal behavior change to societal impact. The following examples illustrate this bandwidth.

Scenarios

Cheating to reach a goal. Paul is sitting in the train on his way home from work. For him, the visualization of the daily steps on his fitness bracelet is an important motivation to stay in motion and healthy. This time, the bracelet shows him that he is still far from reaching his daily step goal because he did not have time to walk enough during the day (cf. Figure 7.5 left). However, if he fails to achieve his goal again, his company will not give him the monthly reward of 50 € extra pay, which he desperately needs to pay for his rent. Therefore, he starts to beat his fist wearing the fitness bracelet against his chest to simulate walking. When he arrives at home he receives a notification from his fitness bracelet that congratulates him of having walked 10,000 steps today even though he has been sitting all day.

Figure 7.5 Visualizations of activity or of nutrition can be persuasive, but also create feelings of guilt or judgment. Left: showing progress toward activity goals on a smartwatch. Right: highlighting the healthiness of food with "stoplight" indicators.

The impact of food choices. Katy is buying groceries for the weekend. When she has sufficient time and energy for shopping and cooking, she sometimes appreciates the mobile traffic light visualization of the nutritional value of any food in the store, which helps her making the right purchase decisions. Today, however, she knows she will not have time to cook a proper meal due to her taking care of her mother who has dementia. She walks up to the frozen food section and picks a frozen pizza and lasagna that she can just quickly warm up in the oven. As always she pays with her online cash system, which immediately depicts information about the types of foods she has bought (cf. Figure 7.5 right). She notices from the red food traffic light next to each item that she has only bought foods that have a high calorie count and she feels bad that she again is eating something unhealthy. Moreover, she is afraid of receiving a message from her insurance company that she needs to start eating more vegetables and healthy food to avoid an increase in her insurance fee, as she has heard happened to others already.

Visualization for good. The Adam family has three kids, and together they try to live an environmentally-friendly and climate-protecting life. When they received their electricity bill from last year, they were astonished to see in a static comparison chart that their energy consumption was even lower than that of an average four-person family. They installed an energy tracking app, eager to reduce their consumption even further and to make a comparison to the families in their neighbourhood. Besides tracking energy consumption for all means of transport the app uses GPS to surface the Adam's family energy consumption relative to those in their neighbourhood. They discover that they are only doing slightly better compared to families around them, and decide to improve on that. They install another app on their ethically produced and fair-traded mobile phone, allowing all family members to see the production methods and supply chains of products they want to buy. While going shopping for clothes, they can easily trace the origin of the product, its transport paths, and the estimated energy footprint associated with it.

Problem Description

There are many benefits to setting goals for oneself and persuasive mobile visualizations assisting in those goals, including following a healthier lifestyle, improving work performance and outcomes, or even contributing to solve societal problems. However, the first example also illustrates that reaching personal goals can sometimes become problematic and lead to personal pressure or even immoral personal decisions. Often visualizations such as the ones shown in Figure 7.5 left depict how far off a person is from reaching a goal. For example, the more color a radial chart contains, the closer one is to reaching a set goal.

If a person like Paul notices that all goals are still far off (their circles are mostly gray, cf. Figure 7.5, left), they might take immediate action, which can be a good motivation and help them lead healthier lives. However, it can also lead to people electing to reach their measured goals through means which do not support the overall, high-level goal. For simulating walking, there are even gadgets like phone cradles[10] to help people reach a specified step count, which can be used to get discounts in a personal health insurance or premium services as a reward. With health insurance companies potentially demanding similar information or goal-setting from their clients in the future, what is currently a private goal and moral dilemma can have more far reaching consequences.

The second example also shows a personal dilemma when buying (un)healthy food. When a visualization depicts such health information during shopping like with Katy's example, people might start to feel stressed over what they are eating. While it is beneficial and effective to classify food into easy to distinguish categories such as green (healthy), yellow (neutral), red (unhealthy) (cf. Figure 7.5, right), people suddenly have to make moral decisions about their lives and perhaps feel guilty about their choices. Again, these are private matters at first, but are subject to abuse by insurance companies, employers, fitness studios etc.

Less far reaching, the fact that other people might simply observe visualizations meant to be rather personal can have an impact. On the negative side, people might find it embarrassing to take some visibly unhealthy food from the shelf or that bypassers observe the visual feedback provided on a personal mobile phone indicating that they have not achieved their goal. On the positive side, if several people have access to a mobile visualization, this might trigger a positive behavior change. As an example, the GenderEQ app [11] provides a simple line graph swinging in the male or female direction over time to indicate speech distribution during a meeting and allowing a team to reflect on whether some members are talking more or less than others. Therefore, raising awareness can be an important goal of mobile visualizations.

---

[10]https://twitter.com/mbrennanchina/status/1128201958962032641?lang=en

[11]https://www.fastcompany.com/3068794/this-app-uses-ai-to-track-mansplaining-during-your-meetings

The third example highlights that mobile visualizations have the great opportunity to make people aware of more than the nutritional value of the food they buy. Individual behavior changes in choosing personal transportation or consuming energy can eventually influence larger problem contexts on a societal or even global scale. For example, the UbiGreen transportation display prototype is an application that semi-automatically senses and reveals information about transportation behavior [29]. People partly considered it to be game-like, engaged with it and saw a great potential for behavior change, but also highlighted the potential for cheating. For a comprehensive overview of persuasive technology for inducing sustainable mobility behaviors, see the state of the art report by Anagnostopoulou et al. [3].

It is both an important opportunity and challenge to design mobile visualizations so that they can help foster personal behavior change and even mitigate global problems like CO_2 emissions and climate change. In the long run, visualizations might even contribute to let what started as personal behavior change potentially result in societal impact. On the downside, people could become socially excluded if they did not use such tools or ignore what is suggested, or governments could abuse such visualizations to influence people in their interest.

Design considerations

Many techniques for developing persuasive visualizations have been proposed in research literature, often including some type of visualization or at least visual display [25, 27]. For a deeper analysis, guidelines for identifying and classifying persuasive elements of interfaces [46] may prove helpful. While not directly targeted at visualizations, criteria like credibility, privacy, personalization, attractiveness, solicitation, priming, commitment, and ascendency might help in developing own persuasive mobile visualizations.

Prior literature has surveyed persuasive techniques in particular application domains, like sustainable mobility behavior [3] or gamified systems for energy and water sustainability [1], which also discuss incentive mechanisms for inducing behavior change and design guidelines. In addition, hundreds of apps promising support for changing habits, attitude, mental and body state, etc., are available for mobile devices and demonstrate the big commercial interest in the behavior change domain.

Balancing information and persuasion. It is worth considering how a visualization can strike a balance between informing people and patronizing them or pushing them into a certain direction. Nudging people's behavior might be in conflict with the idea of an informed society, in which people are able to have access to substantial information and several opinions or arguments and empowered to make their own decisions. Mobile visualizations can offer assistance, but we suggest that people be able to decide how much, when, and in which way they want to leverage these techniques to help change their behavior. For example, in the case of saving the environment and preventing further climate change, mobile visualizations can help trigger behavior change, but should be mindful to avoid crossing the line to get a person's nerves or exhibit an attitude dictatorship.

Considering the impact of framing effects. How data in mobile visualization is framed has been shown to impact people's behaviors. For example, in TimeAware Kim et al. [37] show that a visualization showing how far off a person is from reaching their goal had a greater impact on productivity behavior than highlighting what they have achieved so far (cf. Figure 7.6). However, this framing also introduced stress. As a result of another study investigating the effect of framing on self-efficacy [12], Choe et al. recommend positive framing (highlighting what has already been achieved compared to still remaining). They also found text-only framing led to higher self-efficacy than a text with visual (colored progress bar) framing. Therefore, depending on the design goal, one framing may be preferable over the other, but they should not be treated as equivalent. Other framing choices such as colors and iconography can influence the persuasiveness of mobile visualizations while also generating other emotional responses such as strong sense of drive, stress, or even guilt.

Positive Framing
Productivity-emphasized

Negative Framing
Distraction-emphasized

Figure 7.6 Time Aware by Kim et al. [37] shows a visualization to indicate how far off a person is from reaching their goal. *Figure courtesy of and © Young-Ho Kim, used with permission.*

Letting people decide. When possible, it is important to give people control over the type of information they want to be shown, at which frequency, and even the level of detail. Often it is not good to surface as much objective data as possible. Again, data aggregation might help people to focus on the information they consider relevant to reach a goal. However, people should always have the opportunity to request more details, to compare, even to see other views or arguments. This also includes the visibility to others. In the data physicalization domain, for example, solutions have been proposed which show data significant for a single person or a group of initiated persons in physical form.[12] A knitted blanket (cf. Figure 7.7) or a knitted scarf, for example, could show individuals data encoded in colored stripes, resulting in a pattern that can only be deciphered by the wearer. It is also important to consider that especially for persuasive mobile visualizations one size does not fit all. Persuasive interventions can be personalized with regard to messages and visualizations, and

---

[12]See the website `http://dataphys.org/` for an overview on physical representations of data.

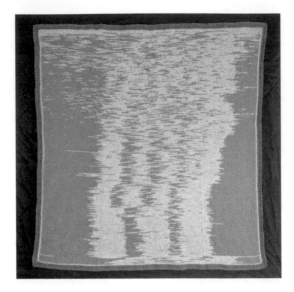

Figure 7.7 Knitted sleep pattern. Each stitch represents 6 minutes of time spent awake or asleep. *Photo courtesy of and © Seung Lee, used with permission.*

the intensity of such persuasive interventions can be adapted to peoples' goals and contexts, thereby increasing the effects of persuasive mobile applications [2].

Balancing personal freedom and societal needs. Some application cases involving mobile visualizations present challenges balancing individual freedom versus societal benefit, which again presents ethical challenges. The example of the world-wide COVID-19 pandemic has demonstrated how the temporal restriction of individual freedom and rights has had a positive impact on the health within the society. As described in many scenarios across the chapter, mobile visualizations played a crucial role in that regard to inform the public. One could argue that visualizations for good could follow a similar path and thereby, even though less drastically, contribute to a better society and world, for example, with regard to the prevalent climate change.

7.5 DISCUSSION

Many of the mobile visualizations scenarios we discussed in this chapter can be addressed with better understanding the people and use cases, careful design, and development of standards. Improving interaction techniques to enable people to further explore data and supporting customization of visualizations on a range of devices are important steps toward improving everyday use of mobile visualizations. But ultimately, well-intentioned designers can avoid many of these pitfalls, and we can collectively build up and develop an interaction language for supporting common mobile visualization tasks.

Other scenarios demonstrate how mobile visualization designers can use the lack of context, interaction, and education to deliberately mislead or misinform people. Others use mobile visualizations to persuade, which can promote help as well as harm. With mobile devices and varied contexts enabling visualizations to become more prevalent, these challenges pose serious concerns. Further understanding how designers are using mobile visualizations to mislead or nudge, and developing techniques and curricula to help address these challenges, we can aim to ensure that mobile visualizations are used to inform and improve society rather than undermine or cause undue stress.

In spite of the presented challenges, the scenarios and considerations we describe still demonstrate the immense opportunity for mobile visualizations to better help people understand and connect with their world and themselves. Increased access and glanceability supports people in understanding and interpreting data closer to the environments under which they need to make decisions, and can support increased passive reflection. Mobile contexts promote an opportunity to share knowledge gained with others. Increased visualization access can help people question and challenge their assumptions and enable deeper access to scientific knowledge and evidence.

We primarily ask future researchers, designers, and developers to consider the potential challenges their mobile visualizations or tools for creating mobile visualizations could promote alongside the benefits. Although we outline specific considerations when addressing the challenges we have surfaced, a more general approach is to integrate conversations around people's interaction, privacy, and ethical concerns into their design process, such as through *value-sensitive design* [28] or involving more stakeholders in the design process.

7.6 CONCLUSION

The ubiquity of mobile devices introduce tremendous opportunities for personal and societal understanding driven by visualization. However, the situational and physical realities of use influence how the data is able to be interpreted and interacted with. Through offering scenarios of use, we have illustrated the complexity of designing effective interactive, ethical, and privacy-conscious mobile visualizations. Although we offer a few considerations for future design based on research systems and commercial tools, there is a need to further study and report on challenges integrating mobile visualizations into everyday life.

REFERENCES

[1] Albertarelli, S., Fraternali, P., Herrera, S., Melenhorst, M., Novak, J., Pasini, C., Rizzoli, A.-E., and Rottondi, C. "A Survey on the Design of Gamified Systems for Energy and Water Sustainability". In: *Games* 9.3 (June 2018), p. 38. DOI: 10.3390/g9030038 (cited on page 230).

[2] Anagnostopoulou, E., Magoutas, B., and Bothos, E. "Persuasive Technologies for Sustainable Smart Cities: The Case of Urban Mobility". In: May 2019, pp. 73–82. DOI: 10.1145/3308560.3317058 (cited on page 232).

[3] Anagnostopoulou, E., Bothos, E., Magoutas, B., and Schrammel, J. "Persuasive Technologies for Sustainable Mobility: State of the Art and Emerging Trends". In: *Sustainability* 10 (June 2018), p. 2128. DOI: 10.3390/su10072128 (cited on page 230).

[4] Baudisch, P. and Chu, G. "Back-Of-Device Interaction Allows Creating Very Small Touch Devices". In: *Proceedings of the Conference on Human Factors in Computing Systems (CHI)*. CHI '09. Boston, MA, USA: ACM, 2009, pp. 1923–1932. DOI: 10.1145/1518701.1518995. URL: https://doi.org/10.1145/1518701.1518995 (cited on page 216).

[5] Bentley, F., Tollmar, K., Stephenson, P., Levy, L., Jones, B., Robertson, S., Price, E., Catrambone, R., and Wilson, J. "Health Mashups: Presenting Statistical Patterns Between Wellbeing Data and Context in Natural Language to Promote Behavior Change". In: *Transactions on Computer-Human Interaction (TOCHI)* 20.5 (Nov. 2013). DOI: 10.1145/2503823 (cited on page 224).

[6] Blascheck, T., Besançon, L., Bezerianos, A., Lee, B., and Isenberg, P. "Glanceable Visualization: Studies of Data Comparison Performance on Smartwatches". In: *Transactions on Visualization and Computer Graphics (TVCG)* 25.1 (Jan. 2018). **Open Access version:** https://hal.inria.fr/hal-01851306, pp. 630–640. DOI: 10.1109/TVCG.2018.2865142 (cited on page 218).

[7] Börner, K., Bueckle, A., and Ginda, M. "Data Visualization Literacy: Definitions, Conceptual Frameworks, Exercises, and Assessments". In: *Proceedings of the National Academy of Sciences (PNAS)* 116.6 (2019), pp. 1857–1864 (cited on page 222).

[8] Boy, J., Rensink, R. A., Bertini, E., and Fekete, J.-D. "A Principled Way of Assessing Visualization Literacy". In: *Transactions on Visualization and Computer Graphics (TVCG)* 20.12 (Dec. 2014), pp. 1963–1972. DOI: 10.1109/TVCG.2014.2346984 (cited on page 222).

[9] Buering, T., Gerken, J., and Reiterer, H. "User Interaction With Scatterplots on Small Screens - A Comparative Evaluation of Geometric-Semantic Zoom and Fisheye Distortion". In: *Transactions on Visualization and Computer Graphics (TVCG)* 12.5 (Sept. 2006), pp. 829–836. DOI: 10.1109/TVCG.2006.187. URL: https://doi.org/10.1109/TVCG.2006.187 (cited on page 217).

[10] Büring, T. and Reiterer, H. "ZuiScat: Querying and Visualizing Information Spaces on Personal Digital Assistants". In: *Proceedings of the Conference on Human Computer Interaction with Mobile Devices and Services (MobileHCI)*. MobileHCI '05. Salzburg, Austria: ACM, 2005, pp. 129–136. DOI: 10.1145/1085777.1085799. URL: https://doi.org/10.1145/1085777.1085799 (cited on page 217).

[11] Chang, K. S.-P., Danis, C. M., and Farrell, R. G. "Lunch Line: Using Public Displays and Mobile Devices to Encourage Healthy Eating in an Organization". In: *Proceedings of the Joint Conference on Pervasive and Ubiquitous Computing (Ubicomp)*. ACM, 2014, pp. 823–834. DOI: 10.1145/2632048.2636086 (cited on page 210).

[12] Choe, E. K., Lee, B., Munson, S., Pratt, W., and Kientz, J. "Persuasive Performance Feedback: The Effect of Framing on Self-Efficacy". In: *American Medical Informatics Association Annual Symposium Proceedings*. **Open Access**

version: https://www.ncbi.nlm.nih.gov/pmc/articles/PMC3900219/. American Medical Informatics Association, 2013, pp. 825–833 (cited on page 231).

[13] Chung, C.-F., Cook, J., Bales, E., Zia, J., and Munson, S. A. "More Than Telemonitoring: Health Provider Use and Nonuse of Life-Log Data in Irritable Bowel Syndrome and Weight Management". In: *Journal of Medical Internet Research (JMIR)* 17.8 (Aug. 2015), e203. DOI: 10.2196/jmir.4364. URL: http://www.jmir.org/2015/8/e203/ (cited on page 219).

[14] Cockburn, A., Karlson, A., and Bederson, B. B. "A Review of Overview+Detail, Zooming, and Focus+Context Interfaces". In: *Computing Surveys (CSUR)* 41.1 (Jan. 2009), 2:1–2:31. DOI: 10.1145/1456650.1456652. URL: http://doi.acm.org/10.1145/1456650.1456652 (cited on page 214).

[15] Consolvo, S., Klasnja, P., McDonald, D., Avrahami, D., Froehlich, J., LeGrand, L., Libby, R., Mosher, K., and Landay, J. "Flowers or a Robot Army? Encouraging Awareness & Activity With Personal, Mobile Displays". In: *Proceedings of the Conference on Ubiquitous Computing (Ubicomp)*. ACM, 2008, pp. 54–63 (cited on pages 214, 221).

[16] Consolvo, S., Libby, R., Smith, I., Landay, J., McDonald, D., Toscos, T., Chen, M., Froehlich, J., Harrison, B., Klasnja, P., LaMarca, A., and LeGrand, L. "Activity Sensing in the Wild: A Field Trial of Ubifit Garden". In: *Proceedings of the Conference on Human Factors in Computing Systems (CHI)*. ACM, 2008, pp. 1797–1806. DOI: 10.1145/1357054.1357335 (cited on page 221).

[17] Correll, M. "Ethical Dimensions of Visualization Research". In: *Proceedings of the Conference on Human Factors in Computing Systems (CHI)*. ACM, 2019, pp. 1–13. DOI: 10.1145/3290605.3300418 (cited on pages 222–224).

[18] Devendorf, L., Lo, J., Howell, N., Lee, J. L., Gong, N.-W., Karagozler, M. E., Fukuhara, S., Poupyrev, I., Paulos, E., and Ryokai, K. ""I Don't Want to Wear a Screen": Probing Perceptions of and Possibilities for Dynamic Displays on Clothing". In: *Proceedings of the Conference on Human Factors in Computing Systems (CHI)*. CHI '16. **Open Access version:** https://escholarship.org/content/qt976075wj/qt976075wj.pdf. San Jose, California, USA: ACM, 2016, pp. 6028–6039. DOI: 10.1145/2858036.2858192 (cited on page 216).

[19] Dohr, A., Engler, J., Bentley, F., and Whalley, R. "Gluballoon: An Unobtrusive and Educational Way to Better Understand One's Diabetes". In: *Proceedings of the Conference on Ubiquitous Computing (Ubicomp)*. ACM, 2012, pp. 665–666. DOI: 10.1145/2370216.2370357 (cited on page 223).

[20] Dörk, M., Feng, P., Collins, C., and Carpendale, S. "Critical InfoVis: Exploring the Politics of Visualization". In: *Extended Abstracts of the Conference on Human Factors in Computing System (CHI)*. **Open Access version:** http://hdl.handle.net/10155/1229. ACM, 2013, pp. 2189–2198. DOI: https://doi.org/10.1145/2468356.2468739 (cited on page 222).

[21] Epstein, D., Cordeiro, F., Bales, E., Fogarty, J., and Munson, S. "Taming Data Complexity in Lifelogs: Exploring Visual Cuts of Personal Informatics Data". In: *Proceedings of the Conference on Designing Interactive Systems (DIS)*. **Open Access version:** https://depstein.net/assets/pubs/depstein_dis14.pdf. 2014, pp. 667–676. DOI: 10.1145/2598510.2598558 (cited on page 224).

[22] Epstein, D. A., Borning, A., and Fogarty, J. "Fine-Grained Sharing of Sensed Physical Activity: A Value Sensitive Approach". In: *Proceedings of the Joint Conference on Pervasive and Ubiquitous Computing (Ubicomp)*. **Open Access version:** https://depstein.net/assets/pubs/depstein_ubi13.pdf. ACM, 2013, pp. 489–498. DOI: 10.1145/2493432.2493433 (cited on page 221).

[23] Epstein, D. A., Lee, N. B., Kang, J. H., Agapie, E., Schroeder, J., Pina, L. R., Fogarty, J., Kientz, J. A., and Munson, S. "Examining Menstrual Tracking to Inform the Design of Personal Informatics Tools". In: *Proceedings of the Conference on Human Factors in Computing Systems (CHI)*. **Open Access version:** https://www.ncbi.nlm.nih.gov/pmc/articles/PMC5432133/. ACM, 2017, pp. 6876–6888. DOI: 10.1145/3025453.3025635 (cited on page 220).

[24] Espeland, W. N. and Stevens, M. L. "A Sociology of Quantification". In: *European Journal of Sociology* 49.3 (2008), pp. 401–436. DOI: 10.1017/S0003975609000150 (cited on page 211).

[25] Fogg, B. J. *Persuasive Technology: Using Computers to Change What We Think and Do*. Morgan Kaufmann, 2002 (cited on pages 227, 230).

[26] Fogg, B. "Persuasive Computers: Perspectives and Research Directions". In: *Proceedings of the Conference on Human Factors in Computing Systems (CHI)*. CHI '98. Los Angeles, California, USA: ACM/Addison-Wesley, 1998, pp. 225–232. DOI: 10.1145/274644.274677. URL: https://doi.org/10.1145/274644.274677 (cited on page 227).

[27] Fogg, B. and Eckles, D. *Mobile Persuasion: 20 Perspectives on the Future of Behavior Change*. Stanford Captology Media, 2007 (cited on pages 227, 230).

[28] Friedman, B. "Value-Sensitive Design". In: *Interactions* 3.6 (1996), pp. 16–23 (cited on page 233).

[29] Froehlich, J., Dillahunt, T., Klasnja, P., Mankoff, J., Consolvo, S., Harrison, B., and Landay, J. A. "UbiGreen: Investigating a Mobile Tool for Tracking and Supporting Green Transportation Habits". In: *Proceedings of the Conference on Human Factors in Computing Systems (CHI)*. CHI '09. Boston, MA, USA: ACM, 2009, pp. 1043–1052. DOI: 10.1145/1518701.1518861. URL: https://doi.org/10.1145/1518701.1518861 (cited on page 230).

[30] Girouard, A., Lo, J., Riyadh, M., Daliri, F., Eady, A. K., and Pasquero, J. "One-Handed Bend Interactions With Deformable Smartphones". In: *Proceedings of the Conference on Human Factors in Computing Systems (CHI)*. CHI '15. Seoul, Republic of Korea: ACM, 2015, pp. 1509–1518. DOI: 10.1145/2702123.

2702513. URL: https://doi.org/10.1145/2702123.2702513 (cited on page 218).

[31] Gouveia, R., Pereira, F., Karapanos, E., Munson, S., and Hassenzahl, M. "Exploring the Design Space of Glanceable Feedback for Physical Activity Trackers". In: *Proceedings of the Joint Conference on Pervasive and Ubiquitous Computing (Ubicomp)*. ACM, 2016, pp. 144–155 (cited on pages 214, 220, 221).

[32] Hauser, H. "Generalizing Focus+Context Visualization". In: *Scientific Visualization: The Visual Extraction of Knowledge from Data*. Edited by Bonneau, G.-P., Ertl, T., and Nielson, G. M. Berlin, Heidelberg: Springer, 2006, pp. 305–327 (cited on page 214).

[33] Hintze, D., Hintze, P., Findling, R. D., and Mayrhofer, R. "A Large-Scale, Long-Term Analysis of Mobile Device Usage Characteristics". In: *Proceedings of the ACM on Interactive, Mobile, Wearable and Ubiquitous Technologies (IMWUT)* 1.2 (2017), pp. 1–21. DOI: 10.1145/3090078 (cited on page 224).

[34] Horak, T., Mathisen, A., Klokmose, C. N., Dachselt, R., and Elmqvist, N. "Vistribute: Distributing Interactive Visualizations in Dynamic Multi-Device Setups". In: *Proceedings of the Conference on Human Factors in Computing Systems (CHI)*. **Open Access version:** https://imld.de/cnt/uploads/Horak-Vistribute-CHI2019.pdf. ACM, 2019, 616:1–616:13. DOI: 10.1145/3290605.3300846 (cited on page 226).

[35] Kay, M., Kola, T., Hullman, J., and Munson, S. "When (Ish) Is My Bus? User-Centered Visualizations of Uncertainty in Everyday, Mobile Predictive Systems". In: *Proceedings of the Conference on Human Factors in Computing Systems (CHI)*. ACM, 2016, pp. 5092–5103 (cited on pages 210, 227).

[36] Kim, N. W., Im, H., Henry Riche, N., Wang, A., Gajos, K., and Pfister, H. "DataSelfie: Empowering People to Design Personalized Visuals to Represent Their Data". In: *Proceedings of the Conference on Human Factors in Computing Systems (CHI)*. ACM, 2019, pp. 1–12. DOI: 10.1145/3290605.3300309 (cited on page 214).

[37] Kim, Y.-H., Jeon, J. H., Choe, E. K., Lee, B., Kim, K., and Seo, J. "TimeAware: Leveraging Framing Effects to Enhance Personal Productivity". In: *Proceedings of the Conference on Human Factors in Computing Systems (CHI)*. **Open Access version:** https://www.microsoft.com/en-us/research/uploads/prod/2016/12/TimeAware-CHI2016.pdf. ACM, 2016, pp. 272–283. DOI: 10.1145/2858036.2858428 (cited on page 231).

[38] Kim, Y.-H., Lee, B., Srinivasan, A., and Choe, E. K. "Data@Hand: Fostering Visual Exploration of Personal Data on Smartphones Leveraging Speech and Touch Interaction". In: *Proceedings of the Conference on Human Factors in Computing Systems (CHI)*. **Open Access version:** https://arxiv.org/abs/2101.06283. ACM, 2021. DOI: 10.1145/3411764.3445421 (cited on page 218).

[39] Klamka, K., Horak, T., and Dachselt, R. "Watch+Strap: Extending Smart-watches With Interactive StrapDisplays". In: *Proceedings of the Conference on Human Factors in Computing Systems (CHI)*. CHI '20. **Open Access version:** https://dl.acm.org/doi/10.1145/3313831.3376199. New York, NY, USA: ACM, 2020, pp. 1–15. DOI: 10.1145/3313831.3376199 (cited on page 218).

[40] Kong, H.-K., Liu, Z., and Karahalios, K. "Frames and Slants in Titles of Visualizations on Controversial Topics". In: *Proceedings of the Conference on Human Factors in Computing Systems (CHI)*. ACM, 2018, pp. 1–12 (cited on page 222).

[41] Langner, R., Horak, T., and Dachselt, R. "VisTiles: Coordinating and Combining Co-Located Mobile Devices for Visual Data Exploration". In: *Transactions on Visualization and Computer Graphics (TVCG)* 24.1 (Jan. 2018). **Open Access version:** https://imld.de/cnt/uploads/Langner_VisTiles_InfoVis17.pdf, pp. 626–636. DOI: 10.1109/TVCG.2017.2744019 (cited on page 226).

[42] Li, I., Dey, A., and Forlizzi, J. "A Stage-Based Model of Personal Informatics Systems". In: *Proceedings of the Conference on Human Factors in Computing Systems (CHI)*. ACM, 2010, pp. 557–566. DOI: 10.1145/1753326.1753409 (cited on page 211).

[43] Lupton, D. *The Quantified Self*. Wiley, 2016 (cited on page 211).

[44] Mamykina, L., Heitkemper, E. M., Smaldone, A. M., Kukafka, R., Cole-Lewis, H. J., Davidson, P. G., Mynatt, E. D., Cassells, A., Tobin, J. N., and Hripcsak, G. "Personal Discovery in Diabetes Self-Management: Discovering Cause and Effect Using Self-Monitoring Data". In: *Journal of Biomedical Informatics* 76 (2017), pp. 1–8. DOI: 10.1016/j.jbi.2017.09.013. URL: http://www.sciencedirect.com/science/article/pii/S1532046417302174 (cited on page 219).

[45] Mishra, S. R., Miller, A. D., Haldar, S., Khelifi, M., Eschler, J., Elera, R. G., Pollack, A. H., and Pratt, W. "Supporting Collaborative Health Tracking in the Hospital: Patients' Perspectives". In: *Proceedings of the Conference on Human Factors in Computing Systems (CHI)*. CHI '18. Montreal QC, Canada: ACM, 2018, pp. 1–14. DOI: 10.1145/3173574.3174224. URL: https://doi.org/10.1145/3173574.3174224 (cited on page 219).

[46] Némery, A. and Brangier, E. "Set of Guidelines for Persuasive Interfaces: Organization and Validation of the Criteria". In: *Journal of Usability Studies (JUS)* 9.3 (May 2014), pp. 105–128 (cited on page 230).

[47] Oinas-Kukkonen, H. and Harjumaa, M. "A Systematic Framework for Designing and Evaluating Persuasive Systems". In: *Proceedings of the Conference on Persuasive Technology (Persuasive)*. Edited by Oinas-Kukkonen, H., Hasle, P., Harjumaa, M., Segerståhl, K., and Øhrstrøm, P. Berlin, Heidelberg: Springer, 2008, pp. 164–176 (cited on page 227).

[48] Pandey, A. V., Manivannan, A., Nov, O., Satterthwaite, M., and Bertini, E. "The Persuasive Power of Data Visualization". In: *Transactions on Visualization and Computer Graphics (TVCG)* 20.12 (2014), pp. 2211–2220. DOI: 10.1109/TVCG.2014.2346419 (cited on page 227).

[49] Peck, E. M., Ayuso, S. E., and El-Etr, O. "Data Is Personal: Attitudes and Perceptions of Data Visualization in Rural Pennsylvania". In: *Proceedings of the Conference on Human Factors in Computing Systems (CHI)*. CHI '19. Glasgow, Scotland Uk: ACM, 2019. DOI: 10.1145/3290605.3300474. URL: https://doi.org/10.1145/3290605.3300474 (cited on page 222).

[50] Pelurson, S. and Nigay, L. "Multimodal Interaction With a Bifocal View on Mobile Devices". In: *Proceedings of the Conference on Multimodal Interaction (ICMI)*. ICMI '15. Seattle, Washington, USA: ACM, 2015, pp. 191–198. DOI: 10.1145/2818346.2820731. URL: https://doi.org/10.1145/2818346.2820731 (cited on pages 217, 218).

[51] Pousman, Z., Stasko, J., and Mateas, M. "Casual Information Visualization: Depictions of Data in Everyday Life". In: *Transactions on Visualization and Computer Graphics (TVCG)* 13.6 (2007). **Open Access version:** https://www.cc.gatech.edu/~john.stasko/papers/infovis07-casual.pdf, pp. 1145–1152. DOI: 10.1109/TVCG.2007.70541 (cited on pages 210, 227).

[52] Rajabiyazdi, F., Perin, C., Oehlberg, L., and Carpendale, S. "Exploring the Design of Patient-Generated Data Visualizations". In: *Proceedings of the Graphics Interface Conference (GI)*. **Open Access version:** https://hal.archives-ouvertes.fr/hal-02861239. Canadian Information Processing Society, 2020 (cited on page 223).

[53] Riche, N. H., Hurter, C., Diakopoulos, N., and Carpendale, S. *Data-Driven Storytelling*. A K Peters Visualization Series. A K Peters/CRC Press, 2018. DOI: 10.1201/9781315281575 (cited on page 227).

[54] Roberts, J. C. "State of the Art: Coordinated & Multiple Views in Exploratory Visualization". In: *Proceedings of the Conference on Coordinated and Multiple Views in Exploratory Visualization (CMV)*. **Open Access version:** https://kar.kent.ac.uk/14569/. Los Alamitos, CA, USA: IEEE, 2007, pp. 61–71. DOI: 10.1109/CMV.2007.20 (cited on page 214).

[55] Segel, E. and Heer, J. "Narrative Visualization: Telling Stories With Data". In: *Transactions on Visualization and Computer Graphics (TVCG)* 16.6 (2010), pp. 1139–1148. DOI: 10.1109/TVCG.2010.179 (cited on page 210).

[56] Shneiderman, B. "The Eyes Have It: A Task by Data Type Taxonomy for Information Visualizations". In: *Proceedings of the Symposium on Visual Languages (VL)*. **Open Access version:** http://hdl.handle.net/1903/466. Los Alamitos: IEEE, 1996, pp. 336–343. DOI: 10.1109/VL.1996.545307 (cited on page 226).

[57]   Siek, K. A., Rogers, Y., and Connelly, K. H. "Fat Finger Worries: How Older and Younger Users Physically Interact With PDAs". In: *Proceedings of the Conference on Human-Computer Interaction (INTERACT)*. INTERACT '05. Rome, Italy: Springer, 2005, pp. 267–280. DOI: 10.1007/11555261_24. URL: https://doi.org/10.1007/11555261_24 (cited on page 216).

[58]   Spindler, M., Schuessler, M., Martsch, M., and Dachselt, R. "Pinch-Drag-Flick vs. Spatial Input: Rethinking Zoom & Pan on Mobile Displays". In: *Proceedings of the Conference on Human Factors in Computing Systems (CHI)*. CHI '14. **Open Access version:** https://imld.de/cnt/uploads/paper425-Pinch-Drag-Flick-vs.-Spatial-Input.pdf. Toronto, Ontario, Canada: ACM, 2014, pp. 1113–1122. DOI: 10.1145/2556288.2557028. URL: https://doi.org/10.1145/2556288.2557028 (cited on page 218).

[59]   Srinivasan, A., Lee, B., Riche, N. H., Drucker, S. M., and Hinckley, K. "InChorus: Designing Consistent Multimodal Interactions for Data Visualization on Tablet Devices". In: *Proceedings of the Conference on Human Factors in Computing Systems (CHI)*. **Open Access version:** https://arxiv.org/abs/2001.06423. New York: ACM, 2020, 653:1–653:13. DOI: 10.1145/3313831.3376782 (cited on page 218).

[60]   Vogel, D. and Baudisch, P. "Shift: A Technique for Operating Pen-Based Interfaces Using Touch". In: *Proceedings of the Conference on Human Factors in Computing Systems (CHI)*. CHI '07. San Jose, California, USA: ACM, 2007, pp. 657–666. DOI: 10.1145/1240624.1240727. URL: https://doi.org/10.1145/1240624.1240727 (cited on page 218).

[61]   Zhai, S. and Kristensson, P.-O. "Shorthand Writing on Stylus Keyboard". In: *Proceedings of the Conference on Human Factors in Computing Systems (CHI)*. CHI '03. Ft. Lauderdale, Florida, USA: ACM, 2003, pp. 97–104. DOI: 10.1145/642611.642630. URL: https://doi.org/10.1145/642611.642630 (cited on page 218).

CHAPTER 8

Mobile Visualization Design: An Ideation Method to Try

Sheelagh Carpendale
Simon Fraser University, Canada

Petra Isenberg
Université Paris-Saclay, CNRS, Inria, LISN, France

Charles Perin
University of Victoria, Canada

Tanja Blascheck
University of Stuttgart, Germany

Foroozan Daneshzand
Simon Fraser University, Canada

Alaul Islam
Université Paris-Saclay, CNRS, Inria, LISN, France

Katherine Currier
University of Calgary, Canada

Peter Buk, Victor Cheung, Lien Quach, Laton Vermette
Simon Fraser University, Canada

CONTENTS

DOI: 10.1201/9781003090823-8

I N many ways, mobile visualization is proliferating. Yet, most visualizations on mobile devices are still drawing from the experiences we have with visualizations on larger screens. In this chapter, we present an ideation methodology that can help us to imagine future mobile visualizations through a human-centered design approach. We begin by outlining the general approach of the methodology and then describe how it was adapted and changed to fit the needs of three groups. This chapter is an experience report about how three different groups adapted a design methodology to suit their circumstances. All the design method adaptions explored were successful in encouraging a wide range of ideas to emerge.

8.1 INTRODUCTION

The goal of this chapter is to offer a simple, generative process illustrated by our experiences with its use, with which designers can derive a rich set of ideas for mobile visualization applications that are meant to communicate data visually in a specific usage context. Designing visualizations for small carryable or wearable mobile devices is not an easy task. Many mobile apps that include graphical data representations adjust and simplify desktop-sized visualizations and make them available with simple interactions. These relatively direct design translations point to possible untapped opportunities for visualization and interaction design. Considering both the technological differences and the usage differences in mobile contexts, it seems extremely likely that these untapped opportunities exist. Concerning technological differences, visualizations for mobile devices can take advantage of novel input modalities that do not exist on desktops: accelerometers, gyroscopes, or personal health related sensors for heart-rate, oxymetry, skin temperature, etc. Through sensors, mobile devices have direct access to data and can provide quick contextual information to viewers. Most carryable and wearable devices also have smaller screens or screens that have completely different form factors than desktop or laptop screens. This opens up opportunities to develop novel dedicated visualizations rather than trying to make existing representation techniques fit. Concerning mobile usage contexts, people's motivation for using mobile visualizations is often much unlike those for stationary office workers sitting in front of larger desktop or laptop screens. In mobile contexts, for example, people: (1) may want to gain better awareness and understanding of their surroundings and current situation, (2) integrate this situational information into their current activities, and (3) understand, share, or analyze data in non-office surroundings with motion, uncontrolled lighting, or noise.

To let go of the limitations that come with designing by translating existing visualizations and adapting them to mobile scenarios, we have devised and explored a flexible design process. This design process can help us to think of mobile visualizations by considering specific contexts of use, mobile-specific tasks, and personal use cases. Specifically, the design process involves stepping into specific usage contexts and tasks, then taking moments to reflect on the current situation and information needs, ideating design ideas, and reflecting on them with others. The goal of the methodology is to create a rich set of different ideas in context of a specific use case. Assessing the "value" of each individual idea, refining it, selecting or discarding it, is a task intrinsic to the motivation of each idea generating group that uses the methodology. This chapter, therefore, does not discuss methods to assess the novelty, effectiveness, or potential success of an idea. We also do not claim that the methodology produces "better" ideas than other methodologies, if that is even something that can ever be claimed about an ideation methodology. Instead, in this chapter we offer a methodology we explored and found useful for generating rich ideas for mobile visualizations that communicate data visually. We detail how the design methodology works in general, how three different design groups adapted it, and provide examples of the richness of the ideas that emerged in five design sessions.

8.2 RELATIONSHIP TO OTHER DESIGN METHODOLOGIES

The basic ideation methodology, which we used for the workshops we describe below, was first explored and then published as a workshop paper [5] with a focus on in situ journaling by a single person. Here, we give more details on the method, relax the frequency of note taking and sketching, and give evidence about how the method can be adjusted and appropriated to different scenarios. The method discussed here still centers around sketching, a method Buxton [4, 7] describes as a distinct form of drawing that supports exploration and communication of ideas about designs. Dedicated "data sketches" have been found and studied on whiteboards [17] and supported in data presentation and exploration interfaces [3, 10, 11] giving evidence that people frequently think and brainstorm with data. As a support mechanism for data visualization ideation, sketching has been in particular promoted as part of the Five Design Sheet methodology [14] or the Visualization Worksheets [12]. Yet, these approaches focus on specific details about a given part of the ideation process such as designing an encoding. Our method is more closely related to approaches for ideation in situated visualization design. Bressa et al. [2] recently discussed a series of seven design workshops that, similar to ours, used a variety of props and sketching sessions to create ideas for situated visualizations. Discussions during ideation centered around several questions that were different from ours, such as where to and how to place the visualizations in the world but surfaced some similar concerns, such as designing simple rather than complex visualizations that can be parsed at-a-glance.

Much of the visualization design ideation advice has tended to focus on specific situations in which factors such as the data, and domain experts are known (see, for example, Sedlmair et al. [15]), or to provide specific details about a given part of the ideation process such as designing an encoding [14]. Our approach takes inspiration from several sources including behavioral sampling [1, 6], repetitive sketching techniques [7], and enactment of scenarios [8]. Within the larger space of ideation our method belongs to the empathic design methodologies [16]. The goal here is for designers to learn how their designs might be experienced in the intended usage surroundings. Many of the techniques that exist to help designers understand these real-world experiences range from simple "what-could-be" observations, role playing, or taking existing prototypes into target environments. Bodystorming [13] is a technique similar to ours as it focuses on design sessions in the intended context of use coupled with discussions and further brainstorming on-site. It has been promoted for the ideation of ubiquitous computing interfaces but follows a different preparation phase as it gives participants specific design questions to target.

On a higher level, our method follows in the tradition of the IDEO Method Cards [9], which intentionally provide a minimal description as a starting point—typically, one image, a title, and 2–3 sentences. The idea is that this minimal description helps trigger within each person or group of people an ideation method that best matches their current needs. In this chapter, we provide more detail, intending to focus on mobile visualization scenarios while still offering considerable flexibility in the execution of the methodology. You will note that each group adapted the method to their personal, current situation, but within these variations, all groups found it a rich idea generator.

8.3   MOBILE VISUALIZATION IDEATION METHODOLOGY

In this section we describe the general ideation methodology that can be followed and adapted to conceive new designs for specific mobile visualization contexts. We have successfully applied this methodology in a variety of mobile visualization scenarios, with small modifications. Three design groups started from a basic list of instructions that were adjusted as needed for the specific situation. We started with some initial ideas for taking a pro-active approach to specific future mobile visualization ideation [5] to develop and explore a flexible mobile visualization ideation methodology in use. Through exploration we have learned a lot about the power of these approaches and the effectiveness of many variations.

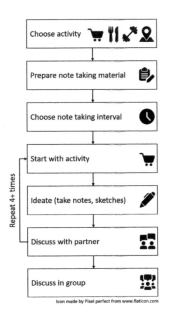

Figure 8.1 General steps of the ideation method.

In general, the ideation activity takes 1–3 hours. It is meant to be done as a paired activity to have another person to share the experience with and discuss ideas with (cf. Figure 8.1). Together both partners *choose an activity* (for example, getting food on campus, going to the mall, going to the gym, going to the library, going home) that is agreeable to both partners as well as the mobile context for which they would like to design (phones, smartwatches, fitness bracelets, etc.). Next, both partners choose and *prepare note taking material* and decide on a note taking procedure. Note taking materials can consist of digital devices, mobile device props made out of other material such as paper or cardboard, or simple notebooks. Once materials and situation are ready, both partners should use a note taking procedure that works for their scenario. Typically, both partners start with their activity and stop after an agreed-upon time interval (*choose note taking interval*), with every 30 minutes being a good first estimate. During every activity gap each partner individually evaluates their information needs in the current situation and sketches a visualization that would address these needs in the current situation for the chosen mobile device (*ideate*). Notes should be added to the sketches so ideas are clearly communicated for later re-assessment of the sketches. After the sketching time *both partners discuss* their ideas and add comments, adjustments, or variations to their notes and sketches. Then, partners continue with the activity for the next time interval and repeat the previous two steps. It is ideal to try the activity at least four times, or more as needed. After the end of the exercise partners meet as a group to go over all their sketches, generate affinity diagrams, and choose the most promising ideas to iterate on further.

8.4 IDEATION ACTIVITIES—MOBILE VISUALIZATION FUTURES

Next, we describe the ideation activities of three different groups to illustrate how one can adapt and adjust the methodology to specific ideation scenarios. The groups involved professors, researchers, and students at Simon Frasier University (Group 1), the University of Victoria (Group 2), and the University of Stuttgart, Inria, and University of Paris-Saclay (Group 3).

All groups started from the basic activities as described in the methodology section (cf. Section 8.3), however, all did some contextual adjustments. Considering that one of the primary motivations of this ideation methodology is to leverage the reality of one's current situation, it seems appropriate to make adjustments as one's context changes. Therefore, the ideation activity part is separated as follows: Section 8.4.1 includes one person's ideation with notes taken in situ; Section 8.4.2 includes one person's ideation when the immediate situation is not conducive to note taking so note taking is done posthoc; Section 8.4.3 covers two people's ideation variations; and Section 8.4.4 contains examples from an in-context activity during which people separated into pairs for specific activities but reassembled regularly and held discussions as a group.

8.4.1 Approach 1: One Person with In Situ Notes

The ideation activities in Group 1 were part of a larger discussion around the challenge of coming up with ideas that were explicitly for mobile visualization. The five participants in Group 1 discussed the simple methodology and there was a fair amount of skepticism as to whether it would make much of a difference. The initial plan was to try the activity in pairs but the reality of long commutes in different directions resulted in much of this exercises being done individually. These one person ideation activities covered specific use cases often inspired by being alone. People had in particular ideas about supporting private choices and about making alone time more interesting. After each person in the group ideated several times during the activity, they re-grouped and discussed the ideas that had emerged. Everyone was surprised and pleased by the amount, the range, and the richness of the generated ideas. The examples mentioned in this section are just a small subset of those we came up with. The following examples are from different people but we retained the first person pronoun in the descriptions of the examples to give a more active and personal sense of the ideation process.

Food Choices and Exercise as Concrete Visualization

I started my ideation activity in a restaurant I visited alone. I am a health-conscious person and wanted help to choose between a meat lover pizza and a cheeseburger that both

tempted me. In this particular moment, I had two information needs: 1) I wanted to see how long I would have to run to burn off each food option and 2) how satiating each food would be—that is, to what extent the food choice would contribute to me feeling full. I sketched a visualization on my phone that would help me answer these two questions and plan my future workout and diet consciously. The sketch shows a hamburger compared to other options which are equal to two slices of pizza! Meanwhile, I can also see how long I should do a specific exercise to burn the calories I gained. On the right side, the satiating power of each of the options is illustrated.

Foroozan Daneshzand
Primary idea generator

What is Nearby?

I would like to enrich the dead time during my commute—such as when I am waiting for or sitting on a bus. I realise that I often miss information about events near where I live. For instance, when walking home, I saw a flyer for the art exhibition of one of my favorite artists. She has been in town and I missed it! Perhaps there are many events, festivals, courses, and exhibitions happening around us which we might be eager to join but we never learn about them. To get information about these types of activities, we need to sit in front of the monitor, spend hours searching and reading about them on different pages. A phone visualization could help us find the best spot in a short time. By sorting the events based on our interests, we can figure out which one is closer to us, people liked the most, is more affordable, etc.

Foroozan Daneshzand
Primary idea generator

Enroute on Transit

My ideation activity was conducted as I took a long hour and a half commute from school to a friend's place. I conducted the ideation activity at the bus stop and while in transit, considering what information would make my commute more interesting as well as informative.

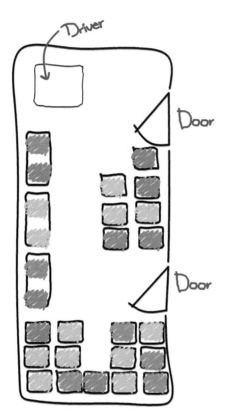

While boarding the bus, I was interested in seeing a bus seat heat map showing the most popular seats on the bus. Such a heatmap would be interesting for me but also bus maintenance staff. During the bus ride I wanted to see status information on my journey including possible delays. I also considered how little I knew about the neighborhoods I was passing through. Commuting is a chance to learn about the neighborhoods and the buildings around us. An interactive visualization can show an overview breakdown of neighborhood data as well as more detailed building level data to find out how these buildings are used. For example, one area might be more business-oriented while another is more residential. Each intersection could also present data on pedestrian traffic or past traffic accidents. All of this information could be presented as an overlay on the route to create an engaging navigation experience. Later, I was transferring from my bus to a train and I noticed that the station felt emptier than usual that day. This got me thinking about how crowded or busy some of the other nearby stations might be. I would like to see whether there are certain stations that I might want to avoid because of overcrowding and at which stations I am more likely to find a seat at and not have to wait for multiple trains to pass before I can board. Once I was on the train, I started thinking about all sorts of train-related data that I would love to have visualized. First, it would be great if I could just see a map showing the real-time location of all the trains active on the system and some extra trivia about each train. The track has a few different train models running on it, some of which are much older than others, so seeing what types of trains there are across the whole transit system would be neat. I would also love to see how the track elevation changes across the system somehow, spanning from several stories underground all the way up to tall bridges and overpasses. Finally, learning more about the particular vehicle I am on could make me feel more connected as a rider because I am not just getting on any train, but a particular one with its own history and maintenance schedule.

Peter Buk, Lien Quach, Laton Vermette
Primary idea generators

Technology Shopping

After a long commute, I arrived at my favourite technology store. With climate change being a hot topic amongst people these days, I pondered about the environmental impact of buying new devices. As a consumer, I realized I knew nothing about the manufacturing process of appliances and electronics. That is when I thought of a new visualization: GreenTech.

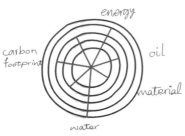

DETAILS ON ENVIRONMENTAL IMPACT

GreenTech would allow people to scan a product to receive information about the manufacturing process and environmental impact the product had. My motivation for this visualization was to bridge the knowledge gap between manufacturers and consumers. By being mobile, GreenTech would allow consumers to access this information quickly, granted that they had a mobile device. Thus, increasing ecological awareness of consumerism. This could help people make more informed decisions while decreasing their carbon footprint. In addition, I wanted a visualization tool that would let me see notable discounts for my store as well as more details about a product and a price history graph to allow for comparison. A feature to see what items have been popular lately at the current store location would be interesting. A similar visualization could be useful for store employees as well.

Lien Quach
Primary idea generator

At the Grocery Store

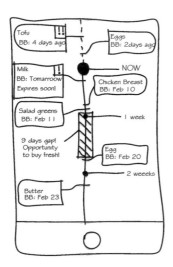

I started my trip with a visit to the grocery store to pick up some ingredients for a shared meal, and a few things to bring home. As I was picking things out, I wished I had a better idea of what was already in my fridge and pantry at home, and in particular when certain things were going to expire. I wanted some way to see how those best before dates clustered over time, and whether there were any multi-day gaps in the near future that might be a good opportunity to stock up on fresh food. Then being able to compare how those dates line up with what is available at the store would be useful! I would also benefit from being able to filter and see whether, for instance, I have a steady supply of eggs to boil up over the next few weeks. I wanted to see a heat map where in the grocery store I typically spend most of my time, to reflect on the types of food I eat and what places I pause a lot to make food decisions (I know I can be rather choosy in the meat aisle!).

Laton Vermette
Primary idea generator

The examples above are just a small subset of the ideas generated by one person using this methodology and taking at least preliminary notes on location. We had 27 ideas and many of them did not include sketches. Authors in this group generally felt surprised and delighted at their and each others ideas when we discussed them as a group after the ideation activity. Everyone came up with ideas, even those who were initially somewhat skeptical.

Bus and train commuting were part of the context explored by all and offered rich opportunities for engagement and empowerment as part of the typical journey. Additional ideas included: Data on how busy the bus route is throughout the day; Alternative times and routes if one route has problems, is too delayed, or too full; Data during bus route, how far along route, typical according to traffic times, insights into real time traffic data along with historic data; Data about the bus/train car you are taking, how long it has been in service, last maintenance; What section of tracks have lower/higher average speeds? What is the noise level inside/outside the train; noise level at this location? Map average "track screech" levels across the entire system; accessibility data (how many flights of stairs? Is the elevator/escalator working? etc.); and Transit payment information, compass card vs credit card.

Other ideas centered around learning about other people, who were on the same bus, in the same store, etc., or alternately taking a broader look at the city, possibly collecting data from a vast range of people. Activity and emotional data could be collected anonymized and visualized so that it is not intrusive, to increase people's empathetic understanding and awareness of the world around them. This could help make the concept of "sonder," the profound realization that every stranger around you is living their own lives just as complex as your own, more possible.

8.4.2 Approach 2: One Person with Post Hoc Notes

Sometimes taking notes in situ is awkward or uncomfortable, such as when one is walking alone at night. Sometimes it is not possible such as when one is riding a bike. However, as the examples below show, this does not mean that these situations are not amenable to good mobile visualization application. However, one has to adapt the above methodology. When sketching is impossible, it is important to still ask oneself the questions outlined in the methodology above: what information need does one have at the present moment and then mentally envisioning a mobile solution. To aid the later sketching of ideas, if possible, one can take quick markers, such as a "pin" in a GPS device or photos from a phone or head-mounted camera, as memory aids about the triggered moments to ideate.

The Green Waver

The activity for this example is bike commuting. With this activity comes constraints that led to several adjustments in the original methodology. First, commuting by bike is usually a single-person activity. Although in this example there was a child present, the child was in a trailer at the back, therefore, this was a one-person ideation process. I set an alarm on my watch to get a notification at a time I knew I would be commuting (once in the morning and once in the evening). Upon being notified, I "visualized" in my head a mobile visualization that I would find handy right at that time. Finally, I sketched the idea once I arrived at work / at home with some rough notes.

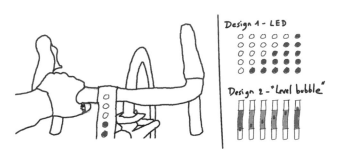

The first ideation was triggered at one of these frustrating times while waiting at a red light. When notified by my alarm, I was thinking about the green wave traffic lights popular in northern Europe. The idea behind green wave traffic [18] is to synchronize traffic lights so that if one maintains a constant speed they will get only green lights. For bikes, the target speed is usually between 15 and 20 km/h. This train of thought made me think of two simple designs, aimed at providing the same information to cyclists. The first design uses a series of LEDs while the second one is more continuous and uses the metaphor of a level bubble. Both ideas are designed to fit on the frame of the bike, always visible when cycling, not requiring to pay too much attention, and most importantly being in line of sight of the cyclist. These designs assume close connection to a phone for computation and network access.

Design 1 uses a series of LEDs to indicate how close one is to the "ideal speed". If the number of LEDs on is too low or too high, the cyclist is too slow or too fast and needs to adjust their speed if they want to benefit from the green wave. Design 1 has the advantage of being relatively simple and cheap to build and implement.

Design 2 is slightly more advanced and uses the metaphor of a level bubble: the bubble in red indicates how "stable" the cruising speed of the cyclist is, and the goal is to keep this bubble as centered as possible. When the bubble is inside the "safe area" the background is green, and when the bubble goes outside the "safe area" the background turns orange to warn the cyclist to adjust their speed.

Charles Perin
Primary idea generator

The Augmented Commuter

The idea for the augmented commuter was triggered from an adrenaline boost after a car had turned right across the bike lane without checking to see whether cyclists were coming. The sketched mobile visualization uses micro-projectors to display information on the ground that is aimed specifically at informing the cyclist only, or other cyclists, pedestrians, cars or bus sharing the road. Such information can include real-time events like sensing a car coming, and historical data like number of recent road accidents at the next intersection.

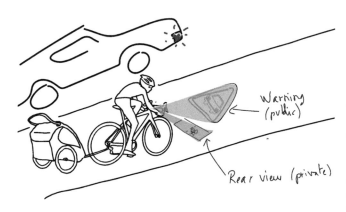

Several micro-projectors can be used to project information on the road or bike lane for both private and shared information. For example, a small view, right beneath the head of the cyclist, is mostly visible by the cyclist only. In this example, it could be used to show a rear-view mirror image, or even a view on their child in the trailer. This mobile visualization might benefit more people than just the bicycle rider and the car driver. In this example, the warning projected on the ground is a type of public display that other cyclists attempting to pass the person if they slow down, can use to understand each other's behavior. Here, the public warning displays information about the car that is about to turn right and might be dangerous for any cyclist on the bike lane.

Charles Perin
Primary idea generator

The ideation exercise conducted during bike commuting differed quite a bit from the original methodology as only one person participated and no in situ note taking was possible. Nevertheless, the performed in situ ideation (in one's mind) resulted in two mobile visualizations that can certainly be of benefit to cyclists.

8.4.3   Approach 3: Two or More People in Discussion

The ideas discussed next arose from pairs conducting the ideation exercise together. Contrary to the original methodology, however, in these pairs one person took the lead and the second person took a more supportive role.

Choosing a Neighborhood to Live

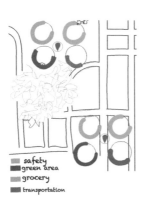

safety
green area
grocery
transportation

We started this activity during the afternoon of a busy day, when my friend and I were looking at some places she might rent. We set out to see places and to help her decide on a place to rent. This is a challenging decision. She had moved to a new country and I have been here for less than a year, so we did not have enough information about different areas, gathering valid and relevant information for different factors was hard and comparing all different options in terms of those factors was harder. A phone visualization showing the ease of access to grocery shops, train and bus stops, green areas, health care centers, the rate of locals about the safety of the area, population and nationalities living there, could help me to make a better decision right at the location.

Foroozan Daneshzand and friend
Primary idea generators

Visualizing Activities and Emotional States

Activity Overview

stabe   stress   unstable

During my daily commute, I sat down near the back of the bus with my friend. We are both on our phones during the bus ride. Getting bored of staring down at a screen, I started to look at the people around me. It was at this moment that I created CityU, a visualization that gathers anonymous data about peoples' current activity and their emotional state. As I surveyed the bus, I noticed that everyone else was on their phones. I got curious about them. "Who are these people? Where are they going?" This train of thought expanded as I considered not only the bus but the city around me. "I wonder what everyone else is doing in the city right now? How is everyone doing right now? What is their emotional state like?" I thought of the ways this data could help the city improve citizens' lives. If the city had a record of high numbers of stressed and mentally unhealthy citizens, they could develop programs to help improve it. I pitched the idea to my friends, who I was commuting with. They loved it and shared their visualization idea to increase city literacy. We thought about the people around us on this crowded ride. Everyone keeps to themselves as they go on their personal commute. We wondered how many are going home, or heading to a late shift. A visualization that shows where people are going and their reason for taking transit at that moment can help connect us momentarily. Of course, such data would be anonymized and aggregated for privacy reasons, but it would still help us feel more connected with our fellow commuters.

Lien Quach and Peter Buk
Primary idea generators

Cooking Dinner for the Group

I had started cooking dinner at my friend's place and it occurred to me that when I am cooking a lot of things at once, due to poor planning, I often end up having to frantically multitask during parts of it to not burn anything or let things get cold before everything else is ready.

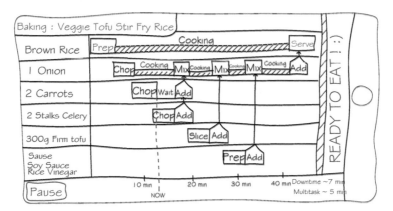

However, there are also some periods of downtime when there is nothing for me to do but wait around or maybe stir a bit. So I got thinking about how useful it would be if I could visualize and plan out the "pipeline" of all my different ingredients and dishes, to schedule when different things will be done and make the best use of my time. I have seen scheduling diagrams that might work well for something like this, showing how long my various foods need to be prepped, cooked, combined, and served for the most effective use of time, and to avoid having to do too many things at once. Maybe I could manually adjust these timings depending on my own personal speeds. Maybe I could also drag different items along the schedule diagram to see if I can make things work better and see updates on how much downtime or multitasking time there is going to be.

Laton Vermette and friends
Primary idea generators

All three of these examples did not use the initial idea of paired ideation, though more than one person was involved. For example, one author essentially suggested the visual decision support for choosing a home, but discussions between the author and her friend formed some of the source of the ideas. In contrast, the idea about visualizing people's activities and emotions, emerged separately from two of the authors and was then discussed together. The third idea about scheduling cooking so that all the parts of the meal are ready at the same time, is mainly a solo idea but it emerged in a social situation with several friends who all had an interest in the meal working out coherently.

8.4.4 Approach 4: Larger Group with Ideation in Stuttgart

The examples reported below were conducted with a group of six people while sightseeing in Stuttgart, Germany. In contrast to the initial instructions, the group chose to stay together throughout the activity and do the design exercises in changing pairs. After each activity the pairs discussed their designs and ideas together randomly, some pairs sketched together, some apart, some sketched just one design and some made multiple sketches. The design exercise focused on smartwatch applications and involved a physical paper prop in the shape of a smartwatch. The group conducted the ideation activity at various locations: at a market hall, the town hall with a famous paternoster elevator, twice in a museum with a historic clock collection, and during lunch. After the ideation sessions three members of the group met to group, categorize, and discuss the different ideas. During the meeting they wrote down observations, grouped sketches, redrew and combined ideas, as well as discussed questions that came up. The following idea descriptions are grouped by the locations where the smartwatch visualizations were thought of.

Stuttgart Market Hall

We created eight sketches, which we categorized into three groups. One group of four sketches was about apps that would help with shopping inside the market hall, such as a shopping list, a budget manager, or a product info display. One sketch described a smartwatch application to find sights in proximity to the wearer's current location. Three sketches concerned apps, which give additional information about the current sight, such as opening or busy time periods and facts about the place, ratings by other tourists, or how one can pay for products (cash or credit). The left image shows a budget manager for souvenirs, money already spent, and how much a current item of interest costs. The middle image is a smartwatch face with an abstracted map background that shows sights in the vicinity. Each icon can be touched for more information. The right smartwatch face gives detailed information about the current sight being visited. The two inner rings show busy times while the wristband (not visible) shows additional information and ratings about the place.

Alaul Islam, Tanja Blascheck, Petra Isenberg, Pantelis Antoniadis, Cristina Morariu, Anne Reuter
Idea generators

Town Hall—Riding the Paternoster

Stuttgart's main town hall has one of the few remaining functional and publicly accessible paternoster elevators, which is a hidden tourist attraction in the city. Here, we collected seven

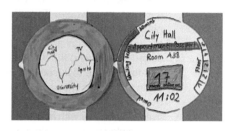

sketches in three different categories. Two sketches focused on a smartwatch app related to elevator riding more generally, with information about which floor one was on, which services are available on the floor, or potentially also the position and waiting time for other elevators. One participant enjoyed the ride on the paternoster and drew an app which would capture his excitement throughout the sightseeing trip—showing a spike during the visit at the paternoster. The outside ring color represents an average level of excitement for the day (left image). Three apps were related to an imagined visit to the town hall for administrative purposes (right image). The purpose of the visit, place and time of the appointment are shown, as well as an average wait time and an indication about how many people (17) are in front in line. All three were focused on way finding in the rather large administrative building of the Stuttgart town hall. One app focused on also showing waiting times for certain services, and one visiting times for a local exhibition.

Alaul Islam, Tanja Blascheck, Petra Isenberg, Pantelis Antoniadis, Cristina Morariu, Anne Reuter
Idea generators

Landesmuseum Stuttgart—Clock Exhibition

Next, we went to a local museum that featured a historic clock and scientific measurements exhibition. Here, we had two ideation sessions during which we collected 12 different

sketches. Three sketches contained an app that would help with the problem of taking photographs of exhibition pieces for memory keeping (left image). Two further sketches included floor plans of the museum with tracking of which rooms one had already visited (second image). Three sketches showed apps that would allow to have a

closer look or get general information about exhibition pieces close by (third image). Two sketches (right image) were concerned with giving an overview, recommendation, and ranking of exhibition pieces in the museum as a guide on what to view next. As we were getting closer to lunch and the end of our sightseeing activities two sketches showed information about upcoming events and the time left for the museum visit.

Alaul Islam, Tanja Blascheck, Petra Isenberg, Pantelis Antoniadis, Cristina Morariu, Anne Reuter
Idea generators

Lunch

To conclude our ideation activity we went for a joint lunch in a local café and after ordering foods and drinks, we did one more sketching session that resulted in nine sketches. Three

sketches were concerned with the day as a whole. Two displayed a history of activities throughout the day and one focused on showing the weather to inform future sightseeing activities. One app showed a daily overview of the sightseeing activities of the day with measures of knowledge or calorie gain and burn (left image). Six sketches were related to the restaurant experience with four focusing on apps that would help to find a restaurant based on price, type of food, or ratings (middle image). One app was related to choosing a menu item based on customer reviews, for example, which dessert other people spoke positively about on public ratings (right image). One app concentrated on more detailed information inside the restaurant such as waiting times, the table one was assigned, restroom information, or other people one could meet based on social media connections.

Alaul Islam, Tanja Blascheck, Petra Isenberg, Pantelis Antoniadis, Cristina Morariu, Anne Reuter
Idea generators

Sightseeing, an inherently mobile activity, was a rich context for the ideation activity. The large group context and extended activity allowed the team to collect a large number of sketches. Going through these sketches with a few team members and grouping the ideas into clusters also helped to uncover interesting questions for the smartwatch visualization context. For example, the group had previously not considered the importance of showing the time. Some participants consistently included a display of time, others did not. From the collected sketches some designs could be used as smartwatch faces (8 sketches) while others might be dedicated apps (28 sketches). One participant wearing a smartwatch with a square display also drew square designs, pointing to a possible limitation of having used a round paper prop. Potentially, 17 of the sketches would also work with a squared smartwatch, but the other half (19 sketches) were designed with a round watch in mind. In hindsight offering a larger variety of smartwatch-sized props might have been useful for coming up with designs that are less focused on a particular display format. However, using the paper prop also gave the opportunity to think into the future. As the wristband could be drawn on several sketches included information displays on the wristbands even though there are currently no consumer watches with wristband displays.

8.5 DISCUSSION

In this chapter we contribute an ideation method for designing mobile visualization as well as examples of using the method to generate designs for a variety of contexts and scenarios.

Our motivation for this project was to start developing methodologies that will encourage us to design mobile visualizations directly by basing the design process on: 1) visualization needs that emerge while we are on-the-go and 2) visualization designs that were thought of directly for on-the-go technology. We want to encourage thinking about mobile visualizations that are initially intended to be used while on-the-go.

In conceiving this mobile visualization design ideation process, we initially thought that we would leverage: context—by performing the ideation in situ; props—making use of actual props, such as one's own phone or smartwatch, or a paper mock up of the intended mobile device to keep the features and limitations in mind; socio-genesis—the ability of two or more people to generate ideas through discussion; enforced repetition—to loosen up our thinking processes by practicing generating new ideas; and immediate journaling and sketching—by taking notes on the spot to take advantage of capturing the ideas while they are fresh.

The initial emergence of these ideas started with a discussion between two of the authors. However, the first enactment was done by just one person and was not that successful. The follow up discussion led to thoughts about possible difficulties. Problems arose from 1) the initial enforced time gap of 15 minutes that was too short and interfered life proceeding such as getting to the next place; and 2) the crowded context made stopping to do an activity awkward and sometimes embarrassing, or in the evening downtown raised issues of personal safety. This experience led to the idea that this might be more successful in pairs, which would bring in the advantages of socio-genesis, and that we should try longer and more flexible time intervals.

At this point we thought that the paired ideation was one of the factors of success. However, as noted in this chapter, the next phase is the fruit of three distinct discussions. One was a group of six people who planned to pair up for the activities, but as circumstances happened many of these were actually done solo. One was always intended as a solo activity. One was discussed and planned as a group, which broke in pairs and re-grouped for discussions.

One author pointed out that while the activities—shopping, commuting—were familiar, doing this activity solo gave her the chance to take her time to think and recall. She queried whether this thinking and recollection would happen less with a partner suggesting that doing this by herself, was more focused on the activity, observing and sketching without distractions. In favour of pairs, one observation was that there was power in discussing the same situation from more than one perspective and that this discussion could challenge assumptions about the features of desired mobile visualizations. It is possible that the paired interactions have more quickly reached a more refined state of ideation, with more of the details thought through and worked out.

We also had a lot of variation in use of props. The idea behind props is to help focus one's mind on the technology in question. This is certainly evident in the group's activities using the circular smartwatch prop, during which most ideas emerged as circular smartwatch possibilities. It is also evident in the group who used their actual cell phone for the solo activities. Here again the ideation results reflect this. Perhaps most interesting in this regard is the ideation while riding on a bicycle. Maybe the lack of props contributed to the innovative suggestions for using technology to provide informative mobile visualizations while riding on a bicycle.

We think that a great deal of flexibility in this ideation methodology is not only possible but should be encouraged and explored. We also think that the two most powerful aspects are the in situ work and the repetition. We think that the context had a significant impact on our design processes. When it was possible to sketch on-site, one could transfer thoughts directly to the sketches, minimizing chance of missing ideas. However, some places were not comfortable enough for sketching, and, if possible, people took quick notes, maybe keywords and a vague sketch that made sense in the context. Sometimes these worked but some people said that quick notes often were too brief and they could not recall the intention when trying to sketch them at home. Another influencing factor related to context is the different observation opportunities each context offers. Riding a bus lends itself to opportunities to observe people for relatively long times in a stable environment. However, observing people while they are shopping might be awkward and uncomfortable, and sketching while biking or driving might be dangerous or impossible. This diversity of contexts requires flexible methodologies that one can adapt. For example, sketching the idea later at home can give more time and tools than when doing the ideation and sketching simultaneously in situ, at the expense of requiring good recall and perhaps more memorization effort. We have explored just a few contexts: transit, shopping, bicycling, and sightseeing. There are countless other possible scenarios to be investigated: isolation, wilderness, and sporting events to name just a few.

8.6 CONCLUSION

We set out to explore a mobile visualization design ideation methodology through a series of activities as a step toward discovering the potential of mobile only visualizations. We note that this chapter is an experience report, where we proposed a methodology but allowed, if not encouraged, people to adapt it to their immediate circumstances. Our combined experiences suggest that a wide range of adaptions are probably viable. Our combined activities suggest a series of possible mobile visualization directions. This offers opportunities for starting mobile visualization designs by thinking about the purpose and the context of the visualization as mobile right from the beginning of the design process. We hope this will encourage the design of new mobile visualizations to break away from the still relatively common tactic of designing simpler and smaller versions of larger desktop visualizations.

In reflecting on all of our activities we suggest that several quite consistent aspects across all the trials that led to a successful design experience with rich ideas:

- Being in-situ: one important part of this methodology is that we tackled the idea at a location of possible use, with the individuals doing the ideation being actually physically present at the given location. While one participant did successfully use imagining of the being in location, we suspect that needing this vivid imagination may not work as well for all people.

- Being at the moment: this idea is essentially a time-wise "in situ." It is our impression that this immediacy was useful in triggering ideas, but as one of our examples show, for some re-imagining a very recent past may also work well.

- The repetition: while the idea of trying to think of a new idea every so many minutes did not appear to be necessary to be rigidly applied, notion of repetition seemed to be generative. That is, getting one idea and then getting another and then another and so on, seemed to be freeing in itself. In a way this took the pressure away. A person did not have to get the perfect idea first, they could just keep going.

- The props: the way different individuals dealt with the device trigger varied from: looking at a physical device (phone or watch); imagining a physical device because current circumstance made pulling one out embarrassing; having a drawing or facsimile of a physical device. All three of these were successful and hint at possibilities of designing for novel devises by being able to draw one or create a mock-up.

- The notes and sketches: we made strong suggestions that note taking and sketching were done immediately, however, in reality this was not always possible. While it may be possible that some nuances were lost, on the whole post hoc notes were also successful.

In take-away we suggest trying this ideation approach bearing primarily in mind: being in situ; being at the moment; and having or creating a device mock-up. We do hope that some of you readers will try these activities. We have found them to be delightfully effective. After we started, ideas just seemed to flow forth. In addition, it seems that a great deal of flexibility can be applied to this methodology without losing its generative power. We are now interested in whether we can further adjust, or invent new ideation methodologies that can help us tease out new ways we can generate ideas that also leverage more of the unique features of common mobile devices, such as their input, output, and sensory capabilities.

8.7 ACKNOWLEDGMENTS

We thank all the people/participants who took part in the ideation method and helped contribute ideas, especially Pantelis Antoniadis, Cristina Morariu, and Anne Reuter from the University of Stuttgart.

REFERENCES

[1] Bolger, N., Davis, A., and Rafaeli, E. "Diary Methods: Capturing Life as It Is Lived". In: *Annual Review of Psychology* 54.1 (2003), pp. 579–616. DOI: 10.1146/annurev.psych.54.101601.145030 (cited on page 243).

[2]   Bressa, N., Wannamaker, K., Korsgaard, H., Willett, W., and Vermeulen, J. "Sketching and Ideation Activities for Situated Visualization Design". In: *Proceedings of the Conference on Designing Interactive Systems (DIS)*. DIS '19. **Open Access version:** http://jovermeulen.com/uploads/ Research/BressaWannamakerKorsgaardWillettVermeulen_situatedvis- dis2019.pdf. San Diego, CA, USA: ACM, 2019, pp. 173–185. DOI: 10.1145/ 3322276.3322326 (cited on page 243).

[3]   Browne, J., Lee, B., Carpendale, S., Riche, N., and Sherwood, T. "Data Analysis on Interactive Whiteboards Through Sketch-Based Interaction". In: *Proceedings of the Conference on Interactive Tabletops and Surfaces (ITS)*. ITS '11. New York, NY, USA: ACM, 2011, pp. 154–157. DOI: 10.1145/2076354.2076383. URL: http://doi.acm.org/10.1145/2076354.2076383 (cited on page 243).

[4]   Buxton, B. *Sketching User Experiences: Getting the Design Right and the Right Design*. Morgan Kaufmann, 2010. DOI: 10.1016/B978-012374037-3/50043-2 (cited on page 243).

[5]   Currier, K., Knudsen, S., Sturdee, M., and Carpendale, S. "Combining Ideation and Journaling to Explore to New Possibilities for Visualization on Mobile Devices". In: *Proceedings of the CHI Workshop on Data Visualization on Mobile Devices*. 2018 (cited on pages 243, 244).

[6]   Dow, S., Fortuna, J., Schwartz, D., Altringer, B., Schwartz, D., and Klemmer, S. "Prototyping Dynamics: Sharing Multiple Designs Improves Exploration, Group Rapport, and Results". In: *Proceedings of the Conference on Human Factors in Computing Systems (CHI)*. ACM, 2011, pp. 2807–2816 (cited on page 243).

[7]   Greenberg, S., Carpendale, S., Marquardt, N., and Buxton, B. *Sketching User Experiences: The Workbook*. Elsevier, 2011 (cited on page 243).

[8]   Iacucci, G., Kuutti, K., and Ranta, M. "On the Move With a Magic Thing: Role Playing in Concept Design of Mobile Services and Devices". In: *Proceedings of the Conference on Designing Interactive Systems (DIS)*. ACM, 2000, pp. 193– 202 (cited on page 243).

[9]   IDEO. *IDEO Method Cards: 51 Ways to Inspire Design*. Product. 2003. URL: https://www.ideo.com/post/method-cards (cited on page 244).

[10] Lee, B., Kazi, R. H., and Smith, G. "SketchStory: Telling More Engaging Stories With Data Through Freeform Sketching". In: *Transactions on Visualization and Computer Graphics (TVCG)* 19.12 (Dec. 2013), pp. 2416–2425. DOI: 10. 1109/TVCG.2013.191 (cited on page 243).

[11] Lee, B., Smith, G., Riche, N. H., Karlson, A., and Carpendale, S. "SketchInsight: Natural Data Exploration on Interactive Whiteboards Leveraging Pen and Touch Interaction". In: *Proceedings of the Pacific Visualization Symposium (PacificVis)*. IEEE, Apr. 2015, pp. 199–206. DOI: 10.1109/PACIFICVIS.2015. 7156378 (cited on page 243).

[12] McKenna, S., Lex, A., and Meyer, M. D. "Worksheets for Guiding Novices Through the Visualization Design Process". In: *Computing Research Repository (CoRR)* abs/1709.05723 (2017). arXiv: 1709.05723. URL: http://arxiv.org/abs/1709.05723 (cited on page 243).

[13] Oulasvirta, A., Kurvinen, E., and Kankainen, T. "Understanding Contexts by Being There: Case Studies in Bodystorming". In: *Personal and Ubiquitous Computing* 7 (2003), pp. 125–134. DOI: 10.1007/s00779-003-0238-7 (cited on page 243).

[14] Roberts, J. C., Ritsos, P. D., Badam, S. K., Brodbeck, D., Kennedy, J., and Elmqvist, N. "Visualization Beyond the Desktop–The Next Big Thing". In: *Computer Graphics and Applications (CG&A)* 34.6 (Nov. 2014), pp. 26–34. DOI: 10.1109/MCG.2014.82 (cited on page 243).

[15] Sedlmair, M., Meyer, M., and Munzner, T. "Design Study Methodology: Reflections From the Trenches and the Stacks". In: *Transactions on Visualization and Computer Graphics (TVCG)* 18.12 (2012), pp. 2431–2440 (cited on page 243).

[16] Steen, M. "Tensions in Human-Centred Design". In: *CoDesign* 7.1 (2011), pp. 45–60. DOI: 10.1080/15710882.2011.563314. eprint: https://doi.org/10.1080/15710882.2011.563314. URL: https://doi.org/10.1080/15710882.2011.563314 (cited on page 243).

[17] Walny, J., Carpendale, S., Henry Riche, N., Venolia, G., and Fawcett, P. "Visual Thinking in Action: Visualizations as Used on Whiteboards". In: *Transactions on Visualization and Computer Graphics (TVCG)* 17.12 (Dec. 2011), pp. 2508–2517. DOI: 10.1109/TVCG.2011.251. URL: http://dx.doi.org/10.1109/TVCG.2011.251 (cited on page 243).

[18] Warberg, A., Larsen, J., and Jørgensen, R. M. *Green Wave Traffic Optimization-A Survey.* Tech. rep. 2008-01. DTU, 2008. URL: https://orbit.dtu.dk/en/publications/green-wave-traffic-optimization-a-survey (cited on page 250).

CHAPTER 9

Reflections on Ubiquitous Visualization

Jo Vermeulen

Autodesk Research, Canada & Aarhus University, Denmark

Christopher Collins

Ontario Tech University, Canada

Raimund Dachselt

Technische Universität Dresden, Germany

Pourang Irani

University of Manitoba, Canada

Alark Joshi

University of San Francisco, USA

CONTENTS

DOI: 10.1201/9781003090823-9

There is a growing demand for data visualization on mobile devices in order to facilitate exploration of locally-relevant data on-the-go. In this chapter, we provide an outlook into the future of mobile visualization which we anticipate will see a growing emphasis on *ubiquitous visualization*. We provide an overview of research in ubiquitous data visualization by interviewing four renowned researchers who have explored data visualization in novel settings with new modalities and technologies that go beyond mobile devices. We report on our discussions and distill important themes and their visions for the future of ubiquitous data visualization. We discuss envisioning scenarios for this emerging research area and reflect on its specific dimensions going beyond mobile data visualization.

9.1 INTRODUCTION AND CONTEXT

This concluding book chapter sets out our vision for moving toward a fuller understanding of *ubiquitous visualization*. While mobile visualizations might connote visual tools for sense-making on small mobile displays, we envision that these mobile visualizations will increasingly move toward ubiquitous visualization: visualization that is available to people everywhere and at any time. The natural leap from mobile to ubiquitous visualization is motivated by the pervasive nature of displays, the ready availability of cloud data, and the growing emergence of displays embedded in our environment. Current mobile visualizations imply having a personal mobile device, such as a smartphone or smartwatch. But as discussed in the previous chapters, some of the limitations of these form-factors such as small display size as well as limited input mechanisms hinder the vast range of applications and scenarios one can imagine when visualizations are ubiquitously accessible. Furthermore, emerging devices including head-worn, flexible or textile displays warrant renewed consideration for how these might be employed for giving access to information displays, at any time and at any place. While mobile devices in current form factors may still form an important part of ubiquitous visualization as a way to have personal rather than shared views, we will increasingly see a variety of different form factors and the wider integration of visualizations in the environment.

Researchers have been envisioning new directions for visualization beyond the desktop [70], leading to the idea of visual analytics everywhere or ubiquitous analytics [26]. Related visions that expand on this include situated and embedded visualizations [51, 62, 97, 99] and immersive analytics [61]. Early prototypes of systems motivated by these new directions have been made possible through the accelerating deployment of novel technologies many of which are becoming consumer ready products. Devices with pervasive displays are no longer necessarily rectilinear and can be free-form [82], dynamically assume a required shape [1], or dissolve into Augmented Reality projections [66, 15]. Furthermore, as users equip themselves with more than one mobile device, opportunities for cross-device visualization create new design opportunities for multi-user and group-based sense-making activities [7]. In addition to enhanced display power, we are also seeing a revitalization and application of multi-sensory input capabilities [60], beyond singular devices, such as a cursor or touch input on smartphones, to include proxemics [4, 24, 44], spatial tangible interaction [55, 59], gaze-input [85], as well as speech [36, 37, 83] for visual sense-making.

While we envision a growing future emphasis on ubiquitous visualization, it is important to acknowledge that much of the early work into what can be considered ubiquitous visualization took place decades ago, even before smartphones became a commodity. Research into *ambient displays* and *calm computing* was motivated by exploring ways to present and visualize contextually-relevant information in the periphery of attention, with the goal of informing people without overwhelming them [92]. Examples include Natalie Jeremijenko's Live Wire [92] (essentially a self-actuated data physicalization [45] of network traffic), the ambient displays developed at the MIT Tangible Media group [100], Information Perculator [38], Tollmar's virtually living together lamp [87], Ambient Devices, Inc.'s Ambient Umbrella [69], Data Fountain [88], and the Power-Aware Cord [33]. Indeed, one might argue that we have come full circle with recent research into ubiquitous visualization returning to the guiding forces behind this early work in the ubiquitous computing community. From the earliest demonstrations of calm computing or ambient displays to the ever growing presence of dot lights in our environment [35] or the potential of future output technologies such as flying displays [17, 81, 101], we cannot overlook the possibility that mobile visualizations might meld and become part of our surroundings. Purposefully and quietly, yet pervasively accessible due to the availability of cloud data, such displays will play a critical role in our every day decision making. Yet despite these advances we still question how best to move forward to realize these visionary proposals? What challenges are we faced with in the process? What has been done, what is next, and what research challenges remain?

This chapter takes a first step toward answering these questions. Unlike methods used for developing content for the previous chapters, we, the authors of this chapter, took a different approach. We first identified papers that have in one way or another broached on the topic of ubiquitous visualization, some of which were cited above. While the authors of these papers did not necessarily explicitly label their work as "ubiquitous visualization," they envisioned many of the prospects supported by this chapter's theme. We decided to interview one author from each of the papers in this initial collection to obtain a handle for how such emerging technologies have impacted their envisioned ideas. The interviews were composed of questions on a general nature about the theme, but also of more specific questions about concepts that the authors alluded to in their work.

While undergoing developments on mobile visualization are still nascent, our interviews enabled us to identify recurrent themes and challenges to be tackled in future research. First, we briefly summarize our approach (Section 9.2). Next, we present the individual interviews with each of the four researchers in detail, covering a common set of questions, and highlighting particular aspects of their relevant and important publications in this area (Sections 9.3, 9.4, 9.5, and 9.6). This is followed by reflecting and discussing overarching and important themes we identified across the interviews (Section 9.7). To better highlight our envisioned future, we provide an overview of possible application scenarios including those that our interviewees highlighted as having much potential for ubiquitous visualization (Section 9.8). Finally, we revisit the dimensions of mobile data visualization from Chapter 1, and discuss how well the vision of ubiquitous visualization is covered by these dimensions (Section 1.2).

9.2 APPROACH

To understand where mobile visualization is heading next, and the opportunities, challenges, and research potential in fusing into ubiquitous visualization, we interviewed four prominent researchers,[1] known for their research in mobile visualization and their vision for new ubiquitous, situated, and mixed reality technologies:

- Wesley Willett, Associate Professor at the University of Calgary, Canada

- Niklas Elmqvist, Professor at the University of Maryland, United States of America

- Sean White, at the time of our interview: Chief of Research & Development at Mozilla, United States of America

- Yvonne Rogers, Professor at University College London, United Kingdom

Two to three authors of this chapter conducted semi-structured interviews with each of our interviewees over videoconferencing. One author led the interview, while one or two other authors took notes. Each interview lasted about an hour and consisted of a set of generic questions, common to all interviews, followed by a set of specific questions that were inspired by how the interviewees' research relates to mobile and ubiquitous data visualization. Interviewees were provided with the questions in advance. Interviews were recorded and transcribed in full.

In the following sections, we describe the relevant background of each interviewee, followed by the outcomes of their interview, structured along the set of generic and specific questions. We decided not to use a coding approach to find commonalities and trends in the interview data. We chose to summarize each interview in full, to present the variety of individual perspectives of each of the interviewees. Each interview consists of editorial summaries interspersed with quotes from the interviewee.

---

[1] *Headshots of all interviewees in this chapter courtesy and © of the respective interviewee.*

9.3 WESLEY WILLETT ON EMBEDDED DATA REPRESENTATIONS

Wesley Willett is an Associate Professor of Computer Science at the University of Calgary where he holds a Canada Research Chair in Visual Analytics and leads the Data Experience Lab. His research interests span information visualization, social computing, new media, and human-computer interaction, and his research focuses on pairing data and interactivity to support collaboration, learning, and discovery.

A notable contribution of Willett's that is of key relevance to this book chapter is his 2017 article on "Embedded Data Representations" [99], co-authored with Yvonne Jansen and Pierre Dragicevic. In this paper, Willett and colleagues contribute a conceptual framework and foundation for thinking about visualizations that are connected to the world in which they are situated. They formalize the notion of physical data referents, or "physical spaces, objects and entities that the data refers to." For example, physical data referents could be the houses that the data in a real estate data set refers to, or the employees described in a company directory. Willett et al. distinguish between visualizations or physicalizations that are either *situated* or *embedded*, where the former display data in proximity to physical data referents and the latter display data so that it coincides with the physical data referent.

What does mobile visualization mean to you? How do you see it being used today?

Willett notes that the term *mobile visualization* has felt a little confusing in the last couple of years. "When I tend to use the term 'mobile,' I am mostly thinking about the form factor of the devices. What it suggests to me is visualization on watches, phones, and tablets. And that's distinct from other terms like ubiquitous visualization and immersive analytics." On how he sees mobile visualization being used today, Willett replies: "If I had to characterize things that I see as mobile visualization right now, it's things like Fitbit tracking, or health data being shown on Apple watches." He then notes that with other things that are more about a vision for visualization in other environments, his tendency has been to use other terms such as ubiquitous visualization or immersive analytics.

What do you see as the benefits of the visualization being mobile?

"From a practical standpoint, mobile visualizations are more accessible by virtue of being on these other hardware platforms. So, in some cases, it's easier for mobile visualizations to be visible in places where people can take action based on them or where they are situated with respect to an appropriate task. There are also a lot of cases where people are creating visualizations on mobile devices just because this is a more convenient software platform."

Continuing on this, Willett points out that with a lot of the current examples of mobile visualizations, it's much more about making the data available in a mobile setting, but "it doesn't necessarily make them inherently more situated with respect to the tasks that they are designed to support." He sees the current generation of mobile visualizations as being more about the fact that "these hardware platforms are with us all the time, rather than doing anything that is really context-aware or embedded in a particular task or application."

How do you envision mobile visualization contextually adapting to aid a user's activity?

Willett says this is the space that he is most interested in: "Thinking about how you can start to embed visualizations into the spaces, and tasks, and even objects or environments where people are actually performing tasks. By connecting visualizations to spaces, we can provide access to data in ways that support specific tasks, and in a way that is very timely and is very situated, helping people experience data in a way that supports decision-making and stimulates reflection." He has mostly thought about this in the context of *personal informatics*, but he also sees much potential in other domains, such as: "Specific tasks in construction or maintenance, where there are clear direct applications of data to measurable tasks that are easy to design around." Willett mentions that embedding data in specialized or everyday tasks is very compelling, but that there is still lots of work to do.

What different application areas and target user groups do you envision in the future for the consumption of data on mobile devices (versus visualizations on the desktop)?

One place where we already have a lot of visualizations that are deeply embedded in the task at hand, according to Willett, is in driving: "Our cars are actually full of little relevant visualizations that are providing specific pieces of data about our current environments and are directly translating into how we drive." Willett explains that we might see many other kinds of operations or settings with that same level of augmentation. Examples include performing surgery or maintenance, brushing your teeth, or making coffee: "These are all tasks where you might be able to bring data to bear in a way that is either interesting personally or allows you to do the task better. And the integration of these visualizations with the tools and the environments could look a lot like the growing integration of visualization into cars." Willett then mentions the example of the large display in a Tesla, and all of the different kinds of information the driver has at their disposal. Rather than just showing speed or RPMs, the display also shows the driver a model of the environment, including the position of nearby vehicles and the current speed limit—things they cannot perceive with their own eyes. Willett explains: "There are many kinds of data that those displays are providing that are incredibly contextually relevant to the task of driving and they're presenting that data via visualizations. I suspect that integrating these kinds of task-specific visualizations into a variety of other contexts could be a really big opportunity for the field." He discusses how this is very much in line with the traditional benefits of visualization (augmenting perception, supporting visual computation, augmenting memory), but doing all of this "in a way that is very grounded in particular spaces, or tasks or tools."

What is the current big thing for mobile visualization? And what do you think will be next?

Willett notes that while Augmented Reality (AR) and Mixed Reality (MR) are currently getting a lot of attention, lots of challenges remain. The more he worked in this space, the less he's convinced that AR or MR is the way forward, at least in many situations. Instead, he thinks screens may be more useful in the short term: "We're thinking about scenarios in which people are using many devices with attached displays, or have many displays that are integrated into their environment. The car analogy actually works really well with this too—the technology that is enabling the tighter and tighter integration of visualizations into cars is still screens, but it is screens embedded in the right places." Willett explains that he feels that integrating visualizations in everyday spaces using projection and displays is more promising in the near term than AR and MR because it avoids many challenges that these technologies present: "And it means that the visualizations become shared objects that people are able to socialize around and examine together. It's also easy to integrate small displays into many existing settings in a way that is technically not that easy for lots of current generation AR tools."

We then mention the LED displays that are integrated in the sidewalks to indicate the green wave on the bicycle paths in Copenhagen[1]. They give cyclists an indication of whether they need to speed up or slow down to go 20 km/h and catch the wave of green traffic lights, requiring no instrumentation. Willett notes: "Exactly. I think that's a really nice example of simple embedded displays. In a lot of cases, the goal of these new visualizations can be really subtle—not providing strictly analytic views, but instead surfacing data in environments in ways that allow people to make good decisions or perform tasks better."

How do you see mobile visualization transitioning to ubiquitous visualization?

"The end goal as I would frame it is: having access to data where and when it's useful." Willett notes that visions of ubiquitous visualization such as ubiquitous analytics [26], are more satisfying to him if they are technology-agnostic. He notes that to make data available in places so that having access to it changes the way you make decisions, there are many design and technology factors to consider: "What is available? What is reliable? What is acceptable from a social perspective? [. . .] My hope is that designers increasingly have access to a variety of different technologies for creating visualizations that live beyond the desktop, and that designers in this space can now focus on creating visualizations that are nicely tailored to real tasks, rather than focusing on particular hardware platforms just because those platforms are the current sexy thing." Looking ahead, Willett notes: "I can imagine twenty or thirty years in the future where everyone has a little display that is projecting into their retina and all of them are perfectly synchronized. Something like retinal displays could become the de facto technology for visualization if it's ultimately cheaper, easier, and more accessible than

---

[1]Streetfilms Snippets – Green Wave LED Lights (Copenhagen, Denmark): https://www.youtube.com/watch?v=6Kx1XZeFkXk

doing something that's physically instantiated in the real world. And that's still an interesting thought experiment for visualization researchers to consider. [...] However, from a practical perspective, there may be lots of other current technologies that we can use to achieve a lot of the same ends."

How does your framework for situated and embedded data representations relate to mobile data visualization? And to the related visions of ubiquitous analytics or immersive analytics?

"So I think of all of these as operating on slightly different levels. I tend to think of the term mobile visualization as a more restrictive concept that is talking specifically about particular hardware platforms. I think of ubiquitous analytics as a broader vision for the integration of data and visualization into a wider range of contexts. Within those, the notion of situated and embedded data representations is more of a tool or framework that lets you think critically about a few specific aspects of these visualizations."

Willett mentions that he sees *situated* and *embedded* as language that facilitates discussing and reasoning about specific design decisions for visualizations that might span a number of different platforms and visions. He notes that it is useful to describe what is different about them, particularly in terms of spatial or temporal indirection. When we asked whether he sees his framework as a conceptual framework to aid design, he answered: "Exactly. The language of situatedness and embeddedness and the discussions that led to that terminology were extremely helpful for me. I think this language helps unpack some of the trade-offs that make visualizations that are connected to the physical world more or less useful and makes it easier to extrapolate from current systems to imagine future designs. This terminology has grounded the majority of the conversations I have had about these kinds of visualizations in the last couple of years."

What propelled the idea of producing a unifying framework for what others may have termed as Situated Analytics or along the lines of ideas proposed by White & Feiner?

"Our paper originated from discussions about a whole bunch of existing visualization systems, including White & Feiner's, that were somehow connected to the physical world. We also considered possible future visualizations inspired by the "Death of the Desktop" workshop at IEEE VIS in 2014 [46]. For example, my submission to that workshop was this "artefact from the future" that imagined visualizations made up of swarms of tiny drones. We ended up using completely different language for it first, like *physically embedded visualizations*, but ultimately preferred language that aligned with some of the earlier literature."

Willett mentions that they were at that time looking at several other related framings, including Dietmar Offenhuber's indexical visualization processes [65] (and subsequent work on autographic visualizations [64]). Willett and his co-authors tried to reason about the differences between the examples to give themselves a language for explaining the differences. Willett continues: "And, that's part of what ended up connecting it back to White & Feiner's work [93] and the work on situated analytics

[26]. It was clear that people were using similar terms but using them to talk about systems that are qualitatively somewhat different."

In your paper, you mention that there is still little empirical evidence for the benefits of situated/embedded visualizations. Since writing the paper, have you been able to identify new insights or evidence for either benefits or drawbacks of these approaches?

"The automobile example is one that I think has become more clear to me in the last couple of years, especially as we've seen new in-dash visualizations that include much more data and are intending drivers to use that data to make driving decisions. I think this is one of the most compelling, real-world, widely deployed evidence for the utility of situated visualization. In my own work, we also thought a lot more about this in the context of personal informatics. That research has felt very satisfying to me, because part of the work has involved building and then personally using lots of new visualizations for self-tracking. [...] This includes a bunch of situated visualizations which I continue to use around the house as part of my daily routine. I feel they aid my ability to reflect, and to do so in everyday settings. That suggests to me that having access to right data can be helpful in lots of domestic settings where we don't tend to think of visualization that much. Our recent work on situating visualizations in the context of construction and maintenance also makes me think that there is a lot of value to be gained by surfacing data in-context for those tasks. At this point, I haven't seen many quantitative studies that have tried to really make the case for the benefits of situated visualizations. However, that's something that we would still benefit from as a community, if only to be able to more concretely articulate their benefits. At least qualitatively, I feel now I have a lot of examples that make a strong case for the approach."

How dependent are embedded visualizations on Augmented Reality (AR), Virtual Reality (VR) or Mixed Reality (MR) technologies? Do you envision other forms of display/interaction techniques being more appropriate for embedded visualizations than the current state-of-the-art in AR/VR/MR hardware/techniques?

"So I think that AR/MR is an interesting technology stack to build these on, and there are a variety of settings and visualization designs that could be difficult to implement using physical displays. On the other hand, I still think the affordances of situating visualizations in physical ways are interesting. In the original VIS paper, we even talk about examples of embedded physicalizations like actuated store shelves that would move in response to sales data. The drone swarm example that motivated a lot of our discussions is another example of how you might create visualizations using technologies that provide more than just a virtual overlay and are instead physically integrated into the space." Willett explains that this has interesting implications for how one might interact with it. For example, is there co-location between sensors or displays, can it actively manipulate the environment? While these questions come up when thinking about technologies that are not AR, Willett notes that for many of these scenarios, this can still be done using an AR overlay as well.

We elaborated on this by referring to modern parking garages where you have LEDs over the parking spaces that show which spots are free as an example that does not rely on AR or MR. Willett replies: "Yes, I think parking indicators are another really interesting example that has emerged in a widespread way in the last five years or so. Every time I see it, I think, oh yeah, that's a great example of an embedded visualization that is quite useful, while also being relatively low-tech. It is really just a simple sensor and one bit of output that are co-located in a space, and then multiplexed through the entire environment so it allows you to make decisions."

What is your perspective on the information density that would be typical for situated and embedded visualizations? Would one typically use glanceable visualizations with very few data attributes, or can you also envision situated or embedded visualizations that present a large amount of data?

"My intuition is that this is a design problem that anyone who is trying to surface information in spaces has to deal with. Any visualization design needs to consider who the viewer is, what the data is, and what the task is. I think that if you have the potential to display information everywhere, then by definition you have to start to make decisions about information density and about attention. That probably suggests that if you are displaying an embedded visualization that covers your whole field of view or appears in many places in the environments, you're likely to want to simplify it or provide more glanceable overviews."

Willett adds that information density isn't the real problem, it's complexity: "If you had an AR overlay showing dense, pixel-level temperature readings for the entire space, that still actually might be fine, depending on the task. It's high-density, but low complexity. But if I have very complicated data that's difficult to visually parse overlaid all over my entire field of view, then that seems likely to be problematic. I think that all visualizations pose problems for attention and that, especially if you're designing systems that can encompass your whole view or can introduce many visualizations at the same time, you're going to have to make decisions. Which visualizations are visible at any given time? How visually salient are they? How do you transition between them?"

You say it also depends on the task and the activities that people are engaged in. In applications for construction or maintenance, maybe in those situations you do actually want to delve into why this machine is not performing as expected, see different charts and explore this in more detail?

"Exactly. The challenge is thinking about how you surface that information, maybe in a staged way. If I am walking into a space with many different pieces of equipment, all of which could potentially have a problem, maybe I need some sort of higher-level glanceable view. Once I've identified the one that is the likely cause of the problem, then I might want to start to pull up more detailed visualizations that highlight particular aspects of that machine and overlay a lot of additional data specific to it. You can think about handling those transitions in many different ways including ones that are driven by locomotion and incorporate notions of proxemics."

While "data" has a big role in embedded visualization, what is the role of people and locations?

"I think that people are, at the end of the day, the most important piece of this. If you have the ability to display lots of data in lots of ways, all over the environment, then at the end of the day, you need to be designing the visualizations in a way that reflects the people that are going to be using them and the tasks that they are going to be performing. The designs need to be tailored to those task and try to help manage people's attention and improve their ability to make sense of that data."

Embedded visualizations seems to be a way to describe and compare different kinds of data representations related to the physical world? Are there other purposes for embedded visualization?

"I think of it in terms of frameworks generally. These kinds of frameworks are useful because they allow us to describe and compare both existing systems and future possible systems. They also make it easier for us to identify points in the design space that haven't been explored. The things that I find most helpful about this framework is that it's given us the ability to discuss the differences between visualizations that are just situated versus ones that are embedded and to think about the level of indirection in those embeddings. This language has shown up in almost every discussion around a visualization system that I have had since, and has been extremely useful." Willett argues that there are still opportunities to expand the framework further in terms of temporal indirection (which was only briefly touched upon in their paper) or semantic indirection, i.e., how compatible the visualization is with the task.

In terms of temporal indirection, we discuss an example where it would be possible to show for a certain location how many cars passed by 30–40 years ago compared to now. Willett replies: "Yes, I think this temporal indirection as a space is ripe for further unpacking. You can consider not only temporal indirection but also temporal aggregation, and also the liveliness of the data. Am I looking at data where I can reach out, make a change to the environment, and now the visualization will change based on that? Am I looking at data that is historical? Am I looking at data that is live but that actually I can't impact? I think that there is still a rich design space here that would be worth providing some more language for."

Is there a kind of "data-oriented proxemics" with Embedded Data Representations?

One of the interviewers seemed to remember that Willett's embedded data representations work [99] quoted Waldo Tobler's first law of geography—"Everything is related to everything else, but near things are more related than distant things.". We mentioned this and noted that it reminded us of theories of and work on proxemics in HCI where the relationships, including even how people face one another, is important for their interactions (e.g. Hall's proxemic zones [34], F-formations [19, 52]). We asked Willett if embedded data representations naturally imply a data-oriented version of existing HCI work in interaction using proxemics [32]:

"I don't know that we ever quote Tobler's law in the paper, but it is something that showed up in some of the presentations that we have given about the work. In hindsight, I think Tobler's law is one of these oft-repeated statements that almost feels like a truism, and I'm not quite sure that it applies neatly here. But I do think that the notion of proxemics and proxemic frameworks map themselves nicely to any discussions around ubiquitous analytics and are definitely compatible with the situated/embedded framing. I think that human spatial perception provides a lot of nice opportunities for using location and attention information to determine which visualizations are shown or what data density you're using. There's definitely a very natural relationship to existing work around proxemics."

To follow up, we asked whether early work in this area such as Vogel & Balakrishnan's work on interactive public ambient displays [89] may be a good match, as well as Isenberg et al.'s work on hybrid-image visualization [43] (of which Willett was also a co-author): "Totally. My sense is that if you look back at the history of proxemics systems, many of the classic examples are data-driven, even if they are not necessarily complex analytic visualizations. I think that when designing visualizations for real environments, using information about where the people are and where their attention is directed to adapt things like the level of detail makes a ton of sense. It would be interesting to think about trying to draw attention to the proxemics literature for the visualization community. Because I don't know how much overlap there is between proxemics researchers and the people working in ubiquitous analytics or situated analytics. My sense is that the overlap might not be huge."

Any final comments or things to add?

"The one other thing I will add, is that I would love to see more work on design futuring in the visualization community. The "Death of the Desktop" workshop at VIS in 2014 was one of the most inspiring sessions that I've been a part of in my entire history in the community. It inspired much of my research and teaching over the past half-decade and left me convinced that these opportunities to actually create artifacts from the future and do design futuring for vis are really fruitful." Concluding our interview, we note that it may be worth organizing a similar provocative design futuring session on the "Death of Mobile."

9.4   NIKLAS ELMQVIST ON UBIQUITOUS ANALYTICS

Niklas Elmqvist is a full professor in the iSchool (College of Information Studies) and Director of the HCIL (Human-Computer Interaction Lab) at the University of Maryland, College Park. His research areas are information visualization, human-computer interaction (often applied to visualization problems), and visual analytics. In much of his research, Elmqvist is concerned with investigating the potential of novel computing environments and styles of interaction for data visualization and analysis purposes, including research on software infrastructures required to support the engineering of these new visualization environments.

Among Elmqvist's notable contributions in the context of this book chapter are his co-authored IEEE Computer Graphics and Applications article "Visualization beyond the Desktop" [70] and his article on "Ubiquitous Analytics" [26], co-authored by Pourang Irani. These articles propose research on visualizations beyond the desktop and *Ubilytics* as situated sensemaking of big data anywhere and anytime, where the analytical process is embedded into the physical environment. This allows analysts to interact with complex data in their offices or in-the-wild, individually or collaboratively, synchronously or not. All of these aspects of Niklas Elmqvist's research and work, i.e., visualization beyond the desktop, ubiquitous analytics, and the engineering of visualizations are reflected in his interview, which is summarized in the following.

What does mobile visualization mean to you? How do you see it being used today?

Elmqvist answers this introductory question: "Data visualization is not designed for specifically sitting in an office, maybe I'd even go further, so not using a personal computer, almost anything that is not using a personal computer, but probably focused on situations where you're on the go, rather than in a fixed setting." He remembers a keynote given by his colleague David Ebert at the Graphics Interface conference in 2008, which was entitled "Mobiquitous Graphics and Visualization". Elmqvist notices that not much mobile visualizations have been developed since then: "We have seen research papers ..., but I don't see there being significant commercial applications with visualizations in the field."

What do you see as the benefits of the visualization being mobile?

Since mobile devices become our personal computers with high screen resolution and a lot of processing power, what sets them apart might be the mobile usage itself. Elmqvist mentions "so what makes the difference is the context of use. And of course, if I am just walking around and looking at sales data, the boundary between a personal computer and a tablet or smartphone in particular is being erased almost entirely, because they are converging. But, if you truly want to take advantage of the fact that you are mobile, then you want to take advantage of some type of context-aware information where you are. [...] Finally, that killer app where you use the location of where the person is in the world is not trivial. It is what makes the difference between a mobile and a normal visualization. But it has to be a form of sense-making that is in-situ, and if you take advantage of location information, and it should somehow uniquely make it easier for you to make opportunistic or serendipitous decisions or analyses that you would need more time or effort to do offline, ex-situ, in an office."

How do you envision mobile visualization contextually adapting to aid a user's activity?

It is an interesting aspect that people do not just look at the data while on-the-go, but the context allows them to discover something completely new or to get some suggestion. Elmqvist reflects: "There is lots and lots of data being collected about the world, especially about cyber-physical systems, things that exist both in the real world and in the digital world. [...] The problem is, the internet, for all its advantages, has the disadvantage that it 'throws away' the real space. There is typically no relation to the real space."

Elmqvist recalls William Gibson's "Neuromancer" novel, where he talks about cyberspace. "It is like a virtual version of the real world. So, everything in the real world has a virtual representation. So that aspect is of course lost in the internet of today. But I think we want to bring back some of it, where the data that is being collected from the real world should be brought back as digital data in the real world, that you can access using a mobile device, some mobile visualization."

He further elaborates on a project turning the University of Maryland campus into a testbed for situated data, where a multitude of information reaching from bus schedules over crime data and safety recommendations up to information about historical buildings is being accessible via smartphone or AR goggles. "Basically, it is about the notion of a real place as an index into the digital world. That is one of the potentials of mobile visualization that it really takes advantage of your spatial location. And that can make decisions easier with less effort. [...]"

What is the current big thing for mobile visualization? And what do you think will be next?

Responding to this question, Elmqvist primarily refers to personal information and emphasizes its big potential. "You tend to see them in things like a smartwatch that captures and displays data. And of course, if you have a Fitbit app or Apple health app that lets you track these information. I think this is certainly a big thing, because it has a personal connection and can make people relate to the data better."

In his NSF project Data World, it is all about personal, recreational use. "So we haven't really looked at professional settings, but my colleague Amitabh Varshney runs the Augmentarium here at UMD, which is all about creating AR experiences. His goals are mostly professional, so that is things like a surgeon wearing AR goggles and they get a visualization of the patient's CAT-scans superimposed on their bodies, or its supporting soldiers in a battlefield [...]. I don't know what the big thing is.

My view is mostly on a personal information space, but I think there's significant potential for applying this to professional settings, too."

How do you see mobile visualization transitioning to ubiquitous visualization?

We then discussed that this usage of mobile visualization in rather professional domains would be a first aspect of that expansion of today's mobile visualizations into future ubiquitous visualizations. Second, it would be to make visualizations far more contextual, to integrate them into real-world contexts. And a third interesting aspect are AR goggles or other augmentation technologies that might play an increasing role in the future. Asked about these potential ingredients on the path to ubiquitous visualization, Elmqvist responded:

"I agree. I think that's the case. I am not one to tell you whether and when AR will actually have a breakthrough, because we as computer scientists have been burned too many times by VR and how hard that has been to get it off the ground. AR is promising, but AR glasses will not be worn by everyone. I think there is a big gap to actually reach that stage. But, having said that, I think of Pokémon Go, that is a good example of integrating the virtual world with the real world. There is much potential for creating these ubiquitous visualization experiences using existing devices that we have. You don't have to invest in huge computer infrastructure, since people already have lots and lots of exciting devices in their pockets."

Which role will Mixed Reality technologies play in the future? What could be alternatives or other enabling technologies?

In this part of the interview, Elmqvist further elaborates on what he calls *ubiquitous visual computing*: "Something that I realized several years ago came from reading Dourish's and Bell's book 'Divining a Digital Future: Mess and Mythology in Ubiquitous Computing'. The whole message of that book is that ubiquitous computing is already here, [...] the notion of ubiquitous computing that Mark Weiser proposed in the 1990s actually has been reached already. It's just that it is a moving target. People tend to think, it is the future. But, if you look at what we have in our pockets and the computing infrastructure we surround ourselves with, it really is the vision that was originally proposed. Yes, the devices are not entirely invisible, and they actually still have displays, [...] they have not disappeared. But, I think that actually points to the notion of not just ubiquitous computing, but *ubiquitous visual computing*.

He argues that instead of thinking 20 years ahead and believing that in 20 years we are all going to wear AR goggles and have clothing that measures everything and speaks to us, we should rather "take advantage of what is already here and open our eyes and realize that there are lots and lots of devices already that we can use to realize this vision of ubiquitous visualization, ubiquitous visual computing, all the pixels that we could be using. That's what I try to do based on my work and based on my ideas of ubiquitous computing."

Some people argue that in the future people do no longer wear bulky AR goggles, but perhaps retina displays or implants reading and producing brain signals. We therefore asked Elmqvist, whether he believes that we still need external displays within the environment or people's hands. "I am a realist and a pragmatist. So that's why I have not considered much of those future devices, I have been focusing on the ones that we have, but you're right, if, for example, you have an AR display or seamless one where you can just put it on the retina [...] there is clearly no need to put any physical displays in our world, as you could 'fake' them. Of course, that would be a game changer."

Elmqvist also referred to the 'Silent Augmented Reality' blog by Dominikus Baur [10], where he described a dystopian vision of advertisements flashing everywhere into people's faces. "If you want visualizations, data and displays available everywhere you need to find a way to not pollute people's virtual space, because then of course they are not going to use it, and you need to be respectful and not disruptive. So some of the things we're planning to look at is how we can create visualizations that are available and that are visible, but are not disruptive. You need to see a difference between virtual and real objects that you do not walk into one or the other. At the same time, you also do not want them to look artificial and attention-grabbing. If we have this future that you think of, there is lots and lots of potentials that we have to find the right ways to do it."

How should software toolkits be designed and how should the entire development be supported in an ecosystem of networked devices?

Multiple, networked devices are key to some of Elmqvist's works including some technology and toolkit support for multi-device environments and visualizations. Asked about an ecosystem of networked devices, he mentioned his Java-based research frameworks Hugin [54] and Munin [6]. "They all forced us to build things on a very low level. The good thing of course was that we could build them for different platforms and operating systems, because a visualization system of the future will consist of many different nodes, running on different types of devices."

"The work that came after was called PolyChrome [5], and more recently Vistrates [7]. In general, we recognized that the unifying layer that all the devices we are interested in seem to have is the web browser." Elmqvist further reasons about a distributed operating system, a display environment that is shared, that runs on many devices simultaneously. "We used to do in the past a lot of that work ourselves, which was very painful, but the ability to just build on web technologies has made life a lot easier. [...] The idea of using web technologies for this type of thing is the same insight that lies behind D3[2] and Vega[3], those visualization libraries that are just again based on web technologies. I think that is the right way to do it."

Are you still missing other ingredients needed to support ubiquitous visualization?

Elmqvist reflects about the challenge of computation on small mobile devices. "Even back when I was thinking about ubiquitous visualization, I had this notion that some of the nodes in the connected environmental devices could be a cloud device that

---

[2]Data-Driven Documents: https://d3js.org/

[3]Visualization Grammar Vega: https://vega.github.io/vega/

have significant computing power. So, essentially you could have a virtual machine in Amazon AWS, waiting for you to send to jobs, and on-demand you could get access to a lot of this computational power as needed, maybe for machine learning as you say or something else." Elmqvist continues: "We have a paper called VisHive [21], which is about: What if you don't have a computer or virtual machine in the cloud. Is there a way you can distribute the work using your local clouded devices? So if I have a smartwatch, tablet, smartphone or laptop, what if we could use those as a mini cluster." He talks about this peer-to-peer approach, where nothing has to be downloaded or installed and everything is just web-based.

Who are the people actually authoring such ubiquitous, distributed and highly adaptive visualizations?

It is already difficult to bring a commercial solution such as Tableau to mobile devices, but it will be much more difficult if they have to bring it to a completely distributed space, which also complicates authoring. Elmqvist agrees and offers one potential solution. "In Vistrates [7], we provide a data flow language, where you drag and drop components, and you connect the outputs of one to the inputs of another [...]." Even though drag-and-drop authoring is already simpler, it is still not trivial and requires an understanding of, for example, data flow. "But it is at least simpler than writing code. If you come across situations where you need a component in Vistrates that doesn't exist in the Vistrates library [...] you can implement an entirely new component from scratch. Or you can take an existing component and branch or fork it and modify it and save it back to the library."

For alternatives of authoring visualizations, Elmqvist then points to the recent work by Arvind Satyanarayan with Lyra [78], or Leo Zhicheng Liu's 'Data Illustrator'[4], or Bongshin Lee's and colleagues' Charticulator[5]. "All these are great examples of drag and drop visualization creation, even for really complex and advanced visualizations that you don't need to choose from a chart gallery."

These examples that Elmqvist provided can be summarized as *End-User Visualization* environments, very much like environments for End-User Software Engineering. In a way, to democratize authoring of visualizations and to make their production accessible to everyone could be a crucial ingredient for ubiquitous visualizations.

Could machine learning or AI help us to provide a solution for contextual adaptation?

Earlier in the interview we had talked about context adaptation for mobile visualizations. One way to achieve this technically is to encode these adaptations manually by programmers, another to achieve this by means of artificial intelligence (AI). Asked about the latter, Elmqvist responds: "With Vistribute [40], we used rules of thumb that we then validated based on a user study. But, how could it be done? It would be exciting if you could take the 'Show Me' feature that Tableau has, which is essentially

---

[4]Data Illustrator for creating infographics and data visualizations without programming: http://data-illustrator.com/

[5]Charticulator for creating chart designs without programming: https://charticulator.com/

Jock Mackinlay's PhD thesis from 1986, implemented 20 years later. There you can say, here is which data I am interested in, and the system is going to tell me how to visualize it most effectively. [...] If we could have a similar approach to not just the visualization themselves and the data, but also the devices that are available so that you can automatically make decisions to optimize depending on the task the person has. [...] I wonder if there are things we could do beyond rules of thumb, maybe, as you said, if we get a big enough training data set to create a machine learning model that can do this for us. We need to collect a lot of real world, in-the-wild data and use the data we collect to figure out what people's preferences are."

How do you expect people to interact with future visualizations? Will there be a mix of technologies, interaction techniques or maybe just speech—what is your opinion?

"As for speech, Arjun Srinivasan at Georgia Tech has done some interesting work there with Orko [84] and related topics. I think there is potential for using speech, but there are always difficulties in interacting using speech alone. So combinations are probably—especially for something as specific as data visualizations – more relevant, where you use touch and speech, or mouse and speech, or keyboard and speech and so on. Some of Arjun Srinivasan's work is interesting because it tries to define the affordances of each modality and how it can be used."

Elmqvist also advocates other modalities beside mouse, keyboard, and even touch. "Pens were out of fashion for a while, but now they have their comeback to some degree. They could be useful for more precise tasks. And I know, [...] you worked on how gaze can be used as an input modality; I think this could be interesting, also using facial expressions." He also considered proxemics in a paper with Sriram Karthik Badam [4]. "Basically, how you relate to other people, whether you look at them, you face them, how close you are to them or to physical objects, whether you hold your phone facing yourself or someone else. All these information could also be useful. If you can capture it, often that means you need an intelligent space, that has cameras to track people in the room."

"We've done some work on gestures and full body interaction, pointing and so on. [...] Providing tactile feedback could be another option. I think all these are potential ways and exciting opportunities. They all have their roles, their strengths and weaknesses, I think we need to figure them out and generate not just a visualization grammar or vocabulary, but also what input devices and output devices we have and how to best map them to the available data and what tasks people want to do."

People's sensory bandwidth is limited, and if they are overwhelmed by interactive visualizations everywhere, shouldn't there be some kind of mindful and respectful use?

People might be overwhelmed by the various options of how to interact with a visualization and no longer know whether to use proximity, gaze, gestures, or speech. Elmqvist argues "We already deal with this in data visualization, because we recognize that people can only see so many visual items at the same time. So there has been a lot of work to minimize clutter and find visual summaries that are not overwhelming. But, it is absolutely true, that the potential for overwhelming the users is even more if you include other sensory modalities, like sound, and everywhere you look there is going to be a bar chart, and everything is going moving and jumping. We have to be respectful of the individuals, find out the best way to do things. Sometimes that may even go so far as to think of the human as the limiting resource we have to manage. And this sounds a little dystopian of course. Just like we think of a computer's memory or rendering performance as a resource we have to manage, we could think about the human's limited resources we have to respect. [...] We might want to manage interruptions and the person's attention. I think it is more about being respectful to human's capacities rather than scheduling, which sounds like we treat the person as a computer. I think, it is more that we respect boundaries."

In your Ubilytics work, you assume that people will actually perform analytics tasks in the wild, but won't they rather deal mostly with easier, glanceable visualizations?

"That's my feeling too, I may be wrong. I have a sense that most people prefer the controlled confines of a space like their office or home for accomplishing more involved tasks, because just how human beings work with the amount of interactions you might have in a mobile setting and things like safety and so on. So yes, I would think that there will be mostly use cases that have to do with opportunistic or serendipitous in-situ decision-making, maybe not so many long-term decisions. Like I said in the beginning, we were trying to find those apps that take good advantage of the fact that people are in a physical space, where the space makes the difference."

Do you envision more interaction happening between people, more collaboration if they use ubiquitous visualizations in the future?

"Most devices are designed for focused use of single users. Smartphones will remain personal devices, because they're so tied up to individuals. 10–15 years ago, new devices came about which were larger, like wall-sized displays or tabletop displays. Because of their orientation and size, they were more inviting for collaborative use. And tabletops and large displays, I am not going to say that they are obsolete, but we see less of them now, because we've moved more to a mobile setting. The question you might want to ask, what is equivalent of a collaborative display or device in an entirely mobile setting. I don't know."

He argued in the following that mobile projections (cf. [22]), even though obviously intended for sharing content or visualizations, are not the right way to do it either. "If it's AR, that is our future, maybe that means that there will be ways where you can signify this is something that not just you see, but also other people see. That allows you to collaborate better. But if you go toward a more physical display future, it's hard to predict. We have one project in our lab where we are looking at displays on devices and projectors on some drones. And some of my colleagues at Maryland had a drone that follows the user, a little like a floating display that follows you around. Very physical, kind of scary. [...] But it could potentially be useful for multiple users."

Niklas Elmqvist concluded the interview with a comment that he was inspired by our discussion and that many things are left to be done in this exciting space.

9.5   SEAN WHITE ON SITUATED AUGMENTED REALITY

At the time of writing, Sean White was the Chief Research & Development Officer for Mozilla. At Mozilla, Sean has championed the development of Mozilla Mixed Reality, including the Firefox Reality browser for VR. He has published pioneering research in the area of augmented reality and visualization, in particular contributing of the notion of *situated visualization* [93].

Situated visualizations, often presented in augmented reality, display data directly within the context where the data is relevant, such as overlaying graphs or visualizations of harmful gas emissions directly over a view of a streetscape. By viewing emissions data in situ, urban designers reported being better able to understand factors causing air quality problems than when viewing a data-annotated map. Interesting findings from the *SiteLens* project included that more literal visualizations such as animated smoke clouds were more effective and relatable in situ over more traditional chart types overlaid on the environment. The disconnect of using stale data in situ was raised as an opportunity which in the ten years since the work is more readily possible with the growth of connected devices, cloud data architectures, and Internet of Things (IoT) sensors in the environment.

White has been engaged with the community including teaching "HCI Issues in Mixed & Augmented Reality" at Stanford, mentoring for Engineers without Borders, and serving on the Steering Committee for IEEE's International Symposium on Mixed and Augmented Reality (ISMAR). We met with him to garner his reflections on ubiquitous visualization, from his industrial research and development perspective.

What does mobile visualization mean to you? How do you see it being used today?

White started by stating his view that visualization is not just communication, but also important to help people think through data, to extend perception/cognition. He said, "Mobile then is the context. It's the ways in which our computational systems extend our abilities to analyze in the context in which it's needed [...] there's a secondary aspect where it's just reachable; that is, I happen to be able to access it while I'm there." White continued to explain that in industry, some initiatives are taking place which build on his early research, such as AR/VR enabled web browsers that can bring visualization into the world around you. For example, embedding temperature sensors in AR headsets to overlay that information in the world around the user.

How do you envision mobile visualization contextually adapting to aid a user's activity?

White believes that by putting the visualization in context the learning and cognition are increased: "There's some reasonable amount of evidence around that. I think it makes more sense when it is situated and you are closer to the sources of data whether that is sensors or other aspects of the world that you're trying to visualize." Mobile visualization generally gives a first-person point of view; the viewer is embedded in the visualization directly. However, "some of the work of Kalkofen [48] gives a sort of third person point of view within a first person point of view."

What different application areas and target user groups do you envision in the future for the consumption of data on mobile devices (versus visualizations on the desktop)?

White envisions immediate applications in industrial and medical environments. In medical applications, he suspects augmented visualizations, where content is projected on the users body, showing veins on the arms could become routine in guiding a nurse when performing blood extractions, for example. Additional means for quickly allowing one to glance at biometric data, such as blood glucose levels at periodic intervals during the day, could be available to patients and also their doctors, the moment the individual steps into the doctor's office. In industrial settings, White envisions visualizations becoming commonplace with advances in LIDAR (LIght Detection And Ranging) technologies. These would enable indoor way finding, a key element for tracking objects in manufacturing plants.

While the above two applications seem to be immediate opportunities, White further envisioned that mobile visualizations would be directed at the masses. At the time of this writing, the COVID-19 pandemic was taking its roots worldwide. White suggested that novel sensors could enable timely COVID-19 tracing. The ability to present information, that is at the same time aesthetically pleasing yet informative could be designed and tailored to the masses to make rapid decisions.

What do you see as key use cases for mobile/ubiquitous visualizations?

White believes an immediate use case is in medicine due to the utilitarian nature of the field, due to it involving in-the-moment decisions, and it being necessary and important. Given that surgeons are already willing to wear glasses as part of their responsibilities, for example for surgery, it may seem like an immediate opportunity for mobile visualization. Similarly, White believes maintenance and repair to be the mechanical version of the needs in the medical fields. In this use case, a mixed reality (MR) web browser could intelligently mash up web content, organize it cohesively, and make it available for remote guidance and remote repair.

What is the current big thing for mobile visualization? And what do you think will be next?

White said, "I would love to see visualization used to ask more questions" and compared it to how mobile visualizations can spark the same degree of curiosity as a piece of good art. Another growing interest is in allowing more views of the data to enable social cohesiveness and collaborative interactions around the visualization. White wishes to see these forms of collaborative spaces to enable creative, social and analytical in-place activities, "to be able to have multiple people visualizing in the space together." White also expects that mobile visualizations will see an evolution as a number of developments converge, particularly with head-worn displays. He expects information to flow more fluidly across multiple modalities including voice, audio and space. Development such as the iPad's LIDAR sensing can lead to interesting ways to incorporate the background and mesh it into the foreground as a whole.

What about scenarios where data can be mobile and with the user? The devices and displays would then be proactive, and adapt to the user, rather than presenting generic information that is the same for everyone?

White alludes to less is more in such scenarios, and to the importance of allowing people to still have the feeling of maintaining control. The idea of subtlety with minimal pre-attentive cues and lightweight hints could be a rich field to explore. He recalls his experience with the first Mac systems where users could just slap hundreds of fonts on a flyer, and thus they did. Over time people took into account perception, aesthetics, and the world generally got better at design. White believes the same is true with current mobile visualizations: navigating those is much like being in a fighter cockpit. Instead, subtle cues, such as those from a friend to indicate in which direction to go while walking down an unknown road together, could enhance one's sense of control while relying on the system and its knowledge of the world and the user's context.

How do you see mobile visualization transitioning to ubiquitous visualization? What does ubiquitous visualization mean to you?

"The pithy answer is: your glasses." White tends to think of it as the distinction of *present-in-hand* versus *ready-to-hand*. "In the best scenario ubiquitous visualization will be present and ready to use as an extension, rather than mobile, which is something I have to pull out of my pocket. We still have a ways to go to get there." White said, "It's a really different usage: when you first start talking to people about mobile visualization, they have a model of always on, always present, always there. Then you get to the realities of it and you have a thing that you can pull out or put on for a moment." White reflected on his work with botanists, who received real benefit from situated mobile visualization using large AR glasses. They were willing to do it because "they cared, because it had a real utility." He said, "All the things we encounter in the world when we are there, are situated. What I am looking for is that mix, where ubiquitous visualization means that I have the option to always be situated in my learning, the things that I create, my interactions with other people." That takes a combination of a lot of new hardware, software breakthroughs, infrastructure, and all the visualizations we would need to create for this platform, but, it would lead to a better way to interact. White stated one of his long-term personal goals "to have us lift up our heads, no longer looking down at our phones. Transitioning to ubiquitous visualization would be part of that. It means we are more human." In contrast to a monocle or other device that has to be pulled out, glasses are already present, breaking down the barrier of interaction inertia.

Has the design and development of mobile visualizations become a key priority in industry?

White confirmed there is recognition in industry that visualization and visual communication are important, along with design, HCI, and user needs. "Visualization in general, but you could consider it mobile visualization, can be powerful for communication, but also for understanding. The industry itself, let's say the mobile phone, device, web-application industries, realize that to make good decisions, you need good visualizations. To make good decisions in the moment, you need mobile visualizations." White reflected on the impact of the mobile revolution—there are fewer people now using desktops than mobile devices; we have now a whole generation who are mobile first. This, White said, is one of the reasons the phone industry is investing significantly in both software and sensors. Phones started as a mini version of a desktop, a metaphorical "horseless carriage" but are slowly transforming "into something more unique, like the Star Trek tri-corder." Situated visualization doesn't have to be constrained to spatially situated, it could be situated through understanding the world, the people around me, the air quality, the impacts of my movements.

In your work, you have also paid attention to how one can best interact with situated visualization in AR (e.g., gestural hints for tangible AR [96], shake menu techniques [95]). What do you think is key in terms of supporting effective interaction when we move to more ubiquitous visualization?

White separated the discussion into the deployment platforms: there is still a broad design space for phones and watches—a lot of experimentation is possible beyond the things we are familiar with. "On the web we build toolkits in an open source way and then suddenly, everbody's using it and building on it. This has not really existed for other kinds of displays. The two I'm thinking of in particular are AR/VR displays and auditory displays." White lamented that for AR/VR displays, the tools built 5 or 10 years ago can't now be used by researchers, students, and industry because the systems are gone. "One of the reasons I like toolkits is for the longevity—there is a platform aspect." Outside of visualization, White thinks the same is true for audio, that there will be a renaissance around the interactions for audio with the new earbud technology. "After that will be the progression from the 100 fonts to a couple," meaning the design will coalesce around key interactions that work well. White advocates for a multi-disciplinary team approach consisting of research scientists, designers, cognitive psychologists. "Artists too. They are always adding in the extra part that other people are not thinking about."

9.6 YVONNE ROGERS ON VISUALIZATIONS FOR SOCIAL EMPOWER-MENT

Yvonne Rogers[6] is the director of the Interaction Centre at University College London (UCLIC), a professor of Interaction Design and the deputy head of department in the Computer Science Department. Former positions include professorships at the Open University, Indiana University and Sussex University; she has also been a visiting professor at University Cape Town, University of Melbourne, Queensland University of Technology,

Stanford University, Apple and UCSD. She is internationally renowned for her work in human-computer interaction, interaction design, and ubiquitous computing. She was awarded a prestigious EPSRC dream fellowship to rethink the relationship between ageing, computing, and creativity. She is passionate about designing computers that are engaging, exciting, and even provocative. She has published over 250 articles, and is a co-author of the definitive textbook on Interaction Design that has sold over 200,000 copies worldwide and been translated into 6 languages.

Several of Yvonne's research projects are of relevance to this book chapter. Yvonne's early work on Ambient Wood [76] within the Equator project explored the use of mobile data collection and visualization as part of an educational experience for children to learn about biology. More recently, Yvonne and her team investigated how to engage communities with data and the Internet of Things in urban settings within the "Intel Collaborative Research Institute (ICRI) on Sustainable Connected Cities". Examples of such projects include Tidy Street [11], PhysiKit, and physical installations to engage citizens with data such as VoxBox [30] and Sens-US [29].

What does mobile visualization mean to you?

Yvonne mentions that mobile visualizations are those that "you might use in person in-situ whilst you are doing another activity as opposed to those that appear on a desktop or a tabletop or a wall that might be shared or used by an individual sitting down or standing."

What do you see as the main use cases of mobile visualization?

Her first experience with mobile visualization was in the field of education in the context of the Ambient Wood project [76]. In that project, students had access to visualizations of data that they were collecting in-situ. Having this at hand "enabled them to couple the data that they were collecting with the learning activity that they were involved in." She also mentions that "We have much more affordable, adaptable, flexible sensing technology than in the old days. You can collect data and visualize it in the moment (both the actual data and the other samples that have been collected).

---

[6]Note that we refer to our interviewee Yvonne Rogers by "Yvonne," as she preferred her first name over "Rogers."

I think in an educational context, particularly for field work, it is a very powerful tool to use."

She thinks that digital healthcare is going to be a use case for mobile visualization where the combination of electronic records and sensing technology will allow healthcare workers and researchers to make decisions in real time. Additionally, fields such as personal informatics, sports, and exercise will benefit, "where people like to see data in the moment and how well they've done compared to other times and periods." Similar to Willett, she also thinks that looking at data in context in the field of retail could be another application area.

What do you see as the benefits of the visualization being mobile?

She mentions that they had an "aha!" moment in the Ambient Wood project [76] where "a simple visualization was shown in the moment. Moisture and light level infographics were used to convey relative levels that were seen by students/users, which they used in their learning activities." Seeing in the moment enabled the students to generate hypotheses on the fly (whether something would be lighter/darker) and take initiative in their own learning. It was much more powerful and fulfilling than just completing tasks.

Recently, Yvonne's PhD student Susan Lechelt has been working with students to think about data collection and what it means in terms of their own data. She had students measure their heart rate, electrocardiogram, and galvanic sweat response (to measure emotional response), and then asked them to answer questions such as "do you fancy X (where X was someone in their class)?" This provided them with readings they could use to determine if the person was telling the truth when answering the questions. Yvonne mentioned that "it got them to think about the reliability and accuracy of the data and not taking it for granted. What does the data they collect represent?" It allows students to collect and sense things about the body and then start questioning what that data means. Learning in those contexts is one of the most powerful uses of data and visualization.

How do you envision mobile visualization contextually adapting to aid a user's activity?

In terms of the visualization contextually providing users cues and hints, Yvonne mentions that walking/cycling apps do a great job of notifying the user when they reach a goal and they also some times encourage the user to keep going. She said that a visualization may "motivate you more" and make you want to keep going.

She referenced the Balance Table [77] project where the authors used a series of LEDs on a tabletop to convey who was talking more or less in a conversation. She mentioned that the "people who didn't speak much didn't like that they were not talking a lot and people who spoke more did not look at the visualization." This kind of ambient display could be used in mobile contexts, such as during remote meetings, showing who is talking or contributing the most. Somewhat controversially, it might be a great way of letting people know—in the form of a peripheral awareness norm—that they should pipe down or speak up.

Yvonne said that we need to be careful with contextually aware approaches to mobile visualization as there are many important considerations such as whether it is the right time to display the right data or the reason why we are providing contextual information to begin with. How would an adaptive interface detect crucial aspects of the person or the environment they are in to make the right decision with respect to showing contextual information? This would be different than previous work on adaptive interfaces that changed based on the completion of a task or adapted to a user's style of interaction.

What do you think is the current big thing and what do you think would be next for mobile visualization?

Yvonne referenced the interactive visualizations that are being developed to visualize the spread of COVID-19 in different countries. She said that it was teaching people to "read graphs and visualizations in a different way." She wondered if new ways of communicating data can be learned and whether individuals were reading those graphs correctly as some of the graphs seen in print and media are fairly complex. It is a great opportunity to think of how to design mobile visualizations that are more accessible to the general public.

She also mentioned that "the current widespread use of visualizations may increase awareness of visualization techniques that they can use in other contexts (e.g., weather, climate change, carbon emission footprint)." She would like to see more examples of accessible visualizations being developed and used to show that the world is getting worse or better (air quality, emissions, deforestation, and so on).

What does ubiquitous visualization mean to you? How do you see mobile visualization transitioning to "ubiquitous visualization"?

Yvonne mentioned that ubiquitous visualization could "include visualizations that appear in the physical environment, such as Picadilly Circus, or on an individual's smartwatch, a public display in a shopping mall, or even in nature, such as a forest. Ubiquitous means anywhere—personal, social, or environment. Some of the early ambient displays might be considered ubiquitous visualizations, for example some of the early art projects that showed the amount of CO_2 emissions by having dynamic visualizations appear on a wall. These were meant to make a statement and provoke the public into action." Many of them did.

What do you see as the most exciting aspects of bringing data and particularly data visualization into people's everyday lives?

Yvonne described her role in the "Intel Collaborative Research Institute (ICRI) on Connected Sustainable Cities," where her team researched how to engage communities in the urban environment and collect data about the environment. She said that the types of visualizations that they developed "were coupled very visibly with the way the data was collected."

She referenced her work on the Tidy Street project [11] and the research of her former PhD student (Lisa Koeman) on *Visualising Mill Road* [58]. She asked people on the street to vote on questions asked each day about topics concerning them (e.g., how safe do you feel?) and then displayed the results in the form of an infographic that was chalked on a street pavement (e.g., the perceived level of safety). Yvonne mentions: "In the Tidy Street project, the goal was to collect the householder's electricity consumption for each day, feed it into an app, and then display the average usage for the street as a public visualization, to get people to act on it to maybe reduce their energy consumption."

She likes to "think about how communities come together and ask questions that they may have not asked and what it means in terms of urban living." She likes to focus on social engagement and empowerment rather than more utilitarian civic engagement related to an individual's neighborhood (e.g., potholes filled, new lampposts). She mentioned how these projects "were more engaging in terms of showing the residents who they were and what they cared about and how safe the streets were and what were the things that troubled them."

She then discussed the PhysiKit [42] project that facilitated the collection of data in people's homes using the Open Source Smart Citizen kit. PhysiKit contained temperature, light, noise, and humidity sensors that could be programmed to notify the user based on user-defined rules. The goal was to get people to think about the consequences of their actions such as the humidity sensor would alert the user to turn on the exhaust fan if the humidity in a room was too high, or if the ambient noise in a room was too high the user would be notified about it. In one particularly interesting example, they played a potted plant on a motor that would rotate the plant based on the light exposure the sensor under it had received that day.

The collected data from the open source Smart Citizen Kit "was presented as a dashboard on a website, so people didn't look at it." The goal with PhysiKit was to get people to think about the consequences of their actions on different sensor readings. They were also given a tangible device they could program to alert them to change in their environment (e.g., when the CO_2 level was high) so they could understand the data in a more meaningful way. She summarized by saying that "Sensing, representing, and acting upon it" are the three coupled things that are common to all of her projects.

Would you like to share any surprising, empowering, or inspiring examples from your team's projects (for example, Tidy Street [11], PhysiKit [42], Roam.io [41] , the lambent shopping handle [49], PlayBats [50], ...)?

Yvonne mentioned the Roam.io [41] project that focused on tracking people on the island of Madeira through their mobile phones and hotspots to help understand the impact of large-scale tourism on the small island. Passersby were very helpful in providing more information beyond what the automated tracking technology offered. This gave the researchers a much better picture of where the tourists went, which parts of the island were visited the most and so on—without identifying any individual people. She also mentioned how her recent research has shown how people are more concerned about data privacy now than they have been in the past. That made her reflect more on the issues related to data collection, storage, usage, and increasing awareness of the users whose data is being collected.

She said that while "General Data Protection Regulation (GDPR) helps in these research projects, privacy has become an increasingly more important concern. While we can and do anonymise our data, we can always collect a lot more. A key question we need to consider more, is what is the minimum amount of data we can collect in order to answer our research question?"

She referenced the project of her current student (Lucy Walsh) that explored how to increase people's awareness of the data being collected about their usage when on a webpage. Part of the project involved developing a tangible device intended to sit on a user's desk that could light up to let them know what data was being collected about them. She said that the next generation of researchers "can think of new ways to alert people about what they are worried about such as the kinds of data being collected."

In a lot of your work (e.g., PhysiKit [42], Voxbox [30], Sens-Us [29], physicality and tangibility play a big role. Do you see this as something that is a nice add-on to have for more engagement, or is that really a key thing to consider?

Yvonne remembers how some of her earlier research started with exploring how to embed the Internet of Things (IoT) technology in a public building to increase awareness of its use. Presenting this back to the inhabitants and visitors of the building as a dynamic visualization can draw their attention to topics, behaviors or other aspects that they would normally overlook. She believes that "something physical is very effective, as it can draw people's attention in ways that a mobile app cannot." She said that her students and she love to build things and incorporating tangibility provides a richer palette (rather than staying only digital).

She predicts that in "in 10 years or so, we may even see plant-based interfaces." She mentioned that there is "plant-based clothing that can change and glow." She said that the next generation of interfaces will be innovative forms of fusing the physical, the digital and the tangible.

With the proliferation of Makerspaces and 3D printers, designing and creating interfaces that are attractive, aesthetic, *and* functional has become more accessible and affordable. Different ways to increase civic engagement and awareness may emerge from such interfaces and some of these may be citizen-driven in line with the increased enthusiasm behind the citizen science movement.

How should we take into account mindful technology for ubiquitous data visualization avoiding things like data addiction?

Yvonne explained that she was on a train recently that stopped at Gatwick airport. There she saw about 20 kids in groups of 4–5 that all had their heads down, looking at their phones. She lamented that "Everyone is looking down at their phones. It would be great if we can design ways to get them to *look up and look out*." One way of doing this, is to create new forms of public mobile visualizations that could shift people's attention from their phones to the environment around them. She said: "For example, in a coffee shop, if we could see how many cups of coffee had been bought that day compared to say, tea, it might get them thinking why is that happening? While seemingly trivial, it can feed into our fascination with factoids. The visualizations might show how much water has been used or saved that day, how many people had brought their one cup, how much the cafe had recycled, how much they had donated to a charity based on the number of lattes sold, and so on. Other topics could also be explored that people might be interested in but which can't currently be seen or conveyed." She urged researchers to think of creative ways to "help people have conversations that don't require always being mediated by your phone."

She mentioned the inspiration for the lambent shopping handle project [49], where a simple LED visualization was integrated with a shopping cart to show certain information about products they were interested in buying such as the number of food miles, whether organic, whether it contained nuts. This enabled shoppers to rapidly see at a glance when comparing different brands for products. She talked about how the prototype they built was featured on the "Gadget Man"[7] show with Richard Ayoade, who "really liked it for the fact that it was integrated into the shopping cart." She added that "When we show the shopping handle to other people, they frequently ask why don't you make it into a mobile app?." She said that "They are missing the whole point about how it's actually embedded into the device itself. It may be too expensive to put it in the handle [now], but it may not be in the future."

How do you see the intersection between (contextual) data collection and the potential for in-situ data visualization?

Yvonne said that "the coupling between data collection and visualization makes it meaningful. If you only provide dashboards that are visualizing what happens in London in terms of air quality, whether the underground is running, etc, people might glance at it once or twice, then forget about it. But if you engage them in the data collection, it becomes much more interesting and meaningful then."

She referenced the Tidy Street [11] project again and said that "if you were engaged personally in reducing energy consumption, then you become much more engaged and motivated to continue." She said that connecting the two (data collection and visualization) makes it more meaningful to the participants.

What do you think about future form factors for visualizations?

Yvonne mentioned that visualizations on a phone or smartwatch will continue for personal use and "they seem to be quite powerful for some people." She would also like to see visualizations that "can be in the environment for people to share and reflect on for groups of people to look at and possibly engage with." In the future, other materials may be used, such as clothing, toys, floors, ceilings and even holograms.

---

[7]https://www.channel4.com/programmes/gadget-man/

Will authoring data visualizations become more "democratic," as you explored in PhysiKit, and will it—like taking photos and video editing—become accessible to everyone? What are the remaining challenges?

Yvonne mentioned 3D printed work by Kim Sauvé [80] where she printed 3D shapes of someone's activity data and then asked them to reflect on it. She also mentioned Khot et al.'s EdiPulse project [53] work on printing 3D shapes from chocolate. She mentioned how "3D printing your own data makes something that is intangible a talking point again."

She also thinks that new 3D authoring tools could be used by people who have difficulty communicating with others. For example, people on the autism spectrum could print their data to "express something that they don't normally express or they find it hard to talk about and maybe through the use of this 3D artifact, they can talk through it and that this could help them communicate better."

There will always be challenges for making our data democratic—not least reassuring people that it is being used for their benefit or society. However, new kinds of visualizations can increase the transparency of how the data is collected and whether it contravenes their privacy rights.

Yvonne's oeuvre has a consistent thread of giving a voice to the people. Her research philosophy goes much beyond just functional things (what can we do for you). Her research group has worked on projects that use technology to raise awareness on important issues and to give citizens a voice, particularly for urban living where people may feel more isolated.

From a methodological perspective, is it time for the visualization community to embrace HCI's "turn to the wild?"

When we asked Yvonne about the relevance of her work on HCI research "in the wild" [75, 72, 20] to the move toward mobile and ubiquitous visualization, where we increasingly see visualizations introduced into a wide variety of different settings and situations, she replied:

"You know what my answer is going to be. Absolutely! It is about time. I think if you really want to understand how people use visualizations, it is important to move out of the lab. I think there is still some important research to be done in the lab in terms of legibility and response time for different kinds of visualizations. But, if you want to see actually how people will use them and reflect upon them in their everyday lives, then you need to go into the world."

9.7 DISCUSSION AND OVERALL REFLECTION

In this section, we reflect on common themes across the four interviews, and discuss what we can learn from them regarding the future of mobile visualization.

9.7.1 Mobile versus Ubiquitous Visualization

We asked all of our interviewees what the the terms "mobile visualization" and "ubiquitous visualization" meant to them. While each interviewee had a different perspective on this, there were some commonalities in their answers. Willett noted that, for him, mobile visualization is mostly about the form factor, about the visualization being shown on a mobile platform such as a phone or tablet. He also noted that even though the data is made available in a mobile setting, this does not always mean that the visualization is more situated with the tasks that it is supposed to support. Elmqvist sees mobile visualization as anything that is not using a personal computer and that focuses on situations where people are on the go. He mentioned that what sets its apart is the on-the-go aspect and supporting decision-making in-situ, which would be harder and require more time to do offline on a desktop device in an office. To Rogers, mobile visualizations are personal visualizations that you might use while doing another activity. While some of our interviewees see mobile visualization as being tied to current (touchscreen-based) mobile hardware platforms, White provided other examples of mobile visualization in AR and MR. White said two aspects of a mobile visualization were important to him: context—the ways in which the mobile visualization can extend our abilities in terms of cognition and learning to analyze data in the situation in which it is needed; and reachability—the fact that one can access it while in that context.

When confronted with the term "ubiquitous visualization," our interviewees had different ways of distinguishing this from mobile visualization. Willett mentioned that the end goal of ubiquitous visualization is to have access to data where and when it is useful. Out of several visions for ubiquitous visualization, he finds the ones that are technology-agnostic more satisfying as they could be realized with technology platforms that are currently available and also with future technology that is still infeasible for the next couple of decades. Good examples of ubiquitous visualization according to Willett are LEDs in parking garages indicating availability of parking spaces and the integrated LEDs in bicycle lanes. To Elqmvist, the key difference is that ubiquitous visualization would be far more integrated into real-world contexts, with possible use of AR or other augmentation technologies. However, like Willett, Elmqvist also mentions that we should consider how we could already achieve ubiquitous visualization with current technologies. Elmqvist mentioned Pokémon Go as a notable example that successfully integrated the real and the virtual world. Rogers notes that ubiquitous visualizations would appear anywhere, in personal settings and social settings, and everywhere in our environment. She notes that some of the early ambient displays could be considered ubiquitous visualizations. A key part of this, according to Rogers, is that these visualizations are meant to make a statement, to provoke the public, or to share with the public. On the other hand, White differentiated between mobile and ubiquitous visualization in terms of the visualization being (in Heidegger's terms) either "present-in-hand" or "ready-at-hand." He gave the example of pulling a phone out of one's pocket versus having access to AR visualizations integrated in one's glasses. While both support visualizations that are "always there." it takes more effort to pull out your phone compared to just turning on the visualization with your AR glasses. White explained that the goal of ubiquitous visualization to him is to have the option to be always situated in one's learning.

These comments suggest that the key aspect of mobile visualization is the ability to access and use the visualization in-situ. Ubiquitous visualization seems to push this idea even further to make the visualization more easily accessible, available, and in particular as noted by our interviewees, more situated within people's activities and settings. Additionally, our interviewees suggested that ubiquitous visualization should also go beyond the personal aspects of current mobile devices and allows for more shared and collaborative use. A common theme in the interviews was that there are few examples of mobile visualizations that really take advantage of being available in a mobile context. Indeed, many mobile visualizations are ports of existing visualizations designed for a smaller form factor, and only take contextual aspects (such as location) into account in a limited way. While location is of course only one of the aspects of context that can be taken into account (other aspects include the social setting, who one is with, and the activities one is engaged in), Elmqvist emphasized the potential of using place as an index into the virtual world of data. Some of the notable contextually-relevant examples that were mentioned by our interviewees include mobile visualizations in car dashboards (Willett), in-situ collection and visualization in an educational context as in Ambient Wood [76] (Rogers), and a mobile AR electronic field guide for botanists [94, 98] (White). This suggests that as part of a move toward ubiquitous visualization, we may initially see more strongly situated mobile visualizations that take advantage of current hardware platforms.

9.7.2 Challenge: Information Overload

Potential information overload is already a challenge with visualization on mobile devices, due to the limited form factor (see Chapter 3). Our interviewees mentioned that this challenge would only be exacerbated as we move more toward ubiquitous visualization. Willett differentiated between information density and information complexity of a visualization and mentioned that the problem mostly lies with information complexity. He mentioned some possible ways to deal with this such as visual summaries, glanceable visualizations, and a staged approach to revealing data. Similarly, Elmqvist brought up the challenge of making visualizations, data, and displays available everywhere without polluting people's virtual space. He argued that designers need to be respectful of the user. White likened current mobile visualizations with being in a fighter jet cockpit. Over time, he expects we will develop a better sense of design and aesthetics, and subtlety in the design of mobile visualizations. Regarding information overload, Rogers mentioned her Physikit project [42], where data becomes visible at certain moments in time to remind people that a certain event occurred, for example, when a certain level of air quality or CO_2 concentration has been reached. In line with Willett's suggestion of a staged approach, a promising way to avoid information overload could be to facilitate opt-in and opt-out choices, as explored in proxemic interaction and interaction with public displays [12, 71], where one would have to explicitly opt-in to or have an option to opt-out of being presented with data visualizations. This also reminded us of prior discussions in the ubiquitous computing and HCI communities with respect to interaction in the periphery [8, 16, 47] and Weiser's notion of calm technology [91]. However, as our interviewee Yvonne Rogers has argued previously, we may also want to design for engaging and playful (rather than calm) experiences [74]. As mentioned above, Rogers argued that she believes a key aspect for ubiquitous visualizations is to provoke and engage people.

Being exposed to ever-increasing data and data visualizations may also have negative consequences. When data is disturbing, being exposed to visualizations of that data may make people anxious. As seen during the COVID-19 pandemic, people reported feeling anxious about news reports and often refrained from following updates about the number of cases or deaths as a result of COVID-19. Chapter 7 on ethics and privacy challenges also discussed "data anxiety" that people may experience in terms of tracking personal health or activity data. This points to a related design challenge for ubiquitous visualization. Depending on the topic, making visualizations available everywhere and at any time may not only overwhelm people in terms of information overload, but may also have negative effects on people's mental health.

9.7.3 Challenge: People Looking Down at Their Mobile Devices

Several of our interviewees also mentioned how it is a common sight to see people just look down at their mobile devices and ignore their surroundings. Our interviewee Yvonne Rogers has previously questioned whether this is what we want from technology [73]. She distinguished between *mindless* interactions in which we are focused on ourselves and look down at our phone and *mindful* interactions in which we are mindful of others and the environment around us. In many ways, this is opposite to what our interviewees envision with ubiquitous visualization. Instead, ubiquitous visualization would aim at bringing us closer to each other and to provide us with more information about the environment in which we are currently residing, making us feel more in touch with it. A few comments from the interviews confirm this. Rogers notes that showing data in-situ could provide talking points to get people to interact socially. White specifically mentioned that one of his personal goals was to break the pattern of people looking down at their phones and he mentioned that transitioning to ubiquitous visualization could be an opportunity to address this challenge and be more human. White mentioned he wants visualizations to ask more questions and spark curiosity, similar to works of art. Rogers also brought up the idea of physical visualizations of data that are human-sized three-dimensional shapes so that people can explore data by walking around it, "more of a museum piece." Similar to Rogers, White also expressed a desire for visualizations that go beyond the personal and enable social cohesiveness and collaborative interactions around the visualization.

Reflecting on these discussion points, there is clearly much potential for ubiquitous visualization break this pattern that we see in current mobile devices by exploring more social, creative, provoking, and engaging aspects of data visualization, rather than focusing on analytic aspects alone.

9.7.4 Opportunity: Mobile Displays as a Way to Envision the Future

While several of our interviewees discuss visions of ubiquitous visualization using advanced technologies such as integrated retina displays or AR glasses, they also argue that we can already realize much of this vision with existing technologies. Moreover, Willett and Elmqvist both cast doubts on whether AR will be the single most optimal technology solution to achieve ubiquitous visualization. Willett notes that while AR and MR are receiving a lot of attention, many challenges still remain. An important challenge of AR/MR that Willett mentions is the difficulty of providing shared experiences using these technologies. Similarly, Elmqvist notes that AR is promising, but that "AR glasses will not be worn by everyone," and that there are still large gaps that need to be addressed to reach that stage.

Instead, Willett and Elmqvist both point to *displays* as a promising technology platform that can be used in the short-term to realize ubiquitous visualization. Willett mentions that embedding increasingly cheaper displays and projections into everyday spaces could be a shortcut to this envisioned future that may still be 20 to 30 years away. Similarly, Elqmvist talks about his vision of "ubiquitous visual computing," which is a version of ubiquitous computing [90] in which devices do not completely disappear nor are display-less or magic. As with making mobile visualizations more integrated with people's everyday tasks, the use of many (small) situated displays [51] may be one of the first ways in which we see practical realizations of ubiquitous visualization. In particular, small, low-cost, and power-efficient e-ink displays have shown promise for exploring and prototyping the use of visualizations in everyday spaces [2, 14]. If the costs of displays continue to decrease, a key difference would be that such displays may not be used as personal devices anymore (as we currently see with current mobile devices). Instead, they could be repurposed and reused many times, depending on the scenario. This is more in line with Weiser's original vision of the "tab" [90] (roughly the form factor of today's smartphone) as a shared and "throw-away" device that one would pick up when needed.

Finally, we want to stress that there are also rich opportunities for ubiquitous visualization that go beyond displays, such as presenting data through physicalization [45], physical actuation as in Jeremijenko's Live Wire [92] or sonification, which we will come back to in Section 9.7.6.

9.7.5 The Web as a Technology Platform

The web is already an essential platform for mobile visualization, with toolkits such as D3 [13] or Vega-Lite [79] that integrate with existing web technologies to enable access to data visualizations on a wide variety of devices. According to some of our interviewees, we can build upon the existing strength of the web as a common platform for mobile visualization when looking at a possible platform to facilitate development of ubiquitous visualizations. Both Elmqvist and White specifically mention the use of web technologies as a generic and widely-available platform that could enable ubiquitous visualization. According to Elqmvist, the key advantage of the web as a platform is that it does not require any specialized software, everything is running in JavaScript in the browser. All one needs is a capable web browser, which more and more devices are nowadays capable of running. Elmqvist noted that the use of web browsers could bring us closer to a distributed operating system, a shared display environment that runs on many devices simultaneously, while noting that this may also mean that some devices may have to offload computation to more powerful nodes due to limited computational capabilities. Similarly, Sean White discussed the opportunities of a mixed-reality web browser (e.g. Firefox Reality [63]) which could intelligently mash up web content for use in particular settings. White contrasted the use of open source toolkits on the web that everyone can use and build upon with the tools for AR/VR that were built 5–10 years ago that cannot be used by researchers, students or industry anymore since the systems do not exist anymore. In summary, this points to much potential for the use of the web as a shared platform to develop future ubiquitous visualization systems, building on the success of prior web visualization toolkits.

9.7.6 How Will We Interact with Ubiquitous Visualization?

As discussed in Chapter 3, visualizations on mobile devices can support a number of different interaction modalities, such as touch, voice and spatial interaction (sometimes even across multiple mobile and stationary devices). A key challenge, however, has been with discoverability and consistency of these interactions: narrowing these possibilities down to common interaction patterns that work well for the activities and tasks at hand. Visualizations also often need to be completely reimagined for mobile use due to differences in display size and resolution, precision in interaction, and the constraints of use on the go (see Chapter 2). To understand what this will mean for interaction with ubiquitous visualization, we asked our interviewees how they envisioned interacting with ubiquitous visualizations. As discussed above, White mentioned the use of AR glasses and having the visualization always at hand, whenever we needed to access it. Proxemics [32] was mentioned by Willett as a possible solution to stage or scaffold the amount of information that was shown to the user and address the risk of potentially overwhelming users. Elmqvist particularly mentioned the use of different input modalities, including speech, body interaction, proxemics, and tactile feedback, and mentions a need to map out what is possible and what is most appropriate for different tasks and purposes. White mentioned the coming renaissance in audio interaction, which will open up audio soundscape design possibilities and may offer opportunities for the sonification of data to accompany or replace visualization when contextually appropriate. While this points to exciting possibilities for interaction with ubiquitous visualization, it may also lead to another way in which users can become overwhelmed, unsure about whether they can expect to use gestures, speech, proxemics or other modalities. In particular, Elqmvist suggests to consider people's limited resources, just like memory and rendering performance, as something that needs to be respected when designing ubiquitous visualizations. Regarding this topic, Rogers sees a lot of promise in physical and tangible interfaces to support engaging and fun experiences, and looks ahead to plant-based interfaces. White notes that we are currently in a phase with lots of design possibilities, many of which will disappear when the design will coalesce around some key interactions that work well.

9.8 SCENARIOS FOR UBIQUITOUS VISUALIZATION

We envisioned a few scenarios for ubiquitous visualization based on conversations at our Dagstuhl seminar "Mobile Data Visualization" as well as the interviews we conducted for this chapter.

Personal informatics is a major theme where information about an individual is crucial to the individual and is provided in a contextualized form. The *Quantified Self* movement consists of individuals who are passionate about collecting high-resolution data about their health, exercise, energy consumption, shopping habits, and so on. For example, a device such as a smartwatch not only captures the data regarding an individual's health, but also allows them to explore it either on the watch itself or on a mobile phone. Mundane tasks such as brushing your teeth, drinking coffee, or shopping could be scenarios in which we may see innovations with respect to ubiquitous visualization. Rather than experiencing visual representations only on a watch/phone, we may see representations on a toothbrush, or a coffee cup, or the handle of a shopping cart. Here one may experience "serendipitous decision-making" rather than conduct detailed analytics that would be performed on a desktop or in a collaborative setting.

We believe that mobile sensors and devices will play a big role in the **retail and sales** sectors. We may see actuated store shelves [99] as well as "smart" stores that may guide customers to various parts of the store based on real-time sales data. Rogers' lambent shopping handle is an example where users can see information about the "distance" a food item has traveled before it reached the supermarket.

Public and private transportation will continue to see situated visualizations for the driver and passengers alike. They may be used to inform the driver and the passengers about the current state of the vehicle and its surroundings. In addition to the standard data on a dashboard of a car, modern cars convey the estimated amount of miles that can be driven on the current level of gas in the tank/charge on the vehicle. Future displays in an automobile will continue to get better and use a variety of sensors (distance, luminosity, acoustic, etc.) to better inform the driver about vehicles, pedestrians, and other situations that the driver may not have noticed. As a difference to mobile visualization as we know it, future traffic scenarios will increasingly involve display functionality integrated into traffic infrastructure and vehicles, but not just shown on mobile devices. We believe that displays will even be integrated into the sidewalk to provide traffic flow information for cyclists and pedestrians as a means of surfacing data in our environments.

Our vision of the future of ubiquitous visualization includes a transformation in the field of **healthcare**, where patients and medical professionals alike will have situated access to all relevant information on mobile applications for rapid decision making. Medicine and healthcare will be completely transformed in the near future due to mobile and ubiquitous visualization. Surgeons and other medical staff will be able to gain deeper insight into the patient's current health conditions before, after, and as they are conducting the surgery—either through augmented reality or through other handheld devices for diagnosis (for example, overlaying CT scan data on patients) and treatment (for example, utilizing adaptive visualizations for post-surgery medication). We envision mobile interfaces to consider multifaceted health data that can be interacted with using multimodal input (touch, voice, force, etc.) and to communicate it via visualizations and even non-visual renderings to other stakeholders regardless of their physical location, a vision also called the Tactile Internet [28].

Cyber-Physical Systems where data is being collected from a variety of entities such as a train or a bus, a toll booth, a water fountain, a trash can, and so on can be visualized seamlessly on situated devices and mobile displays. Some insights from analyzing this data could be conveyed to a casual bystander waiting for the next train or walking past a display in a store to increase their awareness of current urban issues and empower their decision-making.

Crisis management is an overarching theme as a future application domain for ubiquitous visualization. Individuals in a geographic region could be notified on their smart watches/phones/glasses, information about evacuation routes or communicating urgent messages (similar to the Amber alert system in North America that is used to request the public for assistance with finding a missing child.) Car emoji displays (shown on the rear dash) such as the Mojipic[8] could be used to provide helpful information to vehicles behind you in such a scenario. Mobile devices could also be used to increase situational awareness for **improved safety** in personal or public emergency or even military situations. Individual safety can be increased for students on campus by being informed about the location of police officers nearby or zones to avoid. In the future, we may also see personal drones as an informative or collaborative device that can serve to communicate a message to nearby individuals. One such scenario could be when a disabled or elderly person needs **assistance** and the display on the drone can communicate that to the nearby individuals through sound, light, or even notifications on their devices. Drones may also be used in the future for large-scale data collection as well as data aggregation such as in the example in Willett's interview where thousands of drones may go out into a field and provide an overview of specific attributes such as soil moisture.

Construction and **Maintenance** are domains in which we will see larger use of ubiquitous visualization that can provide contextual information on demand to technicians and workers. The mobile device can overlay information onto machinery with level-of-detail representations being displayed on a mobile device or augmented reality glass (creating a so-called digital twin of a physical environments [68]). These systems could also take into account proxemics, for example to show more detailed information as the technician gets closer to some equipment or section of a building.

Communicating emotions and feelings in private and public settings through shape and/or color-changing fabrics could be a reality in the future. In private settings with your family or friends, an individual's smart clothes could communicate happiness,

---

[8]https://mojipic.co/

sadness, anger, and so on through a pattern of the fabric. A shape-changing collar or buttons that grow/shrink in size based on a specific emotion or physical condition (heart rate/blood pressure/blood sugar parameters) would also be a way to provide subtle non-verbal cues.

In a public setting such as a dance club, an individual's clothing may have embroidered displays into the fabric that all work together to communicate their current mood, mental state, or physical state (tired, alcohol consumed, heart rate) to the people around them. While less futuristic, a watch band or other jewellery might be illuminated to communicate feelings or information [57]. There may also be subtle ways of communicating interest in other people at the club through color- or shape-changing fabric.

9.9   REVISITING THE DIMENSIONS OF MOBILE VISUALIZATION

In Chapter 1 the dimensions of mobile data visualizations were introduced as a way to describing existing core cases of mobile visualization, from charts on smartwatches read while running to shared tablet displays used in the field. The experts interviewed have opened up the design space for visualization moving from mobile to ubiquitous, and in this section we will revisit the dimensions to investigate if they require extensions to include the additional factors.

9.9.1   Reflecting on the Dimensions of Mobile Visualization from Our Interviews

The first dimension of mobile visualization is the **data display mobility**. Our experts discussed a range of technologies across all levels of display mobility. Willett proposed that the fastest way to achieve a vision of ubiquitous visualization is from the (relatively) *fixed* ecosystem of in-vehicle screens. This configuration is similar to the edge case of in-cabin displays on aircraft, which are fixed relative to the viewer, but moving through the external world. Rogers suggested similar embedded technologies fixed in the world around us, such as data displayed on coffee shop walls, and expanded out to *movable* displays embedded in shopping cart handles, or even futuristic ideas of data display using plants. White focused on *wearable* see-through displays to augment the world around us with data. And Elmqvist reflected on drones used to display data with *viewer-independent movement*. The typical mobile visualization technology, the *carryable* phone, was the least discussed means to achieving the vision of ubiquitous visualization. Each expert shared the vision that ubiquity means being free to interact with the world around us. Rogers clearly stated, "everyone is looking down at their phones [. . .] we can design ways to get them to "look up, look out."

The second dimension is the **physical display size**, running from *pixel-sized* to *wall-sized*. This dimension did arise in the interviews, including Willett's discussion of single-bit LEDs for biking and parking to White's smart glasses, and Rogers' suggestion of large-scale displays of data in coffee shops or public squares. Willett frames the display size dimension in relation to information density and information complexity, where information that is glanceable may often be desired in situ, and the information density and complexity could adapt to the display size, from small wearable displays to coordinated displays embedded in the environment. This relates to the edge case of micro-mobility through linked display devices, such as two tablets which can be arranged in different configurations on a tabletop, as discussed in Chapter 1. Willett's ecosystem of displays essentially extends this idea into a very large total display size made of many smaller displays in a contextually-appropriate arrangement. What this physical display size dimension from Chapter 1 does not fully cover is the use of *see-through* display technology. For example, AR glasses placed right before the eye, or AR contact lenses, may someday create complete field-of-view coverage for displaying situated data visualizations. Perhaps this calls for another dimension of **display transparency** including levels of *closed-view, video-based see-through*, and *optical see-through* displays, following the terminology of Azuma [3].

The third dimension is the **visualization's reaction to display movement**. This considers how mobile visualizations respond to movement, including direct change (e.g. GPS location data is part of the visualization) and indirect change (user movement induces heart rate which is part of the visualization). In the interviews, we heard consensus that ubiquitous visualization would primarily be situated and contextual, to the location, movement, tasks, people present, environmental factors, etc. In this way, ubiquitous visualization moves beyond responsiveness to movement toward responsiveness to many contextual cues, driven by new types of sensors such as LIDAR, and novel technologies such as fabric-based interfaces [67, 56]. We also heard that it is not only the display movement, but also the **data movement** that may characterize ubiquitous visualization. Data may be *fixed to a single device* in the base case. When the user, rather than the device, is the central factor in a visualization system, the data and visualization views of it can be *linked to the user*, moving from display to display in an augmented environment, or with the user in a wearable system. Data may also *move with the task* across multiple users as needed. As Elmqvist posits, it may be possible to have different levels of sophistication in the various 'nodes' of the device ecosystem, with some devices being compute-heavy (e.g., laptops) while others are displays for the end result (e.g., smartwatches).

The fourth dimension is the **visualization interaction complexity** spanning from *passive interaction* to *highly interactive*. Ubiquitous visualizations may similarly run the gamut of interactive complexities, from passive views of situated data in the environment to highly interactive scenarios responding to multimodal inputs such as speech, mid-air gestures, and interactions on peripheral devices. Furthermore, the system response in ubiquitous scenarios may more often be non-visual (e.g., speech, directional audio, haptics) than in typical mobile visualizations. The vision for ubiquitous visualization interaction in our discussions called to mind Elmqvist's *fluid interaction* [27]—seamless interaction across modalities which does not interrupt the cognitive flow or process of analysis.

The interaction focus in the interviews was on the modality of interaction, and the use of novel technology to enable interaction, such as Willett's and Elmqvist's mention of proxemics on the passive end of the dimension, and ultrasound haptics enabling fluid interaction in the other extreme. Rogers works a lot with tangible and physical interaction to explore the design of interfaces that are attractive, aesthetic, functional and engage people. She thinks the next generation of interfaces will be physical and tangible and looked ahead to plant-based interfaces that could be physical, change their form and appearance (e.g., by glowing). White raised the need for software toolkits that bridge technologies so that we can move beyond one-off prototypes.

The fifth dimension is the **data source** which spans across *captured, connected, and preloaded data*. As we move toward ubiquitous visualization all the scenarios discussed in the interviews were contextual. Contextual awareness enables the situated analytics workflows envisioned in the interviews with White and Willett. This necessarily requires at least some capturing of data such as location, orientation, or other sensor data feeds. Mobile visualization aims to bring data with the user wherever needed; ubiquitous visualization brings the right data to the user at the right time, in relation to the physical, social, and environmental context. As such, it is likely that ubiquitous visualizations will almost always fall under the *combination* level of the data source dimension, combining onboard data with cloud-connected and sensor data. However, our interviewees also mention that contextual adaption is tricky. Rogers stated that we "need to be careful with contextual approaches—is it to bring the right data up at the right time? I haven't seen that many useful adaptive interfaces. [...] Very simple visualizations sometimes are the best."

The sixth dimension is the **intended viewing timespan**, from *glanceable* visualizations to long-term use of *hours or more*. Willett's vision of instrumented multi-screen car environments is actually an extension of the sub-second glance example of an in-car GPS panel discussed in Chapter 1. Like mobile visualizations, ubiquitous visualization will likely span the full spectrum of this dimension. In ubiquitous visualization scenarios, one can imagine glancing at a rich visual notification displayed in the glasses White predicts will become popular, or conducting a deeper analysis of data such as in White's augmented botany field guides [94, 98].

The final dimension is the **intended sharing**, from *personal use* to *general public*. In ubiquitous visualization scenarios, the intended sharing may be highly linked to the display technology, as some technologies such as glasses are personal and viewable by only one person, while others such as displays in the shopping mall are within public view. As Rogers alluded to, the uses of these displays for data display will have to consider their social context. Both Rogers and White suggest that public sharing can become more social, engaging people with each other through data, rather than passive viewing of large displays. Ubiquitous visualization could also be used by *a few people* in groups, for example, field researchers having a first-person view on the same dataset as they roam a forest, or industrial workers seeing personalized data overlays in a factory setting. Ubiquitous visualizations in the environment could be used by *larger groups* in shared workplaces, such as ambient hallway visualizations, or by the *general public*, such as on displays of subway platforms or, as Rogers suggests, in a busy public space such as Picadilly Circus.

The vision for ubiquitous visualization suggests *new levels of this dimension*. First, *linked personal views* in which users have a personal view on a partially or fully shared dataset. These views may be customized to the user's point of view, role, preferences, and interest. For example, two people may be looking at a visualization on their private displays, using preferred color schemes and representation types, but interaction could provide linked highlighting. Ubiquitous technologies may also allow for *hybrid sharing* in which part of the data is shared, e.g. on a wall display, and part of the data is private or user-specific, e.g. overlays displayed in AR glasses. Hybrid sharing could also be achieved through public displays of data in which the included data or the design of the representation is only understandable by a subset of the viewers who possess specialized knowledge.

9.9.2 Expanding the Dimensions with Context

The originally discussed *dimensions of mobile data visualization* embedded contextual awareness within several related dimensions, including *visualization's reaction to display movement, data movement,* and *data source.* A common trend in our interviews was that ubiquitous visualization would be more situated within people's activities and settings. We also discussed opportunities for visualizations to respond and adapt to the changing context. While mobile visualizations may take into account the context through the use of motion sensors and GPS location, or may be personalized to the user, this dimension may achieve more variety in ubiquitous scenarios. We can imagine reframing the contextual dependency into a specific additional dimension for the **level of context-awareness** of the visualization [23]. As a first step, based on our four interviews, we propose that levels of this dimension could be:

non-context-aware The visualization does not change with context.

user context-aware The visualization responds to the user's transient physical or mental state, preferences, or long standing traits.

physically context-aware The visualization is specific to the physical, temporal, or environmental context.

socially context-aware The visualization responds to the number of people in the environment, their social and physical interrelations, tasks, and roles.

combination The visualization has aspects of a combination of user, physical, and social contextualization.

In addition to the type of context awareness, the **response to context** can also vary between passive awareness (which merely suggests and requires user confirmation) and active awareness (where the interface adjustments are autonomously applied) [18]. For example, a passive user context-aware visualization may emphasize the heart rate chart button if user exercise is detected, while an active contextual response would be to simply show the chart directly on the home screen without first prompting. There are interesting considerations and trade-offs to consider between these approaches to embedding context awareness, including interface stability, predictability, and the level of user control [9].

Note that unlike the original dimensions discussed in Chapter 1, a specific instantiation of a ubiquitous visualization could have multiple levels of context awareness through *combination.* For example, an augmented reality visualization for jogging could be responsive to the *physical context* (GPS directions, local traffic), the *user context* (heart rate, breathing), and the *social context* (location and status of runners accompanying the user). Such a head's up visualization would allow the user to safely challenge themselves to reach exercise goals while adapting to changing environmental conditions and staying in sync with their friends.

However, as a caveat, we want to emphasize that delineating "context" in this way is challenging and has long been discussed in the ubiquitous computing community. Dourish noted that the ubiquitous computing literature has mostly looked at context as a representational problem (instead of an interactional problem), and that the sociological critique on context-awareness is that the kind of thing that can be modeled or computationally represented is *not* what context is [25]. According to Taylor, Dourish instead argues that "context is something that is continuously being made and dependent to a large degree on the ever-changing relations between people and the resources they bring to bear in everyday settings" [86]. Similarly, Greenberg argued that context is not a stable set of contextual states, but rather a dynamically evolving situation-dependent construct [31]. Indeed, most successful examples of context-awareness have been confined to quite specific, predictable and low-risk interactions (e.g. location-aware searches to find the local Starbucks, or mobile displays that automatically rotate to portrait or landscape mode depending on how they are held [39]). As mentioned above, our interviewee Yvonne Rogers mentioned that one needs to be careful with contextually-aware approaches.

Perhaps the challenge for ubiquitous visualization research is instead to identify the specific and reliably predictable interactions in which data visualizations can be made incredibly useful by being contextually relevant to the task and setting at hand (e.g., White's example of medical applications to visualize a patient's veins on their arm to support blood extractions), rather than attempting to (automatically) adapt to every possible situation.

9.10 CONCLUSION

In this chapter, we looked ahead to the future of mobile visualization. We anticipate a change from what we describe in this book as mobile visualization toward ubiquitous visualization: Data visualizations will be available everywhere and at any time using a variety of emerging technologies to display and interact with data to support people's activities in a variety of settings. To better understand this emerging topic, we reported on interviews with four renowned researchers who have explored data visualization using new technologies and in new settings in their work. We extracted recurring themes from these interviews to highlight opportunities and challenges in moving toward ubiquitous data visualization. We also discussed envisioning scenarios for ubiquitous visualization and reflect on how moving to ubiquitous visualization will impact the dimensions for mobile data visualization that were identified in Chapter 1. Overall, we hope this chapter provides insights into this exciting emerging research direction that aims at achieving ever-more available and contextually situated data visualizations that fit into people's lives.

REFERENCES

[1] Alexander, J., Roudaut, A., Steimle, J., Hornbæk, K., Bruns Alonso, M., Follmer, S., and Merritt, T. "Grand Challenges in Shape-Changing Interface Research". In: *Proceedings of the Conference on Human Factors in Computing Systems (CHI)*. CHI '18. Montreal QC, Canada: ACM, 2018. DOI: 10.1145/3173574.3173873. URL: https://doi.org/10.1145/3173574.3173873 (cited on page 264).

[2] Alipour, M., Dragicevic, P., Isenberg, T., and Isenberg, P. "Situated Visualizations of Office Noise to Promote Personal Health". In: *Posters of the IEEE Conference on Information Visualization (InfoVis)*. **Open Access version:** https://hal.inria.fr/hal-01857354. Oct. 2018 (cited on page 296).

[3] Azuma, R. T. "A Survey of Augmented Reality". In: *Presence: Teleoperators and Virtual Environments* 6.4 (1997), pp. 355–385 (cited on page 301).

[4] Badam, S. K., Amini, F., Elmqvist, N., and Irani, P. "Supporting Visual Exploration for Multiple Users in Large Display Environments". In: *Proceedings of the Conference on Visual Analytics Science and Technology (VAST)*. Oct. 2016, pp. 1–10. DOI: 10.1109/VAST.2016.7883506 (cited on pages 265, 280).

[5] Badam, S. K. and Elmqvist, N. "PolyChrome: A Cross-Device Framework for Collaborative Web Visualization". In: *Proceedings of the Conference on Interactive Tabletops and Surfaces (ITS)*. ITS '14. Dresden, Germany: ACM, 2014, pp. 109–118. DOI: 10.1145/2669485.2669518. URL: https://doi.org/10.1145/2669485.2669518 (cited on page 278).

[6] Badam, S. K., Fisher, E., and Elmqvist, N. "Munin: A Peer-To-Peer Middleware for Ubiquitous Analytics and Visualization Spaces". In: *Transactions on Visualization and Computer Graphics (TVCG)* 21.2 (Feb. 2015). **Open Access version:** https://www.researchgate.net/publication/273161089, pp. 215–228. DOI: 10.1109/TVCG.2014.2337337 (cited on page 278).

[7] Badam, S. K., Mathisen, A., Rädle, R., Klokmose, C. N., and Elmqvist, N. "Vistrates: A Component Model for Ubiquitous Analytics". In: *Transactions on Visualization and Computer Graphics (TVCG)* 25.1 (Jan. 2019), pp. 586–596. DOI: 10.1109/TVCG.2018.2865144 (cited on pages 264, 278, 279).

[8] Bakker, S., Hausen, D., and Selker, T. *Peripheral Interaction: Challenges and Opportunities for HCI in the Periphery of Attention*. 1st. Springer, 2016 (cited on page 295).

[9] Barkhuus, L. and Dey, A. "Is Context-Aware Computing Taking Control Away From the User? Three Levels of Interactivity Examined". In: *Proceedings of the Conference on Ubiquitous Computing (Ubicomp)*. Springer, 2003, pp. 149–156. DOI: 10.1007/978-3-540-39653-6_12 (cited on page 303).

[10] Baur, D. *Silent Augmented Reality*. Website. Aug. 2017. URL: https://hackernoon.com/silent-augmented-reality-f0f7614cab32 (cited on page 278).

[11] Bird, J. and Rogers, Y. "The Pulse of Tidy Street: Measuring and Publicly Displaying Domestic Electricity Consumption". In: *Proceedings of the Workshop on Energy Awareness and Conservation through Pervasive Applications*. 2010. URL: `https://www.idc-online.com/technical_references/pdfs/electrical_engineering/The%20pulse%20of%20Tidy%20street.pdf` (cited on pages 286, 289, 291).

[12] Boring, S., Greenberg, S., Vermeulen, J., Dostal, J., and Marquardt, N. "The Dark Patterns of Proxemic Sensing". In: *Computer* 47.8 (Aug. 2014). **Open Access version:** `http : / / jovermeulen . com / uploads / Research / BoringGreenbergVermeulenDostalMarquardt_computer2014.pdf`, pp. 56–60. DOI: `10.1109/MC.2014.223` (cited on page 295).

[13] Bostock, M., Ogievetsky, V., and Heer, J. "D^3 Data-Driven Documents". In: *Transactions on Visualization and Computer Graphics (TVCG)* 17.12 (2011), pp. 2301–2309 (cited on page 296).

[14] Bressa, N., Wannamaker, K., Korsgaard, H., Willett, W., and Vermeulen, J. "Sketching and Ideation Activities for Situated Visualization Design". In: *Proceedings of the Conference on Designing Interactive Systems (DIS)*. DIS '19. **Open Access version:** `http : / / jovermeulen . com / uploads / Research / BressaWannamakerKorsgaardWillettVermeulen_situatedvis-dis2019.pdf`. San Diego, CA, USA: ACM, 2019, pp. 173–185. DOI: `10.1145/3322276.3322326` (cited on page 296).

[15] Büschel, W., Vogt, S., and Dachselt, R. "Augmented Reality Graph Visualizations". In: *Computer Graphics and Applications (CG&A)* 39.3 (May 2019). **Open Access version:** `https://imld.de/cnt/uploads/bueschel_cga2019.pdf`, pp. 29–40. DOI: `10.1109/MCG.2019.2897927` (cited on page 264).

[16] Buxton, B. "Integrating the Periphery and Context: A New Taxonomy of Telematics". In: *Proceedings of the Graphics Interface Conference (GI)*. GI '95. Quebec, Quebec, CA, 1995, pp. 239–246 (cited on page 295).

[17] Cauchard, J. R., Tamkin, A., Wang, C. Y., Vink, L., Park, M., Fang, T., and Landay, J. A. "drone.io: A Gestural and Visual Interface for Human-Drone Interaction". In: *Proceedings of the Conference on Human-Robot Interaction(HRI)*. HRI '19. Daegu, Republic of Korea: IEEE, 2019, pp. 153–162. DOI: `10.1109/HRI.2019.8673011` (cited on page 265).

[18] Chen, G. and Kotz, D. *A Survey of Context-Aware Mobile Computing Research*. Tech. rep. TR2000-381. Dartmouth College, 2000 (cited on page 303).

[19] Ciolek, T. M. and Kendon, A. "Environment and the Spatial Arrangement of Conversational Encounters". In: *Sociological Inquiry* 50.3-4 (1980), pp. 237–271 (cited on page 273).

[20] Crabtree, A., Chamberlain, A., Grinter, R. E., Jones, M., Rodden, T., and Rogers, Y. "Introduction to the Special Issue of "The Turn to the Wild"". In: *Transactions on Computer-Human Interaction (TOCHI)* 20.3 (July 2013).

DOI: 10.1145/2491500.2491501. URL: https://doi.org/10.1145/2491500.2491501 (cited on page 292).

[21] Cui, Z., Sen, S., Badam, S. K., and Elmqvist, N. "VisHive: Supporting Web-Based Visualization Through Ad Hoc Computational Clusters of Mobile Devices". In: *Information Visualization* 18.2 (2019), pp. 195–210. DOI: 10.1177/1473871617752910. URL: https://doi.org/10.1177/1473871617752910 (cited on page 279).

[22] Dachselt, R., Häkkilä, J., Jones, M., Löchtefeld, M., Rohs, M., and Rukzio, E. "Pico Projectors: Firefly or Bright Future?" In: *Interactions* 19.2 (Mar. 2012). **Open Access version:** https://imld.de/cnt/uploads/2013/08/2012-Interactions-Picoprojectors_Firefly_Or_Bright_Future.pdf, pp. 24–29. DOI: 10.1145/2090150.2090158. URL: https://doi.org/10.1145/2090150.2090158 (cited on page 281).

[23] Dey, A. K. "Understanding and Using Context". In: *Personal and Ubiquitous Computing* 5.1 (2001), pp. 4–7 (cited on page 303).

[24] Dostal, J., Hinrichs, U., Kristensson, P. O., and Quigley, A. "SpiderEyes: Designing Attention- And Proximity-Aware Collaborative Interfaces for Wall-Sized Displays". In: *Proceedings of the Conference on Intelligent User Interfaces (IUI)*. IUI '14. Haifa, Israel: ACM, 2014, pp. 143–152. DOI: 10.1145/2557500.2557541. URL: https://doi.org/10.1145/2557500.2557541 (cited on page 265).

[25] Dourish, P. "What We Talk About When We Talk About Context". English. In: *Personal and Ubiquitous Computing* 8.1 (2004), pp. 19–30 (cited on page 304).

[26] Elmqvist, N. and Irani, P. "Ubiquitous Analytics: Interacting With Big Data Anywhere, Anytime". In: *Computer* 46.4 (Apr. 2013), pp. 86–89. DOI: 10.1109/MC.2013.147 (cited on pages 264, 269, 271, 275).

[27] Elmqvist, N., Moere, A. V., Jetter, H.-C., Cernea, D., Reiterer, H., and Jankun-Kelly, T. J. "Fluid Interaction for Information Visualization". In: *Information Visualization* 10.4 (2011). **Open Access version:** https://kops.uni-konstanz.de/handle/123456789/18146, pp. 327–340. DOI: 10.1177/1473871611413180 (cited on page 301).

[28] Fitzek, F. H., Li, S.-C., Speidel, S., Strufe, T., Simsek, M., and Reisslein, M. *Tactile Internet with Human-In-The-Loop*. 1st. Academic Press, 2021 (cited on page 299).

[29] Golsteijn, C., Gallacher, S., Capra, L., and Rogers, Y. "Sens-Us: Designing Innovative Civic Technology for the Public Good". In: *Proceedings of the Conference on Designing Interactive Systems (DIS)*. ACM, 2016, pp. 39–49. DOI: 10.1145/2901790.2901877 (cited on pages 286, 290).

[30] Golsteijn, C., Gallacher, S., Koeman, L., Wall, L., Andberg, S., Rogers, Y., and Capra, L. "VoxBox: A Tangible Machine That Gathers Opinions From the Public at Events". In: *Proceedings of the Conference on Tangible, Embedded, and Embodied Interaction (TEI)*. ACM, 2015, pp. 201–208. DOI: 10.1145/2677199.2680588 (cited on pages 286, 290).

[31] Greenberg, S. "Context as a Dynamic Construct". In: *Human-Computer Interaction* 16.2 (Dec. 2001), pp. 257–268 (cited on page 304).

[32] Greenberg, S., Marquardt, N., Ballendat, T., Diaz-Marino, R., and Wang, M. "Proxemic Interactions: The New Ubicomp?" In: *Interactions* 18.1 (Jan. 2011), pp. 42–50. DOI: 10.1145/1897239.1897250. URL: http://doi.acm.org/10.1145/1897239.1897250 (cited on pages 273, 297).

[33] Gustafsson, A. and Gyllenswärd, M. "The Power-Aware Cord: Energy Awareness Through Ambient Information Display". In: *Extended Abstracts of the Conference on Human Factors in Computing System (CHI)*. CHI EA '05. Portland, OR, USA: ACM, 2005, pp. 1423–1426. DOI: 10.1145/1056808.1056932. URL: https://doi.org/10.1145/1056808.1056932 (cited on page 265).

[34] Hall, E. T. *The Hidden Dimension*. Vol. 609. Anchor, 1966 (cited on page 273).

[35] Harrison, C., Horstman, J., Hsieh, G., and Hudson, S. "Unlocking the Expressivity of Point Lights". In: *Proceedings of the Conference on Human Factors in Computing Systems (CHI)*. CHI '12. Austin, Texas, USA: ACM, 2012, pp. 1683–1692. DOI: 10.1145/2207676.2208296. URL: https://doi.org/10.1145/2207676.2208296 (cited on page 265).

[36] Hearst, M. and Tory, M. "Would You Like a Chart With That? Incorporating Visualizations Into Conversational Interfaces". In: *Short Paper Proceedings of the Conference on Visualization (VIS)*. IEEE, 2019, pp. 1–5. DOI: 10.1109/VISUAL.2019.8933766 (cited on page 265).

[37] Hearst, M., Tory, M., and Setlur, V. "Toward Interface Defaults for Vague Modifiers in Natural Language Interfaces for Visual Analysis". In: *Short Paper Proceedings of the Conference on Visualization (VIS)*. 2019, pp. 21–25. DOI: 10.1109/VISUAL.2019.8933569 (cited on page 265).

[38] Heiner, J. M., Hudson, S. E., and Tanaka, K. "The Information Percolator: Ambient Information Display in a Decorative Object". In: *Proceedings of the Conference on User Interface, Software, and Technology (UIST)*. UIST '99. Asheville, North Carolina, USA: ACM, 1999, pp. 141–148. DOI: 10.1145/320719.322595. URL: https://doi.org/10.1145/320719.322595 (cited on page 265).

[39] Hinckley, K., Pierce, J., Sinclair, M., and Horvitz, E. "Sensing Techniques for Mobile Interaction". In: *Proceedings of the Conference on User Interface, Software, and Technology (UIST)*. UIST '00. San Diego, California, USA: ACM, 2000, pp. 91–100 (cited on page 304).

[40] Horak, T., Mathisen, A., Klokmose, C. N., Dachselt, R., and Elmqvist, N. "Vistribute: Distributing Interactive Visualizations in Dynamic Multi-Device Setups". In: *Proceedings of the Conference on Human Factors in Computing Systems (CHI)*. **Open Access version:** https://imld.de/cnt/uploads/Horak-Vistribute-CHI2019.pdf. ACM, 2019, 616:1–616:13. DOI: 10.1145/3290605.3300846 (cited on page 279).

[41] Houben, S., Bengler, B., Gavrilov, D., Gallacher, S., Nisi, V., Nunes, N. J., Capra, L., and Rogers, Y. "Roam-Io: Engaging With People Tracking Data Through an Interactive Physical Data Installation". In: *Proceedings of the Conference on Designing Interactive Systems (DIS)*. ACM, 2019, pp. 1157–1169 (cited on page 289).

[42] Houben, S., Golsteijn, C., Gallacher, S., Johnson, R., Bakker, S., Marquardt, N., Capra, L., and Rogers, Y. "Physikit: Data Engagement Through Physical Ambient Visualizations in the Home". In: *Proceedings of the Conference on Human Factors in Computing Systems (CHI)*. ACM, 2016, pp. 1608–1619 (cited on pages 289, 290, 294).

[43] Isenberg, P., Dragicevic, P., Willett, W., Bezerianos, A., and Fekete, J.-D. "Hybrid-Image Visualization for Large Viewing Environments". In: *Transactions on Visualization and Computer Graphics (TVCG)* 19.12 (2013). **Open Access version:** https://hal.inria.fr/hal-00844878, pp. 2346–2355. DOI: 10.1109/TVCG.2013.163 (cited on page 274).

[44] Jakobsen, M. R., Haile, Y. S., Knudsen, S., and Hornbæk, K. "Information Visualization and Proxemics: Design Opportunities and Empirical Findings". In: *Transactions on Visualization and Computer Graphics (TVCG)* 19.12 (Dec. 2013). **Open Access version:** http://www.kasperhornbaek.dk/papers/InfoViz2013_ProxemicVisualization.pdf, pp. 2386–2395. DOI: 10.1109/TVCG.2013.166 (cited on page 265).

[45] Jansen, Y., Dragicevic, P., Isenberg, P., Alexander, J., Karnik, A., Kildal, J., Subramanian, S., and Hornbæk, K. "Opportunities and Challenges for Data Physicalization". In: *Proceedings of the Conference on Human Factors in Computing Systems (CHI)*. CHI '15. **Open Access version:** https://hal.inria.fr/hal-01120152. Seoul, Republic of Korea: ACM, 2015, pp. 3227–3236. DOI: 10.1145/2702123.2702180 (cited on pages 265, 296).

[46] Jansen, Y., Isenberg, P., Dykes, J., Carpendale, S., and Keefe, D. F. *Death of the Desktop: Envisioning Visualization Without Desktop Computing*. IEEE Visualization Workshop. 2014. URL: http://dataphys.org/workshops/vis14/ (cited on page 270).

[47] Ju, W. *The Design of Implicit Interactions*. 1st. Morgan & Claypool, 2015 (cited on page 295).

[48] Kalkofen, D., Mendez, E., and Schmalstieg, D. "Interactive Focus and Context Visualization for Augmented Reality". In: *Proceedings of the Symposium on Mixed and Augmented Reality (ISMAR)*. IEEE. 2007, pp. 191–201 (cited on page 283).

[49] Kalnikaite, V., Rogers, Y., Bird, J., Villar, N., Bachour, K., Payne, S., Todd, P. M., Schöning, J., Krüger, A., and Kreitmayer, S. "How to Nudge in Situ: Designing Lambent Devices to Deliver Salient Information in Supermarkets". In: *Proceedings of the Conference on Ubiquitous Computing (Ubicomp)*. UbiComp '11. Beijing, China: ACM, 2011, pp. 11–20. DOI: 10.1145/2030112.2030115 (cited on pages 289, 291).

[50] Kaninsky, M., Gallacher, S., and Rogers, Y. "Confronting People's Fears About Bats: Combining Multi-Modal and Environmentally Sensed Data to Promote Curiosity and Discovery". In: *Proceedings of the Conference on Designing Interactive Systems (DIS)*. ACM, 2018, pp. 931–943 (cited on page 289).

[51] Kawsar, F., Vermeulen, J., Smith, K., Luyten, K., and Kortuem, G. "Exploring the Design Space for Situated Glyphs to Support Dynamic Work Environments". In: *Proceedings of the Conference on Pervasive Computing (Pervasive)*. Edited by Lyons, K., Hightower, J., and Huang, E. M. **Open Access version:** `http://jovermeulen.com/uploads/Research/KawsarVermeulenKortuemLuyten_pervasive2011.pdf`. Berlin, Heidelberg: Springer, 2011, pp. 70–78. DOI: 10.1007/978-3-642-21726-5_5 (cited on pages 264, 296).

[52] Kendon, A. "Spacing and Orientation in Co-Present Interaction". In: *Proceedings of the Conference on Development of Multimodal Interfaces (COST)*. COST '09. Dublin, Ireland: Springer, 2009, pp. 1–15. DOI: 10.1007/978-3-642-12397-9_1. URL: `https://doi.org/10.1007/978-3-642-12397-9_1` (cited on page 273).

[53] Khot, R. A., Pennings, R., and Mueller, F. "EdiPulse: Supporting Physical Activity With Chocolate Printed Messages". In: *Extended Abstracts of the Conference on Human Factors in Computing System (CHI)*. ACM, 2015, pp. 1391–1396 (cited on page 292).

[54] Kim, K., Javed, W., Williams, C., Elmqvist, N., and Irani, P. "Hugin: A Framework for Awareness and Coordination in Mixed-Presence Collaborative Information Visualization". In: *Proceedings of the Conference on Interactive Tabletops and Surfaces (ITS)*. ITS '10. Saarbrücken, Germany: ACM, 2010, pp. 231–240. DOI: 10.1145/1936652.1936694. URL: `https://doi.org/10.1145/1936652.1936694` (cited on page 278).

[55] Kister, U., Klamka, K., Tominski, C., and Dachselt, R. "GRASP: Combining Spatially-Aware Mobile Devices and a Display Wall for Graph Visualization and Interaction". In: *Computer Graphics Forum* 36.3 (June 2017). **Open Access version:** `https://mt.inf.tu-dresden.de/cnt/uploads/Kister_GraSp_EuroVis17.pdf`, pp. 503–514. DOI: 10.1111/cgf.13206 (cited on page 265).

[56] Klamka, K., Dachselt, R., and Steimle, J. "Rapid Iron-On User Interfaces: Hands-On Fabrication of Interactive Textile Prototypes". In: *Proceedings of the Conference on Human Factors in Computing Systems (CHI)*. **Open Access version:** `https://imld.de/cnt/uploads/rapid_iron_on_user_interfaces_chi2020_klamka.pdf`. Honolulu, Hawaii, USA: ACM, Apr. 2020. DOI: 10.1145/3313831.3376220 (cited on page 301).

[57] Klamka, K., Horak, T., and Dachselt, R. "Watch+Strap: Extending Smart-watches With Interactive StrapDisplays". In: *Proceedings of the Conference on Human Factors in Computing Systems (CHI)*. CHI '20. **Open Access version:** https://dl.acm.org/doi/10.1145/3313831.3376199. New York, NY, USA: ACM, 2020, pp. 1–15. DOI: 10.1145/3313831.3376199 (cited on page 300).

[58] Koeman, L., Kalnikaité, V., and Rogers, Y. ""Everyone Is Talking About It!" a Distributed Approach to Urban Voting Technology and Visualisations". In: *Proceedings of the Conference on Human Factors in Computing Systems (CHI)*. ACM, 2015, pp. 3127–3136 (cited on page 289).

[59] Langner, R., Horak, T., and Dachselt, R. "VisTiles: Coordinating and Combin-ing Co-Located Mobile Devices for Visual Data Exploration". In: *Transactions on Visualization and Computer Graphics (TVCG)* 24.1 (Jan. 2018). **Open Access version:** https://imld.de/cnt/uploads/Langner_VisTiles_InfoVis17.pdf, pp. 626–636. DOI: 10.1109/TVCG.2017.2744019 (cited on page 265).

[60] Lee, B., Srinivasan, A., Stasko, J., Tory, M., and Setlur, V. "Multimodal Interaction for Data Visualization". In: *Proceedings of the Conference on Advanced Visual Interfaces (AVI)*. AVI '18. Castiglione della Pescaia, Grosseto, Italy: ACM, 2018. DOI: 10.1145/3206505.3206602. URL: https://doi.org/10.1145/3206505.3206602 (cited on page 264).

[61] Marriott, K., Schreiber, F., Dwyer, T., Klein, K., Riche, N. H., Itoh, T., Stuerzlinger, W., and Thomas, B. H. *Immersive Analytics*. Vol. 11190. Springer, 2018 (cited on page 264).

[62] Moere, A. V. and Hill, D. "Designing for the Situated and Public Visualization of Urban Data". In: *Journal of Urban Technology* 19.2 (2012), pp. 25–46. DOI: 10.1080/10630732.2012.698065. URL: https://doi.org/10.1080/10630732.2012.698065 (cited on page 264).

[63] Mozilla. *Mozilla Mixed Reality: Firefox Reality*. https://mixedreality.mozilla.org/firefox-reality. [Online; accessed 18-May-2020] (cited on page 297).

[64] Offenhuber, D. "Data by Proxy—Material Traces as Autographic Visualiza-tions". In: *Transactions on Visualization and Computer Graphics (TVCG)* 26.1 (2020), pp. 98–108 (cited on page 270).

[65] Offenhuber, D. and Telhan, O. "Indexical Visualization—The Data-Less In-formation Display". In: *Proceedings of the Conference on Ubiquitous Comput-ing (Ubicomp)*. Vol. 288. New York: Routledge, 2015, pp. 288–303 (cited on page 270).

[66] Parker, C. and Tomitsch, M. "Data Visualisation Trends in Mobile Augmented Reality Applications". In: *Proceedings of the Symposium on Visual Information Communication and Interaction (VINCI)*. VINCI '14. Sydney NSW, Australia: ACM, 2014, pp. 228–231. DOI: 10.1145/2636240.2636864. URL: https://doi.org/10.1145/2636240.2636864 (cited on page 264).

[67] Poupyrev, I., Gong, N.-W., Fukuhara, S., Karagozler, M. E., Schwesig, C., and Robinson, K. E. "Project Jacquard: Interactive Digital Textiles at Scale". In: *Proceedings of the Conference on Human Factors in Computing Systems (CHI)*. ACM, 2016, pp. 4216–4227. DOI: 10.1145/2858036.2858176 (cited on page 301).

[68] Prouzeau, A., Wang, Y., Ens, B., Willett, W., and Dwyer, T. "Corsican Twin: Authoring in Situ Augmented Reality Visualisations in Virtual Reality". In: *Proceedings of the Conference on Advanced Visual Interfaces (AVI)*. **Open Access version:** https://hal.archives-ouvertes.fr/hal-02614521. New York: ACM, 2020, 11:1–11:9. DOI: 10.1145/3399715.3399743 (cited on page 299).

[69] Resner, B., Gandhi, P., Negroponte, N., Dredge, R., and Rose, D. "Weather Forecasting Umbrella". US Patent App. 11/699,314. Nov. 2007. URL: http://appft.uspto.gov/netacgi/nph-Parser?Sect1=PTO1&Sect2=HITOFF&p=1&u=/netahtml/PTO/srchnum.html&r=1&f=G&l=50&d=PG01&s1=20070256716.PGNR. (cited on page 265).

[70] Roberts, J. C., Ritsos, P. D., Badam, S. K., Brodbeck, D., Kennedy, J., and Elmqvist, N. "Visualization Beyond the Desktop–The Next Big Thing". In: *Computer Graphics and Applications (CG&A)* 34.6 (Nov. 2014), pp. 26–34. DOI: 10.1109/MCG.2014.82 (cited on pages 264, 275).

[71] Rodriguez, I. B. and Marquardt, N. "Gesture Elicitation Study on How to Opt-In & Opt-Out from Interactions with Public Displays". In: *Proceedings of the Conference on Interactive Surfaces and Spaces (ISS)*. ISS '17. Brighton, United Kingdom: ACM, 2017, pp. 32–41. DOI: 10.1145/3132272.3134118. URL: https://doi.org/10.1145/3132272.3134118 (cited on page 295).

[72] Rogers, Y. "Interaction Design Gone Wild: Striving for Wild Theory". In: *Interactions* 18.4 (July 2011), pp. 58–62. DOI: 10.1145/1978822.1978834. URL: https://doi.org/10.1145/1978822.1978834 (cited on page 292).

[73] Rogers, Y. "Mindless or Mindful Technology?" In: *Proceedings of the Symposium on Engineering Interactive Systems (EICS)*. EICS '14. Rome, Italy: ACM, 2014, p. 241. DOI: 10.1145/2607023.2611428. URL: https://doi.org/10.1145/2607023.2611428 (cited on page 295).

[74] Rogers, Y. "Moving on From Weiser's Vision of Calm Computing: Engaging Ubicomp Experiences". In: *Proceedings of the Conference on Ubiquitous Computing (Ubicomp)*. Springer. 2006, pp. 404–421 (cited on page 295).

[75] Rogers, Y., Marshall, P., and Carroll, J. M. *Research in the Wild*. Morgan & Claypool, 2017 (cited on page 292).

[76] Rogers, Y., Price, S., Fitzpatrick, G., Fleck, R., Harris, E., Smith, H., Randell, C., Muller, H., O'Malley, C., Stanton, D., et al. "Ambient Wood: Designing New Forms of Digital Augmentation for Learning Outdoors". In: *Proceedings of Conference on Interaction Design and Children (IDC)*. 2004, pp. 3–10 (cited on pages 286, 287, 294).

[77] Rose, D. *The Balance Table*. Product Website. Accessed June 2020. 2016. URL: https://enchantedobjects.com/#/balance-table/ (cited on page 287).

[78] Satyanarayan, A. and Heer, J. "Lyra: An Interactive Visualization Design Environment". en. In: *Computer Graphics Forum* 33.3 (June 2014), pp. 351–360. DOI: 10.1111/cgf.12391. URL: http://onlinelibrary.wiley.com/doi/10.1111/cgf.12391/abstract (visited on 03/27/2015) (cited on page 279).

[79] Satyanarayan, A., Moritz, D., Wongsuphasawat, K., and Heer, J. "Vega-Lite: A Grammar of Interactive Graphics". In: *Transactions on Visualization and Computer Graphics (TVCG)* 23.1 (2017), pp. 341–350. DOI: 10.1109/TVCG.2016.2599030 (cited on page 296).

[80] Sauvé, K., Houben, S., Marquardt, N., Bakker, S., Hengeveld, B., Gallacher, S., and Rogers, Y. "LOOP: A Physical Artifact to Facilitate Seamless Interaction With Personal Data in Everyday Life". In: *Companion Proceedings of the Conference on Designing Interactive Systems (DIS)*. ACM, 2017, pp. 285–288 (cited on page 292).

[81] Scheible, J. and Funk, M. "In-Situ-Displaydrone: Facilitating Co-Located Interactive Experiences via a Flying Screen". In: *Proceedings of the Symposium on Pervasive Displays (PerDis)*. PerDis '16. Oulu, Finland: ACM, 2016, pp. 251–252. DOI: 10.1145/2914920.2940334. URL: https://doi.org/10.1145/2914920.2940334 (cited on page 265).

[82] Serrano, M., Roudaut, A., and Irani, P. "Visual Composition of Graphical Elements on Non-Rectangular Displays". In: *Proceedings of the Conference on Human Factors in Computing Systems (CHI)*. CHI '17. Denver, Colorado, USA: ACM, 2017, pp. 4405–4416. DOI: 10.1145/3025453.3025677. URL: https://doi.org/10.1145/3025453.3025677 (cited on page 264).

[83] Setlur, V., Battersby, S. E., Tory, M., Gossweiler, R., and Chang, A. X. "Eviza: A Natural Language Interface for Visual Analysis". In: *Proceedings of the Conference on User Interface, Software, and Technology (UIST)*. UIST '16. Tokyo, Japan: ACM, 2016, pp. 365–377. DOI: 10.1145/2984511.2984588. URL: https://doi.org/10.1145/2984511.2984588 (cited on page 265).

[84] Srinivasan, A. and Stasko, J. "Orko: Facilitating Multimodal Interaction for Visual Exploration and Analysis of Networks". In: *Transactions on Visualization and Computer Graphics (TVCG)* 24.1 (2018). **Open Access version:** https://www.cc.gatech.edu/~john.stasko/papers/infovis17-orko.pdf, pp. 511–521. DOI: 10.1109/TVCG.2017.2745219 (cited on page 280).

[85] Steichen, B., Carenini, G., and Conati, C. "User-Adaptive Information Visualization: Using Eye Gaze Data to Infer Visualization Tasks and User Cognitive Abilities". In: *Proceedings of the Conference on Intelligent User Interfaces (IUI)*. IUI '13. Santa Monica, California, USA: ACM, 2013, pp. 317–328. DOI: 10.1145/2449396.2449439. URL: https://doi.org/10.1145/2449396.2449439 (cited on page 265).

[86] Taylor, A. S. "Intelligence in Context". In: *Proceedings of the Conference on Intelligent Environments (IE)*. Apr. 2006, pp. 5–7 (cited on page 304).

[87] Tollmar, K., Junestrand, S., and Torgny, O. "Virtually Living Together". In: *Proceedings of the Conference on Designing Interactive Systems (DIS)*. DIS '00. New York City, New York, USA: ACM, 2000, pp. 83–91. DOI: 10.1145/347642.347670. URL: https://doi.org/10.1145/347642.347670 (cited on page 265).

[88] Van Mensvoort, K. *Datafountain: Money Translated to Water*. 2005. URL: https://www.koert.com/work/datafountain/ (cited on page 265).

[89] Vogel, D. and Balakrishnan, R. "Interactive Public Ambient Displays: Transitioning From Implicit to Explicit, Public to Personal, Interaction With Multiple Users". In: *Proceedings of the Conference on User Interface, Software, and Technology (UIST)*. UIST '04. Santa Fe, NM, USA: ACM, 2004, pp. 137–146. DOI: 10.1145/1029632.1029656. URL: https://doi.org/10.1145/1029632.1029656 (cited on page 274).

[90] Weiser, M. "The Computer for the 21st Century". In: *Mobile Computing and Communications Review* 3.3 (1999), pp. 3–11 (cited on page 296).

[91] Weiser, M. and Brown, J. S. *Designing Calm Technology*. [Online; accessed 10-May-2020]. Dec. 1995. URL: https://calmtech.com/papers/designing-calm-technology.html (cited on page 295).

[92] Weiser, M. and Brown, J. S. "The Coming Age of Calm Technology". In: *Beyond Calculation*. Springer, 1997, pp. 75–85. DOI: 10.1007/978-1-4612-0685-9_6 (cited on pages 265, 296).

[93] White, S. and Feiner, S. "SiteLens: Situated Visualization Techniques for Urban Site Visits". In: *Proceedings of the Conference on Human Factors in Computing Systems (CHI)*. New York, NY, USA: ACM, 2009, pp. 1117–1120 (cited on pages 270, 282).

[94] White, S., Feiner, S., and Kopylec, J. "Virtual Vouchers: Prototyping a Mobile Augmented Reality User Interface for Botanical Species Identification". In: *Proceedings of the Symosium on 3D User Interfaces (3DUI)*. IEEE, 2006, pp. 119–126 (cited on pages 294, 302).

[95] White, S., Feng, D., and Feiner, S. "Interaction and Presentation Techniques for Shake Menus in Tangible Augmented Reality". In: *Proceedings of the Symposium on Mixed and Augmented Reality (ISMAR)*. IEEE, 2009, pp. 39–48 (cited on page 285).

[96] White, S., Lister, L., and Feiner, S. "Visual Hints for Tangible Gestures in Augmented Reality". In: *Proceedings of the Symposium on Mixed and Augmented Reality (ISMAR)*. IEEE, 2007, pp. 47–50 (cited on page 285).

[97] White, S. M. "Interaction and Presentation Techniques for Situated Visualization". AAI3373578. PhD thesis. USA: Columbia University, 2009 (cited on page 264).

[98]   White, S. M., Marino, D., and Feiner, S. "Designing a Mobile User Interface for Automated Species Identification". In: *Proceedings of the Conference on Human Factors in Computing Systems (CHI)*. CHI '07. San Jose, California, USA: ACM, 2007, pp. 291–294. DOI: 10.1145/1240624.1240672. URL: https://doi.org/10.1145/1240624.1240672 (cited on pages 294, 302).

[99]   Willett, W., Jansen, Y., and Dragicevic, P. "Embedded Data Representations". In: *Transactions on Visualization and Computer Graphics (TVCG)* 23.1 (Jan. 2017). **Open Access version:** https://hal.inria.fr/hal-01377901, pp. 461–470. DOI: 10.1109/TVCG.2016.2598608 (cited on pages 264, 267, 273, 298).

[100] Wisneski, C., Ishii, H., Dahley, A., Gorbet, M. G., Brave, S., Ullmer, B., and Yarin, P. "Ambient Displays: Turning Architectural Space Into an Interface Between People and Digital Information". In: *Proceedings of the Workshop on Cooperative Buildings (CoBuild)*. Berlin, Heidelberg: Springer, 1998, pp. 22–32 (cited on page 265).

[101] Yamada, W., Yamada, K., Manabe, H., and Ikeda, D. "ISphere: Self-Luminous Spherical Drone Display". In: *Proceedings of the Conference on User Interface, Software, and Technology (UIST)*. UIST '17. Québec City, QC, Canada: ACM, 2017, pp. 635–643. DOI: 10.1145/3126594.3126631. URL: https://doi.org/10.1145/3126594.3126631 (cited on page 265).

Index

3D Touch, 80

A/B test, 182
accelerometer, 15, 41, 70, 120, 213, 242
accessibility, 77, 152, 249
aesthetics, 163, 167–169, 284, 294
aggregation, 46, 192, 231, 273, 299
ambient light, 41, 167
ambient visualization, 152
animation, 42, 49, 184, 187
annotation, 11, 36, 42, 47–50, 75, 78, 79, 125
aspect ratio, 45, 68, 86
augmented reality, 4, 37, 69, 88, 89, 95, 96, 113–115, 120, 121, 131, 212, 264, 269, 271, 278, 282–285, 299, 303
    handheld, 69, 120, 126
    mobile, 69, 86, 90, 93, 95, 111
autographic visualization, 93

behavior change, 152, 185, 194
bimanual interaction, 74, 76, 217
brushing and linking, 46, 92, 217

calm technology, 157, 295
casual information visualization, 156, 210, 227
CAVE, 21, 123, 127
clutch, 76, 77, 79, 94
collaboration, 93, 129, 267, 281
color scale, 93, 212
color scheme, 161, 219, 220, 302
context-aware, 55, 268, 276, 303
contextual inquiry, 182
controlled experiment, 91, 180, 181, 187, 194
crowdsourced experiment, 165, 187
customization, 93, 213, 214, 221, 232

data
    geo-spatial, 120
    large-scale, 299
    personal, 11, 68, 89, 193, 210, 211, 218, 219
    physicalization, 6, 82, 231, 265, 267, 295, 296
data tracking, 156, 163, 182, 190, 267, 276, 295
depth perception, 129
design
    ideation, 243, 257, 258
    methodology, 243
    mobile-first, 36, 50
details-on-demand, 10, 50
detection
    face, 41
    gaze, 54
    grip, 95
    hover, 95
    pose, 94, 95
device
    handheld, 15, 74, 95, 120, 125, 126, 137, 299
    orientation, 54, 85
    ultra-small mobile, 179
    wearable, 15, 54, 69, 94–96, 193, 242
discoverability, 70, 85, 91, 96, 192, 297
display
    head-mounted, 21, 128, 216
    large-scale, 300
    mobility, 3, 5–7, 300
    movement, 3, 8–9, 301
    non-stereoscopic, 118, 122–124, 134
    peripheral, 152, 157, 161
    resolution, 13, 19, 68, 95, 96, 114, 167, 179, 185, 196, 214, 275, 297
    size, 3–5, 34, 35, 38, 41, 48, 52, 89, 96, 264, 297, 300